A DRIVE DOWN MEMORY LANE:
The Named State and Federal Highways of Michigan

By LeRoy Barnett, PhD

MICHIGAN

III

State Highway Commissioner Charles M. Ziegler does the ribbon-cutting honors at the Stephenson Highway in Oakland County. See related text on page 204.

A DRIVE DOWN MEMORY LANE:
The Named State and Federal Highways of Michigan

By LeRoy Barnett, PhD

Le Roy Barnett

The Priscilla Press
Allegan Forest, Michigan
2004

Please direct any questions or comments
about this publication to the author at
9713 Looking Glass Brook Road,
Grand Ledge, MI 48837-9270

ISBN 1-886167-24-9

Printed By:
Sheridan Books, Inc.
Chelsea, MI

DEDICATION

To my wife who, with this volume and most of my
other books, has in truth been an unnamed co-author;

and

to the buyer of this publication who, by making this
purchase, has helped to support research into the
fascinating realm of Michigan history.

TABLE OF CONTENTS

FOREWORD

Between 1905 and 1930, Michigan built a network of highways on what were once Native American paths and military, wagon, plank and farm-to-market roads. The age of mud was over; the age of concrete and asphalt was beginning.

In Michigan, we have a long-standing tradition of naming our highways. From the earliest days, most of our early roads shared a name with a prominent person, or a meaningful geographical feature. US-12, designated as a U.S. Heritage Trail in 2004, was referred to as the Chicago Road, and before that, was known as the Sauk Trail, one of the most important migration routes for settlers into Michigan territory.

Giving names to our highways is a way of connecting people with the land. By the 1920s, the state and federal governments had developed a national numbering standard to replace the common practice of naming highways. But naming highways is a popular tradition that continues to this day. The state Legislature has named sections of the interstates for a wide variety of individuals and organizations prominent in Michigan history. They range from former President Gerald Ford (I-196 in Grand Rapids) to auto pioneers Walter Chrysler (I-75 in Detroit), Edsel Ford (I-94 in Detroit), David Buick and Louis Chevrolet (I-69 in Flint) and labor leader Walter P. Reuther (I-696 from Farmington Hills to St. Clair Shores).

The process to select memorial highways was legislated in 1999.

We are delighted that this long-standing tradition continues in Michigan. Indeed, if you live in the metro Detroit area, it is not uncommon to wake to the sounds of your radio traffic reporter talking about the Jeffries Freeway, or the Lodge Freeway. If you live in Grand Rapids, you may hear reference to the Gerald R. Ford Freeway or the Paul Henry Freeway. In Lansing, commuters travel on the Olds Freeway. It's a connection to the past, to our state's heroes and founders.

Esteemed Michigan historian LeRoy Barnett has written about "A Drive Down Memory Lane," the first book ever to comprehensively address the state's memorial highways. He captures a rich background of highway history that has made Michigan a leader in transportation. As the Michigan Department of Transportation celebrates its centennial anniversary in 2005, we have much to be proud of and many stories to share.

Mr. Barnett's book is a great resource for highway buffs, and for people who want to learn more than the memorial highway sign has space to tell. Happy traveling!

Gloria J. Jeff
Director
Michigan Department of Transportation

PREFACE

We live in a digital age. Nearly everything today is assigned numbers. This is particularly true for citizens of the United States, who have phone numbers, driver's license numbers, social security numbers, PIN numbers, health insurance card numbers, and a host of other serial integers that constitute our transaction identities. We are increasingly becoming like the wailing prisoners in folk songs, who musically lament that as incarcerated criminals they are known by a number and not a name.

A similar situation has occurred with the roads of North America. Once known solely by name, they are for the most part now just stretches of hardtop bearing numbers on signs. The present arrangement can not be faulted for its simplicity and efficiency, as distinguishing highways by different digits makes it easy to follow a route or transportation system to one's intended destination. But reducing motorways to a cipher or two often deprives them of their character or historical context, and this does a disservice to the trunk line, the people who use it, and the region through which it passes.

If most of us harken back to our high school days, we can probably remember studying about some of the more important routes in the evolution of our nation.* One of the earliest of these paths was Braddock's Road, a 115-mile passage from Cumberland, Maryland, to Pittsburgh, Pennsylvania, that was laid out by forces under the command of General Edward Braddock in 1755. Another famous trail to Pittsburgh was Forbes Road, built by soldiers following General John Forbes to the three-rivers junction in 1758.

Many U.S. history books make reference to the Wilderness Road, a 700-mile-long course marked out and cleared by Daniel Boone starting around 1775. This mountainous track enabled the frontier wayfarer to travel from the upper reaches of the Potomac River in West Virginia to Louisville, Kentucky, on the Ohio River. Another Bluegrass connection was Zane's Trace--built by Ebenezer Zane in 1797--which linked Wheeling, West Virginia, with Maysville, Kentucky, 226 miles distant.

Two other well-known eastern pioneer arteries were the Natchez Trace--which ran 550 miles from Nashville, Tennessee, to Natchez, Mississippi--and the Cumberland Road (also called the National Turnpike). This latter route was built by the federal government beginning around 1818 from Cumberland, Maryland, to Vandalia, Illinois, pretty much along the line of contemporary US-40. For more than a century the 667-mile-long road was "the most traveled route between the East and the trans-Allegheny West."

As settlement advanced beyond the Mississippi, that far region of our country blazed its share of legendary roads. Probably the earliest of these paths was the Sante Fe Trail, established about 1822, which extended 770 miles from Independence, Missouri, to Sante Fe, New Mexico. Later, the trans-montane Spanish Trail was created which covered the 1,200 miles between Sante Fe and Los Angeles, California. Together, this road duo formed a combine that nearly stretched from the Father of Waters to the Pacific Ocean.

To the north of these two routes was the renown Oregon Trail, which was active from about 1842 to 1869. This 2,000-mile pair of ruts in the dirt enabled hardy settlers to travel from Independence, Missouri, to Portland, Oregon, or points in between. The Bozeman Trail was another famous route in the West, this course of passage covering 967 miles from Kearney, Nebraska, to a destination or cutoff not far from Bozeman, Montana.**

As recently as sixty years ago the U.S. was still building roads more familiar as names than numbers. A case in point is the Alaska Highway, constructed in the early 1940s between Dawson Creek, British Columbia, and Fairbanks, Alaska. This route was established on an emergency basis as a land bridge to what is now our remote 50th state. The remarkable engineering achievement was deemed necessary to counter Japanese forces who had invaded the Aleutian Islands and were thought at one time to threaten the mainland of North America.

The major routes built in the eighteenth and nineteenth centuries on this continent were generally called "road," "trail," "trace," or "turnpike." Not until the twentieth century did the word "highway" come into common usage. The first celebrated channel of traffic to bear this name was the Lincoln Highway, created in 1913 as a link between New York and San Francisco on a course approximated by contemporary Interstate-80. While the main route of the Lincoln Highway did not pass through Michigan, the organization's headquarters were in the "Motor City" and its first president was Detroit businessman Henry B. Joy.

The next principal road in the United States to carry the title of "highway" was the Dixie Highway, constituted in 1915 as a route from Miami, Florida, to Sault Sainte Marie at the foot of Lake Superior. It can fairly be said that this year approximately marks the beginning of the memorial highway era in our state in the modern sense of the word. Granted, the following pages will identify some Michigan roads of remembrance that predate this moment in time, but the regular appearance of trunk lines in tribute to people and things begins in this period as shown by Appendix 3.

The era of naming rather than numbering motorways was quite limited, as by 1926 the state and federal governments had both established digital systems for distinguishing their respective ribbons of concrete. Thereafter, all trunk line pavements were assigned a number designation, even though some routes continued to carry or were subsequently assigned a name as well. It is the Michigan roads bearing this sort of double-identity that will be the subject of this volume's attention.

About 250 memorial or named state and federal highways in Michigan have been recognized by this study over the six years the research effort was underway. These roads fall into a half-dozen basic categories. Forty-six percent of the routes included in this book are named after people, 23% have a military or patriotic theme, 14% recognize a geographical area, site or feature, 9% honor a place, town or region, 3% credit Indians, and 5% are of a miscellaneous nature. All letters of the alphabet are represented by names of memorial highways with the exception of X, Y, and Z.

Since nearly half of the highways included in this book are named after people, it is appropriate to analyze the makeup of this population. Most of the roads in this category honor politicians (37%), with the remainder paying tribute to businessmen (16%), military personnel (12%), public servants (10%), pioneers (9%), clergy (5%), social advocates and activists (4%), explorers (3%), and men of letters (2%).

Of the highways in Michigan that have identities other than numbers, twelve are Interstates, sixteen are U.S. trunk lines, and seventy-six are state designated routes. This means that 83% of Michigan's Interstate arteries have been given a name in addition to digits, 92% of "US" roads have been similarly treated, as have about 50% of the "M"-designated ribbons of concrete. It is not uncommon for a specific motorway to have received more than one christening since the practice officially started in 1913. To illustrate this fact, I-75 has a dozen different titles along its course, US-31 has been given fifteen alternate monikers over the years, and M-46 bears ten distinct appellations throughout its length.

While the term named or memorial "highway" is regularly used in this text, less than half of the entries are titled so. In descending order of frequency, the breakdown shows that the designated state and federal motorways of Michigan bear the following identifiers: Highway (40%), Road (13%), Trail (13%), Freeway (6%), Avenue (4%), Drive (4%), Parkway or [Paved]way (4%), Pike (3%), Street (3%), Boulevard (2%), Expressway (2%), Lane (2%), Route (2%), Interchange (1%), and Overpass (1%).

It has often been asked, "What's in a name?" In the case of Michigan highways, the answer is "Quite a bit." For example, most of the "Roads" in this book are or originally were in rural settings. Conversely, nearly all of the "Avenues", "Boulevards" and "Streets" are in urban areas. All of the "Expressways" were early limited-access arteries in Detroit, while all "Freeways" postdate 1957. Most of the "Drives" are of a tourist or recreational nature, while all of the "Lanes" are associated with memorial tributes. And finally, whereas all of the "Pikes" came early in our motoring history, this name was soon replaced by "Trail" which seemed to offer a sense of adventure and discovery to the potential Michigan driver.

There are named or memorial state and federal highways in all of Michigan's counties. Those with the fewest--just two--are Gladwin, Lake, Missaukee, Montmorency, and Oscoda. The county with the most routes carrying distinction beyond a number is Wayne, which has 60 such thoroughfares. In the Upper Peninsula, the most represented counties are Chippewa and Mackinac with eighteen named roads each. About 30% of the entries in this book are urban and the remainder are to varying degrees rural. Eighty-five percent of the featured roads are in the Lower Peninsula, 11% in the Upper Peninsula, and 5% cover both sides of the Straits.

Since 1913 when record keeping began, at least one memorial or named highway has been created every year except in 1936, 1943, 1950, 1956, 1960-62, 1964-65, 1968, 1970, 1979, 1982-83, and 1987. The most roads labeled in any given year was eleven in 1917, the time when Rand McNally began creating identities for many drives around the country. The second greatest number of arteries named in one year was 2001, when eight new trunk lines were designated during a recodification of all the memorial highway statutes.

Today, nearly all named or memorial highways must be approved by the Michigan Legislature. Since the most important elections occur in even-numbered years, cynics might assume that most state or federal roads are named at this time as lawmakers theoretically attempt to curry favor with the voters or with special interest groups. To the contrary, however, analysis shows that 56% of all highways in our two peninsulas have been created during odd-numbered years.

Thirty-eight memorial or named highways have been proposed for Michigan but were not officially established. The actual count of candidates in this class is almost certainly far higher, but will never be known because of the lengthy amount of time that has passed since such ideas surfaced and the local or limited regional nature of many of these movements. Also, some of these concepts can be spawned in a cavalier fashion while others have a serious basis. It is impossible now to track down all of these aspiring roads of remembrance that never made the grade, though all that have been discovered are represented in the Postscript.

Historically speaking, most of the memorial highways across our two peninsulas were established by the Michigan legislature. In modern times, that is just about the only way a designa-

tion can be made. There were periods when state lawmakers were not inclined to participate in this exercise, the decade of the 1960s being a prime example. Lately, however, any reluctance to go this route seems to have disappeared, and both chambers of the Capitol in Lansing have been approving new roads of remembrance in the twenty-first century at the average rate of five per annum. With approximately a quarter-thousand memorial and named highways already existing in Michigan, at the present rate of increase the number will double in just the next half century.

It should be noted, in conclusion, that Adopt-a-Highway programs at the state and county levels will allow roadside pickup volunteers to dedicate their efforts in memory of an individual or group. It is not uncommon, for example, to see signs along the pavement saying, in effect, that the next two miles of right-of-way are cleaned or groomed in memory of Person X. In these situations, the routes benefiting from contributed labors in remembrance of some human, pet, or other entity are not considered to be memorial highways by this book.

Also, the purview of this book does not include drives created for purposes beyond typical point-to-point motoring. An example of a named automobile route omitted from this work is the "Southwest Michigan Wine Trail," a circuit followed by those wishing to visit the wineries of Berrien County and vicinity. Another instance of an ignored vehicular path is the "Allegan County Heritage Trail," a loop that can be traced by people wishing to see twenty-eight historic sites in the district. And a final illustration of a disregarded route is the "Historic Women of Michigan Theme Trail," a travel guide to nineteen places in the state that are of significance to women's history.

*Internationally, some famous named routes are the Silk Road (Asia), Appian Way (Italy), Burma Road (World War II), and the Ho Chi Minh Trail (Vietnam War).

**Some familiar western trails--like the Chisolm and the Goodnight-Loving--were cattle trails, not vehicular trails (other than for chuck wagons and such).

INTRODUCTION

Every day people driving in and through Detroit pass over freeways named Lodge, Jeffries and Fisher. Who are these people and why are there expressways in their honor? Travelers elsewhere in Michigan encounter highways called the Dixie, Red Arrow and Meridian. How did these roads come to bear these titles and what do the names mean?

Clearly, some people, organizations and events were once deemed worthy of recognition, as evidenced on the transportation landscape. But the bases for these tributes have not been handed down to the current era. Consequently, much of Michigan's motoring heritage has been lost in the fog of passing time.

Attempting to find the origins of a name for any particular stretch of concrete is an exceedingly difficult task. Since designating roads can be done at the local or state level, there is no single place that keeps records of these actions. For this reason, a study of highway etymology can be a most frustrating exercise.

It would be nice if there was just one source people could go to for facts on the background and origins of Michigan's principal named roads. What's needed is a compilation that explains the meaning of the unfamiliar words that identify many of the major highways that crisscross the state. This volume attempts to accomplish that goal.

Much of Michigan's motoring legacy has been forgotten. It is still remembered by mute road signs but has slipped the minds of passing generations. In an effort to recapture that missing part of our history, this work reacquaints us with the people and things that were once deemed so important they should be immortalized on the travel maps of this state.

With this compendium, travel can be more than getting from point A to point B. It can become a learning experience, an opportunity to satisfy curiosity, and a glimpse into Michigan's past as seen through the windshield. If driving about this state elicits questions, there should be a place to go for answers. In most cases, the desired explanation can be found between these covers.

Given the thousands of city streets, county roads, state trunklines, and federal highways in Michigan, some limitations had to be placed on an effort of this nature. To keep the project to manageable proportions, with a few exceptions for famous local trails the following pages restrict their attention to those numbered routes beginning with the letters M-(Michigan), US-(United States), and I-(Interstate).

These thoroughfares are the most heavily used stretches of pavement in the state and are thus likely to be the roads most familiar to readers. Furthermore, to have one of these major arteries designated in honor of a person or group can be considered one of the highest tributes possible in the realm of Michigan travel and a form of recognition worthy of a book.

This publication is organized alphabetically by the name of each road. Anyone wishing to access this book by the number of a route should consult the appendix section in the back. Tables at the end of this volume also track the establishment of named or memorial trunk lines chronologically and geographically.

A one- or two-page narrative vignette has been prepared for each of the highways featured in this book. Insofar as the historical record permits, these sketches include background information about the road, the reason for naming the motorway, the authority under which the christening was made, and the date this act was dedicated. Following the story of each trunkline there appears the coordinates of the route as found on the official state highway map issued by the Michigan Department of Transportation.

In many cases, the parties involved in naming a certain highway are now deceased and could not be consulted for background information, leaving old newspapers as the sole sources for particulars about some roads. In other instances, individuals who played a role in designating a particular Michigan trunkline are still living but for reasons that were never expressed refused to cooperate with this project, depriving future inquiring minds of their knowledge of the subjects. On a happier note, many more people who were participants in or witnesses to these events did offer their input, and to them the author expresses his gratitude for helpful details that were shared.

Aside from the large number of people who deserve acknowledgment in general for assistance rendered to the author, there are a few individuals whose contributions to this work merit specific mention. Carolyn Damstra (Michigan History Magazine), Mark Harvey (Michigan Bureau of History), Chris Byron and Gordon Olson (Grand Rapids Public Library), Patrick Morris (Newberry Library), Charles Hyde (Wayne State University), the staff at the Burton Historical Collections, Pete Hanses and Gary Eiseler (Michigan Department of Transportation), Caroline Scholfield (private researcher), Judy Huxmann (layout and design specialist), personnel at various County Road Commissions, and the crews at the State Archives, the MDOT Photo Lab, the Burton Historical Collection, and the Library of Michigan all played major roles in the creation of this volume.

Special praise is also in order for Larry and Priscilla Massie, who had such confidence in the worth of this book that they helped get it into print through personal contributions and the services of their Priscilla Press in the Allegan Forest.

Important assistance was also received from the MotorCities National Heritage Area organization, which generously underwrote a part of the publication costs with an award from its Mini-Grant Program.

In conclusion, some words are in order about the title of this book. A number of possibilities were considered, among them being (in alphabetical order): Driving the Paths From the Past; From Trails to Trunklines; Glancing in the Rearview Mirror--A Look Back at Special Michigan Highways; Highways of History; Highways of Honor; History in Concrete and Blacktop; History Over the Hood; Michigan History Through the Windshield; Our Motorway Heritage; The Roads Paved With Good Intentions; and Wheeling Through the Past. The chosen title was partially suggested by the staff at the MotorCities National Heritage Area. Those designations considered but rejected are revealed so as to help give potentially interested parties a better idea of the nature of this volume. Regardless of its name, as one travels through this book it is hoped that the reader enjoys a trip down Michigan's memory lanes.

**STAY
BETWEEN
BOOK
COVERS**

ADLER MEMORIAL HIGHWAY

Detroit Area

Morris Adler was born in Russia in 1906 and was brought to the United States seven years later by his parents. As an adult, he followed in his father's footsteps and became a conservative rabbi.

In 1938, Adler accepted the pulpit of Shaarey Zedek in Detroit. Under his leadership, the congregation grew into one of the largest in the country.

Within the Detroit Jewish community, Adler was viewed as a leader and expert in the field of adult Jewish education. Beyond the local religious scene, he held a number of important offices in organizations associated with his faith.

Adler was also considered a spokesman outside of ecclesiastical circles. Among the many capacities in which he served were stints with the Michigan Fair Election Practices Commission and the Governor's Commission on Higher Education. On 12 February 1966, while presiding at Sabbath services in his synagogue, Rabbi Adler was shot by a mentally ill youth. The best efforts of the medical profession could not save the clergyman, and he died of his wounds a month later.

The citizens of Michigan, and even those of the nation, were shocked by this tragedy. Governor George Romney, reflecting the public mood, declared Adler's funeral a day of mourning throughout the state.

The Michigan legislature sought some way of paying tribute to a man who had contributed so much to his religion and society in general.

The method arrived at was manifested in the form of House Concurrent Resolution 309 of 1966.

By virtue of this action, it was "resolved by the House of Representatives (the Senate concurring), that the portion of Northwestern Highway between the intersections of 8-Mile Road and Telegraph Road, currently designated as Interstate Highway I-696, is designated as Adler Memorial Highway, as a memorial to the late Rabbi Morris Adler of Southfield."

Some adjustments to this tribute were made in 2001 when the Legislature passed Act 142. This updated statute declared that "the portion of highway M-10 located in Oakland county between the intersections of US-24 and M-102 shall be known as the 'Adler Memorial Highway'."

And so appropriate recognition was given to a man who had lived gently but died violently. By this gesture the people of Michigan, working through their elected officials, helped to show that individuals of good will shall be remembered by a society who benefits from their presence, despite the efforts of evil to deprive us of their services.

Coordinates: Southeastern Michigan Enlargement C-D/6-7

ALGONQUIN TRAIL

Today, trunk line M-25 is a beautiful shoreline drive around the circumference of Michigan's Thumb. Running from Port Huron to Bay City, it is shown as a scenic route on nearly every highway map of our state.

But a road that exists main-ly for tourists is going to have a hard time competing for limited highway funds when pitted against more utilitarian thoroughfares. After all, no large towns are situated along the course of the coastal motorway and there are more direct land routes connecting the upper St. Clair River with Saginaw Bay.

This was the problem faced by the Thumb of Michigan Association, as it worked to encourage travelers to take M-25 while at the same time convincing the Highway Department to improve the road.

Believing that some catchy name would help its cause, the Association ran a contest in 1927 to see who could pick a fitting title for the road. The winner of the competition received $10 for coming up with the descriptive and euphonious phrase, "Blue Water Scenic Drive."

While the judges had done their jobs well, the motoring public was largely unresponsive to the lure of the words. Believing this problem was due to the label and not the product, in 1929 the Thumb of Michigan Association teamed up with the Southeastern Michigan Tourist and Publicity Association to rechristen M-25.

The replacement name chosen for the lake shore road was "Algonquin Trail." And to help promoters market the route, it was extended to run 270 miles around the Thumb from Bay City to the Ohio border. It still followed M-25 from Bay City to Port Huron, but from there south it took M-29 to New Baltimore, M-3 from New Baltimore to Detroit, M-85 from Detroit to Rockwood, and approximately I-75 from Rockwood to the state line.

Algonquin was a new name for the road, but not a stranger to the Michigan scene. It had already been applied to a township, two hamlets, a lake, a waterfall and two parks, plus served as the basis for such town names as Algansee, Algoma and Algonac.

As a term, Algonquin applied to those native Americans that belonged to a certain linguistic family. With the exception of the Winnebagos around Green Bay, this group included nearly all of the tribes in the western Great Lakes region. Thus, the "Algonquin Trail" was named in tribute to the Indians of the Midwest.

Unfortunately, such a noble gesture was to be short-lived. For just six months after the Algonquin Trail was created, the Great Depression began and the money supply became tight. Soon, no funds were available for advertising the route and the number of tourists who could afford to travel any scenic highway declined significantly.

Thus, without publicity and broad-based pleasure driving, the Algonquin Trail soon faded from the motoring lexicon. Today, the roads to which the name once applied are again carrying traffic of all sorts, but no longer do they pay honor to the Indians of Michigan.

Coordinates: I-K/12-14

AMERICAN LEGION MEMORIAL HIGHWAY (I-75)

The American Legion is the largest veterans association of its kind in the world. It was founded by Americans in Paris, France, just after World War I, but it was not incorporated by an act of Congress until 1919.

Originally, only American soldiers, sailors, marines and nurses who had served on active duty in World War I were allowed to be members. However, in 1942 the Legion amended its charter to allow World War II veterans to join. Korean War veterans became eligible for admission in 1950, and Vietnam War veterans were first accepted in 1966.

Today, the American Legion has about 2,600,000 people on its rolls distributed among approximately 1,600 posts. Working collectively, the members attempt to advance the interests of veterans, benefit the nation through useful projects, and encourage support of the Armed Forces.

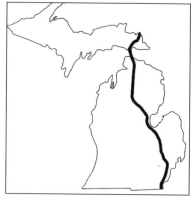

It is not surprising that an organization of this nature would have a Michigan road named in its honor. Such recognition was first bestowed in

1969 when, on the Legion's fiftieth birthday, the state legislature passed a concurrent resolution (HCR 21) "designating Interstate Highway 75 as the American Legion Memorial Highway."

Twenty-two signs along the route of I-75 were supposed to note that the freeway was a memorial to the American Legion. Unfortunately, it took the organization's members over three years to create and pay for the six-foot markers, and then the State Highway Department did not finish installing them until the end of 1972.

By 1984, "many of the plaques had fallen into disrepair. Some people thought that the best way to ensure that the memorial plaques were properly maintained was to place the designation of I-75 as American Legion Highway into statute and [then] to require the Department of Transportation to provide suitable markers."

The desired law would remove

from the private sector the burden of maintaining the commendatory signs and instead put the obligation to do so upon a government agency that specializes in much matters. This goal was accomplished in 1984 when Public Act 174 was passed by the legislature, once again designating the length of I-75 as the American Legion Memorial Highway and reassigning responsibility for the markers.

The new legislation gave the American Legion Memorial Highway and its roadside indicators the same status as nearly all similar designated routes in Michigan. As one observer noted, "if the membership of the American Legion could survive World Wars I and II, Korea and Vietnam, it's nice to see the state see to it that [the organization's] signs will survive the effects of time."

Coordinates: C-N/10-13

- -

AMERICAN LEGION MEMORIAL HIGHWAY (ANN ARBOR)

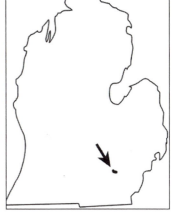

Not long after the state built a trunk line bypass south of Ann Arbor, someone suggested that the cut-off for what was then route M-17 be made a road of remembrance. This idea was embraced by the local American Legion Post, and in January of 1930 the members of that body committed themselves to making the newly-paved artery "a living memorial to soldiers and sailors who gave their lives in the World War."

This goal would be achieved by setting out 400 elm trees 50 feet apart on either side of the highway. Since the trees would be purchased and planted by Legionnaires, and since their national organization was founded for the benefit of World War I veterans, the avenue would be called the American Legion Memorial Highway.

The State Highway Department gave its blessing to this proposal, and by early April all of the two-inch diameter saplings had been put in place. Bronze plaques were installed at the base of each tree to indicate the name of the departed soldier in whose memory it had been planted.

This tribute to Ann Arbor's fallen soldiers was dedicated on 30 May 1930, when over a thousand people gathered to view the completed project and honor the veterans for whom it had been undertaken. Those present were told of future plans to erect suitable monuments at both ends of the highway to indicate its memorial character to those approaching for either direction.

Much has changed since that ceremony in 1930. Today, the trees have all succumbed to Dutch elm disease, the route is no longer a trunk line highway, and few people realize the avenue was ever a memorial road. All most people know is that the street is a heavily travelled thoroughfare called Stadium Boulevard.

Coordinates: Southeastern Michigan Enlargement F/1

AMVETS MEMORIAL HIGHWAYS

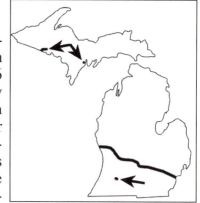

AMVETS is the abbreviated title of a national organization known as the American Veterans of World War II, Korea and Vietnam. Founded in 1944, its stated aims are to promote world peace, preserve American ideals, and help veterans to help themselves.

Membership in this association is open to all citizens of the United States who served honorably in our nation's armed forces since 1940. There are about 1,600 local posts scattered across the country, collectively comprised of around 250,000 members.

The first effort to associate the AMVETS name with a road came from the organization's Post 123 in Escanaba. This chapter petitioned the legislature to assign the acronym to that portion of routes US-2, US-41, and M-35 that extend south 1.1 miles from county road 426 to the northern city limits of Escanaba. The politicians in Lansing endorsed this idea in 1959 under authority of Public Act 144, which declared the highway to be "Amvets Memorial Drive" (spelled "AmVets Memorial Drive" by PA 142 of 2001).

The second attempt to name a trunk line after this veterans group occurred when members of its Post 74 asked that a portion of Business Route I-94 in Kalamazoo be designated AMVET Memorial Parkway. The Michigan legislature granted this request in 1963 through House Concurrent Resolution 13 (modified to "AmVets Memorial Parkway" by PA 142 of 2001).

The third endeavor to honor

American Veterans occurred on 30 May 1976 when Iron County Road 436 from about Iron River west to the Wisconsin border was dedicated as the Amvets Memorial Highway. Although action relating to county roads would seem to be outside of the purview of this book, the most easterly portion of this route was, until 1933, a part of trunk line US-2.

The last move to tie AMVETS to a road began in 1990, when the Michigan legislature passed House Concurrent Resolution 134 which named all of I-96 as the AMVETS Memorial Highway. While this measure gave the veterans group some well-deserved recognition, it "did not provide for signs to be placed anywhere along the freeway." To correct this oversight, in 1994 the legislature passed Public Act 124. This statute prescribed that it was the duty of the state Transportation Department to provide for the erection of suitable markers upon the route indicating the name of the AMVETS Memorial Highway. The final effort at fine tuning was conducted under PA 142 of 2001, when the Legislature slightly changed the spelling of the road to "AmVets Memorial Highway."

Coordinates: D/6; Kalamazoo Inset; D/3; K-M/8-13

ARCTIC-TROPIC OVERLAND TRAIL

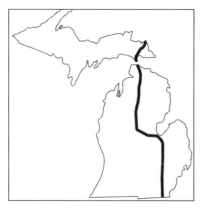

As we learned in grade school, in the global method of location-finding the equator is zero degrees latitude and the north pole is ninety degrees latitude. This review of our early geography lessons is necessary to remind us that 45 degrees of latitude--the imaginary horizontal line midway between the widest part of the earth and its very top point-- runs through parts of Michigan.

This line of demarcation was initially identified for the

benefit of Michigan's motorists in 1940 at a point just north of Menominee along US-41, where a roadside monument declared that viewers were equally between the equator and the north pole, the distance being 3107.47 miles north or south. People standing at this site would be midway between the arctic and the tropics.

Though the marker near Menominee was the first time the Northern Hemisphere's dividing line had been made known to travelers, people had for decades been aware of the fact intellectually. It was this awareness that gave rise to a proposal to develop a highway between the two climatic extremes of torrid and frigid.

In December of 1916 the Saginaw Board of Trade announced its idea of sponsoring an international Arctic-Tropic highway to run from Miami, Florida to James Bay in northern Ontario. The organization's intent was to create the greatest north/south road on the continent, stretching from Biscayne Bay to nearly Hudson's Bay, a distance of more than 2,000 miles.

In Michigan the proposed route approximately followed contemporary US-23 from Toledo to Saginaw, US-10 from Saginaw to Clare, US-27 from Clare to just south of Grayling, and I-75 from around Grayling to Sault Ste. Marie.

Tracing this course, the envisioned motorway closely paralleled but did not strictly duplicate the newly born Dixie Highway which also linked the cool waters of the Great Lakes with the warm waters of the Gulf Stream.

Though the Arctic-Tropic highway was still being talked about as late as 1918, it never survived to see the 1920s. Not only was the route overshadowed by the success of the closely-aligned Dixie Highway, but its goals were much too ambitious to be successful. For while it is nice to be a dreamer, the Saginaw Board of Trade's brain child was about a century before its time, as not even now is it possible for one to drive a vehicle from warm and sunny Miami to the subpolar region around James Bay, Ontario.

In 1916 the businessmen of Saginaw believed that tourists, the curious, and those in search of mineral riches would be interested in driving along their envisioned Arctic-Tropic Overland Trail. If this class of wayfarer, or anyone else, wishes to take the trip today, they had best be prepared to walk or ride the train over the last 150 miles of the road's contemplated northern extent for the high-latitude portion of the highway has yet to be built.

Coordinates: C-N/10-13

ARTHUR VANDENBERG MEMORIAL HIGHWAY

Many of the memorial highways in Michigan are named for people who were prominent in their time but are relatively unknown today. Such may said to be the case with a once-famous resident of this state, Arthur Hendrick Vandenberg.

In the first half of this century, Vandenberg was a powerful figure in American politics. His stature may be gauged from fact that he was the only Republican senator in the populous states of the Midwest to survive the Roosevelt sweep of 1934. And in the 1946 elections, he easily won his seat "without making a political speech or an appearance in the state in behalf of his campaign."

Vandenberg was born in Grand Rapids on 22 March 1884, where he was educated in the public schools. After studying law for one year at the University of Michigan, he returned to his

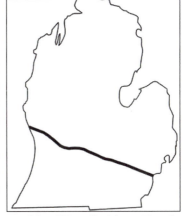

home town to work at the Grand Rapids Herald. In 1906, at the age of 22, he was made editor and general manager of the newspaper, positions he held until 1928.

When the Honorable Woodbridge Ferris died in 1928, Vandenberg was appointed to succeed him in the US Senate. After moving to Washington, Vandenberg became known as a leader of the "isolationist bloc" in foreign policy and an opponent of Roosevelt and his New Deal on the domestic scene.

As one of the Republican luminaries, Vandenberg was considered by his party as a likely prospect for higher office. But he declined the GOP vice-presidential candidacy in 1936, and at the national convention in 1940 he received only 76 votes for the presidential nomination.

World War II had a significant impact on Vandenberg and his world view. During the course of this conflict he realized that the United States could no longer insulate itself from events overseas, but had to take a leadership role in global affairs. This change in philosophy made him a major player in shaping US foreign policy during the remainder of his political career.

In his new role as a leader in crafting international legislation, Vandenberg became one of the most significant figures in postwar Congress. He helped draft the United Nations' charter and was instrumental in securing the Senate's almost unanimous ratification of that document. Vandenberg also guided the Marshall Plan for European recovery through the Senate and he helped lay the groundwork for establishment of the North Atlantic Treaty Organization.

After Vandenberg died on 18 April 1951 in Grand Rapids, many people wanted this state to pay tribute to its famous native son. The Michigan legislature obliged in 1952 by passing Public Act 70 which declared US-16 between Detroit and Muskegon to be the Arthur Vandenberg Memorial Highway. Route US-16 disappeared in the Fall of 1962 upon completion of I-96, and so a road of remembrance gradually passed from memory like the person it was meant to honor.

Coordinates: K-M/8-13

A marker along the route of the Blue Star Memorial Highway as photographed in 1949 at a roadside garden adjacent to US-31 south of Traverse City. See related text on pages 32-33.

BAGLEY ROAD

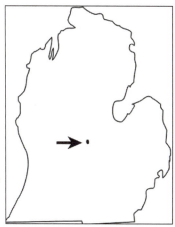

Though John Judson Bagley was born on 24 July 1832 in Medina, New York, he became a resident of Michigan when he moved to this state with his parents in 1840. Settling first in Constantine and then later in Owosso, Bagley began working in country stores at the age of thirteen. By the time he was 21, Bagley had started his own tobacco firm in Detroit, a manufacturing concern that eventually earned him a fortune as "one of the Midwest's largest producers of chewing tobacco."

As a prominent Detroit businessman, Bagley was active in local government. At various times he served as a police commissioner, city councilman, and member of the municipal board of education. He was also a driving force behind some of the town's commercial establishments, helping to found the Michigan Mutual Life Insurance Company (performing for several years as its president), aiding in the incorporation of the Wayne County Savings Bank, plus serving as director of the American National Bank, vice president of the American Exchange National Bank, and president of the Detroit Safe Company.

Bagley's energies were also evident in political circles, where he participated in the formation of the Republican Party at Jackson, Michigan. Later, he was twice elected our state Governor on the GOP ticket, serving successive terms in 1872 and 1874. Thereafter, he retired to a relatively short business and civic life before dying in San Francisco on 27 July 1881. He is buried in Detroit.

During his time as Michigan's chief executive, Bagley achieved a number of notable accomplishments. Among these successes were overseeing the beginning construction of our present state capitol, reorganizing the state militia, creating the offices of Fish Commissioner, Railroad Commissioner, and Board of Public Health, and developing the Public School for Dependent Children in the town of Coldwater for youngsters who were wards of the state.

Because of these and other achievements, Gratiot County officials decided in April of 1942 to name one of their north/south roads in honor of John Bagley. Fortunately for the ex-Governor, the most southerly twelve miles of this thoroughfare happened to coincide with the route of trunk line US-127, giving the former chief executive a federal memorial highway in Michigan.

Coordinates: K/11

BASE LINE ROAD

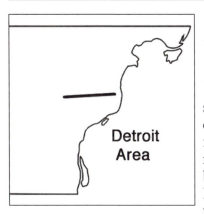

Detroit Area

In 1815 Congress decided that a survey should be conducted of the land in Michigan Territory which had been ceded by the Indians. The frontier of this nation was inexorably moving cross-continent, and by then pioneers were increasingly interested in settling down near the western Great Lakes.

In order for a survey to occur, it was first necessary to establish two standard lines from which all measurements would be taken. These two axes were known as a principal meridian (to run north and south) and a base line (to run east and west).

To create this basic coordinate system, on 18 April 1815 the federal government hired Alexander Holmes to lay out the base line at a rate of $3.00 per mile. His instructions were to run the line from a point of his choosing somewhere north of Detroit.

Holmes waited until Fall was well advanced before starting his work, probably because by then the mosquitoes were gone and the leafless trees made it easier to sight his transit. However, by waiting until late in the year to undertake his task, Holmes traded one set of problems for another.

Writing in mid-November, he said "we have been wading in ice and water for three days and are completely worn out." About a week later he penned, "we have suffered almost ever[y] difficulty that could be expected for mortals to endure." Despite this adversity, by 1816 Holmes had finished setting off the baseline from Lake St. Clair west to about Base Line Lake between Livingston and Washtenaw counties.

It eventually took six other surveyors to finish running the base line the rest of the way across the state. Not until May of 1827 was the 173rd mile of this axis finally established on the shore of Lake Michigan. By then, it was starting to serve as the northern boundary of the second tier of counties in a Michigan increasingly growing in population.

As Michigan developed, it was necessary to create a road network that would serve its transportation needs. With this goal in mind, in 1827 the Territorial Legislature enacted a law declaring that all township highway commissioners were "required to cause to be opened a public road on the line of each section of land in their respective townships."

Since normal section lines are one mile apart, this statute meant that a checkerboard pattern of roads would be built across Michigan at one mile intervals. Because of this regular spacing, Wayne County residents named the east-west roads for their approximate distance from De-

troit. Under this arrangement, the surveyors' base line was called Eight Mile Road.

To many people the base line was special, and not just another one of the main highways north of Detroit named in ascending numerical order. To bestow appropriate significance upon the street, on 28 December 1926 the Wayne County Road Commission changed its title to Base Line Road. Two years later the State, in what might be considered a gesture of respect, gave it another identity as trunk line M-102, an honor it still holds today.

As the boundary line between three counties--and as the linear demarcation between Detroit and the northern suburbs--Base Line Road has come in the eyes of some to represent a barrier rather than an avenue of movement and communication. In an effort to overcome this negative impression, certain parties have suggested a new start to regional interaction by rechristening Base Line Road.

Some of the new names that have been seriously proposed are Tri-County Boulevard, City-County Boulevard, East-West Avenue, Industry Avenue, Gordie Howe Avenue, Coleman Young Boulevard, Metro Detroit Drive, and Michigan's Way. Other ideas stem from a lighter vein, like Motown Parkway, The Great Divide, Jimmy Hoffa Highway, Motor City Raceway, and Pothole Road. The thoroughfare under its name of Eight Mile Road was also honored in the title of the autobiographical motion picture film by the famous Michigan rock star, Eminem. Whether route M-102 is called Eight Mile Road or one of the above alternative choices, it will always remain the one and only base line in Michigan.

Coordinates: Southeastern Michigan Enlargement D/6-10

BAY CITY HISTORIC HERITAGE ROUTE

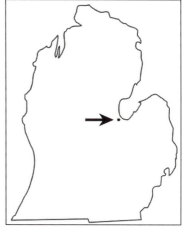

Basically put, there are two kinds of roads in our state: those that are mainly used for getting from here to there, and those that receive use in part because they offer an enjoyable experience or a scenic ride. For decades the functional or utilitarian highway has received most of the funds and attention from the Department of Transportation, but beginning in 1993 additional emphasis started to be placed on pavements that people take for sightseeing and recreation.

This modification in priorities came about on account of a new law that sought to advance the development and promotion of drives that expose people to some of the special natural and cultural characteristics that make up our two peninsulas. It was noted in the statute that certain portions of Michigan's trunk line system are uniquely endowed with these amenities adjacent to the roadside. In these cases, it was felt, wayfarers should be encouraged to use the highways for the pleasurable experience of just traveling rather than as a route to a particular destination.

When the legislative bill as finally approved included historical significance among the resources to be emphasized, Bay City realized it could easily participate in the program. For along 1.5 miles of its Center Avenue (M-25) from near downtown east to about the municipal limits, the community had one of Michigan's most outstanding collections of architecturally significant residences and institutional buildings.

The lavish structures date from the early 1870s forward, when some of Bay City's most affluent families began to build homes along the tree-lined street that ultimately became one of the town's principal east/west thoroughfares. These wealthy people displayed their fortunes in their dwellings, erecting elegant Victorian mansions on well-spaced sites with broad lawns and ample set-backs from the road.

Eventually, as the well-to-do continued to move to this prestigious address, 262 opulent buildings occupying a combined 113 acres were constructed along or near what came to be called Bay City's "Grand Promenade." Fortunately, most of these estates remained in the hands of prosperous people over the years and they were generally well-maintained up to the present era.

In the 1970s, Bay City officials realized they had to take steps to preserve these examples of the town's finest architecture. To accomplish this goal, they first worked to get many of the structures on the National Register of Historic Places. Next, they helped with successful efforts to have the entire locality designated an historic district.

Continuing these local preservation labors, when the Historic Heritage Highways act was passed in 1993 Bay City was the second municipality to qualify under the program, receiving official recognition for its unique Center Avenue neighborhood on 13 August 1997. This designation was dedicated on October 23 of that year, and because of that ceremony today a special symbol on the official state highway map guides motorists to a Michigan trunk line through Bay City's most impressive residential area.

Coordinates: Bay City Inset

BICENTENNIAL FREEDOM WAY

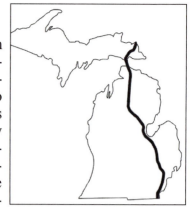

It is common knowledge that the American Colonies proclaimed their freedom from British rule through an instrument called the Declaration of Independence. It may not be common knowledge, however, that there was a highway in Michigan named in honor of this event.

The United States celebrates its birthday on July 4 because on that date in 1776 the Second Continental Congress adopted the final draft of a document that irrevocably severed our bonds with the mother country.

As the 200th anniversary of this event approached, members of the Michigan legislature looked for an appropriate way to recognize the occasion. One of the ways adopted was through passage of Senate Concurrent Resolution 216 of 1975 which made I-75 "the Michigan Bicentennial Freedom Way."

The longest freeway in Michigan is I-75 which travels from the Ohio line, over the Mackinac Bridge, to the international border at Sault Ste. Marie. The last link in this 395-mile highway opened 1 November 1973 when the stretch between Roscommon and West Branch was finished.

With the completion of Michigan's "Main Street" fresh in their minds, the solons in Lansing picked I-75 for special Bicentennial designation because it passed through the state's two oldest cities (Detroit and Sault Ste. Marie), both of which were established prior to the American Revolution.

Another contributing factor in the selection of this route was that the freeway's number--75--coincided with the year in which the American Revolution began. Contrary to what some drivers may think as they bump along this interstate today, certain stretches of the road have not existed unmaintained since colonial times.

Also having some bearing on the choice for Bicentennial route was the earlier decision of the Department of State Highways and the Department of Natural Resources to release in 1976 a road log or trip-book for I-75 identifying the points of interest along its course. Having this publication available meant that no additional promotional pieces had to be created for the celebration.

The final determinant in throwing the official spotlight on I-75 was the recognition that, of all the highways in Michigan, it was the only one that was a segment of an interstate that extended the full length of the Nation (it ends in Miami, Florida, which, despite not reaching to the Keys, was far enough to make the point).

These combined elements were what prompted the legislature to give special recognition to I-75 for just the Bicentennial year. Thus, in addition to being featured on our country's 200 birthday, I-75 also became the only known memorial road in Michigan to be purposely limited to a single year's duration.

Coordinates: C-N/10-13

BLOSSOM HIGHWAY

Charles William Post--the man who invented Post cereals and helped to make Battle Creek famous--had some ideas for things besides breakfast foods. One of his notions was a scheme on how to maintain Calhoun County roads at no cost to the taxpayers.

In 1914 Post suggested that two-year-old cherry trees be planted sixty feet apart on both sides of the road between Battle Creek and Marshall. This project would require setting out 17,600 saplings and, after expenses of about $200 per mile to remove existing vegetation, cost a total of around $14,500 to implement.

The purpose of this exercise was two-fold. First, the presence of the trees would greatly enhance the beauty of the road by creating in season an avenue of flowers between two of Calhoun County's major towns. Second, according to the reasoning of Mr. Post, the yield from these trees would help pay for repairs to the bordering road.

Under the Post plan, highways lined with fruit trees could produce enough revenue to provide for their own upkeep. This roadside linear forest would be looked after by county officials while they also maintained the intermediate pavement. Then at harvest time nature's bounty could be auctioned off to the highest bidders, generating an anticipated income of from $425 to $500 per mile to help reimburse the public coffers.

Whatever the merits of this idea, it was not well received. The county road commissioners were not at all interested in becoming pomologists, and abutting property owners along the route expressed concern about motorists stopping to climb in the trees and eat the fruit. Consequently, the proposal never bore fruit.

But fifteen years later a modified version of Post's suggestion was floated by a Battle Creek newspaper. Eliminating the original part about harvesting the fruit for public financial gain and expanding the scope of the enterprise, the daily editorialized on 5 May 1929 that fruit trees should be planted all along the route followed by I-94 today, making the entire road the Blossom Highway.

Envisioned by this idea was a scenic lane of shade and flowers from New Buffalo to Detroit that would attract tourists, highlight the region's large fruit-growing industry, and create for local residents "a route of sweetly-scented and delicately-tinted trees." Since the trunk line was often used as a gateway to our state, implementing the recommendation would also serve to properly introduce travelers to Michigan by exposing them to an enchanted pathway trimmed with a "bower of blossoms."

The concept of turning Michigan's principal east/west thoroughfare into an alluring drive with a romantic-sounding name was well received in many quarters, with newspapers in Ann Arbor, Grand Rapids, and Chicago coming out in support of the cause. But the State Highway Department insisted that the road be known solely by a number designation, and so the Blossom Highway was nipped in the bud.

In the 1950s, during the annual Blossom Festival in St. Joseph and Benton Harbor, "Blossom Trails" were established for people to follow if they wanted to view the area's fruit orchards in bloom. Though some of these vehicular paths did coincide with federal highways, the Trails were only temporary and never carried official government status.

Coordinates: M-N/7-13

BLUE & GRAY TRAIL

In 1929 a monument was dedicated in Pomroy, Ohio, to John Hunt Morgan, the famous Confederate cavalry general. As individuals who fought on both sides of our Civil War met there to celebrate this occasion, they collectively resolved that something should be done to help bring the two opposing regions of the conflict together.

After some deliberation, it was decided that a highway connecting the tidewater of the Atlantic Ocean with the fresh water of the Great Lakes would help to bind the former combatants together. This proposed link between Dixieland and the Midwest was envisioned as a future artery of traffic and friendship between the North and South.

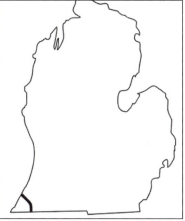

During the War Between the States, those fighting for the North usually wore blue uniforms and men comprising the Confederate army wore gray. In honor of the soldiers who served on either side in this great struggle, it was decided that the contemplated road should be known as the Blue & Gray Trail.

Initially, the memorial route was planned to

run from Norfolk, Virginia, west to Muskegon via such Michigan towns as Hillsdale, Marshall, Battle Creek, Hastings and Grand Rapids. Though there was much local support for this idea, the State Highway Commissioner refused to allow the chosen path to carry the name of Blue & Gray Trail. He insisted that Michigan roads be assigned a number only.

For some years the promoters of the paved tribute to Civil War soldiers tried to change the Highway Commissioner's mind, but with no success. Finally, in an effort to resolve the matter and fulfill their dream, the sponsors of the Blue & Gray Trail abandoned the projected diagonal course across southern Michigan and adopted US-33 as their memorial motorway.

The newly chosen trunk line did have some mileage in our State, but much less than that initially allotted by the group to Michigan. US-33 was confined solely to Berrien County, crossing our border with Indiana just north of South Bend and passing through Niles and Berrien Springs en-

route to its terminus at St. Joseph on the shore of Lake Michigan (a path generally followed by contemporary US-31).

Thus the Blue & Gray Trail, which for nearly a decade sought to define its configuration, was formally established in 1938. The 838-mile highway was so long it had to be dedicated twice. The first ceremony took place at Richmond, Virginia, on 2 May 1938 while the western end was officially opened with a celebration at St. Joseph five days later.

Today, US-33 still connects part of the eastern seaboard with the Great Lakes region as it passes through the states of Virginia, West Virginia, Ohio, and Indiana. But the soldiers of the Civil War are no longer honored by the road (this status having been forgotten), as that privilege has passed on to the annual Blue & Gray football game played each Christmas day in Montgomery, Alabama.

Coordinates: N/7-8

BLUE STAR MEMORIAL HIGHWAY

The Blue Star Mothers of America--a body chartered by the Congress of the United States in June of 1960--is an organization dedicated to the memory of the men and women who have served this country as members of the Armed Forces. Practicing members display a flag with a blue star for each member of their family who is on active duty.

The origins of this female fraternity can be traced back to January, 1942, when Army Captain George H. Maines ran a newspaper article in the Flint Journal requesting information from mothers about their children serving in the armed forces. More than 1,000 women responded to this call, and by 8 March 1942 the Blue Star Mothers of America, Inc., were formed with chapters in Michigan and eight other states.

Admission to the association is limited to mothers whose sons and daughters have served (or are serving) in the U.S. military. Originally the goals of the group were "to bring our sons home, to ensure they received the benefits they

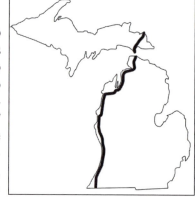

deserved, help service member's families, help each other and to be there if something happened." Over the years the purpose of the society has grown, and now members often serve as volunteers in Veterans' Administration hospitals helping to care for the needs of patients and work to promote civil defense.

Because of the noble nature of this group, the State Highway Commissioner was encouraged to name a road after them. Consequently, Charles M. Ziegler declared that US-23 and US-31 from the southern border of Michigan to Mackinaw City, and US-2 from Saint Ignace to the Soo, would be called the Blue Star Memorial Highway.

This kind gesture was met with "a roar of protest" by the Spanish-American War veterans, who pointed out that in 1945 the legislature had dedicated US-23 as a memorial to their war efforts.

The Commissioner quickly bowed to the "heated protests" from the Spanish-American War soldiers and agreed to leave US-23 solely to the veterans of 1898. The remaining two trunk lines were together named the Blue Star Memorial Highway, an act that was formally dedicated at Mackinaw City on 10 October 1948.

The flap over mistakenly including US-23 in the original plan disquieted some people, who felt such a problem might occur again. Therefore, in a move to ensure that no confusion arose in the future, in 1952 the Michigan legislature passed Public Act 71 officially sanctioning the Blue Star Memorial Highway. This gesture was repeated in 2001 when the state's lawmakers approved Act 142 which once again averred that US-31 was to bear a name in tribute to the esteemed Blue Star Mothers.

Coordinates: C-N/7-11

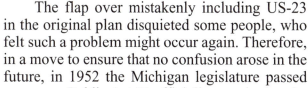

BLUE WATER HIGHWAY (M-21)

For decades the only way for the public to travel the few hundred feet from Port Huron, Michigan across the St. Clair River to Sarnia, Ontario (or visa versa) was on a comparatively slow ferry boat. This floating highway link was sufficient to accommodate the traffic load until the mid-1920s, by which time the number of automobiles trying to move between Canada and the United States had overloaded the waterborne transportation system.

A study conducted in the summer of 1927 showed that so many people wanted to make the Port Huron/Sarnia crossing that it would pay to build a bridge at the site. Since such a span would be crossing an international boundary, Congress had to approve the idea which it did under Public Law 312 of 1928.

For a couple of years thereafter private interests tried to obtain financing for the project, but the necessary funds could not be raised, particularly after the onset of the Great Depression late in 1929. It eventually became clear that the desired bridge could only be built with public support, so in 1935 the Michigan Legislature passed Public Act 147 creating a state commission to do just that.

Ground-breaking ceremonies took place on 24 June 1937, with construction starting on both shores and proceeding outward over the water. By 24 May 1938

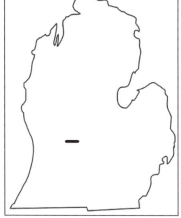

the steel was all in place, and on 8 October of that year the bridge was dedicated and opened to traffic.

What motorists received was a $3,000,000 span that soared 152 feet above the surrounding landscape, stretching for 1.25 miles as a lasting symbol of peace and interaction between the US and Canada. Since the structure offered excellent views of beautiful Lake Huron and the St. Clair River, it was appropriately named the Blue Water Bridge.

This bridge became an important crossing for those seeking to avoid the congestion of the Ambassador Bridge at Detroit or find a shortcut route between mid-Michigan and southwestern Ontario. One of the main arteries that carried this traffic was trunk line M-21, a highway that then

extended westerly across our state from Port Huron through Ionia to Holland connecting the blue waters of Lake Huron with the blue waters of Lake Michigan.

In 1947 and 1948, officials in Ionia County began to name and mark all of the roads within their boundaries to make it easier for drivers to reach their destinations. Seeing their portion of M-21 as part of the interlake system to benefit from the construction of the Blue Water Bridge, county authorities decided to call the route the Blue Water Highway, a gesture apparently approved by the State Highway Commissioner in November of 1948.

Coordinates: K-L/ 9-10

BLUE WATER HIGHWAY (US-25)

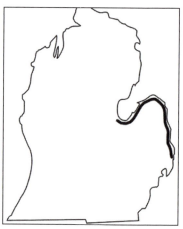

The Blue Water Bridge links Port Huron with Sarnia, Ontario, at the mouth of the St. Clair River. When the $3,000,000 span was finished in 1938, it was a cause for celebration and pride throughout the southern Lower Peninsula.

With connections at this important border crossing no longer dependent upon slow ferry boats, the number of people attracted to this locality increased greatly. Unfortunately, some of the area's roads were not up to the challenge of accommodating the increased traffic.

One of these inadequate highways was US-25. This route started in Miami, Florida, and proceeded north through Monroe, Detroit, and Port Huron, terminating at the tip of Michigan's thumbnail, Port Austin. For its entire course this federal transportation artery was paved, with the exception of the forty miles between Grindstone City and Port Sanilac.

In an effort to correct this embarrassing situation, 300 Thumb-area men met at Harbor Beach on 1 December 1938 for the purpose of promoting the improvement of US-25 north of Port Huron. Agreeing to work for a common cause, those in attendance sought a name for their new organization and its adopted shoreline highway.

With the completion of the bridge between Port Huron and Sarnia fresh in their minds, the delegates declared themselves to be the Michigan Blue Water Highway Association and the road they championed was christened the Blue Water Highway.

It was necessary to put "Michigan" in their name because Ontario already had a Blue Water Highway, route 21, running from about Sarnia to Owen Sound. Given the success of this Canadian Lake Huron shore road in attracting motorists, the people along the east coast of the Thumb hoped that similar good fortune would smile on them.

For the purpose of the Michigan Blue Water Highway Association was not just to get the last gravel stretches of US-25 turned to concrete, its goal was also to entice travelers to drive the upper reaches of that route and visit the area it served. To draw the desired tourists, the organization worked to make the road one of the most beautiful in the United States.

Engaging in a two-pronged attack, the Association first got a commitment from the State Highway Department to fully pave US-25 by 1944. Next, it set about preserving and upgrading the aesthetic qualities of the ninety-mile drive that almost continuously had Lake Huron in sight.

Landscaping was done all along the trunk line, though no trees or shrubs were planted on the east side which would tend to obscure the lake view. Some attractive right-of-way was purchased to prevent it from being developed, selected spots were acquired for scenic turnouts, roadside parks were built, camping grounds established, and other improvements made to areas adjacent to the route.

Just as it seemed the Blue Water Highway effort was going to be a success, everything was interrupted by World War II. By the time the conflict was over, other matters had captured the attention of local residents and the concerted effort to upgrade the region's main road was left in the dust as public interest shifted to what were viewed as more important issues.

In 1973, as the sort of last act in a tragedy, even US-25 was decommissioned with the route reverting to state control as M-25. But the unfinished efforts of the Blue Water Highway Association had not been in vain, for its enhancements of one of the Michigan's longest shore-hugging avenues left a positive Thumbprint on the beckoning hand formed by the Lower Peninsula.

Coordinates: I-K/14

BLUE WATER TRAIL

As the old saying goes, it is possible to have too much of a good thing. A prime example of this observation's merits can be found in Michigan, which has a Blue Water Bridge (Port Huron) and two Blue Water Highways (parts of trunk lines M-25 and M-21). What the state didn't need was another road called "Blue Water," but the words apparently have an irresistible charm.

Succumbing to the lure of the phrase, in August of 1940 the non-profit Blue Water Trail Association was formed to promote a waterfront drive from Chicago to Detroit. Supported by the 25 principal towns along the way, the designated course along two of the Great Lakes was envisioned to become one of America's most popular travel routes.

Entering Michigan at Menominee, the motorway followed M-35 from Menominee to Escanaba, US-2 from Escanaba to St. Ignace, and I-75 from St. Ignace to Sault Sainte Marie. After crossing the Straits, the itinerary continued in the Lower Peninsula along US-23 from Mackinaw City to Bay City, M-25 from Bay City to Port Huron, M-29 from Port Huron to near New Baltimore, and I-94 from about New Baltimore to Detroit.

People wishing to take a ride on this thousand-mile-long odyssey would enjoy one of our nation's greatest outdoor show places, running along the picturesque western and northern shores of Lake Michigan and the western coast of Lake Huron. In addition to scenic pleasures for the eye there were educational benefits for the mind, as the trip led to many famous frontier sites in the Midwest and followed paths tred centuries ago by Indians, French explorers and trail blazers, fur traders and voyageurs, and soldiers of the War of 1812.

With so much to recommend it, the enterprise was endorsed by Michigan's highway commissioner and businessmen along the route looked forward to the economic stimulus vacationers would bring to their communities. But the travelers and benefits barely materialized because before the Association could undertake a full-scale advertising campaign World War II came to this country, sharply curtailing leisure-time activities.

With survival of the United States at stake, attention was understandably turned from tourism to defense and the production of armaments. By the time hostilities creased five years later, it was too late for the Association to recover from the hiatus. So, while the Blue Water Trail took people on a track steeped in historic legends of former centuries, due to the interruption brought by the Second World War the named road itself is now a thing of the past.

Coordinates: C-M/5-13

BLUEWATER CIRCLE DRIVE

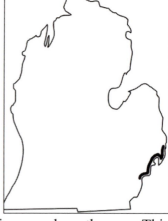

When World War II ended, North Americans not only wanted to pick up where they left off in civilian life, they tried to make up for lost time. With gas and tire rationing ended, manufacturing plants turning out automobiles once more instead of military equipment, and full employment in the economy, people could once again engage in the favorite pastimes of a Sunday spin in the family car and the motoring weekend or extended vacation.

To guide these pent-up, four-wheeled wayfarers on their outings, in 1947 Canadian Joe M. Harrison and the Chatham, Ontario, Chamber of Commerce put together a scenic circuit for travelers to follow. Called the Bluewater Circle Drive (but also known in some quarters as the Michigan/Ontario International Circle Drive), the route was supposed to attract trip-takers to the interesting sites to be found on both sides of River and Lake St. Clair.

Since this regional vehicular roundabout was conceived in Canada, its focus was understandably on the sights, features, activities and tourist services of southwestern Ontario. Nevertheless, Michigan did get some of the attention. The U.S. portion of the Circle Drive started in Port Huron and followed M-29 to its terminus. At that point it approximately traced the route of contemporary I-94 south to Jefferson Avenue, a road that marked the Bluewater's course into downtown Detroit. From the waterfront of the Motor City one could find bridge and tunnel connections to Windsor, where the Canadian part of the orbital itinerary started back north through Chatham to Sarnia.

A guide book was published annually by promoters of the Circle Drive, a printed release that highlighted places of interest and gave advertising space to businesses along the way. This complimentary handout included a small section on Michigan until about 1972, when our state was dropped from the publication and the Circle Drive ceased to exist as an international entity. According to one of the former officers, "with changes in our life styles and progress and improvements in highways it was no longer attractive [for leisure motorists to take a holiday jaunt] around the original Bluewater Drive route."

The guidebook that once escorted people as they moved along the International Circle path still exists today as the "Bluewater Visitor Guide," but the text is devoted solely to Ontario attractions. And while the Canadian portion of the highway still gets attention in the recreational press, the Michigan segment of what was once the Bluewater Circle Drive has long since been forgotten under its old name by the travel industry and the motoring public.

Coordinates: K-M/14

BOHN HIGHWAY

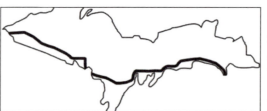

The State Administrative Board was established in 1921 for the purpose of exercising supervisory control over all government departments, boards and commissions above the county and regional level.

So far as can be determined, on only two occasions has this body ever named a state road after an individual. One of these actions occurred on 1 July 1924, when the Board resolved "that the Michigan trunk line highway designated as Number Twelve shall be hereafter known as the Bohn Highway."

This route we know today as US-2, the major east/west highway in the Upper Peninsula. The reason Bohn's name was associated with this road is because he was one of the most prominent citizens in the region.

Frank Probasco Bohn came to the area in 1890 and then moved to Newberry, his permanent residence, in 1898. There, he served as village president from 1904 to 1919, member of the school board from 1908 to1914, President of the Newberry State Bank from 1909 to 1941, member of the state senate from 1923 to 1926, and representative to Congress from 1927 to 1933.

As a physician, Bohn practiced medicine from 1890 until 1923. He was

also a trustee of the Newberry State Hospital for 20 years, the institution's president for twelve years, and a member of the State Hospital Commission from 1935 to 1937.

After a distinguished career, Bohn died at his home in Newberry on 1 June 1944 as the town's "most popular and highly respected resident." His "funeral cortege was one of the largest ever witnessed in Newberry," a fitting tribute to one of the community's most important citizens. With his demise also died the memory of the ancestor of US-2 having once been called the Bohn Highway, a road known today by a number and not a name.

Coordinates: C-D/1-11

BERNIE BORDEN MEMORIAL OVERPASS

Most people have to die in order to qualify for a road of remembrance. By its very name, "memorial highway" signifies that the person being honored is deceased. Wouldn't it be nice, though, if those being given such a tribute could receive and enjoy it while they are still alive. It would be the equivalent of presenting them with flowers while they can appreciate them, rather than putting pretty bouquets around their casket. Fortunately for Bernard Pollard Borden, he did not have to pass away in order to learn how much his community appreciates him.

Born in 1929 in Clio, Michigan, Bernie graduated from the local school system in 1947 and immediately enrolled at what is today Ferris State University. There, between 1948 and 1951, he participated in the Kappa Alpha Phi fraternity and played varsity baseball. After taking time out from his studies for a stint with the US Navy in the Korean War, Mr. Borden graduated from Ferris in 1956 with a Bachelor's degree in Pharmacy.

For the next ten years Bernie worked for various chain pharmacies before opening his own store in Clio in 1966 (just about the only independent pharmacy left in Genesee Coun-

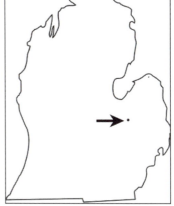

ty). In his capacity as a local businessman, Borden helped to sponsor many community activities, volunteered for numerous projects, supported a variety of athletic teams, and donated nearly $20,000 to the Clio School District. In addition, he served on the Clio Downtown Development Authority, Clio Planning Commission, and Clio Area Chamber of Commerce.

Through these and other gestures, Borden came to be viewed as a "model citizen for the Clio-area community." Wishing to recognize this local hero for his years of involvement, it was suggested that the bridge at the intersection of I-75 and M-57 (Vienna Road) be named in his hon-

or. This idea was subsequently officially endorsed by such governmental entities as the City of Clio, Clio Area School Board, Forest Township Board, Thetford Township Board, Vienna Township Board, and the Genesee County Board of Commissioners.

But because this matter involved naming a Michigan and a U.S. highway, the permission of the Legislature was also required to give Borden his due. The necessary approval from the State came via Public Act 142 of 2001, and the overpass was subsequently dedicated before over 200 people at the Vienna Township Hall on 27 September 2001. On that day the people of northern Genesee County established "a fitting tribute to an individual who has contributed his time and resources to efforts that have benefited the residents of Clio and surrounding townships."

Coordinates: K/12

BOY SCOUT TRAIL

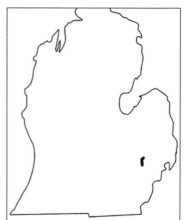

The Boy Scouts originated in England in 1907. They were founded by a Lieutenant General in the British Army who had served a tour of duty in South Africa. Taking the uniform and slogan of the South African constabulary, he created an association designed to instill in male minors such attributes as sound character and good citizenship along with moral and physical fitness.

The British officer who developed the Scouts categorized the membership into three levels based mainly upon age. The Cub Scouts were for juveniles aged 6 to 10, the Boy Scouts were for youths between 11 and 17, and the Explorers were for adolescents between 14 and 20. The lads within these various classes were banded into different-sized units called dens, packs, patrols, troops and councils. Based upon individual performance, participants could advance through the ranks from Tenderfoot (lowest) to Eagle Scout (highest).

The Boy Scouts of America were formally organized on 8 February 1910. Because the movement was so successful in teaching its followers responsibility, leadership, self-reliance, service to others, and chivalrous behavior, in 1916 the organization received a federal charter from the Congress of the United States. Today in this country there are about 4,500,000 Boy Scouts guided by 1,500,000 adult leaders. These individuals share the same goals as over 7,000,000 other Scouts worldwide in more than 130 countries.

Because of the Boy Scouts' noble mission, they have many supporters across the country. Within our two peninsulas, their boosters wanted to concurrently show their support for such fellowship, promote the causes embraced by the

brotherhood, and help with the training of its enrollees. These wishes, they concluded, could best be done by establishing a memorial highway for the association.

The idea for this approach occurred in January of 1924, and initially the name of "Eagle Scout Trail" was favored. Upon further reflection, however, this title was deemed too narrow and not sufficiently representative of the entire Michigan membership. Before long the most logical solution was arrived at, and in April of that year the Oakland County Road Commission officially declared what was then part of trunk line M-24 the "Boy Scout Trail."

The motorway given this designation began at the intersection of Oakland and Baldwin avenues, proceeded due north to Clarkston Road, and then turned east to the town of Orion. The portion of this route within the city of Pontiac had already been christened Baldwin Street--and the passage of this resolution did not change that status--but in the rural areas this new name applied.

And so the backers of Scouting in Michigan achieved their desire of touting a favored cause while helping its adherents learn "a proper regard for road signs, the beautifying of the highways by planting trees, a knowledge of the cities and towns connected by the highways, and intelligent directing of strangers and tourists coming to this vicinity." One could almost say that they created a concrete example for Boy Scout advocates in other states to follow.

Coordinates: L/13

BRISTOL ROAD

Rarely is a state trunk line so short it does not even appear on the official Michigan highway map. Such, however, is the case with route M-121. This approximately two-mile-long connecting link between I-69 and I-75--serving as an access path to Bishop Airport--is so abbreviated it can only be found on the detailed inset map for Flint and vicinity (it is the eleventh shortest state highway in Michigan).

The road itself was created in June of 1836 when it was authorized by local government officials. It evolved from an east/west rural trail to an increasingly important country drive until 1935, when a segment from Dort Highway west to about its present terminus was officially incorporated into the state's transportation network.

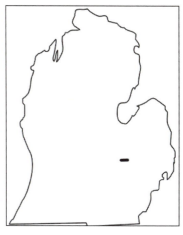

The road is said to draw its name from Anson and Deborah Bristol, who immigrated from New York state to southeastern Flint Township sometime in the 1840s. The locality where they and other kin built their homes became informally known as Bristol Settlement, an unincorporated community that once existed near the sites of Bristol Cemetery and the Bristol Methodist Episcopal Church, both of which were also founded by the pioneer family group.

Today, Bristol Road is one of the major thoroughfares in the Flint metropolitan area, well known to nearly all of the region's motorists. But the people for whom the highway was named have long since departed and been forgotten. Still, numerous signboards along the route bear testimony to their former presence in the vicinity and more or less constitute posted memorial markers to an otherwise obscure Genesee County pioneer family.

Coordinates: Flint Inset Map

BROCKWAY MOUNTAIN DRIVE

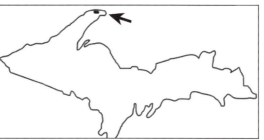

He was one of the pioneer setters of Copper Harbor (1846), postmaster of the town (beginning in 1851), resident agent for a number of the mines in the district, Upper Peninsula state road commissioner (starting in 1859), and well-known regional entrepreneur. For these and other reasons, one of the most prominent natural features in the Keweenaw Peninsula was named for him (Brockway Mountain). And, later, when a road was built upon this elevated landform, a highway bore his name as well.

Daniel D. Brockway--the man whose accomplishments were summarized above--was born in Morristown, Vermont, on 2 May 1815. After the passage of some years, he moved with his family as a child to the Midwest, where they in time settled in Washtenaw County, Michigan, in 1831. After reaching manhood, Brockway learned a number of crafts, talents which the federal government found so desirable it hired him as blacksmith and mechanic to the Indian Department of Lake Superior.

Accepting this position, Brockway arrived at Sault Ste. Marie on 19 June 1843 enroute to his appointed station at L'Anse. After waiting over six weeks for a vessel to carry him west, the brig John Jacob Astor finally arrived and conveyed him to his destination in five days (the distance can be driven today in less than five hours). For three years Brockway taught his skills to the Indians for a salary of $600 per annum before tiring of the job and deciding to move on.

The year was 1846, and copper fever was

sweeping much of the country. The valuable tawny metal had been found lying about parts of the Northern Peninsula and Brockway wanted to get in on some of the action. Loading his wife and three small children into an open boat, with the help of two Indians he followed the rocky coast of Lake Superior toward the setting sun, eventually coming to shore permanently at Copper Harbor in early May.

Copper Harbor at the time was little more than a small tent village, so Brockway set about building the first permanent structure which served as his residence and a hotel. His hostelry was called "The Brockway House" and it gave shelter and hospitality to nearly all of the early men on the Keweenaw Peninsula. As host to this stream of explorers, miners and scientists, Brockway became popular with visitors and local residents alike, a fact which no doubt lead to his name being applied to an elevation just a few miles west of his adopted home. By the time he died at Lake Linden on 9 May 1899, the Brockway name had become almost legendary in the copper mining district.

The Brockway name would become further immortalized just thirty-four years later when the Great Depression forced the U.S. government to sponsor public works projects in order to help the unemployed. Instead of giving people welfare payments, relief for the jobless came in the form of paychecks for labor performed on various federally-authorized construction ventures. One of these enterprises, built under the direction of the Keweenaw County Road Commission, was a 9.5-mile long highway between Eagle Harbor and Copper Harbor via Brockway Mountain.

About 300 men were assigned to work on this motorway in the Spring of 1933. The laborers made 25 cents per hour, and all of their efforts were manually done as the only extra help on site was a team of horses. Amazingly, the road was finished and open for traffic in October of 1933, through some touchup work was required the following year and the route was not given a hard surface until 1938. So, with just a few months of toil and an investment of less than $30,000, the Brockway Mountain Drive was born.

The highway quickly became one of the most popular drives in the Midwest, attracting tourists from all over the country. At about 735 feet above the level of the surrounding waters, the top of Brockway Mountain afforded a scenic panorama of the northern Keweenaw Peninsula and its environs. From its heights people enjoyed seeing in one view the azure of Lake Superior and its rock-bound coast with pebbled coves, the contrasting green wooded hills and valleys, and the picturesque settlements nestled along the distant shorelines.

As a county road, it may seem inappropriate to include the Brockway trail in this book. The reason for its existence can be traced to the construction of present-day M-26 which partially parallels the Mountain Drive. Though this state highway was officially brought into the trunk line system as M-129 in July of 1933, the entire route was not finished and opened to traffic until October of 1934. There is some evidence to indicate that while the northern portion of this coastal highway was being built to Copper Harbor, Brockway Mountain Drive served as temporary M-129 for about one year.

Coordinates: A/5

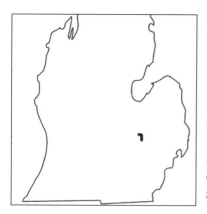

BUICK FREEWAY

Though his name has been put on millions of automobiles, David Dunbar Buick died almost forgotten and impoverished in Detroit on 5 March 1929. Until cancer made him too sick to work, he was a "forlorn old man" eking out an existence as an instructor at the Detroit School of Trades.

Born 17 September 1854 in Arbroath, Scotland, Buick moved with his parents to Detroit at the age of two. A few years after his father died in 1860, Buick was forced to quit school and help augment the family income. Working at a variety of jobs, he gained valuable experience that would serve him well as an adult.

By the mid-1880s, Buick was in the plumbing supply business, where he patented a process for bonding porcelain to cast iron. This created the white bathtub, the rights to which (along with his business) he sold to a firm known today as American Standard, an outfit that still makes the product found in nearly every home.

Taking his earnings from this deal, Buick eventually began working on gasoline engines. This effort gradually led to the automobile, which Buick began to manufacture in Detroit in 1902. In need of additional capital by the following year, Buick joined with the well-funded Flint Wagon Works and moved his plant from Detroit to Flint.

William Durant was brought in to manage the struggling Buick Manufacturing Company, and by 1908 he had made the firm the number-one builder of cars in the country. This Flint assembly plant and Buick nameplate was the rock upon which Durant founded General Motors in 1908.

Meanwhile, Buick's interest in the company he started had been bought out in 1906, allegedly for $100,000. He subsequently lost all this money by seeking oil and gold in California, investing in Florida real estate, and manufacturing carburetors in Michigan.

Despite his later financial failings, Buick had done a lot to get Flint started as a manufacturing center. Consequently, when the city's Commissioners considered christening a downtown freeway, they decided to honor the automotive pioneer by naming the road after him. The highway, route I-475, went right by the Buick plant, and most of the people employed there would use the north/south interstate in getting to work.

This decision was blessed by the Michigan Legislature through House Concurrent Resolution 22 of 1969, and the deed dedicated twice as the

highway was opened in two parts on 9 November 1973 and 26 September 1974.

Things changed, however, shortly before the third and final segment of I-475 was scheduled to be finished. A local politician, wishing to honor not just car manufacturers but automobile workers as well, proposed that Buick's name be removed from the freeway and the route commemorated instead to the UAW.

This idea was approved by the legislature via House Concurrent Resolution 622 of 1980, and by this action Buick's name was transferred to route I-69 in Flint to form the Chevrolet-Buick Freeway. So even though he no longer had a road just to himself, the "hometown" of Buicks still did the car's founder right by giving him shared billing on one of the city's principal transportation arteries. Ironically, the memory of a penniless soul was preserved in a freeway that cost a fortune to build.

But a little more than two decades later things got slightly better for David Buick, thanks to the generosity of the Michigan Legislature. The lawmakers in Lansing passed Public Act 142 of 2001 which enlarged the amount of pavement set aside in Buick's honor by declaring that "highway I-69 in [all of] Genesee county shall be known as the 'Chevrolet-Buick Freeway'." With this statute the size of Buick's linear concrete memorial grew from being city-wide to county-wide in scope, a dimension more fitting for a man of his fame.

Oddly enough, this same Public Act also designated another Flint-area motorway in Buick's memory. Section 21 of the measure proclaimed that "the portion of highway I-475 that is in Genesee county shall be known as the 'David Dunbar Buick Freeway'." Thus, the man whose name is synonymous with an up-scale General Motors vehicle now is remembered by two major roads in the city his car helped to build.

Coordinates: Flint Inset

CAIRN HIGHWAY

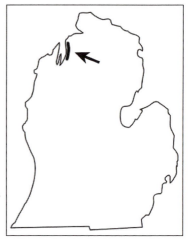

At the beginning of the 1900s, many parts of interior northwestern Lower Michigan were relatively valueless cutover lands unsuitable for cultivation. In developed areas primarily along the shorelines, summer resorts existed but rivalry and jealousies prevented these enterprises from coordinating their activities for mutual advantage. And many of the businesses that catered to people on vacation had accommodations and service that were substandard for the industry. Within just a few decades, one man had managed to correct most of these major problems.

The individual who worked this magic was Hugh J. Gray, a person hailed as the father of Michigan's tourist and resort trade. Born 6 September 1868 at Lakeside near the town of New Buffalo, as a young adult Gray became employed with the some of our state's major railroad companies and rose to the rank of regional passenger agent. Because of his skills in inducing tourists to ride the Pere Marquette lines to resorts served by that railroad, in 1917 Gray was hired as secretary/manager of the newly formed Michigan Tourist & Resort Association (later the West Michigan Tourist & Resort Association).

The purpose of this organization was to entice travelers and recreationists to make western Michigan their destination. Gray accomplished this goal by:

- being instrumental in the creation of the Manistee National Forest;
- leading in the development of the state park system;
- originating the idea of maintaining out-of-state tourist offices in populous centers to stimulate business for West Michigan;
- organizing conducted tours for newspaper editors and others in the media, thus gaining much free publicity;
- helping to develop festivals and special events throughout the year to attract visitors;
- aiding in the development of hotel management courses at what today is Michigan State University; and
- gaining appropriations from state government for the purpose of tourist advertising (beginning in 1929).

As the leading figure in turning Michigan into a summer haven and playground, many in the tourist business who benefited from his labors felt that Gray deserved some kind of recognition for his successful efforts to promote the attractions of our state. After some consideration, it was finally decided to honor the man with a cairn composed of 83 large stones, one from each Michigan county. The boulders were assembled a few miles north of Kewadin along highway US-31 in Antrim County, where they were cemented into a pyramid twelve feet square at the base and fourteen feet high. This lasting tribute to Gray and his achievements was dedicated in a special ceremony at the site on 28 June 1938.

When Hugh Gray died in Grand Rapids on 4 March 1943--and for years before and after--his cairn was a popular stop for motorists traveling along one of the main thoroughfares in West Michigan. In fact, the marker was so renown that IT became the center of attention and the man it honored was gradually forgotten. Even US-31 in Antrim County was named the "Cairn Highway" rather than something more fitting like, say, the "Hugh Gray Trail." Eventually even the memorial cairn became pretty much lost to the public mind, because in 1959 the route of US-31 in that vicinity was straightened and thereafter the stone marker was bypassed by all but local traffic. Today the monument to Hugh Gray still stands on what is now a county side road, and the name of

"Cairn Highway" still appears on official maps, but few people remember for whom the rock pile exists or why some Antrim County roads have "Cairn" in their name.

Coordinates: F-G/9

CAPITAL TO CAPITAL HIGHWAY

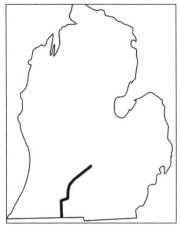

When the modern vehicular communications network of Michigan was in its developmental phase during the first two decades of the twentieth century, the road that went from Lansing south to Marshall and Coldwater ultimately made its way to Indianapolis, just like contemporary I-69. Because this early route connected the seats of government for Michigan and Indiana, about 1920 its promoters decided to name it the Capital Pike or, more commonly, the Capital to Capital Highway.

But when our national highway system was implemented in 1926 and the route became federal highway US-27, its assigned course went only as far as Fort Wayne before dropping southeasterly to Cincinnati, Ohio. With the road no longer connecting the State Houses of Michigan and Indiana, it became inappropriate to call it the Capital to Capital Highway and that name was abandoned.

But one group's loss became another group's gain, for when US-27 was diverted away from Indianapolis another trunk line became the connecting link between Michigan's capital and its political counterpart south of the border. This new path was M-78, a highway that ran from Lansing down through Charlotte, Battle Creek, Athens, Leonidas and Sturgis to the state line where it met with paved roads that extended on to Indianapolis.

Realizing that the title "Capital to Capital Highway" had been surrendered by its originators, the backers of M-78 south of Lansing adopted the name in 1926 as the identity for their thoroughfare. Like the supporters of other transportation arteries around the state, the road's proponents lobbied government to improve their favorite avenue and encouraged motorists to drive the route to their destinations.

These efforts were partially rewarded when, in 1930, the stretch of M-78 between the state capital and Battle Creek was finally paved, making it the principal approach to Lansing from the southwest. But while they were successful in getting funds for road construction, the route's backers failed to get the Highway Department to approve their special designation for the trunk line.

As the ensuing economic depression left the champions of M-78 with diminishing funds for furthering their cause--and as decreasing state budgets made government less open to new initiatives--the effort for officially naming the Capital to Capital Highway gradually died. Today, the only remaining signs of this noble endeavor are the main streets called "Capital Avenue" in Bellevue and Battle Creek, former segments of the great envisioned motorway between Lansing and Indianapolis.

Coordinates: L-N/9-11

CARLETON ROAD

A town in Monroe County bears his name, as do various schools, roads, and a bridge. Historical markers have been erected in his honor. Buses traveling between Hillsdale and Adrian frequently stopped at his birthplace enroute so passengers could see the old farmstead. The state legislature mandated that he be remembered in all public schools on his birthday.

Do these honors relate to the famous Michigan aviator Charles Lindbergh? Perhaps a distinguished favorite-son politician like George Romney? Maybe a native manufacturing genius like

Henry Ford? No, it's "just" about a poet who appealed to the common folks.

William (Will) McKendree Carleton was born in a farmhouse two miles east of Hudson, Michigan, on 21 October 1845. After attending the local schools of the neighborhood and graduating from Hillsdale College in 1869, he became a journalist.

While working as a newspaperman in 1871, Carleton heard a Hillsdale attorney describe a divorce he was handling between a local farmer and his wife. Struck by the tragedy of the situation, Carleton wrote a poem about the incident entitled "Betsy and I Are Out." So powerful was this verse that it was said to have been the means of reuniting many estranged couples of the times.

Just a short while later, basing a poem upon a Hillsdale County facility, Carleton wrote "Over the Hill to the Poorhouse." This was the story of an elderly mother abandoned by her children and forced to seek public assistance. The rhyme was so touching that "superintendents of poor houses reported that their inmates were decreasing in numbers because children were withdrawing their parents from these institutions, shamed into filial duty by this ballad."

These poems permanently turned Carleton's career from prose to poetry, and he gave up journalism to devote himself full-time to authorship and lecturing. His metered writings and sentimental speeches earned him vast sums of money, but he invested his re-

turns poorly. When he died in Brooklyn, New York, on 18 December 1912, his net worth was less than $5,000.

Because of his enduring popularity, a Will Carleton Memorial Association was founded in 1915. After convincing the Michigan legislature to designate October 21 as Will Carleton Day, the organization began lobbying to have M-34 declared "Carleton Road." This effort eventually met with success through the passage of Public Act 113 of 1925 (on 14 October 1927, the Wayne County Road Commission named the motorway following the Wayne/Monroe County boundary the "Will Carleton Drive").

The official scope of the paved tribute to one of Michigan's favorite poets was expanded by Public Act 142 of 2001 which declared that "the portion of highways US-223 beginning at the intersection with US-23, M-34, and M-99 extending northwest through Monroe, Lenawee, Hillsdale, and Calhoun counties to the city of Homer shall [all] be known as 'Carleton Road'." Thus, though Michigan giants like Charles Lindbergh, George Romney or Henry Ford do not have a state or federal highway named for them within our borders, we did bestow such an impressive honor upon a simple poet whose words struck a sympathetic chord in the hearts of the little people.

Coordinates: N/10-12

CASS COUNTY VETERANS MEMORIAL HIGHWAY

As World War II drew to a close, members of the Daughters of the American Revolution in Cass County decided to initiate an effort to honor the 3,082 local men and women who did military duty during that conflict.

After careful deliberation, the most suitable tribute was deemed to be a memorial highway along the nine-mile stretch of M-62 between Cassopolis and Dowagiac. This route was chosen because it would link the county seat with the county's only city.

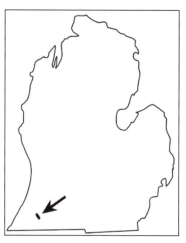

Funds for the project were raised through popular subscription. As an incentive to contribute, anyone donating $10 or more was allowed to dedicate a tree to a specific Cass County soldier, whether that person be living or dead.

To further encourage donations, the supporters of the enterprise formed a non-profit corporation on 14 December 1945. By this action, they claimed that anyone who made a contribution automatically became a member of the corporation, a status that presumably allowed them to deduct the expense from their income tax.

Concurrently with fund raising, the organizers worked out an arrangement with the office of State Highways. An agreement was reached under which the Department would do all of the designing and landscaping free of charge if the citizens of Cass County would buy or donate the necessary seedlings and nursery stock.

The trees chosen for the parkway were mainly tulip, pines, and maples, with some shrubs included as pleasing accents. With more than $7,000 eventually raised from various private sources, there were ample plantings to beautify both sides of the road along its entire length.

Since the highway was in honor of all soldiers who served in World War II, a decision was made to build a specially landscaped site midway along the route to recognize the 87 Cass County veterans who gave their lives in that struggle.

It was originally planned to have all of this work done sometime in 1946. However, the mysterious theft of some of the trees coupled with a severe summer drought prevented this goal from being realized.

Consequently, the small memorial park and associated roadside plantings were not in place until early summer of 1947. With the work finally completed, on June 29 of that year about a thousand people showed up to help dedicate the project to its intended purpose.

A representative of the Highway Department was on hand to accept the gesture on behalf of the citizens of Michigan, and the residents of Cass County expressed satisfaction with the living tribute they had made to their men and women who served in uniform.

Coordinates: N/8

CENTER LINE HIGHWAY

In 1913 the West Michigan Pike was formed to carry motorists along the eastern shore of Lake Michigan. Then, in 1915 the East Michigan Pike was created to accommodate those who wished to drive along the western coasts of Lakes Erie, St. Clair and Huron. Not surprisingly, by the summer of 1916 there was talk about establishing a middle north/south route descriptively called the Central Michigan Highway.

This tentative title was bestowed because the proposed road bisected the Lower Peninsula and it followed the path of the Michigan Central Railroad for much of its distance. While the idea for such a highway was sound, at the time tourists--the principal long-distance travelers on these routes--were more attracted to the Great Lakes than they were to inland waters.

A break for the planned Central Michigan Highway came when the United States entered World War I. With this country involved in global hostilities, improved transportation to and from the military reservation at Grayling became a high priority with government.

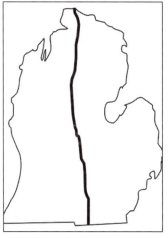

Taking advantage of the opportunity presented by this national emergency, the Central Michigan Pike Association was formed at Gaylord on 1 February 1918. Its purpose was to work for the construction of a first class road from the northwestern Ohio border almost straight up over 300 miles to Mackinaw City, passing by Camp Grayling on the way.

The name chosen for this mid-course thoroughfare was the Center Line Highway, and at a meeting in Ithaca in November of 1919 the Highway Commissioner approved the general path of the route as a state trunkline. We know the road today as a combination of US-127 from Lansing to about Grayling, and then I-75 from Grayling to the Straits.

The name Center Line Highway never seemed to stick, and by the early 1920s some motorists were beginning to refer to it as the "Inland Lake Route." A little later, in May of 1925, the Detroit Bar Association recommended naming the meridian traffic channel the "Lewis Cass Highway" after Michigan's famous governor and national statesman. While Cass certainly merits having some major stretch of concrete paying him tribute, the people authorized to designate highways failed to heed this proposal.

A few years later, in 1929, the legislature was asked to declare the route the "Main Street of Michigan." Though no formal action was taken,

the name did catch on as an unofficial title for the highway that runs up the center of our state road maps. In fact, as recently as 1973 the Department of Transportation was still sometimes referring to the north/south artery by that name.

But it is hard to beat the convenience and precision of numbers, so eventually the trunkline designations prevailed and the various alternative titles fell into disuse. Now motorists traveling right up the middle of southern Michigan are driving a Center Line Highway that is, arguably, the state's Main Street, but no one would recognize the route by those names.

Coordinates: E-N/10-11

CENTRAL MICHIGAN INTERNATIONAL HIGHWAY

In 1917 a group of regional boosters formed the Central Michigan Pike, a highway running from Port Huron to Holland. This named road, now represented by various state trunk line and Interstate route numbers, survived until the mid-1920s, when its personal identity was largely replaced by two digits on a diamond-shaped sign.

Though the title "Central Michigan Pike" gradually disappeared from the transportation scene, the goodwill of the phrase persisted across the south-central Lower Peninsula. Much of the motoring public remained pleasantly familiar with the name and continued to associate it with east/west travel.

Hoping to take advantage of this amicable legacy, the Central Michigan International Highway Association was formed on 22 May 1934. Trying to capitalize upon an already respected name, the group sought to establish a land link between the harbor cities of Port Huron and Muskegon.

The proposed road would stretch almost in a straight line across the lower-middle portion of the state. On a contemporary map, it mainly followed I-69 from Port Huron to Davison; M-15 from Davison to Otisville; M-57 from Otisville to US-131; US-131 north to Cedar Springs; and M-46 from Cedar Springs to Muskegon.

This highway, generally running about ten to fifteen miles north of its inspiration, the old Central Michigan Pike, was said by its originators to offer a number of benefits. The route would create a less-congested avenue for cross-state traffic, establish a new outlet to shipping centers, and open up rich agricultural land to markets.

These positive effects, maintained the promoters, could be realized if the Central Michigan International Highway (it did, after all, offer access to Canada at Port Huron) could be made into a state trunk line. Much of the laid out course at the time was simply known as County Road 500, and that relatively minor status did not allow the major monetary investments necessary to bring the route up to high standards.

The Association, despite operating under the financial handicap of the Great Depression, actively lobbied politicians and state government in support of its cause, and also engaged in public relations work among the citizens and communities along its path. These efforts paid off in late December of 1937 when the Highway Department designated much of the route trunk line M-57.

With its mission thus fulfilled and other issues starting to compete for regional attention, the Central Michigan International Highway and its sponsoring organization slipped into history. The success of the Association in reaching its goal during a

period of national economic hardship is even more impressive when one considers the nature of the product the group was trying to market: not too long ago a stretch of M-57 in Gratiot and Saginaw counties was reportedly voted the most boring highway in the Lower Peninsula.

Coordinates: K/8-14

CENTRAL MICHIGAN PIKE

As early as 1832, the citizens of Michigan were beseeching government to build a highway from Port Huron west to the navigable reaches of the Grand River. This request was finally granted by Act 83 of 1843, which authorized the construction of a "wagon road" along the desired route.

This frontier track was slowly improved over the decades into a serviceable avenue of transportation. Eventually, it became one of the principal arteries for movement laterally across the Lower Peninsula.

Shortly after the turn of the last century, communities along this thoroughfare found themselves competing for road-building dollars with other towns and their preferred highways. Something was needed to tip the scales in this contest to favor the local channel of traffic, and a solution to this problem came from the great map-making firm, Rand McNally.

A.E. Nissen, an employee of the company's auto trail map department, was promoting the establishment of trunk lines across the country. He told representatives of settlements along the Holland/Port Huron axis that if they designated and marked the road that linked them together, experience had shown that their chances of getting funds for highway improvement would increase.

To pursue this suggestion, delegates from places all along the line congregated in Owosso on 18 September 1917. There and then they formed the Central Michigan Pike Association for the purpose of creating a "motor trail" from Port Huron to Holland.

The chosen route, reportedly recommended by the state Highway Commissioner, closely followed contemporary I-69 from Port Huron to

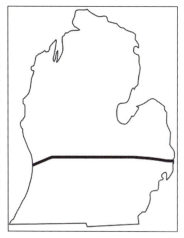

Flint, M-21 from Flint to Grand Rapids, and then I-196 from Grand Rapids to Holland. It was agreed that the name of this connection between Lake Huron and Lake Michigan should be the Central Michigan Pike.

A sort of motto--the Lake to Lake Route-- was chosen for the highway and an emblem selected for its identity. It was decided the road's mark would have a two-inch white band at top and bottom with a 14-inch black band in between. On the black background would appear the monogram CMP in white.

This symbol was to be placed on telephone poles adjacent to the Pike, at all intersections and about every 1,500 feet on the straight-away, at a cost to local communities of $3.00 per mile. The painting project started in late October at Holland and proceeded east to port Huron. When the marking project was finished, Rand McNally began showing the route on its maps.

The Central Michigan Pike appeared on travel guides until the mid-1920s, when it was dropped in favor of route numbers. The reason for this was not only the trend toward digitizing trunk line identification, but also some confusion within Michigan about which highway was to be called "Central."

It seems another Central Michigan Pike Association was formed in Gaylord in February of 1918 to promote a north/south road up the center of the state. Though this group characterized its adopted road as the Center Line Highway, the names were sufficiently similar to cause confusion in people's minds. The result was trouble for both organizations, ultimately contributing to their demise.

Today, the Central Michigan Pike-

C M P

-a road that was neither central nor a turnpike--is remembered only by antiquarians and students of old maps. To all others, it could just as well be a species of fish. Such is the fickle nature of life in our state's transportation history.

Coordinates: K-L/8-14

CESAR E. CHAVEZ AVENUE/WAY

In the mid-1990s, about 8% of Pontiac's population was of Mexican-American heritage. Many of these Hispanics lived along Oakland Avenue, also known then and now as Business Route US-24. On 7 September 1995, the leaders of this ethnic community convinced the city council to rename Oakland Avenue from Wide Track Drive to Telegraph Road as Cesar E. Chavez Avenue. This act was dedicated three weeks later in special roadside ceremonies. Designating a famous Pontiac street for someone who never lived in Michigan may seem somewhat strange, but with a little explanation the gesture can be understood.

Cesar Estrada Chavez was born 31 March 1927 in North Gila Valley near Yuma, Arizona. When his parents lost the family farm and store in the financial disaster called the Great Depression, they collectively became migrant field workers harvesting crops in the American Southwest.

Seeking to escape the difficult life of a field hand, at age 15 Chavez joined the United States Navy and served a two-year stint in the western Pacific during World War II. After his discharge from military life, he briefly returned to agricultural labor before becoming an activist promoting such causes as voter registration campaigns, citizenship drives, better educational opportunities, and improved social services.

In 1962, Chavez turned his attention away from mainly urban issues and toward the plight of people working in the fields. He formed the National Farm Workers Association, our country's first bargaining agent for migrant and seasonal field workers. Later, this organization affiliated with the AFL-CIO and became the better-known United Farm Workers of America.

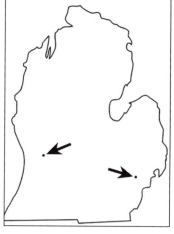

In support of his union's members, Chavez led nationwide boycotts of grapes, lettuce, wines, and other agricultural products. Through this technique, he was able to raise the wages and improve the working conditions of over 100,000 field hands while helping to inspire the Chicano civil rights movement of the 1960s.

Chavez's efforts to raise cultural pride and promote workers' rights were ended by a heart attack at San Luis, Arizona, on 23 April 1993. Nearly 50,000 mourners attended his funeral and millions more watched on television. In 1994, President Clinton posthumously awarded him our nation's highest civilian honor, the Medal of Freedom.

The large Mexican-American community in Grand Rapids, acknowledging Chavez as one of their heroes, looked for some way "to recognize the compassion, courage and steadfast commitment of" the man who gave so much to them. With Grandville Avenue serving as the most well-traveled thoroughfare in the Latino neighborhood, the local citizens decided to change the name of this road in the hope that seeing "Chavez" on the street signs would "encourage people to follow his example of seeking peaceful solutions to social and political problems."

The first step of this goal was accomplished in 2001 when the Grand Rapids commissioners approved changing Grandville Avenue to Cesar E. Chavez Way between Franklin and Wealthy streets. Then in the following year the Michigan Legislature passed Public Act 361 which officially extended Cesar E. Chavez Way from Franklin Street south to Clyde Park Avenue (a stretch also known as Business Route I-196). This gesture by the state lawmakers was dedicated on 21 September

ber 2002, a day in which all of the non-polar world had an equal amount of daylight and darkness. A rather appropriate astronomical event for a man who spent most of his adult life working to promote equality.

Coordinates: Grand Rapids Inset.

CHARLES J. ROGERS INTERCHANGE

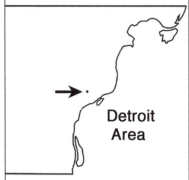

Detroit Area

In the realm of transportation, Michigan has memorial highways, bridges, and airports, but it has only one memorial interchange. This unusual feature can be found where I-75 and the Davison Freeway (M-8) meet in Detroit, and it is called the "Charles J. Rogers Interchange."

Charles J. Rogers was born on 24 January 1890 in Ireland. At the age of 23 he came to America, settling in the Motor City. He served with the 106th U.S. Army Engineers during World War I, and with this unit he supervised the building of roads, railroads, and barracks at various places in Europe. After discharge from the military he worked for various Detroit car manufacturers before starting his own construction company in 1920

This family business grew quickly, and eventually Rogers was involved in such famous southeastern Michigan projects as the J.L. Hudson (downtown) store, the Kern's Building, Book Tower Building, United Artists and Michigan theaters, the American sides of the Windsor Tunnel and the Ambassador Bridge, and the Willow Run bomber plant.

In the more recent era, his company's work included Hudson's Northland and Eastland shopping centers, the City-County Building in Detroit, Cobo Hall, the Detroit Greyhound Bus Terminal, Michigan Consolidated Gas Company headquarters, and many automobile manufacturing facilities.

But the Charles J. Rogers Construction Company was also one of the largest roadbuilding enterprises in Michigan, fulfilling contracts for many miles of freeway throughout the state. It is mainly for this reason that, slightly more than a year after Mr. Rogers died on 23 April 1970, the Michigan legislature passed a concurrent resolution (SCR 150 of 1971) naming a freeway interchange after a man who had built so many such structures during his remarkable career.

Coordinates: Southeastern Michigan Enlargement D/8

CHEVROLET FREEWAY

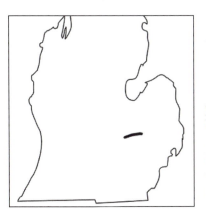

While probably everyone in America has heard of Chevrolet, very few people are familiar with the man behind the name. And since there are about as many cars with this French moniker than there are vehicles bearing the patronym Ford, it only seems fitting that a few words be said on behalf of the little-known European.

Though born near Bern, Switzerland, on Christmas day in 1878, Louis Joseph Chevrolet spent most of his youth in France. He immigrated to the United States in 1900, where he worked for a variety of vehicle manufacturers.

Around 1905, Chevrolet began participating in automobile races. He won many of these contests and set speed records on nearly every important track in the United States, becoming one of the earliest famous racecar drivers in this country.

Eventually tiring of the race circuit, he turned to designing automobiles and engines, organizing in 1911 the Chevrolet Motor Company. The following year his factory was moved from Detroit to Flint, a relocation that helped to develop the Genesee County seat into a car-manufacturing center.

Chevrolet sold his plant and nameplate to William Durant in 1915 who, the next year, brought the Company into the General Motors organization. The division has been with the firm ever since, accounting for the greatest portion of its total sales.

After selling out to GM, Louis Chevrolet built racing cars, competitively operated speedboats, and designed aircraft before ill health forced him to retire from business in 1936. An inventor, highly skilled driver and mechanical genius, Chevrolet died in Detroit on 6 June 1941.

The Flint City Commission, meeting on 4 November 1968, was trying to decide what name should be applied to limited-access highway M-78, the new freeway being built through town. Realizing that the road would pass by most of the five Chevrolet plants then in Flint, the board decided to christen the urban trunk line after the man, not the car.

These sentiments were passed on to the Legislature, and in 1969 it obligingly passed House Concurrent Resolution 22 declaring M-78 within Genesee County the Louis Chevrolet Freeway. The western segment of the road was dedicated on 2 September 1970 and the eastern portion was similarly opened on 21 December 1971.

Louis Chevrolet had this trunk line all to himself until 1980, when the lawmakers at the Capitol made a few changes. Since M-78 no longer passed through Genesee County, and since there was a desire to treat equally two automotive names of significance to the region, the Legislature approved House Concurrent Resolution 622 making route I-469 in Flint the Chevrolet-Buick Freeway.

There is not now and there never has been a route I-469 in Flint. The crafters of the measure meant to say I-69, but the mistake was not caught until December of 1998. In that month the legislature passed Senate Concurrent Resolution 102 which once again established the Chevrolet-Buick Freeway, this time bestowing the honor upon the correctly numbered highway.

But the story was not yet finished. Apparently there was a feeling in some quarters that Chevrolet deserved to have more lanes of traffic bearing his name than could be found within the Flint city limits. Consequently, in 2001 the Legislature passed Public Act 142 which specified that henceforth "highway I-69 in [all of] Genesee county shall be known as the 'Chevrolet-Buick Freeway'."

Coordinates: Flint Inset

CHICAGO ROAD

Prior to the time Michigan became a state, the federal government was largely responsible for funding internal improvements in the Lower Peninsula. Expenditures of this nature usually involved bettering land communications, and the first project authorized by Congress that fell within our boundaries was constructing the Detroit to Toledo road.

This highway was mainly built for military reasons. But other roads were needed for the primary purpose of giving settlers access to the interior of Michigan. Thus, the second national route to be developed in our domain was the Detroit to

Chicago road.

This undertaking gained approval through the actions of Michigan's third delegate to the U.S. House of Representatives--the first priest to ever to serve in that body--Father Gabriel Richard.

In March of 1824, Father Richard filed a petition with Congress for money to fund the creation of a graded land-link between Detroit and Chicago. And in January of 1825 he made his first and only speech on the floor of the House in an effort to persuade his colleagues of the project's merits.

Richard's words were convincing, and on 3 March 1825 the existence of the Detroit to Chicago road was established by federal law. The survey of the route was completed late in the same year, and construction begun in 1829.

The course of the highway followed a major Indian track between southern Lake Michigan and the Detroit River called the Sauk Trail. With work starting on the eastern end of this ancient path, the road was not finished to the Indiana border until late in 1835.

Though the Detroit to Chicago road was finally established in fact, what to call it has been in question for much of this century. The highway departments prefer to assign it just a number, dubbing it M-23 in 1916, then US-112 in 1927, and changing it again to US-12 in 1962.

Other interests prefer a title for the road. During the 1920s, the DAR

endorsed calling the route the "Gabriel Richard Highway," after the man who was literally and figuratively its "Father." And seeking to highlight the road's heritage, bills have been introduced in the Michigan legislature to name it the "Great Sauk Trail."

To this day the route suffers from an identity crisis. In Wayne, Washtenaw and Lenawee counties it is called the "Michigan Road," while in Hillsdale, Branch and St. Joseph counties it is known as the "Chicago Road." Berrien County, marching to a different drummer, has christened it the "Pulaski Highway."

In determining whether to identify the road by a number, name or destination, perhaps the best solution is to call the highway by the term most commonly used by historians who have erected plaques and monuments to the trunk line. These markers, scattered along the length of the pavement from Detroit west to White Pigeon, consistently refer to the route as the Chicago Road or Turnpike.

During the twenty-first century this route has started to take on a new identity. In May of 2001 the portion of this hardtop through Saline became known as a Historic Heritage Route, a title similarly bestowed in October 2002 upon the segment serving Clinton village and township. In 2004 the entire length of US-12 took on the mantle of Historic Heritage Corridor, the first highway in Michigan to bear this name.

Coordinates: M-N/7-13

CHIPPEWA MEMORIAL PIKE

When Europeans first came to the New World, they found a population of Algonkian-speaking Indians living in the area around the Ottawa River in what is now east central Canada. At the time of their contact with the French, these native Americans occupied the important position athwart the trade route between the Ottawa River (major tributary of the St. Lawrence River) and Georgian Bay in Lake Huron. This intermediate location and their natural talents made this tribe major traders and middlemen, thus accounting for their name "adawa" (Odawa or Ottawa), meaning to trade or buy and sell.

The Ottawa became friends and allies of the French. Since the French and Iroquois Indians were at war, this made the Ottawa targets for the Iroquois warrior confederacy. The numeri-

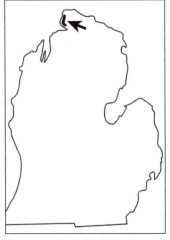

cally superior Iroquois attacked the Ottawa nation and drove the people from their homelands west to the Straits of Mackinaw district. After living in that area for some years, most of the remaining tribe members relocated in 1742 to the Cross Village region, making contemporary Emmet County "the Ottawa capital of the Midwest."

As residents of the northwestern Lower Peninsula, the Ottawa made important contributions to the culture and economy of the territory. With one of the largest Indian populations in the state, the tribe's women produced substantial quantities of high-quality arts and handicrafts like woven baskets, quillwork, pottery, jewelry, beaded items, paintings, sculptures, carvings, and buckskin clothing. They were also responsible for harvesting surprising amounts of berries and maple sugar for sale in local markets.

The men also contributed their share. At various times in the evolving whiteman's world the Ottawa males served as trappers, hunters, guides, packers, boatmen, fishermen, lumbermen, farm workers, and winter mail carriers (when it was necessary to deliver the mail using snowshoes since there were no open roads and ice had temporarily ended navigation). The Ottawa "braves" also catered to Michigan's tourist trade by performing for the benefit of visitors in various plays and pageants, conducting periodic public pow wows, and reenacting popular tribal rituals.

The Ottawa men were also warriors. Not only were they formidable adversaries in olden days, they also proved their mettle in the more modern era. During World War I, for example, 1,029 men from Emmet County answered the call of their country and served in uniform. Of this number, 49 (4%) were Ottawa Indians fighting for a nation that had treated them at times in less than honorable ways. As an expression of appreciation for this act of sacrifice and forgiveness, the Emmet County Board of Supervisors on 15 October 1920 named the Harbor Springs to Cross Village shoreline drive the "Chippewa Memorial Pike."

When the earliest government surveyors came to Michigan they found an Indian trail already existing between present-day Cross Village and Harbor Springs. The first atlas of our state shows that by 1873 this path had become a road, although by contemporary standards it would not be so generously characterized. Wishing to upgrade this picturesque route, on 25 June 1919 the Emmet County Road Commission announced it would rebuild the road so it could accommodate motorists.

The task of making the Chippewa Memorial Pike suitable for automobiles was roughly finished in 1921 and upgraded to the highest standards in 1923. Because of the beautiful vistas along this winding stretch of road, in 1927 Michigan's Highway Department said it would take over the route if a right-of-way 300 feet wide could be acquired along the wooded sections of its course to preserve the natural scenic qualities. By 1933 it had become clear that it would never be possible to obtain property rights to a swath that wide, so the state accepted the road as it existed and on 1 January 1934 declared the shoreline avenue through the "tunnel of trees" to be trunk line M-119.

And so it is by a three-digit number and not a name that the famous high-bluff road along Lake Michigan's western coast is known today. The memorial name of appreciation bestowed years ago by the Emmet County supervisors has long since been forgotten, as it never seemed to catch on with the white community. The resident Indians never cared much for it either, for the well-intentioned county fathers mistakenly named a tribute to the Ottawas after their Chippewa brethren.

Seventy years after the picturesque coast-hugging road was turned over to the state by Emmet county, local citizens there succeeded in getting the spectacular stretch of pavement declared a Michigan Scenic Heritage Route. This special

designation was celebrated at a ceremony in the Indian settlement of Cross Village on 28 June 2003, a date that more or less represents the dedication of an alluring highway honoring one of our most famous groups of Native Americans.

Coordinates: E/10

CHIPPEWA TRAIL

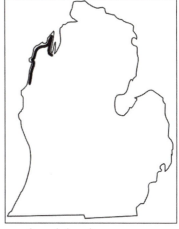

In former times the Chippewa (or Ojibwa) Indians were the most populous tribe in the land that became Michigan, and they remain so today. In the Upper Peninsula they occupy reservations at Bay Mills, Keweenaw Bay, L'Anse, and Lac Vieux Desert, with large numbers also living on Sugar Island. South of the Straits the Chippewa have reservations at Mount Pleasant and Suttons Bay.

The Chippewa were the first natives seen by Europeans when the white man came to this area in 1622. Our woodland Indians got along well with these newcomers and helped them establish control over the western Great Lakes region by serving as hunters, trappers, guides and warriors. As allies of the French and then the British, the Chippewa became one of the largest tribal groups in North America with a territory covering 1,000 miles from east to west, extending from Lake Huron to North Dakota.

The word "Chippewa" means puckered up from roasting, a term derived from the peculiar seam the tribe members sewed on their moccasins. In addition to their noted skills in working with animal skin and needle, these people were also expert with the canoe, as fishermen, and in the use of birch bark to make things like boxes, baskets, and covers for wigwams. The Chippewa were also preeminent as gatherers of wild rice, and even now they harvest much of the wild rice that is eaten in this country.

As the dominant group of native Americans in our region, it is not surprising to find their tribal name well represented on the landscape. In Michigan the word "Chippewa" has been given to one county, three townships, one hill, one waterfall, a harbor, one lake, a river, two creeks, three communities, a state forest, and two points along the Great Lakes shoreline. "Ojibwa," the alternative name for the tribe, appears on one lake, a mountain, and an island.

Though not well known, "Chippewa" also appeared on the Michigan landscape as a named highway. This event occurred on 25 February 1930, when the M-22 Association bestowed this title upon the scenic route that runs from Manistee to the tip of Leelanau County and back south to Traverse City.

For months the M-22 Association had sought a name that would appropriately describe its highway and lure tourists to drive the road. While the group was meeting at the Chippewa Hotel in Manistee, the magic term just suddenly came to mind.

The image of an Indian head was chosen as a symbol for the route, and plans were made to print 25,000 copies of a promotional brochure for distribution to tourists. But economic realities interfered with the sponsor's dreams, and a deepening national recession curtailed efforts to publicize the highway. Today, M-22 still remains one of the most popular scenic routes in Michigan, but the name "Chippewa Trail" exists only in history.

Coordinates: G-H/8-9

CHRISTOPHER COLUMBUS FREEWAY

Italians have been in Michigan for nearly all of the state's recorded history. The first person of this nationality to reside here was Alfonso de Tonti (Tonty), one of the early military commanders at Detroit, who came here with Cadillac in 1701. He, it is also said, was the father of the first white child born in Michigan, presumably making an Italian the initial European brought forth within our present boundaries.

There were other Italians who came to Michigan after Tonti, but most immigrants from the native country did not arrive here until the beginning of the twentieth century. One of these transplants, reflecting upon the cross-Atlantic movement of his people from the Old World to the North American Midwest, observed that "poverty drove them from the land of their birth, and they thought the New Land would give them opportunities they had not at home."

Continuing with his reflections, the commentator noted that his fellow-Italians "were not warriors who came to conquer; they were not capitalists who came to invest their money; they were laborers, mostly men and women whose sole capital consisted in a sturdy pair of arms and a determination to get enough of this world's goods to sustain them and their families. They were usually young men and women, just married, who desired to start their families in the new land of promise."

These Italian newcomers to the United States and Michigan often started out as common day laborers, small-time storekeepers, peddlers of fruits and vegetables, and factory workers. Before long they were heavy in the building trades and widely employed in the shops, railroads, shipbuilding industries and auto firms around greater Detroit. Eventually their culture and cuisine became a part of the American mix, as evidenced by our national love for Italian art, music, and foods such as pasta, wine and pizza.

Like other foreign groups that came to our shores, the Italians of southeastern Michigan tended to congregate together in a sort of former-countryman colony. This ethnic neighborhood was largely in Detroit east of Woodward Avenue in the area around Harper and Gratiot avenues. As whites increasingly left the Motor City after World War II, the Italians joined the exodus by mainly moving from Wayne County into adjacent southern Macomb County, where they are concentrated today.

One of the individuals representing these people in the Michigan legislature from 1975 to 1994 was Sal Rocca, a man born in Rome in 1946. After coming to the United States, he made his home in Sterling Heights and later graduated from Macomb Community College. Proud of his Italian roots and wishing to honor the heritage of his constituents, Rocca searched for some way to pay tribute to his homeland and the people it sent to America.

Noticing that a state highway in his district had not been given a name, Rocca introduced House Concurrent Resolution 694 of 1978 for the purpose of giving the road an appropriate title.

His colleagues in the Legislature concurred with his proposal, and thus the portion of M-53 between the City of Sterling Heights and the Village of Washington came to be called the Christopher Columbus Freeway.

Coordinates: L/13-14

CLARA BARTON
MEMORIAL HIGHWAY

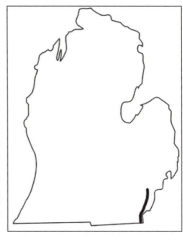

Christened Clarissa Harlowe Barton, we know her today as Clara Barton. Born at North Oxford, Massachusetts on 25 December 1821, she was a brilliant child who was teaching school at the age of 16.

When a throat ailment forced her to give up her role as educator in 1850, she subsequently went to Washington DC to look for work. In recognition of her talents, she was given a job in the Patent Office, becoming the first woman to hold a clerical position in any US government department.

Barton remained a public employee until the Civil War broke out in 1861, when she resigned her position and devoted herself full-time to supporting the Union troops. After some initial resistance from civil and military authorities because of her gender, she was eventually allowed into the hospitals where she nursed those soldiers in need of medical attention.

In addition to ministering to the sick and wounded, Barton secured supplies and provided food for her patients, bestowing her care upon Reb and Yank alike. In a short time she became widely known as the "Angel of the Battlefield."

During the four years of the Civil War, Barton worked side by side with the field surgeons, enduring the rigors of a soldier's life. Frequently under fire, her clothing was pierced by bullets and torn by shrapnel but she was never wounded. Appropriately, by the conclusion of hostilities her fame had become national.

After the Civil War Barton returned to the federal payroll, organizing and working for four years in the bureau responsible for finding missing soldiers. She first identified and marked the graves of Union men who had succumbed at Andersonville Prison, and she laid out the grounds of the national cemetery there. Then Barton devoted the rest of her time to tracking down thousands of other dead combatants and preparing records on their respective burial sites.

In 1881, Barton founded and became the first president of the American Red Cross. The first project undertaken by this aid-giving body was to offer assistance to those Michiganers who were affected by the 1881 fire that swept across the Thumb region of our state.

After a distinguished career as a public servant, care-giver, humanitarian and relief organizer, Barton died at Glen Echo, Maryland, just outside our nation's capital, on 12 April 1912. At the time of her passing in her ninety-first year, she had become one of the world's best known women.

In tribute to her many accomplishments-- and perhaps in belated gratitude for her assistance after the fire of 1881--the Michigan legislature passed Public Act 80 of 1954 making US-25 from the Ohio boundary north to Detroit the Clara Barton Memorial Highway. Over time US-25 was discontinued in our state, so in 2001 our lawmakers took corrective action in the form of Act 142 which avowed that route M-125 "and the portion of US-24 beginning at the intersection of M-125 and extending north to I-96 in Wayne county shall be known as the 'Clara Barton Memorial Highway'."

Coordinates: M-N/13

CLEVELAND AVENUE/STREET

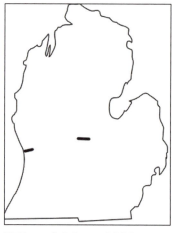

Who was the first Democrat elected President after the Civil War? Who is the only President ever married in the White House? Who was the husband of the youngest woman ever to be First Lady (age 22)? Whose daughter (Ruth) was born in the White House and had a famous candy bar named after her as a baby? The answer to all of these questions is Stephen Grover Cleveland.

Born 18 March 1837 in Caldwell, New Jersey, Grover Cleveland (he dropped his first name while still a boy) received a traditional education until the age of fourteen, when his father died and he had to help support his family. After a few years employed in a general store, Cleveland moved to Buffalo, New York, and began there the study of law. He eventually succeeded in mastering this line of inquiry and was admitted to the bar in 1859.

Cleveland's political career began soon after he became a lawyer. He was first appointed assistant district attorney of Erie County, New York, in 1863 and then took time out to serve as local sheriff during 1870-1874. After holding these relatively minor posts for some time, Cleveland's star began a rapid assent as he was elected Mayor of Buffalo in 1881, Governor of New York in 1882, and President of the United States in 1884.

After losing a bid for reelection in 1888, Cleveland returned to his private law practice until the campaign of 1892, when he defeated Benjamin Harrison and once again occupied the

White House as the only President to serve two nonconsecutive terms (22nd and 24th in succession). Cleveland left politics in 1896 and retired to Princeton, New Jersey, where he made his home for the rest of his life. He died there at the age of 71 on 24 June 1908.

Thirty-four years after the ex-President's demise, the leaders of Gratiot County decided to name most of their north/south roads after Michigan governors and their east/west roads after former U.S. chief executives. It was Grover Cleveland's good fortune to have his name fall on two lanes of traffic that had previously been designated trunk line M-57, thus qualifying him for inclusion in this listing of our state's memorial highways.

Favorable lightning struck twice for Grover Cleveland, as in April of 1946 Ottawa County decided to partially follow the example of Gratiot and designate some of its east/west highways after previous U.S. presidents and Michigan governors. Again it was a stroke of luck in the chronological listings that had Cleveland's name fall upon a trunk line road, giving him a second state memorial thoroughfare in the form of route M-104.

Coordinates: K/10-11; K/8

CLINTON TRAIL

Since there are four townships, a county, a river, and two settlements in the Lower Peninsula named after DeWitt Clinton, it should not be surprising that there is a state road in the man's honor, as well. But this situation begs the question, "Why?" The answer lies in the fact that

Clinton probably did more than any other person to make Michigan and the Midwest accessible to settlers in the early 1800s.

Born at Little Britain, New York, on 2 March 1769, DeWitt Clinton developed into one of the greatest personalities of his time. At various stages of his adult life he served as mayor of New York City, state representative and senator, U.S. Senator, plus lieutenant governor and governor of New York State.

Clinton's connection with Michigan comes from his sponsorship of the project to build the Erie Canal. Work on what was jokingly referred to as "Clinton's Ditch" began in 1817 during his first year as governor. Still governor, he presided at the formal opening of the Canal in 1825.

Upon completion of the Erie Canal, settlers had a cheap and easy means of travel from the East to the Great Lakes region. Following this man-made waterway, tens of thousands of pioneers got on boats for a trip West to the promising Territory of Michigan.

As people followed the Erie Canal to new homes in frontier Michigan, a need arose to develop the internal transportation network. To help with this effort, in 1834 Congress authorized the expenditure of $8,000 to build a road from northern Lenawee County to Grand Rapids. Because the chosen path began in the town of Clinton, the new road was dubbed the Clinton Trail.

The survey of this route ran

northwesterly to Jackson and then generally through wilderness on to its destination. The road was built diagonally across Eaton County since, at the time, there were no settlements to deflect its course. Later, when Charlotte was founded, a square-cornered cutoff to the town was constructed and part of the old road eventually disappeared.

The remaining portions of the original Clinton Trail stayed generally under local jurisdiction until 29 June 1926, when the highway was officially adopted into the state trunk line system as route M-50. Signage denoting this status was in place by mid-August of that year, but no official ceremonies were held to mark the occasion.

The closest thing to a formal dedication ceremony occurred on 23 April 1937, when government officials accepted two identical bronze tablets from the Eaton County Federation of Women's Clubs. These markers, soon after fixed to boulders, were placed as memorials at the points where the Clinton Trail enters and leaves Eaton County.

Coordinates: L-M/10-11

CLOVERLAND TRAIL

It is said that teams hauling hay to the lumber camps south of Lake Superior inadvertently scattered clover seed along the way. Some of this seed took root, grew and spread, eventually leaving red and white

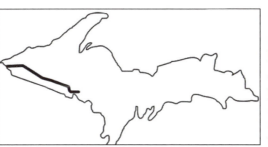

clover blossoms along many of the roads. The Upper Peninsula Development Bureau, seeking to capitalize upon this situation, took to calling the territory it represented "Cloverland."

When, late in 1915, the 100-mile stretch of road between Ironwood and Iron River was finally finished, the editor of the Ironwood newspaper suggested that it be called the Cloverland Trail. This name would appropriately characterize some flower-flanked segments of what is now US-2 and reinforce the theme established by the group promoting Upper Peninsula development.

The dedication of this imaginatively-dubbed highway took place on 22 July 1916, when over 1,500 people met where the road crossed the Gogebic/Iron County boundary to celebrate the completion of the six-year construction project. Three bands were on hand to provide day-long entertainment, and those tiring of endless music amused themselves with socializing, games and athletic events.

An occasion of this nature also called for a picnic, and in a display that would have made locusts blush the attendant multitudes munched or quaffed 1,500 pounds of meat, 800 loaves of bread, 250 pounds of butter, 20 bushels of potatoes, 20 gallons of pickles, 12 crates of celery, 70 pounds of coffee, and similar quantities of other foods. There were no reported fatalities from over-eating.

The Cloverland Trail received a great deal of publicity, a fact that was not lost upon those seeking to entice visitors to our Northern Peninsula. Consequently, they soon extended the name to include all of US-2 from Ironwood to Escanaba. Not content with this accomplishment, they next decided to apply the title to all trunk line routes in the UP.

The green cloverleaf was chosen as a logo, and the Upper Peninsula Development Bureau received permission from the State Highway Department to place the symbol along appropriate thoroughfares. Between 1920 and 1922, the sign of the cloverleaf was placed all over main arteries in the UP, as the emblem was painted on adjacent posts, bridges, barns, billboards, and other prominent places.

These actions turned out to be counterproductive, for the advertising campaign had declared so many roads to be Cloverland Trails that the term became meaningless. Seeking to establish a new identity, in 1927 the Upper Peninsula Development Bureau began phasing out Cloverland in favor of a better theme, Hiawatha Land.

CLOVERLAND TRAIL

Today, motorists in the UP no longer ride over Cloverland Trails, envisioning flower-dotted meadows with honeybees droning in the sunshine surrounded by the sweet fragrance of blossoms wafting on a summer breeze. Instead, and more appropriately, they tour Hiawathaland, where they drive along paths once tread by moccasined feet that pass by verdant forests, scenic lakes, murmuring waterfalls, and rugged coasts. They travel the real Upper Peninsula, not one created by a publicity agent looking for a catchy name that could apply to any place promising greener pastures.

Coordinates: C-D/1-11

COLGROVE HIGHWAY

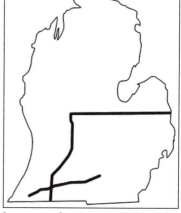

Most memorial roads in Michigan are transportation arteries identified by a single state or federal trunk line number. A major exception to this rule is the Colgrove Highway. This route, designated by the state legislature in 1921 as Public Act 350, is a mishmash of five different roads that seem to have been thrown together in an effort to please nearly every regional interest in the southern Lower Peninsula.

In a simplified form, the Colgrove Highway follows (better have a Michigan map handy):

US-131 from the Indiana border north to Kalamazoo

M-43 from Kalamazoo north to Woodbury

M-66 from Woodbury north to Edmore

M-46 from Edmore east to Port Sanilac

As a sort of afterthought, the legislature also threw into the pot M-60 from Niles east to Jackson. Together, these routes amount to about 400 miles of road.

The person to whom the highway pays tribute is Philip T. Colgrove, a lawyer once prominent in Hastings. Though well-known in Michigan's legal circles, Mr. Colgrove was not honored because of his skills in jurisprudence. Nor was he given recognition because of his service as Barry County prosecutor (1882-1888) and state senator (1889-1890).

Rather, a complex mix of motorways bears his name because for 20 years he ably served as the first president of the Michigan Good Roads Association. Furthermore, as an attorney, he helped craft the statute that created the State Highway Department in 1905.

When Philip Colgrove passed away on 10 February 1930 at the age of 72, portions of the state's transportation network still bore his name as well as various assigned trunk line numbers. But despite his many accomplishments, after death he gradually faded into obscurity as did his association with certain routes. Today, his name can no longer be found on the state highway maps, even though the law remains on the books that calls for specific roads to be designated in his honor.

This legal protection, however, may not permanently save the memory of Mr. Colgrove. In the year 2000 a bill was introduced in the Michigan legislature (SB 1149) to repeal the law that established highways in his name. While this measure did not pass, it does indicate that the days of this memorial route may be in jeopardy.

Coordinates: J-N/9-14

COLUMBUS MEMORIAL HIGHWAY

Detroit Area

Rated as one of the best navigators of all times, he started the first European settlement in the New World, introduced the horse and Christianity to the Western Hemisphere, was the first person to make four round-trip transatlantic voyages, and by some accounts discovered America. The man, of course, is Christopher Columbus.

Born in Genoa, Italy, in 1451, Columbus received little or no formal education as a youth. By age fifteen he had gone to sea, acquiring considerable sailing experience first as a deckhand and later as a sailor. His maritime adventures took him throughout the Mediterranean region, as far north as Iceland and as far south as the African coast near the equator.

Around the age of 34, he went to Lisbon, Portugal, where he studied the making of maps and charts along with such subjects as navigation, geography and hydrology. It was probably at this time that he developed the idea of sailing west to reach the Far East.

For centuries, Asia's lucrative commodities such as drugs, gems and spices had attracted European traders. Since it was very difficult to reach Asia overland, most of these products had to be purchased from Moslem middlemen at considerable cost. Europeans longed for a sea route that would allow them to purchase goods directly.

When Columbus proposed to the king and queen of Spain that they sponsor his voyage west to what he was sure would be the riches of the East, they put up the venture capital to finance the operation. Consequently, as we all learned in a school rhyme, in 1492 Columbus sailed the ocean blue in the Nina, Pinta, and Santa Maria.

After a lengthy voyage into the unknown, Columbus encountered a number of islands in the Caribbean Sea which he mistook for Indies, a fact that explains why he called the aboriginal peoples "Indians." Following explorations of the region, he returned to Spain with products of the new lands along with seven captured natives to prove he had reached a part of the planet previously unknown to the Old World.

These discoveries produced a sensation in Europe, and Columbus received a hero's welcome and the highest honors for his work. Grand receptions were held in his behalf, and his royal patrons bestowed rewards that included impressive titles, noble status, special privileges, not to mention the usual money and property.

Three more times Columbus ventured forth to the New World, but these expeditions were disappointing failures compared to his initial success. He died in relative obscurity at Valladolid, Spain, on 20 May 1506, still convinced he had reached the long-sought Indies.

Despite his confusion, the Michigan legislature thought the Italian mariner deserved some kind of recognition for putting us on the map. In tribute to this accomplishment, our lawmakers put the discoverer of America on the map by

passing Public Act 86 of 1955, which made nearly all of highway M-102 (Eight Mile Road north of Detroit) the Columbus Memorial Highway (reconfirmed by PA 142 of 2001).

Coordinates: Southeastern Michigan Enlargement D/6-10

COOLIDGE HIGHWAY

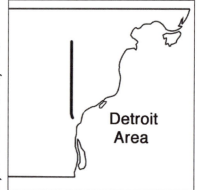

Detroit Area

It's all a little confusing, but today Southfield Road is also known as M-39. Before Southfield Road first bore this route identifier in 1962, the two-digit trunk line number was assigned to Schaefer Road about two miles to the east. And before Schaefer Road bore its present name, it was for a time christened Coolidge Highway. All of this calls for an explanation.

John Calvin Coolidge successfully ran for the office of U.S. President in 1924, then dwelled in the White House during what historians have referred to as this country's "Roaring Twenties". As times were good during his administration, Coolidge was a popular chief executive who, not surprisingly, had a number of things named in his honor. One of these gestures of recognition came from metropolitan Michigan, where various units of government cooperated to create a major ribbon of concrete called Coolidge Highway.

The effort to salute the President began in the Detroit Common Council on 27 October 1925 when its members, looking at the major developing artery known today as Schaefer Road, predicted that "this road will be one of the greatest highways on the west side of the city of Detroit." Because of its bright future, it was felt that this avenue "should bear a great name." "Whereas," the Council concluded, "it is confusing at the present time to have this road known by several different names, therefore be it resolved...to name such portions of the road as passes through the city of Detroit, Coolidge Highway, in honor of and after Calvin Coolidge, who as President is administering the affairs of the United States in such a manner as to promote our general prosperity and elicit the universal commendation of our people."

At about this same time coordinating measures were introduced in other venues along the route. In Oakland County the idea was readily accepted and the new moniker adopted. Concurrently, the Dearborn municipal council also considered altering the name of Schaefer Road to Coolidge Highway. This initial attempt was frustrated by protests from members of the Schaefer family. But eventually persistence paid off for those favoring change, and by March of 1931 the Dearborn city fathers had become convinced that motorists would be best served if the entire route bore the uniform "Coolidge" title.

No sooner had this conclusion been reached than it was effectively negated by action of the Detroit Common Council. A number of citizens in the Motor City were unhappy having Coolidge's name on one of the area's principal pavedways. With Coolidge now out of office and the country in the depths of the Great Depression, there was little opposition to restoring a famous local name to the road. Thus, on 14 April 1931 Detroit's governing body declared "that the name of the street and highway now known as Coolidge Highway within the limits of the City of Detroit be and the same is hereby changed to and shall hereafter be known as Schaefer Highway." Their counterparts in Dearborn did the same, removing the Coolidge name from the Wayne County transportation network.

Today, twelve miles of the Coolidge Highway still appear on the road maps of Oakland County, serving as a faded reminder of the thoroughfare's former glories. But Coolidge the man and most of his namesake drive in southeastern Michigan both died in the early 1930s, leaving each of them more notables of the past than historic symbols in the present.

Coordinates: Southeastern Michigan Enlargement B-E/7

COOLIDGE TRAIL

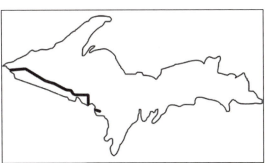

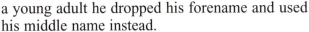

Nicknamed "Silent Cal" for his infrequent pronouncements, John Calvin Coolidge was president of the United States during much of the "Roaring 20s." Born at Plymouth Notch, Vermont, on 4 July 1872, as a young adult he dropped his forename and used his middle name instead.

After graduating from Amherst College in 1895, Coolidge went on to study law, being admitted to the bar in 1897 and subsequently opening a private practice. Very soon he entered the political arena, in which he gradually rose through a wide variety of government posts.

In succession, Coolidge served in the state of Massachusetts as city councilman (1899-1900), city solicitor (1900-1901), court clerk (1903), member of the house of representatives (1906), member of the general court (1907-1908), mayor (1909-1910), member of the senate (1911-1915), lieutenant governor (1915-1918), governor (1918-1920), and vice president of the United States (1920-1923).

When President Warren G. Harding died in office on 2 August 1923, Coolidge became the sixth vice president to become President upon the death of a chief executive. After serving out the remainder of his predecessor's term, in 1924 Coolidge was elected to spend four more years in the White House with the slogan "Keep Cool With Coolidge."

As the Coolidge presidency drew to a close in 1928, he sought to isolate himself from the political wrangling in Washington. To do this, he decided to spend the summer fishing and relaxing along the Brule River in northern Wisconsin at a site about 35 miles southeast of Superior and a few miles south of Brule.

As soon as the public heard that the president and his wife would be vacationing just south of Lake Superior, thousands of people made plans to visit the area in the hope they might catch a glimpse of the first family. The curious citizenry, joined by hundreds of media-types, created a tremendous influx of humanity into the northwestern Great Lakes region.

Hoping to capitalize upon this potential business opportunity, the Iron Mountain Chamber of Commerce attempted to entice motorists to reach the Brule area via Dickinson County. To do this, it declared US-141 from Green Bay to Crystal Falls, and US-2 from Crystal Falls to Brule, to be the Coolidge Trail.*

Signs were erected along the roadsides directing people to the route, and advertisements boasted that the course saved 67 miles over any other path to the summer White House. The town of Iron Mountain even built a municipal tourist camp so that travelers would have a free place to stay as they journeyed north from such population centers as Chicago and Milwaukee.

The tourist boom was short-lived, however, for when the President left the Brule River in September the throngs of gawkers disappeared with him. Things in Iron Mountain quickly returned to normal, and as Coolidge retired from politics a few months later the trail named in his honor was on its way to becoming a relic of past events. By the time former president died on 5 January 1933 at age 60, the Coolidge Trail had succumbed too.

*As an aside, it should be noted that in May of 2001 the Michigan Department of Transportation designated the portion of this route between Crystal Falls and Iron River an Historic Heritage Route.

Coordinates: C-D/1-4

"CURLEY" LEWIS MEMORIAL HIGHWAY

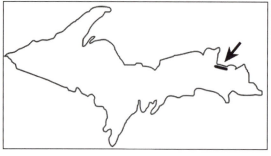

Born in Alma, Michigan, on 8 May 1895, Irwin L. Lewis remained a resident of the Gratiot County area until about 1934, when he left the Lower Peninsula to start a new life in Paradise, near the eastern extremity of Lake Superior. There he opened a tavern, a business which eventually expanded into a restaurant, gift shop, and motel.

As a major local entrepreneur, Lewis quickly became a person of some influence. Because of his stature in the community, he was at various times elected as Supervisor of Whitefish Township, County Road Commissioner, and Chippewa County Supervisor.

Whether in his capacity as a politician or as a private citizen, Lewis had a passion for improving tourist-attracting highways. Throughout his life in the North Country he worked to upgrade the regional transportation system in an effort to make the area more accessible to sightseers. His success in this endeavor was such that it is said about a half-dozen roads in the eastern Upper Peninsula are due in total or in part to the lobbying efforts of this man.

As Lewis approached the end of his career, beneficiaries of his ceaseless advocacy for better motorways looked for some way to honor him. The most appropriate thing, they agreed, was to assign his name to a route that owed its existence to his effectiveness in getting funding for the project.

The road that was chosen to convey this tribute was Federal Forest Highway 42, an eighteen-mile section of shoreline-hugging pavement along Whitefish Bay. Its gently curving two-lane path meanders through forests of beech, maple, birch and cedar, forming a beautiful connecting link between Dollar Settlement and trunk line M-123 to the west.

The Chippewa County Road Commission promoted this gesture of recognition in August of 1981, an idea that was supported two months later by the Michigan legislature in the form of House Concurrent Resolution 401. Though Mr. Lewis died in September before he could personally receive this salute, the memorial highway was dedicated in his name at roadside ceremonies on 15 October 1981.

While many visitors drove the ribbon of concrete bearing the name of Mr. Lewis, the locals felt that something more was required to give people a true sense of what awaited them along the trail. Consequently, on 28 July 1983 the Chippewa County Road Commission officially modified the title of the route to I.L. "Curley" Lewis Memorial Highway Scenic Lakeshore Drive. Were he alive, Mr. Lewis would not mind the shared billing, as he helped set the example for promoting the eye-catching assets of Michigan's Lake Superior realm.

Coordinates: C/10

CUSTER ROAD

As early as 1826 the citizens in and around extreme southeastern Michigan were sending appeals to their elected representatives for a road inland from the port of Monroe. They noted that a path for horse-drawn vehicles from the head of Lake Erie "through Monroe westwardly in the most eligible route...is in the opinion of your Memorialists an object of great importance, not only to the people of this Territory, but to the nation at large."

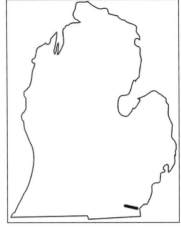

The signers of these petitions observed that this district was "rapidly settling with an industrious, enterprising, and valuable population. The surplus produce of all that rich country bordering upon the River Raisin...must at no distant period find an Eastern market; and the facility afforded by a road leading from that country to the head of the Lake [Erie] for transporting their surplus articles must be obvious."

In concluding their pitch, the various endorsers noted that "the proposed road would not only shorten the distance to the Lake [Erie] some fifty miles, but would open to the eye of the emigrant a first rate country for settlement. It would increase the value of the public lands through which the proposed road would pass, and in the event of a war would afford a safe and easy avenue from Lake Erie to Lake Michigan, through which military stores and ordnance might be transported from one post to another without the exposures usually incident to a frontier in time of war."

This collective voice was heard by the Territorial Legislature, which on 23 June 1828 passed a law authorizing just such an internal improvement. Unfortunately, the resident lawmakers had no money with which to build a track into the forested wilderness, so the following year they petitioned the federal government for funds to do the job. This appeal was finally acknowledged on 4 July 1832, when Congress approved a statute authorizing the undertaking and earmarked $15,000 for the wagon route

The surveying of this road

took place in 1833 with construction commencing soon after. When the originally allotted funds failed to finish the project, on 30 June 1834 Congress appropriated $10,000 more, thus enabling the endeavor to be completed in 1835 to Cambridge Junction. In 1836 the Michigan legislature approved an extension of the route from contemporary US-12 northwest to Marshall, but this road was never built.

The trail from Monroe to the interior remained rather primitive into the early twentieth century, when residents of the region again resorted to signing petitions for redress. They wanted the Michigan Highway Department to make improvements to this important but substandard artery, and their desires were met in November of 1915 when the route was incorporated into the state trunk line system as M-50.

With the promise of better things to come in the way of transportation facilities, it was deemed appropriate to give the old highway a new name. Previously, the most easterly fourteen miles of the route had been known as the Monroe-Dundee Road. With the state poised to upgrade its condition, local authorities decided in late March of 1916 to also enhance the street's image by changing its title to "General Custer Road" in honor of the hometown military hero George Armstrong Custer.

With these preliminary actions completed, surveys to improve the thoroughfare were finished and bids were let for the necessary reconstruction efforts in April of 1916. In a relatively short time the then eighty-year-old road was brought up to contemporary standards, turning it into one of the region's most heavily used routes to the inner reaches of the far southeastern Lower Peninsula.

Coordinates: N/12-13

CUSTER TRAIL

He was advanced four grades in a single jump to become the youngest brigadier general in the Union Army during the Civil War. It is said that he never lost a cannon or color yet captured more guns, flags and prisoners than any other general at his level. He was the commander who stopped Lee at Appomattox and to whom the flag of truce was delivered along with overtures of Confederate surrender. And he was one of the few officers present when the South formally capitulated at Appomattox court-house, receiving as souvenirs for his contributions to this end the white towel used by the Rebels as a flag of truce and the table on which the surrender agreement was written. He was George Armstrong Custer.

Born at New Rumley, Ohio, on 5 December 1839, Custer was educated in the local schools until the age of ten, at which time he moved to Monroe, Michigan, to live with his half-sister. He finished his secondary education at Monroe and then received an appointment to the Army school for engineers at West Point. His conduct at the military academy was rather nonconformist and unfocused, factors which help to explain why he graduated last in his class in 1861.

Within three days of leaving West Point Custer took part in the first major land engagement of the Civil War, the Battle of Bull Run. In this and subsequent encounters he displayed a dash, daring, courage and initiative that eventually made him one of the Union's most celebrated military personalities.

Exhibiting the fearless style and aggressive behavior the military looks for in its top brass, Custer is reported to have personally secured the first battle flag captured by the Army of the Potomac during the War Between the States. In the course of bravely leading his troops in battle and exposing himself to enemy fire, Custer had ten horses shot out from under him but received just one wound to his body.

When, in June of 1863, he was given command of the Michigan Cavalry Brigade, Custer was just 23, prompting the nickname "Boy General." He attired himself in colorful uniforms that included golden spurs, a crimson necktie and lots of gold

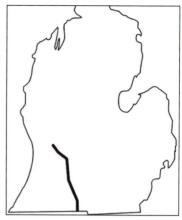

braid ornamentation. While some criticized him for these excesses, he claimed with a degree of justification that his eye-catching appearance made it easier for his men to see and follow him in battle.

When the Civil War ended in 1865, Custer congratulated his men on having "never been defeated." This achievement, coupled with his flamboyant style of leadership, made him an idol to his soldiers and a hero in the North, a position of attention he relished. This love of the limelight may have influenced Custer in his ill-fated decision to attack 8,000 Sioux warriors with a few hundred U.S. Cavalrymen at the Little Big Horn River on 25 June 1876.

Because of his widespread popularity and his connection with Michigan, it is not surprising that there would be a highway in this state named in Custer's honor. The trunk line of tribute was established in 1917 as a route between Grand Rapids and Fort Wayne, Indiana. In Michigan the course ran south on contemporary M-37 to Battle Creek and then along what are now secondary roads through Union City, Coldwater and Kinderhook to the border.

The traffic along this motorway was apparently never very heavy and its promoters not very effective, for by 1930 the highway was said to be "originally known as the Custer Trail." Still, it lingered on in an abbreviated form, as a 1949 publication noted it had been reduced to a Battle Creek-Fort Wayne connector that was "less frequently referred to by name."

In the end, the Custer Trail met the same fate as its human inspiration, just not as abruptly. The promotion of these honorary routes required people along their paths to contribute to yearly advertising campaigns. As enthusiasm and funding waned, as the identifies of the roads gradually declined in favor of trunk line numbers, and as the development of the state transportation network bypassed part or all of the desig-

nated itineraries, it became impossible to maintain the viability of most named highways. Today, the only place one can find Custer or his Trail is in the annals of the past.

Coordinates: L-N/9-10

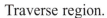

D. H. DAY HIGHWAY

It was said, at the time of his death on 17 April 1928, that he was "probably the best known man in Northwestern Michigan." He had spent most of his career helping to build western Leelanau County, and in the process became the principal business and civic leader of the region. His name was David Henry Day, and his life was synonymous with development of the Sleeping Bear Dunes area.

Born in New York state in 1858, Day came to Glen Haven, Michigan, in 1878 as shipping agent for the Northern Transit Company. Here he took up permanent residence and soon made a mark for himself on the local scene. Over the next fifty years he operated a general store at Glen Haven and served as the town's postmaster. Using his considerable influence, he helped to get the Lifesaving Station built at nearby Sleeping Bear Point.

Eventually, Day moved into the lumbering business, buying a sawmill at the west end of Glen Lake and constructing a 2.25-mile railroad from the mill to the Glen Haven wharf. This narrow-gauge line carried forest products to Lake Michigan, where Day's dock and water transportation company received the freight for export to Great Lakes markets. To help promote the logging industry, Day served as head of the National Hardwood Lumbermen's Association for many years and was instrumental in founding the Michigan Hardwood Association.

In the course of acquiring raw material for his sawmill, Day purchased about 8,000 acres in Leelanau County. As the wood on these lands was cut, the properties were often systematically replanted in a manner that served as a national model for timber conservation and reforestation. Other parts of these real estate holdings were used for agriculture, with Day operating one 400-acre farm that included over 5,000 cherry trees. The success of this orchard helped to establish fruit growing in the economy of the Grand

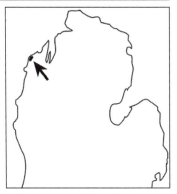

Traverse region.

As President of the Western Michigan Development Bureau for many years, Day was interested in attracting people and investment to the region. With this purpose partially in mind, he helped to create Day Forest Estates as a summer resort development near Glen Lake and gave a valuable 32-acre tract of land to the state which became D.H. Day State Park near Glen Arbor. This generous act was so popular with the public that Day was made the first chairman of the State Park Commission. His donated campground was eventually incorporated into the Sleeping Bear Dunes National Lakeshore.

Day was also designated Leelanau County's "overseer of highways." In his efforts to improve overall local communication, he was "responsible for laying the cable from Sleeping Bear to South Manitou Island." Day is also said to have planned, supervised, and personally paid for improving the road from Glen Haven to Empire, a stretch of highway that later became part of trunk line M-22.

Because of Day's work to improve transportation in northwestern Michigan, not long after his death the Traverse City Chamber of Commerce suggested that a segment of M-22 be named in his honor. Though then-Governor Fred Green expressed his support for such an idea, the Legislature never acted on the proposal.

Not until slightly more than seventy years later did the effort revive to name a road in honor of Day. In October of 2000 the Leelanau County Board of Road Commissioners passed a resolution in support of making all of route M-109 the "D.H. Day Highway," a short but pleasant drive that passes the cemetery where Day is

buried. The Michigan Legislature responded favorably to this suggestion by passing House Bill 6031 of 2000, but the measure never took on the force of law because of a pocket veto by Governor John Engler. This temporary setback was remedied the following year with the passage of Public Act 17, and the long-awaited Day memorial highway was finally made official with a ceremonial bill signing in Traverse City on 15 July 2001.

Coordinates: G/8

DAVISON LIMITED HIGHWAY

Detroit Area

Detroit is crisscrossed with a number of freeways named after individuals. The first of these to be constructed was the "Davison Limited Highway." The reason for this number-one ranking lies in the fact that Highland Park is surrounded by the city of Detroit. Of the 30 parallel streets that ran east and west in Highland Park, only Davison passed from border to border within the enclave and made connections with Detroit thoroughfares.

Davison was an old road that was named after Jarad Davison, an English immigrant who was one of the early settlers in the area. By 1940, this former country lane could no longer accommodate the traffic load it had to bear. As the sole east/west connector for Detroit traffic, Davison road congestion almost approached gridlock during rush-hour periods. Surveys showed that 96% of the motorists on Davison were just driving across Highland Park, without a local destination, in an effort to get from one side of the city to the other.

To remove this cross-town bottleneck, it was proposed to build a six-lane, limited-access highway through the middle of Highland Park. The necessary right-of-way would be obtained by acquiring a continuous half-block of property all along the south side of Davison Avenue for its entire length. This project was approved by the Highland Park City Council on 17 March 1941, when they agreed to pay $100,000 of the cost of the enterprise with Wayne County, with contributions from state and federal governments picking up the rest of the total $3,400,000 tab.

Construction on the Davison connector started in the summer of 1941. Plans called for an expressway 1.3 miles long recessed 12 to 17 feet below grade level. To accommodate this excavation, 69 buildings were to be torn down and another 63 moved. World War II began about six months after ground was broken, but this turn of events just accelerated construction. Due to its proximity to plants engaged in defense work, the road was judged to be a military access highway. This designation gave the Davison highest priority status for the allocation of scarce building materials.

Rushed to completion because of its importance to war industries, the Davison Limited Highway was opened to traffic at 4:00 p.m. on 25 November 1942. There were no dedication ceremonies, since authorities felt that the national emergency required more essential activities.

With the widened Davison artery an accomplished fact, journeys through Highland Park that once took a quarter of an hour or more could now be made in 3 to 4 minutes. And with the inauguration of this non-stop superhighway, Michigan acquired the first depressed expressway in the United States outside of the New York metropolitan area.

In 1997, the Department of Transportation assigned trunk line number M-8 to the Davison

highway, but appropriate signage was not installed along the route until the year 2000. Also in 1997 Senate Bill 749 was introduced in the state legislature for the purpose revoking the Davison title and rechristening the road as the "Father William Thomas Cunningham Freeway." While this measure unanimously passed the upper chamber, mercifully it was never voted on by the House. Consequently, the Davison remains to this day the oldest named limited access highway in Michigan.

Coordinates: Southeastern Michigan Enlargement D/8

DETROIT INDUSTRIAL EXPRESSWAY

Detroit Area

One bit of good economic news for southeastern Michigan in pre-war 1941 was that a huge bomber manufacturing plant was going to be built by the Ford Motor Company on the outskirts of Ypsilanti. The bad news was that the region's existing infrastructure could not supply a complex of that size with its required amounts of labor and material. Subsequent construction of the Willow Run Expressway took care of transportation needs in the vicinity of the plant, but better highway facilities were needed to improve the arteries between industrial Detroit and the new military airplane factory along the Wayne/Washtenaw County border.

Research showed that most of the fabricated parts and sub-assemblies would have to be trucked to the bomber-building site from Detroit. The bulk of these components emanated from Ford plants in Dearborn, Highland Park, and the industrial colossus at River Rouge, requiring a paved link between the various manufacturing complexes. In a sense, a high-speed road would be needed as part of an assembly line for the production of giant four-engine aircraft.

Studies also revealed that most of the manpower to run the bomber factory would have to come from Detroit and its immediate suburbs. Three-quarters of the 100,000 anticipated employees were expected to use private conveyances to reach the work site, meaning that at shift changes an estimated 140 buses and 8,330 cars would be trying to cover some of the distance between Ypsilanti and the Motor City.

Recognizing the need for an improved route to handle these heavy vehicle loads, on 17 January 1942 the War Department approved and authorized the construction of the first continuous limited access highway in Michigan. "Designed for safe travel at speeds up to 100 miles per hour," the sanctioned Detroit Industrial Expressway was to cover the distance parallel to the

Wabash Railroad from about Romulus east to the Detroit city limits at Michigan and Wyoming avenues.

Some construction on the project started immediately, though grading activities did not begin until 12 May 1942 mainly due to wet soil conditions. While contractors had problems getting sufficient labor and material, the forces marshaled for the undertaking were soon characterized as "one of the greatest concentrations of men and equipment ever assembled for a road job." For example, a typical week in December of 1942 included on site about 750 people, 238 trucks, 40 large shovels, and 31 cement mixers.

These crews were in essence building one of the nation's first interstate-type trunk lines within a 300-foot right-of-way and on both flanks of a 140-foot safety median. Each side of the divided highway had two twelve-foot lanes poured nine inches thick over two feet of sand base with twelve-foot shoulders. Because of metal shortages, no reinforcement bars were used saving 38 tons of steel per mile of road. The pavement surface stood about three feet above ground level, except for the most easterly 2.5 miles which were depressed because it was easier to go under the web of streets and railroad crossings rather than over the cross traffic.

Construction was from west to east along sixteen miles of contemporary route I-94 in Wayne County. The job--starting at about what is now exit 194--was opened to exit 199 on 5 December 1942; to exit 204 on 2 February 1943; to about exit 208 on 8 December 1943; and to the terminus at exit 210 on 9 March 1945 (the road's day of dedication). With final trimming and clean-up, the entire project was not finished until August 1945.

The "biggest single road job under construction in the United States in 1943 and 1944" was never meant to be just a feeder channel to the Willow Run bomber plant. Planners had anticipated that the approximately $20,000,000 undertaking would be

part of a postwar inter-regional artery linking Chicago with Detroit and Port Huron. In 1958 the Detroit Industrial Expressway was officially made part of I-94, turning a highway built to help make weapons of war into a motoring path for peaceful travel and commerce.

Coordinates: Southeastern Michigan Enlargement: F-G/5-7

DETROIT-LINCOLN-DENVER HIGHWAY

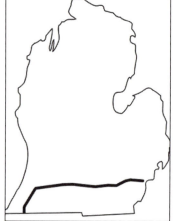

In May of 1911 a group of good roads enthusiasts on the Great Plains met to form an organization to promote the creation, improvement and use of a motorway across the states of Nebraska and Colorado. Named after the major cities along its course, the highway was rather presumptuously christened the "Omaha-Lincoln-Denver Transcontinental Route."

By 1920 these men had largely accomplished their original goal and were seeking some way of extending the length of the road to match its geographically inflated title. In that year the drive became more deserving of the term "transcontinental" when it expanded its point of origin 750 miles east to the Motor City and changed its name to the Detroit-Lincoln-Denver Highway.

The path taken by this new road essentially followed contemporary I-94 from Detroit to Paw Paw and then M-51 south from there to the Michigan/Indiana border. While the headquarters of the sponsoring association remained in Lincoln, Nebraska, it did open a district office in Detroit to deal with promotional affairs in this state.

The official symbol of the highway was two feet high--consisting of three-inch black stripes above and below an eighteen-inch white band--with the monogram DLD in black letters centered in the middle portion. This route identification icon was painted on telephone poles, fence posts, trees, or other exposed objects along the way making it possible

for sojourners to remain on track in what was then a poorly marked interstate transportation network.

Those who ventured forth along this national highway, particularly in its more primitive and less-settled western portion, were not assured of having a pleasurable experience behind the wheel. This fact prompted some travelers to joke that the letters DLD stood not for the major connected cities but for "Dry, Long and Dusty" or "Damn Lonesome Drive."

While the condition of the motor trail did not substantially change to merit some better nicknames, the fate of the group promoting the road did undergo a rapid alteration a few years after the DLD was founded. This transformation began late in 1925 when the federal government designated much of the Detroit-Lincoln-Denver Highway "US-38" and began discouraging the use of words and titles to describe the route.

Although cartographers continued to put the emblem of the DLD Highway on road maps for a few more years, its days as a named route were quickly passing. By around 1930 the use of numbers for most trunk lines was widely accepted and the title Detroit-Lin-

coln-Denver passed into the history books as a curiosity of another era. The sponsoring organization was disbanded, its multi-state membership went on to other pursuits, and today DLD may just as well stand for a Delegation Long Defunct.

Coordinates: M-N/8-13

DEWAYNE T. WILLIAMS MEMORIAL HIGHWAY

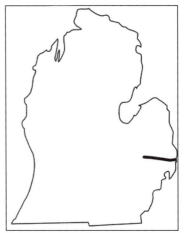

DeWayne Thomas Williams was the only Michigan Marine serving in Vietnam to be awarded the Medal of Honor, the highest military tribute offered by this nation.

Williams was born 18 September 1949 in Brown City, Michigan. Upon graduation from Capac High School, he enlisted in the U.S. Marine Corps Reserve at the age of 18. He received a discharge in January of 1968 to enlist in a regular Marine Corps unit.

After undergoing basic military training at Camp Pendleton, California, Williams was sent to Vietnam and assigned duty as an Automatic Rifleman with Company I, 3rd Battalion, First Marine Division.

On the night of 18 September 1968, his 19th birthday, PFC Williams went on combat patrol with his unit. While moving into position, his scouting party came under enemy fire.

Williams was wounded in the ambush but, recognizing the danger to his patrol, he immediately began to crawl forward to a good firing position. While he was advancing with other members of his unit, a grenade landed in their midst.

Immediately realizing the mortal danger this device posed to his fellow-soldiers, Williams fell upon the grenade and took the full impact of the explosion with his body. By giving up his life, Williams prevented the other members of the patrol from incurring injury and possible death.

Because Williams made the ultimate sacrifice, the men he saved were able to successfully defeat the attackers and hold their position until assistance arrived. After the battle, Williams' body was returned to the States and buried in St. Mary's Cemetery at Saint Clair, Michigan.

In recognition of Williams heroism, the Michigan legislature passed House Concurrent Resolution 690 in December of 1976 declaring that when M-21 west of Port Huron became a freeway, the road would be named in his honor.

True to its word, when the eastern portion of I-69 was finished, the legislature remembered the gallant acts of a Michigan soldier. Under color of Senate Concurrent Resolution 914 of 1984, the section of M-21 between Lapeer and Port Huron was declared to be the DeWayne T. Williams Memorial Highway.

The trunk line was dedicated in a special ceremony on 4 December 1984. On hand was the family of Private First Class Williams, justifiably proud of the recognition DeWayne had received from the grateful citizens of Michigan.

As time passed, the number M-21 was eventually removed from the expressway between Flint and Port Huron. Since this turn of events technically erased this road of remembrance from the transportation landscape, the Legislature was

forced to take remedial action. In 2001 it passed Public Act 142 which stated that "the portion of highway I-69 beginning at the eastern city limit of the city of Lapeer and extending east to the western city limit of the city of Port Huron shall be known as the 'DeWayne T. Williams Memorial Highway',"

Coordinates: K/13-14

DEXTER TRAIL

Starting at a point about three miles northwest of Unadilla, and running thence to about Mason, is a highway called the Dexter Trail. Then, about six miles northwest of DeWitt, one again encounters the Dexter Trail which terminates near Lyons. One could logically assume that these are remnants of the same road, but history tells us that such a conclusion would be wrong.

While both of these trails came into existence at about the same time, the southern stretch seems to have the older genealogy. As early as 1828 the Territorial legislature authorized a road to run from Dexter to the principal meridian (a survey line that passes near Mason). Not until 1837, however, did our ancient lawmakers specifically establish a route to connect the towns of Dexter and Mason along the approximate course of the present Dexter Trail.

The basis for naming the road is uncertain, but its origin can be reduced to about three possibilities. First, nearly everyone using the trail was either coming from or going to Dexter, so the name of the town was naturally bestowed upon the route. Second, when first created in 1828 (and for eight years thereafter), nearly the entire length of the road was in what was then a much enlarged Dexter Township. The third option is that it was named for Samuel William Dexter.

Sam Dexter was born in Boston on 18 February 1792. After graduating from Harvard University, he came to Michigan in June of 1824. A man of means, he quickly acquired substantial land holdings here and upon them located such settlements as Byron, Dexter, and Saginaw. Settling in the town bearing his surname, Dexter was the community's first postmaster, the county's first judge, publisher of the county's first newspaper, and a regent of the University of Michigan. Clearly worthy of having a trail named in his

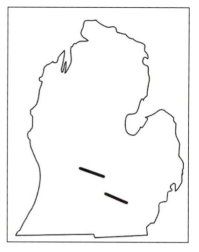

honor, Samuel Dexter died at home on 6 February 1863.

Ironically, the northern Dexter Trail is also named for a Samuel Dexter, although this one was born in Rhode Island on 5 December 1787. He came to Michigan in May of 1833 leading a company of 63 people who were to help colonize a town he founded called Ionia.

This party of settlers left Detroit and traveled on a northern branch of the Grand River Trail through Pontiac and then west to a point just beyond present-day DeWitt. In this vicinity they left the established route and set out through the wilderness toward Ionia, cutting a road through the woods as they went. The path cleared by the pioneers subsequently became known as the Dexter Trail.

This second Samuel Dexter went on to become the first justice of the peace in Ionia County, the first county judge, and a receiver of public moneys at the Government Land Office in Ionia. With his name firmly established in Michigan history and transportation nomenclature, the western Samuel Dexter died in Ionia on 6 August 1856.

And so it came to pass that two prominent Easterners with the same name--both founders of Michigan towns and leaders in the local judiciary system--left their marks upon the our state's network of rural arteries. Yet it is ironic, as one commentator noted, that "for all their similarities, neither the roads nor the men ever met."

Coordinates: L-M/10-12

DICKMAN ROAD

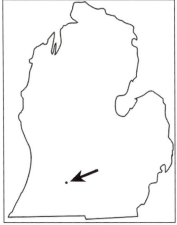

It is unusual for a district to name a road after someone who spent just three months in the area, but that is what happened in northwestern Calhoun County. To find an explanation for this peculiar situation it is necessary to go back to 1917 when Camp Custer was created just west of Battle Creek.

The first commandant of this military reservation was Joseph Theodore Dickman. Born on 6 October 1857 in Dayton, Ohio, Dickman was a career officer who graduated from West Point in 1881. He spent many years stationed at garrison outposts in the western United States where, in due course, he was promoted up through the officer ranks. By the beginning of World War I, Dickman had reached the grade of Major General.

Seeking a high commissioned soldier to oversee the building of Camp Custer, the Army put Dickman in charge of the base and the 85th Division that was to be trained there. Arriving on 25 August 1917, the General quickly directed construction of the cantonment which, in appreciation for his labors, named its main street after him.

Dickman had little time to savor this honor, for exactly three months after his arrival in Battle Creek he was ordered to leave Camp Custer for overseas duty as eventual commander of the Third American Army. He remained in Europe with his troops until July of 1919, when he returned to the United States bearing war decorations from five nations.

Having answered his homeland's call to duty, Joseph Dickman retired from the Army after 45 years of service on 6 October 1921. He died in Washington DC on 23 October 1927 of a heart attack at the age of 70.

Meanwhile, with the exception of a name change from Camp Custer to Fort Custer, not much was happening at the post west of Battle Creek. This situation began to change in 1940 as America started to gear up for what eventually became World War II.

One of the top priorities in preparing for possible hostilities was to improve access roads to military bases around the country. Congress made a special appropriation for this purpose, and the first project funded with these monies was the reconstruction and expansion of Dickman Road.

By now the original Dickman Road had become a rather narrow, 2.33-mile long ribbon of worn out concrete. Using part of the federal allocation for military highways, Fort Custer's main street was completely rebuilt and expanded to four lanes by the end of 1940.

The next order of business was to extend Dickman Road from the boundaries of the military post into the town of Battle Creek. Work on this project started in October of 1940 and restricted travel was possible over the route two years later. Officially, however, the 3.2-mile civilian stretch of Dickman Road was probably opened on 23 February 1943, the date the city council gave that name to the eastern end of the highway.

From its inception, the new and expanded Dickman Road had a numerical designation. It was labeled route US-12A until July of 1943, when this form of identification was dropped (action made official in 1952). The thoroughfare was known solely by its given name until 1964, when the eastern part of the street became Business Route I-94. The western portion was brought into the state trunk line system in 1971 as M-96, a status that finished making Dickman Road one of Michigan's memorial highways.

Coordinates: Battle Creek Inset

DISABLED AMERICAN VETERANS HIGHWAY

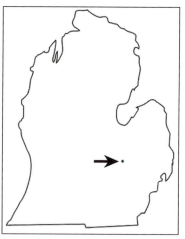

At the end of World War I, 1,300,000 veterans were left with permanent injuries, battle scars, gas-seared lungs, or chronic illnesses. Believing that somebody should help provide for the welfare of these ex-soldiers and their dependents, an organization called the Disabled American Veterans was formed in Cincinnati in 1920.

Membership in the DAV was limited to those honorably discharged men and women who were wounded, gassed, injured or permanently handicapped in the line of duty while in service. By joining together, they were better able to ensure that disabled veterans secured the compensation and other benefits to which they were entitled.

Given its noble constituency and cause, the ranks of the DAV quickly grew and its influence became national in scope. Finally, in 1932, Congress granted a charter to the group, officially recognizing it as the representative body for those individuals suffering from service-connected ailments.

As time passed and subsequent conflicts ensued, the DAV extended membership to those armed forces veterans who incurred disabilities during World War II, Korea, Vietnam, and other engagements. Today, the service organization has 2,162 chapters in the United States and a membership of slightly over one million.

The DAV continues to look after and promote the welfare of those who suffered physical and emotional damage in time of war. It provides all services to disabled veterans and their families at no charge to beneficiaries. The organization receives no government funds, deriving all of its income from membership dues and contributions from an American public grateful for the sacrifices of those who were injured while on military duty.

Because of the good work performed by the DAV and the price paid on behalf of liberty by its members, some citizens of Burton, just south of Flint, proposed that a local thoroughfare be named in honor of the organization and those whom it represents. This idea was carried to the Legislature in the form of House Concurrent Resolution 344 of 1990, which approved naming Bristol Road in Genesee County the Disabled American Veterans Highway.

Ordinarily this business could have been handled by the County Road Commission or the County Board of Supervisors, but since part of the designated route was state trunk line M-121, the matter needed the blessing of government officials in Lansing. Once these procedural matters had been tended to, the promoters of the memorial highway saw that it was properly initiated with a roadside dedication ceremony on 31 October 1990.

The linear extent of this road of remembrance was truncated about a decade later through the actions of the Michigan Legislature.

The lawmakers at the state Capitol performed this surgery through Public Act 142 of 2001 which simply stated that "Highway M-121 in Genesee county shall be known as the 'Disabled American Veterans Highway'," with no reference to Bristol Road.

Coordinates: Flint Inset

DISABLED AMERICAN VETERANS MEMORIAL HIGHWAY

Detroit Area

Established nearly eighty years ago, the Disabled American Veterans is a private, non-profit organization that is comprised of, staffed by, and works for individuals disabled in wartime. Its membership and focus is limited to those who were wounded, physically compromised to any degree, or left with a long-term illness while serving on active duty in the US Armed Forces.

Since it is not a government agency, the DAV derives its support entirely by dues and donations. These funds enable the group to provide free help to over 200,000 veterans and members of their families each year. Some of the services rendered include guidance to ex-soldiers in getting entitlements, appropriate health care, job training, and other earned benefits. In addition, members of the DAV annually devote millions of hours volunteering to work with their former comrades-in-arms confined to VA hospitals.

Given the noble nature of this organization and its many accomplishments, it is not surprising that its wishes would be well received in the Michigan legislature. Such was the case in early 1995 when the 1,500 members of the Livonia DAV collectively requested that a local highway be named in their honor.

Representatives of the chapter proposed that, since it was the 75th anniversary of their parent body, the four-mile stretch of I-275 between 8 Mile Road and I-96 be designated the "Disabled American Veterans of Livonia Memorial Highway." This idea was given form as House Bill 4725, a measure that was actually approved by both chambers of the legislature.

The bill needed only the governor's signature to become law, but this the chief executive refused to do. In explaining his veto, John Engler correctly noted that the legislature had already named another Michigan street for the DAV (Bristol Road south of Flint), and a second one would just lead to confusion. Furthermore, the governor explained that the bill asked the state to honor a local organization, something more appropriately done by the host community.

Despite this setback, another bill was soon introduced in the Michigan house on behalf of the Livonia DAV chapter. This second effort was slightly modified to eliminate the objections raised by John Engler. Most importantly, it proposed to name I-275 north of I-96 the "Disabled American Veterans Memorial Highway," a concept more inclusive than its predecessor.

This idea was quickly passed by the legislature because it dealt with most of the first bill's weaknesses by making the special designation on behalf of all Disabled American Veterans rather than just a small part of that population. Furthermore, the legitimate concern that this was the second DAV memorial highway was relieved by noting that it was the first "interstate" highway to receive the title.

With the governor's mind now put at ease, he approved Public Act 185 of 1996 to create in southeastern Michigan another Disabled American Veterans Memorial Highway. This gesture was dedicated on 16 September 1996 at the Livonia City Hall in the presence of many ex-servicemen on whose behalf the road was named.

Coordinates: Southeastern Michigan Enlargement D/5

DIX AVENUE

Detroit Area

There are a number of stories explaining the origins of Dix Avenue. One of the most popular accounts claims that the road is named for an early settler in southeastern Michigan called Captain John Dix (Dicks). This individual established the village of Dixboro (just east of Ann Arbor) in 1825. This John Dix, besides platting the community that bore his surname, also owned in the town a saw mill, grist mill, and general store in addition to serving as local postmaster. These investments and positions apparently were not enough for Mr. Dix, however, for it is said he sold his Michigan interests in 1833 and emigrated to Texas where he had a successful career.

While this scenario makes sense, according to the legendary historian Silas Farmer it is not correct. Mr. Farmer avers that the John Dix from whom Dix Avenue receives its name apparently came to the Detroit area decades before the founder of Dixboro ever set foot on our soil. The date of his arrival in Michigan is unknown, but he was here sufficiently early to receive private claim 117 along the Rouge River. The problem with this version of events is that the real estate owned by John Dix number two is miles distant from the course of Dix Avenue.

A more likely explanation is that Dix Road is indeed a tribute to J. Dix, but the forename is probably Ja-

cob and not John. Jacob (apparently the brother of John) also had a private claim (number 41) along the Rouge River, and a bridge crossed this stream at the southern margins of his lot. When a wagon path was built across Jacob Dix's property and over this bridge in 1842, the carriageway was appropriately given the name of the land owner through which it passed.

The condition of this cart trail gradually improved over the years, so by 1887 its title was changed from Dix Road to the more impressive Dix Avenue. Its evolution as a transportation artery continued to progress to the point that by 1913 it was brought into the system of primary highways maintained by the Wayne County Road Commission. It reached the penultimate status in 1932 when it was incorporated into the federal trunk line network as US-25, a position it held for 35 years until the construction of urban interstates in Detroit led to the bypassing of Dix Avenue and its retirement from the list of our state's numbered thoroughfares.

Coordinates: Southeastern Michigan Enlargement F/8

DIXIE HIGHWAY

In 1913, William Sydnor Gilbreath helped lay out the first continuous improved road across North America, a 3,300-mile track stretching from New York City to San Francisco. This transcontinental route was promoted by the Lincoln Highway Association, a Michigan organization headquartered in Detroit.

After Gilbreath had finished establishing this great east/west trail, he decided to create the nation's first north/south interstate motorway. His plan was to link the Great Lakes with the Gulf and thus connect the summer playgrounds

of the Midwest with the winter resorts of Florida.

This idea, coming fifty years after the end of the Civil War, was also meant to commemorate a half-century of peace between two previously hostile regions. With the development of an intersectional highway, residents of the North and South could feel that they all lived on the same street.

As originally conceived by Gilbreath, his road between America's top and bottom would start at Chicago and end at Miami. And when a sponsoring organization called the Dixie Highway Association first met in 1915 to consider his plan, the "Windy City" terminus was given approval.

Once our state's governor, Woodbridge Ferris, heard of this decision, he sent two representatives to the Association's headquarters to plead for Michigan's inclusion. So convincing was the presentation of these men that the Dixie Highway route was soon changed so that its most northerly extent reached the Straits of Mackinaw.

The Michigan delegation had done such a good job of selling our state to the Dixie Highway group that the body decided to allocate more than 900 miles of its system to Michigan. This figure rose to over 1,000 total miles when, in 1917, the Dixie Association approved extending its length to reach the Canadian border at Sault Ste. Marie. Later, another 100 miles was added when an alternative path was established in the southwestern part of the Lower Peninsula.

The route of the Dixie Highway in Michigan consisted of two divisions. The eastern section (about 700 miles long) essentially took the course of contemporary I-75 from Toledo to Standish, where it diverted via US-23 to Macki-

naw City. After crossing the Straits, it continued north along M-134 and M-129 to the Soo. There was also a scenic loop to the eastern unit that followed present I-94 from Detroit to Port Huron and then M-25 around the thumb to Bay City.

Michigan's western division of the Dixie Highway (around 550 miles in length) began at Mackinaw City and took US-31 south to the Indiana border. An interior extension branched off at Grand Haven and proceeded inland to Grand Rapids, down to Kalamazoo, and then southwesterly through Dowagiac and Niles to South Bend.

Despite having the second greatest share of the Dixie Highway (only Georgia had more miles), Michigan was the first to finish building its portion of the system. The entire distance between the Soo and Miami was completed in 1925, and in 1929 the full length was finally paved and the route dedicated by its "father," Mr. Gilbreath.

Gilbreath, who had become manager of the Detroit Automobile Club in 1916 and executive vice president of the Automobile Club of Michigan in 1927, died in Detroit on 13 October 1936.

And, after its project was completed in 1925, the Dixie Highway Association also passed away, with only a few road names in Monroe, Oakland, Saginaw, St. Clair, Antrim and Chippewa counties currently serving as testaments to the organization's efforts to make a land bridge between North and South.

Coordinates: C-N/7-14

DORT HIGHWAY

On the east side of Flint once existed a north/south street called Western Road. This avenue was christened not for its direction or placement relative to some point, but in honor of a pioneer family in the area. Nevertheless, the name of the thoroughfare was the cause of much confusion, and local sentiment grew in favor of a change.

In June of 1925, a proposal was brought before the Flint City Council to alter the geographic misnomer Western Road to something less likely to befuddle motorists. Not surprisingly, members of the Western family fought this idea,

putting the matter to rest until November when it was announced that the state was going to turn Western Road into a trunk line (US-10) and make it the eastern bypass route around Flint.

With Western

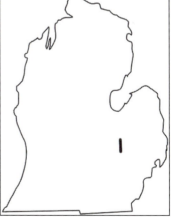

Road slated to change from a byway to a highway, the number of people potentially exposed to a misleading name was about to increase significantly. This new situation eventually prompted the City Council to take corrective action, and on 2 August 1926 it passed a resolution changing Western Road to Dort Highway.

The person being recognized by this gesture was Josiah Dallas Dort, a local man who had contributed generously to various Flint charities, philanthropies, and public institutions. He had also been largely instrumental in developing the park and boulevard system of the city, so it was fitting that a road be named after him.

J. Dallas Dort had been a Michigan man all his life, being born in Inkster on 2 February 1861 and raised in the community. His connection with the city that ultimately celebrated his name began in October of 1886 when he started the Flint Road Cart Company for the purpose of manufacturing horse-drawn vehicles.

In 1895 the Flint Road Cart Company was reorganized into an expanded firm called the Durant-Dort Carriage Company, one of the chief industries of Flint and one of the largest builders of non-motorized vehicles in the world. With fourteen plants in the US and Canada, it produced over 50,000 buggies and wagons annually.

As the years progressed, it became clear that transportation was increasingly turning to self-propelled con-

veyances. Therefore, in 1914 the Durant-Dort Carriage Company ceased operations and was replaced on 1 January 1915 with the Dort Motor Car Company.

The Dort line of automobiles was late on the scene in the revolution that was taking place in personal transport. This tardy entry into an already highly competitive field, coupled with the economic recession following World War I, led to the demise of the Dort Motor Company on 9 September 1923.

The strain of trying to save his firm and the pain of its termination took a toll on Dort's health, almost certainly contributing to his death in Flint on 17 May 1925. Though his last business venture had not been successful, he was still viewed by the town's residents as "the most beloved citizen in Flint's history."

While vehicles carrying the Dort nameplate no longer travel the streets of Flint, the man who manufactured them is remembered by the city through signboards on one of its principal thoroughfares. And such a tribute is only fitting for a person who played a major role in the settlement's early industrial prosperity, was a leader in its business affairs, and reigned as one of the dominant figures in the community.

Coordinates: Flint Inset

DR. MARTIN LUTHER KING, JR., DRIVE (BENTON HARBOR)

There are more memorial state and federal highways in Michigan named for Dr. Martin Luther King, Jr., than for any other person. The total would be even greater, had not the Legislature twice rejected bills to change route M-1 (Woodward Avenue) to "Martin Luther King Memorial Highway."

One of the roads named for this famous black leader is in the southwestern part of our state. It was officially designated by a local governmental body and then subsequently approved by the Michigan Highway Department.

The story begins in 1969, when the decision was made to build a M-139 extension just east of

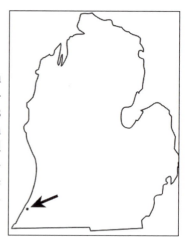

St. Joseph-Benton Harbor. Upon hearing of plans for this project, the Benton Township Board went on record in favor of naming the new road "Dr. Martin Luther King, Jr. Drive or Place, etc."

By November of 1972, as work on the road progressed, the Benton Township Board of Trustees petitioned the State Highway Department. They requested that the M-139 extension be named "Dr. Martin Luther King, Jr. Drive."

At the same time, the Board also contacted the Berrien County Road Commission to see how it felt about the idea. "The Road Commission recommended that the Township, in the interest of keeping the street signs to a practical size, consider naming the street 'Martin Luther King Drive'."

This proposal was approved by the Township on 2 January 1973, and the matter of a suitable name was settled. All that remained was to have a dedication ceremony upon completion of the new boulevard.

The Twin Cities Area Chamber of Commerce contacted the Highway De-

partment about such an event in September of 1973. Since the overture was so late in the construction year, and because so many other roads were already scheduled for opening formalities, it was decided to postpone the dedication until King's birthday in 1974.

Thus, on January 15, at the intersection of M-139 and Britain Avenue, the northbound section of the state trunk line was officially consecrated in memory of Martin Luther King, Jr. It was the first Michigan numbered highway to bear the civil rights leader's name.

Coordinates: Benton Harbor Inset

DR. MARTIN LUTHER KING, JR. MEMORIAL HIGHWAY (ALBION)

O n 13 March 1963, Dr. Martin Luther King, Jr., came to Albion College to speak about justice, integration, and racial harmony. During his visit he said that "We must learn to live together as brothers or perish as fools."

In September of 1984, a group of Albion citizens began an effort to have one of the town's streets named in memory of the deceased civil rights leader. By the end of that month they had convinced the city council to take the desired action, with the only question being which street would receive the new designation.

This last detail presented a major difficulty for Albion government officials, since most municipal streets were already named after famous people or had residents and business along their flanks quite satisfied with the present state of affairs and not interested in a change of address.

The ensuing debate over which street would be renamed threatened to tear the community apart. Finally, in a spirit of compromise that would have greatly pleased Reverend King, a solution to the problem was found that made all sides of the controversy happy.

Some conciliator recalled that when Dr. Martin Luther King, Jr., came to Albion, he travelled along the

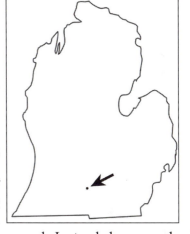

length of Business Loop I-94. It would be appropriate, then, to name this access route in honor of this great American leader.

The beauty of this idea was that no city streets would have to be renamed. Instead, large roadside signs noting the memorial highway status would be placed at regular intervals along the five-mile trunk line, which formed the two major entrances to the community.

The Albion city council readily agreed to this Solomon-like solution, officially designating the highway at a meeting on 3 December 1984. Since the proposed avenue of tribute was a state trunk line, the blessing of the legislature was sought before any final action was taken.

The solons in Lansing were happy to be a part of this constructive affair, and expressed their pleasure in June of 1985 by passing Senate Concurrent Resolution 42 declaring business loop I-94 to be the Dr. Martin Luther King, Jr., Memorial Highway.

Signs announcing this fact were erected on 23 August 1985, but the road was not dedicated until 3 May 1986. On that date the mayor of Albion proclaimed MLK Highway Day, and the citizens of the town united in celebrating the legacy of a man who worked to bring all races together in common purpose.

Coordinates: M-10

DUNES HIGHWAY

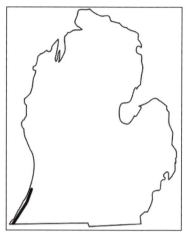

Until the early 1920s, it was not easy to travel from Chicago to west Michigan. People wishing to make the journey either rode the train, took a passenger boat across Lake Michigan in the shipping season, or drove a very roundabout way on poor roads.

The reason for this situation was a stretch of nearly virgin territory between the Indiana towns of Gary and Michigan City. This uninviting terrain was a mixture of marshes and sand hills that ran along the southern tip of Lake Michigan for 25 miles.

The area was unsuited for agriculture, so few settlers were attracted to the region. Furthermore, along the lake front in this district there were no harbors or facilities for accommodating boats, a fact that led industry to find more desirable sites elsewhere.

Because of its undeveloped nature, this tract of swamps and sand dunes formed a barrier to land transportation between motorists in the Windy City and the summer resorts of western Michigan. To eliminate this obstacle, in November of 1923 Indiana finished building a good road through the district allowing vehicles to easily travel to and fro along the south shore border area.

This construction project was a celebrated engineering feat that immediately attracted large numbers of drivers from all over the Midwest. Given the American inclination to name things of importance or popularity, this new link in east-west communication was appropriately called the Dunes Highway.

As motorists flowed into Michigan along Indiana's recently poured pavement, it soon became clear that roads in the Wolverine State could not accommodate the sudden surge in vehicles. In order to handle the increased traffic, Michigan was in turn forced to build its own Dunes Highway.

The first segment of this road-building construction project was the distance from New Buffalo to St. Joseph. This route was surveyed in 1926, contracts let in 1927, and the job completed by 1929. Immediately thereafter attention was turned to the northern section which ran from St. Joseph to South Haven, an enterprise that was surveyed in 1929, contracted in 1930, and finished the following year.

Michigan's version of the Dunes Highway approximately followed I-94 from the Indiana border north to around Scottdale, and then US-31 from Scottdale up to South Haven. With the usual ritual of speakers, handshakes, patriotic music and ribbon cuttings, this shore-hugging path to resort country was dedicated on 14 October 1931.

Today, throngs of people from the greater Chicago area still travel Lake-front trunk lines to reach the well-known cooling breezes, sandy beaches, and scenic grandeur of southwestern Michigan. But long forgotten is the name of the road that first attracted Illinois motorists to this picturesque playground along the Dunes Highway.

Coordinates: M-N/7-8

EARLE MEMORIAL HIGHWAY

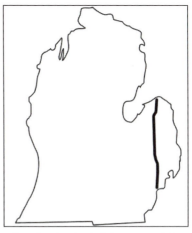

Highway M-53 leaves Detroit and runs north 115 miles to Port Austin. Nearly everywhere along its course the trunk line is known as Van Dyke Road. But in a few places the route is called Earle Memorial Highway. Therein, as the old saying goes, lies a story.

Horatio Sawyer Earle came to Michigan from Vermont in 1888. He quickly made his mark in this state as a proponent of transportation improvements and pavedways. With others, he was one of the founders of the Michigan Good Roads Association and was the organization's first president.

In 1903, with prodding from Earle and others, the legislature passed a law creating the State Highway Department. As recognition for his lobbying efforts, Earle was tapped to be the first Highway Commissioner.

When the law under which Earle was appointed was declared unconstitutional, he served in the position for two years without pay until the legislature could take corrective action. Once a modifying law was passed in 1905, Earle was officially appointed to a four-year term.

As Highway Commissioner, Earle decided that the first mile of state reward road would be built at Cass City near the middle of the Thumb Region. The people of the area were so grateful for this gesture that they formed an association to name M-53 the Earle Memorial Highway. After years of promoting their cause, the supporters of this idea finally got their wish when, in April of 1939, then Highway Commissioner Murray Van Wagoner officially designated M-53 as the Earle Memorial Highway.

Two years later, the Michigan

legislature followed suit with a blessing of its own by passing an act (PA 118 of 1941) that recognized Earle as "the father of good roads in the state of Michigan." The statute went on to observe that he had "laid out and instigated M-53, a great artery of traffic serving agricultural districts and tying them in with the great metropolitan district of Detroit." The law did not, however, actually name the trunk line in his honor.

Unfortunately, Earle did not live to personally receive these accolades, for he died on 25 December 1935. Nor did he live to see his trunk line finished, as the last stretch of pavement was not completed until October of 1940.

From 1940 through 1957, every official state highway map of Michigan identified M-53 as the Earle Memorial Highway. But the road lacked the official imprimatur of the Legislature. This problem was addressed by Public Act 142 of 2001, which asserted that "highway M-53 extending from the city of Detroit north to M-25 in Huron county shall be known as the 'Earle Memorial Highway'." Despite the eventual granting of this formal recognition, and despite his years of public service and the past efforts to acknowledge his deeds, today almost nothing remains on the transportation landscape as tribute to "Good Roads" Earle.

Coordinates: I-L/13-14

EAST MICHIGAN PIKE

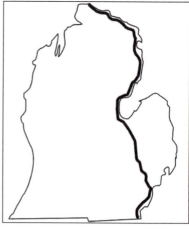

The West Michigan Pike, predecessor to US-31 in Michigan, debuted in 1913 and was an instant success in gaining name recognition and in attracting automobile travelers to the western coast of the Lower Peninsula. Hoping that lightning could strike twice, in September of 1915 Detroit interests decided to try and duplicate the success of the West Michigan Pike by creating a corresponding road along the eastern shores of our state.

The vision was to establish a 370-mile thoroughfare from Toledo to the Straits of Mackinac along the border of adjacent lakes Erie, St. Clair and Huron that would meet the West Michigan Pike at its terminus in Mackinaw City. With such a road in place, a complete highway circuit of the Lower Peninsula would be created enabling people to go from Detroit to the Straits in just two days or drive the entire 800-mile circuit in five days.

Before such a route could be formally established, it was first necessary to do some missionary work to be certain all affected parties were fully informed of the enterprise and encouraged to support it. Thus, the Detroit backers of this plan began annual tours along the path of the proposed highway giving pep talks about good roads in general and spreading enthusiasm for the development of a counterpart to the West Michigan Pike.

Initially, the idea was to have a shoreline avenue that went from Detroit through Mount Clemens and Port Huron, then northwest via Vassar to Bay City and on to points along the Lake Huron coast. However, conditions of the roads in the Thumb region were so bad that the route of the already-established Dixie Highway was selected instead from Detroit to Bay City by way of Pontiac and Flint.

With the course of the companion to the West Michigan Pike chosen, it only seemed right to call the sister-road the East Michigan Pike. So, on 24 May 1917 the East Michigan Pike

Association was formed for the purpose of creating a major transportation artery for the eastern Lower Peninsula and, indirectly, developing the area served by that highway.

Since this was the era before standardized road signs, the path of the East Michigan Pike had to be identified by colored bands on nearby telephone poles. This method of route marking was ostensibly invented by Detroiter William B. Bachman, who a few years earlier had devised a system of assigning a different set of tinted symbols to each route so motorists could follow the proper trail.

The design chosen for the East Michigan Pike was three four-inch bands colored yellow, white and blue, with the initials EMP stenciled on the middle white ring. In 1919 Bachman himself is said to have marked the portion of the East Michigan Pike that ran from Toledo to Detroit.

Unfortunately, the color code identifying the East Michigan Pike did not last long. The promoters of the EMP had made the mistake of choosing the same route for their road as did the backers of the Dixie Highway. In the competition for name recognition, the Dixie forces easily won out, eventually sending the words East Michigan Pike to the realm of obsolete phrases.

Now, all the colored bands that once covered Michigan's roadside poles have been erased by passing time, including those of the East Michigan Pike. But the successor highway to the EMP still offers some color to motorists in the blue emblem of I-75 from Toledo to Flint and the black-and-white shield of US-23 from Flint to the Straits of Mackinac.

Coordinates: E-N/11-13

EDSEL FORD EXPRESSWAY

Detroit Area

As early as 1939, Detroit began making plans for an east-west limited access highway through the center of the city. During this preliminary stage, the road was given the rather generic name of Cross-Town Motorway.

The idea for such a route began changing from dream to reality on 23 October 1945, when federal funds were finally authorized for the project. Almost immediately, acquisition of the right-of-way began.

By this time the unofficial name of the new superhighway had changed to Harper-McGraw Expressway, after two major streets along its path. But this description seemed to lack imagination, so a more meaningful title was sought.

Initially, there was support to name the road after Roy Chapin, the deceased Michiganer who had served as President of the Hudson Motor Car Company and as Secretary of Commerce in the Hoover administration.

The Detroit Common Council, however, decided someone else deserved the honor. On 23 April 1946, it passed an ordinance designating what is now I-94 within the city boundaries as the Edsel Ford Expressway.

Born in Detroit on 6 November 1893, Edsel Bryant Ford was the only child of Henry and Clara (Bryant) Ford. He began to work at his father's automobile manufacturing plant in

1912, where he spent time in all the major departments of the firm.

Edsel was quick to master the business, and at the young age of 22 he became the corporate secretary. Several years later he also assumed the post of company treasurer.

On 31 December 1918, after the resignation of his father, Edsel was elected president of the Ford Motor Company. He held this office until his premature death on 26 May 1943 at his home on Lake St. Clair.

It was a combination of stomach cancer and undulant fever that killed this popular and talented man at the age of 49. Sorrow over Edsel's early passing undoubtedly influenced the decision of Detroit city officials to name one of their first freeways after him.

Construction on the newly christened Edsel Ford Expressway started in January of 1947, and the first concrete was poured on 9 October 1950. When the initial section of road was opened to traffic on 9 July 1951, it was fitting that Mrs. Edsel Ford was there as guest of honor to cut the ribbon.

Coordinates: Southeastern Michigan Enlargement D-E/8-10

FISHER FREEWAY

Detroit Area

Michigan has memorial highways named after people, organizations, groups, things and events, but just one road honoring an entire family. These celebrated individuals, all male, are known by relatively few singularly, but together their name is famous worldwide.

The seven men our state has commemorated with linear concrete were all born in Ohio, sons of a man who specialized in building horse-drawn coaches and wagons. As youngsters, they were trained in their father's shop as blacksmiths and carriagemakers.

As the automobile industry began to develop in and around Detroit, the eldest of these brothers left home for the Motor City where their skills were in high demand. After briefly working in car manufacturing plants, the siblings joined forces in 1908 to create a firm bearing their family name, the Fisher Body Company.

This new establishment was a pioneer in the development of interchangeable parts, the building of closed auto bodies, and the use of finishing lacquers instead of paint or varnish. It also placed strong emphasis on quality production, a trait that soon made the slogan "Body by Fisher" a hallmark of craftsmanship.

As the family business rapidly grew, it required the attention of all seven brothers to operate. Under their guidance, the corporation became the largest manufacturer of automobile bodies in the world. In 1926 General Motors purchased the giant enterprise for over $200,000,000 and allowed the Fishers to remain as managers of the concern.

Eventually, some of the brothers went on to assume leadership roles within the parent company, serving as directors and top executives at the GM headquarters. Collectively, they also invested some of their great wealth in the local community, constructing the Fisher Building with its "golden towers" in 1929 and adding the famous Fisher Theater in 1961, establishing the National Bank of Detroit in 1933, and donating millions of dollars to charitable causes.

Because of their many contributions to the Greater Detroit area, sentiments were strong to recognize the

Fisher brothers in some appropriate fashion. An opportunity to realize this goal arose when, in June of 1958, the city was planning a portion of urban I-75 called the Fort-Vernor Expressway.

Seventeen prominent citizens of Detroit petitioned the Common Council to suggest that the proposed highway be named in honor of the Fisher brothers, Alfred, Charles, Edward, Frederick, Howard, Lawrence, and William. The committee to which this appeal was sent quickly gave its approval, and the Fisher Freeway was born.

Construction on the ten-mile-long segment began on 26 November 1963 and the first section was finished on 12 December 1967. When the final link was opened on 17 September 1970, the entire freeway was formally dedicated to seven captains of Detroit industry. With this act the name of Fisher, in many ways synonymous with the car-making business, became identified with one of the roads inspired by the automobile.

Aside from its unique standing as the sole route commemorating a family, the Fisher Freeway is also unusual in apparently being the only Detroit expressway without official status. The idea to name part of midtown I-75 for the Fishers received such immediate popular acceptance that no evidence can be found to show that city government ever bothered to pass a resolution approving the designation.

Coordinates: Southeastern Michigan Enlargement E-F/8

FITZGERALD MEMORIAL HIGHWAY

For eighteen years--from 1940 through 1957--the Fitzgerald Memorial Highway appeared on official state road maps. Today, all that exists of this route is a seldom-noticed marker at the junction of M-43 and M-100.

The story begins with Frank Dwight Fitzgerald, a native of Grand Ledge, Michigan. The son of a legislator, Fitzgerald received his education in the public schools of Michigan.

Fitzgerald worked as a clerk in the state legislature from 1913 to 1919, when he was appointed deputy secretary of state. He left this job in 1923 to become business manager of the Highway Department, a position he held for seven years.

In 1930, Fitzgerald was elected secretary of state and re-elected to the

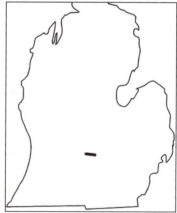

post in 1932. Two years later he ran as a Republican for governor and won. However, his attempt for a second term as chief executive was unsuccessful, as he was defeated in the election of 1936.

Two years later, Fitzgerald made a successful comeback bid in the 1938 gubernatorial race. Unfortunately, just a few months after he took office he succumbed to a heart attack, becoming the only Michigan governor to die in office.

About six months after Fitzgerald's death on 16 March 1939, the aldermen of his home town met to discuss a suitable memorial for their "first citizen." They proposed to the state highway commissioner that the road between Lansing and Grand Ledge be named after the former governor.

The highway commissioner responded favorably to this idea, and on 18 September agreed to name the 11-miles of M-43 the

Frank D. Fitzgerald Memorial Highway. The route of acclamation would be a four lane thoroughfare connecting the ex-governor's home town with the Capitol City where he worked. The designated road, trunk line M-43, was dedicated to Fitzgerald at ceremonies on 15 June 1941.

Sixty years later, Public Act 142 of 2001 gave the Legislature's official blessing to this tribute by professing that "the portion of highway M-43 beginning in the city of East Lansing and extending west to the city of Grand Ledge shall be known as the 'Frank D. Fitzgerald Memorial Highway'." No contemporary street signs bear witness to this gesture, though, as all along its length the memorial highway is known today as Grand River Avenue and Saginaw Street.

Coordinates: L/10

FLINT TRAIL

Of all the non-interstate national highways in Michigan, none has had more names bestowed upon it than US-23. Over the years, segments of this long north/south route have borne fifteen different titles, most of which remain unfamiliar to contemporary travelers. One of these now-forgotten monikers is the "Flint Trail," an identifier assigned to the stretch of road between Toledo, Ohio and Flint, Michigan, now followed by this federal trunk line.

The city of Flint gets its name from the Flint River which flows through it in a great U-shaped bend. The bed of this stream is rocky in places, which early on caused the waterway to be christened after some of the stones that line its bottom. It is not uncommon for a road connecting two points to be designated after one of its termini, and in this case the odds favored the seat of Michigan's Genesee County rather than the town to the

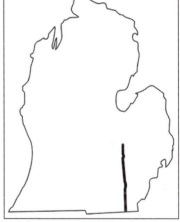

south along the banks of Ohio's Maumee.

The "Flint Trail" appears to be a name bestowed by employees of the Rand McNally Company late in 1917 to the approximately hundred-mile distance between Flint and Toledo. The term apparently had no regional support, and so the moniker can only be found on the 1918 edition of the Chicago firm's detailed highway maps. One might say that the trail named for Flint quickly faded into history because it failed to strike a spark with locals or the motoring public.

Coordinates: K-N/12

FORD ROAD

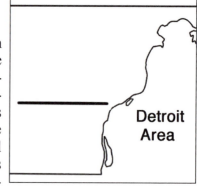

Detroit Area

Running east out of Detroit towards Ann Arbor is route M-153, also known as Ford Road. Given the many Ford Motor Company facilities in close proximity to this highway, most people would understandably assume that the highway is named for the corporate founder, Henry Ford. They would be wrong.

Ford Road was actually named for Henry Ford's father, who was one of the local residents requesting that the highway be built in December of 1894. The petitioners had their appeal quickly approved by the township board, and construction commenced not long thereafter.

Henry Ford's father, William Ford, was born in 1827 near Cork in southern Ireland. He came to America in 1847, and settled in Dearborn Township the same year.

A farmer in the old country, William continued to pursue this occupation here in Michigan. However, he was also a skilled carpenter, and much of his time was spent practicing this craft for regional businesses and neighbors.

William's frequent carpentry jobs required him to often travel about the area, an aspect of his work that was not greatly inconvenient for a bachelor. But when he married Mary Litogot on 25 April 1861 in Detroit, he felt obligated to adopt a life style more suitable to that of a husband.

William bought a farm at what is now the intersection of Ford Road and Greenfield Avenue and seriously took up the business of raising crops and a family. It was here that Henry Ford was born on 30 July 1863, the second of six children and the couple's first son.

As William settled down, he became more active in public affairs. At various times in his life he served the local community as road commissioner, member of the school board, justice of the peace, and church warden.

As a hard working and honest man in service to his neighbors, William became prosperous and popular within the greater Dearborn area. It is not surprising that, in tribute to his accomplishments, the citizenry would name a road in his honor before his death in March of 1905.

Ford Road remained under township control until 29 August 1924, when the Wayne County Road Commission assumed responsibility for it. The street switched to state jurisdiction on 2 December 1930, the date the route was declared to be a trunk line highway.

In 1934 M-153 was developed by the state as a thoroughfare between Detroit and Ann Arbor that would bypass the slow urban traffic that caused congestion along Michigan Avenue. It is ironic that a relief route like Ford Road eventually became so popular that it in turn had to be replaced by the modern Interstate highway. But it remains in heavy use today named, as someone noted, "for one Ford and traveled by cars named after another."

Coordinates: Southeastern Michigan Enlargement E/2-7

FORT CUSTER MEMORIAL HIGHWAY

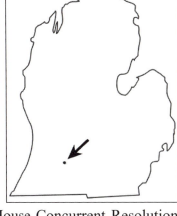

Camp Custer, just west of Battle Creek, was established in the summer of 1917 as part of the mobilization effort for World War I. It was named after General George Armstrong Custer, a famous former resident of Michigan.

The purpose of the Camp was to train soldiers to fight in Europe. During the first 1.5 years of its existence, about 90,000 troops were processed and given basic combat instruction at the facility.

Following the Armistice late in 1918, the Camp became a demobilization center. Over 100,000 men passed through the installation as they changed their status from soldiers to civilians.

In 1940, the Army began to reactivate the largely mothballed facility and changed its name to Fort Custer. When World War II began, the training base was once again used to prepare recruits for combat duty.

Not long after hostilities ended in 1945, activities at Fort Custer were scaled back and the installation returned to a quiet mode. Government officials were hard pressed to find some constructive use for the under-utilized post.

As early as the late 1950s, a movement commenced to create a national cemetery at Fort Custer. This goal was achieved on Memorial Day of 1982, when the desired burial ground was officially opened.

Because of the important role Fort Custer played in Michigan history, in 1988 the state legislature passed House Concurrent Resolution 677 to commemorate the post.

The method chosen to honor the installation was "to rename that section of M-96 between the I-94 business loop and the Village of Augusta as the Fort Custer Memorial Highway." The designated five-mile stretch of road ran through what had formerly been part of the old military reservation.

On 27 May 1988, a simple ceremony was held to dedicate the trunk line and erect signs at both ends of the route. By virtue of this action, a section of M-96 and Dickman Road became a tribute to the soldiers who had trained at Fort Custer and the veterans who are buried on its grounds.

Coordinates: M/9

FORT STREET/ROAD

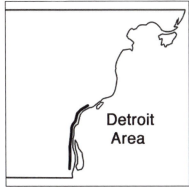
Detroit Area

Almost since the day of its founding, Detroit had a fort. Though its name changed over time, a defensive structure of some type existed to protect the settlement until the 1820s. In that decade, the encroachment of a growing community led the federal government to abandon the bulwark and redeploy the troops to Green Bay, thus leaving the town for the first time without soldiers.

In 1826, Congress generously granted what was left of the post and its surrounding reservation to the city of Detroit. The following year members of the municipal council had the land surveyed and laid out into streets, with one of the principal thoroughfares not surprisingly given the name of West Fort Street (East Fort Street was not created until 1835).

As the Wayne County region developed, West Fort Street grew as well, gradually extending its reach south to about the Monroe County line. Within the confines of the Detroit city limits, the route was given the suffix "Street," but in the suburban or rural areas it was customarily called "Road," as is the case today.

Though Fort Street did not begin as a major transportation artery, by 1898 its traffic had become such that it was widened to one hundred feet and made a feeder route for the city from the south. Soon it acquired "gateway" status--evolving into the principal means by which vehicles entered Detroit from downriver points--and it became in the first decade of the nineteenth century a major route controlled by the Wayne County Road Commission.

By the early 1920s, Fort Street was an industrial boulevard hosting along or near its flanks such firms as Cadillac Motors, the famous Ford Rouge plant, Timken Roller Bearings, Pennsylvania Railroad shops and yards, Michigan Steel Corporation, and others. In 1923, a local newspaper story on the road called it "one of the

longest business streets in the world" and an important stretch of the famous Dixie Highway.

When the federal government first assigned numbers to trunk lines in 1926, it decided that Fort Street/Road was so significant it should be designated US-25. This route number remained until 1956, when completion of part of the nearby Detroit-Toledo Expressway shifted much of Fort Road to Michigan's jurisdiction and the new owners provided their own identifier, M-85. When the downtown portion of US-25 was upgraded to interstate quality in 1972 and turned over to the state, part of it was rechristened M-3. Since it was confusing to have the same street bear two different numbers along its length, in March of 2001 all of Fort Street/Road that has trunk line status was given the designation M-85.

Coordinates: Southeastern Michigan Enlargement E-H/7-9.

FRED L. KIRCHER FREEWAY

One of the biggest problems in identifying the state and federal memorial highways in Michigan is that just about any governmental unit can designate one. Roads have been named for prominent individuals by Congress, the state legislature, state highway commissioners, state administrative boards, county boards of supervisors, county road commissions, township boards of supervisors, and city councils.

With this many possible sources to research, it is highly unlikely that we will ever know the actual number of state and federal trunk lines in Michigan that pay tribute to some deserving individual. A good example of the problem can be found in Lansing with the Fred L. Kircher Freeway.

It is unlikely that more than a few dozen people living in Michigan today have ever heard of Fred Kircher (aside from family members), and fewer still know that his name has been given to that portion of US-127 located "within the corporate limits of the City of Lansing."

The person of honor was born in Cissna Park, Illinois, on 18 November 1891. He arrived in Michigan in 1910, but his path did not lead to

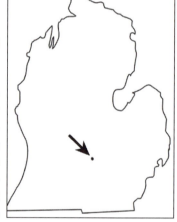

Lansing until seven years later.

Locally, Kircher was employed by the New York Central Railroad, where he worked his way up to yardmaster. He remained in this post until 1930, when he left transportation to open his own petroleum business. Meanwhile, he was first elected as alderman in 1923 and at every subsequent election, holding that office through 1938.

In 1939 Kircher began his tenure as the newly elected Lansing representative to the state legislature. He was returned to the Capitol three more times, serving in that capacity until 1946.

Upon leaving the legislature, Kircher was again elected to the city council in 1947, remaining a part of that body for a total of 27 years until his death on 7 April 1960. At the time of his passing he was also serving his 23rd year with the Ingham County Board of Supervisors.

Some years after his demise, the Lansing City Council sought to establish "a more tangible expression of its appreciation to the late Fred L. Kircher for his outstanding service to

his community." The method used by this body on 5 September 1967 was to unanimously name the town's only north/south freeway after the man respectfully known as "the dean of Lansing aldermen."

Coordinates: Lansing Inset

FULTON STREET

When the town of Grand Rapids was first platted in 1836, it included a number of streets along the Grand River with nautical or hydraulic names. In addition to avenues called Canal, Bridge, Water, Fountain, Ferry and Pearl (for the little white treasures sometimes found in the clams that lived in abundance on the adjacent stream beds), there was also Fulton, in honor of the man who pioneered in making the steamboat a practical and financial success.

It was appropriate that Fulton--creator of the first commercially successful water craft with motive power--be included in the mix of Grand Rapids' original street names. The town, after all, was at the head of navigation for the adjacent Grand River, though on some rare occasions vessels were able to overcome the rapids there and serve communities upstream. Parties began digging a canal around this navigation hazard in 1835 and completed the enterprise fifteen years later, but the necessary locks for raising and lowering ships were never installed.

Early Grand Rapids was heavily dependent upon Fulton's invention, as rivers were the main arteries of commerce in frontier Michigan. The first steamboat began service on the Grand River in 1837, and only five years later it was said that merchandise could be freighted by water from New York City to Grand Rapids in just two weeks time. Steamboat connections between Grand Rapids and Lake Michigan were so important they remained active until the last vessel was retired in 1917.

The person hailed by Fulton Street--Robert Fulton--was born near Lancaster, Pennsylvania, on 14 November 1765. From childhood he demonstrated a keen

mechanical aptitude, and as an adult he was recognized as a skilled gunsmith, artist, inventor, and engineer. In 1807 he built and operated the Clermont along the waters connecting New York City and Albany, introducing regularly scheduled steam navigation and self-propelled passenger service to the world. Before he died in New York on 24 February 1815, he had designed thirteen more steamboats and had a fleet of five packets plying the Hudson River.

As a path for the movement of land traffic, Fulton Street evolved in concert with the settlement of Grand Rapids. As the urban area grew along the fifteen-foot falls of the Grand River, the road honoring the father of the steamboat expanded eastward with it, eventually even outpacing the city limits and reaching the common boundary of Kent and Ionia counties.

Fulton Street's status as a major link between town and country was elevated in December of 1925 when it was informally made a part of route M-21. The road, which required improvements to meet its enhanced designation, was graded to trunk line standards in 1927, paved in 1928, and officially made a part of the state highway system in June of 1929. The new thoroughfare quickly became at the time the third most heavily used cross-state motorway in Michigan (then connecting Port Huron with Holland), showing that the Fulton name could be successful whether carrying traffic on land or water.

Coordinates: L/9

G. MENNEN WILLIAMS HIGHWAY

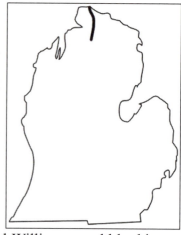

In 1976, the Michigan Legislature passed Senate Concurrent Resolution 559 as a tribute to a man one renown columnist has called "Michigan's Politician of the Century." The person being honored was G. Mennen Williams and the form of the recognition was a memorial highway.

"The commitment and dedication of this loyal citizen to the State of Michigan," said the commendation, "certainly merit the naming of a certain portion of Interstate 75 in his honor. Just as Interstate 75 connects Michigan's Lower and Upper Peninsulas, so the life of this remarkable public servant is inextricably linked to the progress of Michigan and its people." Therefore, concluded the solons in Lansing, "a fifty mile portion of Interstate 75 beginning at the South end of the Mackinac Bridge would be named the G. Mennen Williams Highway."

Gerhard Mennen Williams was born in Detroit on 23 February 1911. His affectionate nickname was "Soapy Williams" a moniker derived from his family background. His mother was the daughter of Gerhardt Mennen, the founder of the Mennen brand of shaving lather and skin preparations.

Williams began his education in Detroit, but moved on to later graduate from Princeton University in 1933. Immediately thereafter he attended the University of Michigan, where he received his law degree in 1936. After serving in a variety of legal capacities, Williams joined the Navy in 1942. He spent four years in the service, leaving as a lieutenant commander with ten battle stars.

With his formal education finished, Williams set out on a political career. He met with early success, winning his first contest for governor in 1948. He was elected to this post for an unprecedented six terms, initiating "the longest Democratic control of the governor's office since the Republican Party was founded in 1854."

In 1960, Williams announced he would not run for a seventh term and, instead, would seek some other public office. His new job was revealed after the November elections of that year when President John F. Kennedy, making his first major appointment, said Williams would be his assistant secretary of state for African affairs.

Williams held this position for six years and then was named U.S. Ambassador to the Philippines in 1968. After nearly a decade abroad, he left federal government service in 1969 and returned to his home in Michigan.

In 1970, Williams ran for and was elected to the Michigan Supreme Court. He remained a member of this judicial body until the end of 1986, when he retired from the bench at the age of 75.

Though Williams no longer participated in legal proceedings, he did not entirely abandon jurisprudence. When he died in Detroit on 2 February 1988, he was on the teaching faculty at the University of Detroit's School of Law. After a fifty-year public career, the man had earned a memorial highway, appropriately located near the Mackinac Bridge which was built during his administration as state governor.

Williams' road of recognition was left undisturbed for a quarter-century, when some slight tweaking was done to its authorizing language. Rather than have his memorial extend a

stipulated distance from the Mackinac Bridge, the state's legislators thought a more precise boundary was needed. Accordingly, in 2001 they passed Public Act 142 of 2001 declaring "the portion of highway I-75 in Cheboygan and Mackinaw counties shall be known as the 'G. Mennen Williams Highway'."

Coordinates: E-F/10-11

GARY PRIESS MEMORIAL HIGHWAY

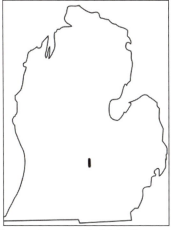

About once every three days in the United States a law enforcement officer is killed in the line of duty. In Michigan, one of our state troopers is killed while in uniform approximately once every two years. Some of these deaths are due to accidents and some are caused by hostile action. But in either case a member of one of the world's most dangerous professions is dead in the course of protecting the American public.

When a policeman or woman is lost, it is not uncommon for the community they served to remember them in some special way. A plaque conspicuously displayed is popular, as are memorial markers or monuments of modest design. Rarely resorted to, except in the most unusual circumstances, is naming a highway in honor of the deceased. Because Gary Neil Priess was an unusual man and a highly popular trooper, he has a trunk line of tribute in Michigan bearing his name.

Priess was born 2 December 1956 at Newberry in the Upper Peninsula. He grew up along the Lake Superior shore and graduated from Northern Michigan University with a Bachelor's degree in criminal justice. In 1982 Priess moved south to St. Johns, the seat of Clinton County, where he took a job with the DeWitt Township Police Department.

By the turn of the century, Priess was the senior patrol officer on the

16-member DeWitt Township police force. On 25 January 2000, while conducting a routine traffic stop along route US-127 north of Lansing, he was hit and killed by the errant driver of a passing tractor-trailer. A few days later nearly 1,000 people attended his funeral to pay their respects and say good-bye to one of the most popular cops in Clinton County.

As time passed, the citizens for whom Priess worked searched for some way of tangibly expressing their appreciation for his positive impact on their collective lives. Eventually, a significant number of people decided an appropriate gesture would be to name part of the highway where he was killed in the policeman's honor. To accomplish this goal, a local legislator introduced a measure to name twelve miles of US-127 from the Ingham/Clinton County line north to Price Road in remembrance of Priess. This noble idea was signed by the Governor in February of 2002 as Public Act 5 and the deed was dedicated at a roadside ceremony on August 14 of the same year.

Coordinates: L/11

GERALD R. FORD FREEWAY

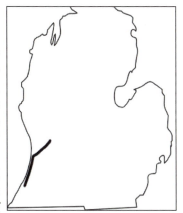

Michigan has two Ford freeways, a fact that could cause a lot of confusion were they not on opposite sides of the state. In Detroit there is the Edsel Ford Freeway (I-94), named after Henry Ford's son. And in southwestern Michigan there is the Gerald R. Ford Freeway (I-196), named for the 38th president of the United States.

Though Gerald Rudolph Ford was born 14 July 1913 in Omaha, Nebraska, he grew up in Grand Rapids, Michigan. While at South High School, he was an all-city football center for three years and also made the all-state team. As a high school senior, he was chosen the "most popular" member of his class.

Ford continued his football success at the University of Michigan where, in 1934, he was selected the Wolverine's most valuable player and, in 1935, played in the college all-star football game. He graduated from the U of M in 1935 with a Bachelor of Arts degree.

Ford turned down offers from professional football teams in order to attend Yale Law School. He graduated from that university in 1941 in the top third of his class. Shortly thereafter he joined the Navy as an ensign, serving a total of 47 months. He was discharged in 1946 as a lieutenant commander and then returned to Grand Rapids to practice law.

In 1949 Ford entered politics, winning the first of many elections to the U.S. House of Representatives. When Vice-President Spiro Agnew resigned his position on 10 October 1973, President Nixon nominated Ford to fill the vacancy. Later, when Nixon resigned his office, Ford became President on 9 August 1974.

Ford finished serving what remained of Nixon's term and then ran against Jimmy Carter in 1976 to seek a full term of his own. Ford lost in a close election, becoming the only president who never won a national election.

Because of Ford's outstanding career, and because he is the only president to hail from Michigan, it was deemed appropriate to name a highway after him. When a new freeway was about to be completed in his old congressional district, the opportunity was not allowed to pass.

By authority of Senate Concurrent Resolution 415 of 1974, I-196 from Benton Harbor to Grand Rapids was designated the "Gerald R. Ford Freeway." This was the first public facility to be named for the President and the first interstate in western Michigan to be named for a person.

Due to the press of official business, Ford was not able to attend the dedication ceremonies on 11 December 1974. The President delegated his three brothers to represent him at the occasion, which featured his name on road signs temporarily colored maize and blue in honor of Ford's alma mater.

Later, when Ford had left public office, a second dedication ceremony was held for I-196. This time the former president was able to be present, and on 8 August 1978 he gave his personal blessing to the Gerald R. Ford Freeway.

Strange to say, this tribute to a famous Michigander was slightly truncated by the state Legislature in 2001. It approved Public Act 142 that year which said that "highway I-196 in Kent, Ottawa, and Allegan counties shall be known as the 'Gerald R. Ford Freeway'." For reasons that cannot be explained, this new law omitted the small portion of the route that passes through Berrien County.

Coordinates: L-M/8-9

GLACIAL TRAIL

As the glaciers of the last ice age began to melt about 14,000 years ago in a gradual withdrawal to the arctic, they uncovered what is now Saginaw Bay and southern Lake Huron long before they retreated from the St. Lawrence River Valley. With the present exit for Great Lakes waters blocked, the flow from this slowly-forming drainage basin had to find another route to the sea.

Unable to move north to the Straits of Mackinac by the presence of the still massive ice front, the waters of developing Lake Huron and Saginaw Bay flooded down the lowest available channel at that time. This discharge route--generally occupied today by the Maple and Grand Rivers--ran westward across the Lower Peninsula and into a gradually emerging Lake Michigan. From there the effluent went down the Illinois River to the Mississippi River, which ended like now in the Gulf of Mexico.

As the waters of embryonic Saginaw Bay and Lake Huron coursed across the palm of

Michigan's mitten, they carved out a broad east/west channel. Over time this valley was cut down by erosion to the point that its maximum elevation was just 72 feet above the levels of the two freshwater seas at either end. When the current drainage paths of the Great Lakes were finally freed by the receding ice sheet, the load carried by the cross-state stream bed greatly declined leaving behind three smaller water courses known today as the Bad, Maple and Grand Rivers.

This trans-peninsular lowland from prehistoric times was used as a transportation artery by those seeking an easy and intermediate travel route from the western shores of Lake Huron to the eastern shores of Lake Michigan. It is understandable then why as early as 1835 Michigan settlers were petitioning their government to build a ship canal along the path of the old glacial spillway.

The proponents of this undertaking said that, because most of the present linking waterways were already navigable, all it would take is a canal 14 miles long to connect two of the largest river systems in Michigan. The construction of such a shipping aid would facilitate regional transportation, provide an alternative to the long and dangerous Mackinac passage, and allow east/west commerce to continue before and after ice had choked off movement at the Straits.

In response to these appeals, in 1837 the Michigan legislature began authorizing expenditures for building what was generally called the Saginaw-Grand canal. Work all along the length of this internal improvement was soon commenced, but only one mile was finished before the state ran out of funds to complete the project after spending $50,000. Most of the building materials were just abandoned in place or were appropriated by local residents.

Though the distance between Saginaw and Grand Rapids was never joined by a canal along the course of the old ice age channel, as time progressed many people thought it would make a good route for a road. This idea was finally given voice on 19 April 1919, when a former Michigan Congressman proposed that such a highway be built and that it be called the Glacial Trail.

The contemplated motorway was to closely follow the surveyed path of the canal, running from Saginaw westwards through St. Charles, Brant, Ashley, Maple Rapids, Lyons, Ionia, and Lowell to Grand Rapids. Of the total route, only that portion in Ionia and Kent counties was ever built, forming part of trunk line M-21 today. The eastern half of the Glacial Trail was never constructed, its existence apparently getting the cold shoulder from state and local officials.

Coordinates: J-L/9-12

GOLD STAR MEMORIAL HIGHWAY

Soon after the start of World War I, a custom arose in the United States of displaying flags at homes, places of business, schools, churches, etc. These banners were in addition to the Stars and Stripes that waved over most private and public buildings at that time.

The special pennants were called Service Flags, and a blue star was placed on the ensigns for each member of a family or organization who was serving in the Armed Forces.

Not long after the introduction of this practice, the question arose as to what should be done when someone represented by a blue star on a flag died while in service to their country. In response, the decision was made to replace a deceased soldier's blue star with a gold star as a sign of tribute to one who made the ultimate sacrifice for liberty.

Consequently, when St. Joseph County, Michigan, 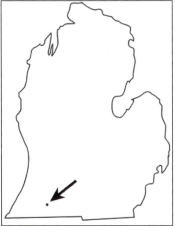 decided to recognize its citizens who lost their lives in World War I, it elected to do so by creating a Gold Star Memorial Highway.

This idea, generated by local chapters of the Daughters of the American Revolution and American Legion posts, was to consist of 100 black walnut trees and four Norway spruce along old US-131. The designated portion of the road ran for 1.5 miles from the southern city limits of Three Rivers into the country towards the Indiana border.

After getting permission from the county road commission and the state highway department to mark the trunk line, the sponsors acquired the desired trees from the Forestry De-

partment at the Michigan Agricultural College (now MSU). Local school children did the planting as class projects.

With great solemnity, the finished project was dedicated 4 May 1924. On that day, people of the region paid tribute to their fallen soldiers by consecrating roadside trees in their honor along one of the busiest routes in St. Joseph County. As one person noted, "they lined the route with trees, but they named it after the stars."

Coordinates: N/9

GRAND HIGHWAY

Given their names, it was almost a foregone conclusion that someone would eventually come up with the idea. That is, the notion of connecting Grand Haven and Grand Rapids with a "Grand Highway." This seemingly inevitable proposal was finally put forth on 7 November 1914 when the Grand Highway Association was established at Spring Lake.

This non-profit organization declared its purpose to be the construction of a 30-mile concrete highway between the two "Grand" cities. Funds to underwrite this enterprise were to be raised from annual membership dues of $10 per person. For those donors with more money or visions of immortality, the Association promised to "dedicate a section of this highway and erect columns to suitably mark any such section as a memorial to any name, cause or institution that the giver may desire."

The course of this Grand Highway generally followed the paths of contemporary trunk lines M-104 and I-96. Starting in Grand Haven, the road passed through Spring Lake, Nunica, Dennison, Coopersville, and Marne before entering Grand Rapids by way of Leonard Street. The circuit was marked out by black and white rings painted on telephone poles, causing the motorway to sometimes be called the "black and white line." Later, five-feet-high white concrete posts were placed along the route to keep drivers on the right track.

The Association agreed to pay the respective

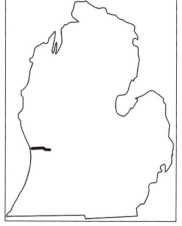

county road commissions $1,000 for every mile of highway that was built between the two grand cities. After about one year of promotional efforts, nearly three miles of pavement had been put in place. This accomplishment nearly consumed all available funds, so to help extend its meager resources the Association with mixed success tried to get thirty cement companies to each donate sufficient concrete to build 100 feet per mile of new road.

To help create more support for its plans, the Association convinced the Ottawa County Road Commission to build "object lesson" segments at various points along the Grand Highway. These were isolated 100-foot strips of concrete that served as demonstration patches of how the entire drive would look if more people agreed to back the good-roads cause.

Records do not indicate whether or not this approach had the desired effect of bringing in additional street-building funds. But the act of paving a stretch of road did have an interesting byproduct. One local newspaper reported that farmers along finished portions of the Grand Highway were "sprucing up their homes and premises. Nearly every farm shows signs of remodeling, rebuilding, painting or some improvement over the old appearance of things."

Though off to a fast start, the work of the Association quickly slowed down. There were a variety of factors contributing to this decline, among them being difficulty with fund raising and the distraction caused by World War I. Another problem was a lack of focus. Before the organization was a year old its directors were talking about extending the Grand Highway 150 miles to Detroit, intersecting along the way the town of Grand Ledge and following Grand River Avenue into the Motor City.

For these and other reasons, the

Grand Highway name survived for only a few years. But the logic that spawned the route was sound, for in a short time without a promotional group behind it the link between Grand Haven and Grand Rapids was finished and declared a trunk line in 1919-1920. The entire distance became US-16 in 1926 and in 1940 the extreme western segment was made M-104 when part of the main artery was diverted northwest towards Muskegon. Since 1961 the interstate network has let traffic bypass most of the original motorway, but despite its reduced stature from years past the old road is still a Grand Highway.

Coordinates: K/8-9

GRAND RIVER AVENUE

When the first Europeans came to what is now Michigan they found a number of Indian footpaths crisscrossing the territory. One of these routes--running from contemporary Detroit northwestward to the mouth of the Grand River--was appropriately called the Grand River Trail.

These tracks through the wilderness were used by early whites and Indians as a means of communication, but as time passed and settlers began moving to Michigan's interior the paths proved inadequate to accommodate the vehicles used by most pioneers. Consequently, as early as 1825 Congress was receiving petitions from citizens asking the national government build a good road into the "Grand River Country."

Many residents of the southern Lower Peninsula wanted Washington to construct a highway from the Detroit River to the Grand River so that newcomers could more easily reach the hinterlands and products from farm and forest could more readily pass to market. But at the time most federal politicians felt that public monies should not be spent on aiding parochial road projects, so petitions for improving the Grand River Trail were not acted upon.

Eventually, however, those promoting the creation of a better trans-peninsula route learned that the U.S. government did endorse the building of roads for national defense and internal im-

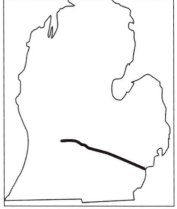

provements of broad regional importance. Consequently, on 4 July 1832, they got Congress to approve an act making the Grand River Trail one of five military highways radiating out from Detroit (the other streets being Woodward, Gratiot, Michigan and West Jefferson).

Officers working with the War Department surveyed the road pretty much along its present course, and by the time Michigan became a member of the Union in 1837 about sixty miles of the route had been built westward out of Detroit. As a state, Michigan had no money to continue the project or improve upon that which had already been done, so for nearly a decade it petitioned Congress for help in finishing the job.

Finally realizing that the resources to complete the Grand River Trail would have to come from local sources, the legislature began passing laws designed to get the road improved. Beginning in 1844 it enacted a number of statutes handing over portions of the highway to private companies who, in turn for making the needed repairs, would be allowed to charge tolls on all who used the route. These firms--levying fees of up to

10 cents for a wagon and six cents for a rider and horse--remained in existence collecting fees until shortly after the turn of the last century (only those persons going to or from churches or funerals were exempt from paying).

After the various toll road franchises had expired, the Grand River Trail (by then widely known as "Avenue" due to an 1871 name change in Detroit) reverted back to public control. Thus, when the legislature passed the trunk line highway act of 1913, the old coast-to-coast Indian path became adopted into the state's new motorway system as route M-16.

As their periods of control over Grand River Avenue drew to a close, the toll firms deferred all maintenance leaving a trail desperately in need of repair. To put the old turnpike back into shape, the State Highway Department had prisoners pave most of the stretch between Farmington and Lansing with the rest of the route being built by private

contractors. The entire length of road was eventually given a hard surface and opened to traffic on 7 August 1926, becoming "the first paved highway across the state."

One year later Grand River Avenue was designated US-16, the only Michigan road to have the same number first as a state and then as a federal highway. As a national transportation artery, use of the thoroughfare grew until it could no longer handle the traffic load it was forced to bear. Consequently, its course was made one of our first Interstate routes (I-96), with the initial section opening in 1957 and the last leg being completed on 21 November 1977.

Today, one can travel from the Ambassador Bridge to Lake Michigan on a paralleling Interstate replacement to Grand River Avenue. But the old highway still largely survives as a street serving local needs, no longer a way to quickly get from one side of the state to the other but remaining a path of history.

Coordinates: K-M/8-13

GRAND TRAVERSE MEMORIAL HIGHWAY

President Warren G. Harding, speaking in 1923, said "I find myself altogether responsive to a request for an appeal to the people to plant memorial trees along the important public highways and acknowledging [those lives that] were sacrificed in the [First] World War. It would be not only the testimony of our sentiments, but a means to beautify the country which these heroes have served so well."

Our nation's chief executive continued by saying that "a general adoption of the plan would, in the coming years, be noted as one of the useful and beautiful ideas which our soldiers brought back from France. The splendid avenues of France have been among the great delights of the travelers there, and a similar development would equally add to the beauty and attraction of our country."

Taking these words to heart was the Grand Traverse County Federation of Women's Clubs, which decided to sponsor a tree-lined memorial

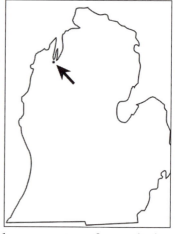

highway in honor of the local men who lost their lives in World War I. The place selected for this tribute was just south of Traverse City along a stretch of old route US-31 near the top of Rennie Hill.

The plan was to have one tree for each deceased soldier, with a tag attached bearing the name of the person to whom it was dedicated. The initial planting appropriately occurred on Arbor Day of 1923, when 42 maple saplings were set in place on both sides of the southern approaches to the city not far from the Garfield Township Hall.

The dedication of this gesture took place on May 4 in the presence of 200 people. An account of the ceremonies, along with a complete record of the trees and who they commemorated, was filed with the county clerk for permanent preservation.

Almost annually after this event additional maples were planted along the highway as new sponsors were found to purchase additions in the name of deceased veterans. And every Memorial Day small flags would be placed along the rows of trees in honor of the sons of Grand Traverse who had died in service to their country.

Despite the care sponsors devoted to the site, there were problems with the memorial. The area chosen was not well suited for growing trees, and many of them died and had to be replaced each year. Also, wayfarers seemed to find the flags irresistible, and "by the end of the summer the more patriotic of the passing motorists had stolen them all."

As late as 1935 an attempt was still being made to maintain the living tribute, but the long-term fate of the project was becoming clear. Today, the Grand Traverse Memorial Highway is all but forgotten in the region of its birth. Fortunately, the same cannot be said about those the road was to honor, and that is the most important legacy of the effort.

Coordinates: Traverse City Inset

GRATIOT AVENUE

All of the major forts in Michigan were built on the shores of the Great Lakes or their connecting rivers. Consequently, these structures were supplied by ships that regularly tended to the needs of the military's outposts.

However, this system worked only if the United States controlled our interior freshwater seas. If some other nation managed to dominate the Great Lakes--as Britain did in the Revolution and during the War of 1812--then the various forts would be at the mercy of the enemy.

In an effort to ensure that, in the event of hostilities, some of the most important Michigan garrisons could be supplied by land, on 2 March 1827 Congress authorized the building of a military road from present-day Detroit to Port Huron. Construction on this route began at Detroit in 1829 and was completed to Mount Clemens within two years. The entire 57-mile-long course was finished in 1833.

The destination of this road was an enclosure called Fort Gratiot. This installation was strategically situated at the southern end of Lake Huron, about a thousand feet from where the St. Clair River commences.

Soldiers began building the structure in May of 1814 to help American interests control a crucial water link between the Great Lakes. Since the engineer in charge of construction was

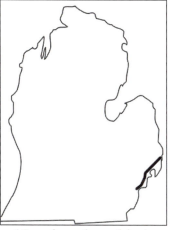

Charles Gratiot, the fort was named in his honor.

Charles Gratiot, Jr., was born into a prominent family on 29 August 1786 at what is today St. Louis, Missouri. A rather precocious youngster, he entered West Point at age 17 and graduated in just two years as a second lieutenant.

It was while serving as a career officer in the War of 1812 under General William Henry Harrison that Gratiot was ordered to build the stronghold that later bore his name. Through the successful completion of this and other assignments, Gratiot was eventually brevetted a brigadier general and made Chief of all Army Engineers.

Gratiot left the military in 1838 and became a clerk in the United States General Land Office. He retained this position until shortly before his death in St. Louis on 18 May 1855, at the age of 69.

Gratiot's fort survived him by a quarter-century, as it was finally abandoned in 1879. But his name lives on in the title given to the overland route that was built to connect Detroit with the defensive works that he erected at contemporary

Port Huron.

This artery of transportation began life as a stump-strewn and seldom-used military track that was called Gratiot because it was the route to or from Fort Gratiot. But over time it gradually evolved from a rough earthen road to a corduroy road, plank road, toll road and gravel road to a fully paved, heavily traveled, multiple-laned street called federal highway US-25.

When I-94 was finally completed on 1 February 1967, much of the traffic on Gratiot Avenue was diverted to the paralleling freeway and its status was downgraded to that of a state trunk line. Despite this decline in use and importance, the street is still one of the major and most historically significant thoroughfares in Southeastern Michigan.

Coordinates: K-M/14

GREAT LAKES AUTOMOBILE ROUTE

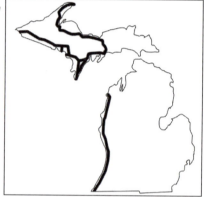

This highway was established by the Upper Peninsula Development Bureau in 1917 as "a circular journey along the banks of Lakes Michigan and Superior and Green Bay...." Because of the spherical nature of the trip, the route's motto was "When you start you're on the way home."

The path of this highway passed through Michigan, Wisconsin, Illinois and Wisconsin, with about two-thirds of the mileage being in the Wolverine State. To encourage tourists to follow this circuit, 50,000 pamphlets were prepared and distributed at various travel-related facilities across the region.

In Michigan, the Great Lakes Automobile Route (sometimes called the Great Lakes Tour) began at the Indiana border near New Buffalo and proceeded north along US-31 to Manistee. From there it followed M-22 to Frankfort, where drivers boarded the Ann Arbor Railroad car ferry for a trip to Manistique in the Upper Peninsula.

Once disembarking at the Schoolcraft County seat, excursionists could take two routes out of Manistique. One course followed M-94 to Munising, then M-28 from Munising to Marquette, and finally US-41 from Marquette to Copper Harbor. The second option went from Manistique to Ironwood along US-2, with alternative stretches from Escanaba to Menominee along M-35 and US-41 or between Crystal Falls and Iron Mountain along M-69 and M-95.

The Great Lakes Automobile Route appears not to have lived to see its first anniversary. The reasons for its quick demise are mainly two-fold. First, it appeared on the scene just about the time

America was entering World War I with its ensuing gas rationing, tight budgets, and national focus on fighting rather than recreation. Second, it included too many roads in the Upper Peninsula, embracing practically every trunk line west of Manistique. A Great Lakes circle drive was a good idea--a concept revisited many times thereafter--but this first one was short-lived because of bad timing and an inability to focus on just a single road in the Upper Peninsula rather than many.

While the original goal of the Great Lakes Automobile Route was to get people to drive around Lake Michigan, it got distracted from its mission by including side trips leading motorists up to Lake Superior. In 1927, the Escanaba Chamber of Commerce began promoting a more focused trip called "Looping the Lake." This circuit of Lake Michigan was to follow US-31 in the Lower Peninsula and US-2 and US-41 in the Upper Peninsula. While the idea was initially well received, it did not survive the onset of the Great Depression.

When large amounts of federal money started being used to stimulate the national economy, Wisconsin interests suggested in 1934 that Washington finance a road encircling Lake Michigan as a means of offering work to the unemployed.

This route was named the Lake Michigan Shore Drive, but funds to build such a thousand-mile highway were never available given more compelling priorities.

Coordinates: A-N/1-8

GREAT LAKES INTERNATIONAL HIGHWAY

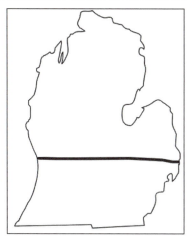

In October of 1928, a group of businessmen met in Owosso to create an association to promote what they named the Great Lakes International Short Route. This was a trunk line running almost horizontally across Michigan from Port Huron to Grand Haven, mainly known at the time as M-21.

Someone driving the route today would still travel in a nearly straight-line course across the state, but due to the building of Interstates the route numbers have been changed. Under contemporary signage, the highway would follow I-69 from Port Huron to Flint, M-21 from Flint to Grand Rapids, I-96 from Grand Rapids to Nunica, and M-104 from Nunica to Grand Haven.

The highway was called "international" because it was part of a system that went from Niagara Falls, New York, to Madison, Wisconsin, via Ontario and Michigan, a distance of nearly 600 miles (about 200 across Canada, 200 across Michigan, 100 across Lake Michigan, and 100 into Wisconsin). In Madison the road met what was called the National Parks Highway, a trail that went all the way to the Pacific coast.

The promoters called it the "short route" because, by taking the Grand Trunk car ferry ride between Grand Haven and Milwaukee, motorists would save 150 miles over driving the all-land distance on an east/west cross-country trip through Michigan. Furthermore, such an itinerary would shorten driving time by avoiding the congestion encountered in such large cities as Cleveland and Chicago.

Although individuals and corporations could and did join the group promoting the road, its most important members were cities along its course. These were the entities most likely to benefit from travelers' use of the route, so the various communities adjacent to the highway were charged dues in proportion to their populations.

The members of the association agreed on a slogan--The Scenic Highway to Niagara Falls--but they had trouble with the title of their product. Surveys had shown that the public could not tell if the Great Lakes International Short Route was a railroad, airplane connection, or steamship line. Since it was obviously none of these things, in December of 1928 the name of the route was changed to the more descriptive Great Lakes International Highway.

To publicize and market this motorway, over $6,500 was spent on advertising stickers, newspaper space, magazine articles, guide maps, promotional folders, radio announcements, and an annual release called the International Tourist. These promotions reached 76 cities in 21 states, with the result that 1929 traffic over the route increased by 29% above that of the previous year.

Just when it looked like the Great Lakes International Highway was poised to become one of the major lateral routes across mid-Michigan, it was hit by the Great International Depression. The stock market crash of late 1929 soon deprived the sponsors of the money they needed to lobby for improvement of the route and encourage travelers to follow its path. The association did not survive past 1930, and with its demise quickly passed most memories of the named highway it promoted.

Coordinates: K-L/8-14

GREEN ARROW ROUTE

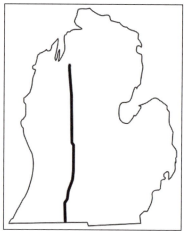

As the Mackinac Bridge approached completion, there was anticipation that traffic to and from the Straits region would increase significantly. Communities along the various north/south feeder routes looked forward to greatly improved business as these expected motorists sought local services.

In the western and central part of the state, the main approach roads to the Bridge would be US-31, US-131, and US-27. This meant that of all the major cities in the region, Battle Creek would be the only one without a highway serving people traveling up and down the Lower Peninsula.

In an effort to correct this problem, in March of 1957 the associate editor of the Battle Creek Enquirer and News proposed that M-66 be popularized as an alternate route from Indiana north to the Bridge. To do this, it was felt that some attention-getting name had to be found for the road so drivers would be lured to its path.

After some period of deliberation, it was decided to dub the road the Green Arrow Route. This appellation was perhaps subconsciously derived from a competing form of transportation, the Pennsylvania Railroad. For years this company operated a famous passenger train parallel to M-66 called the Northern Arrow, some favorable association in the public mind that would certainly do the highway backers no harm.

Officially, however, the "Green" part of the road's title represented the color of the forests through which drivers would pass if they followed the route. The "Arrow" portion represented the early days of Michigan and signified the land of Indian legends that motorists could access by driving the featured highway. A secondary meaning was that M-66 went straight as an arrow from one end of the Southern Peninsula to the other.

It would take more than a catchy name to make travelers leave the principal arteries in favor of M-66. In recognition of this fact, the supporters of the Green Arrow Route declared it to be the most direct and scenic path to vacation country. Furthermore, the road avoided most of the major cities, thus offering less congestion and a minimum amount of traffic.

Despite these alleged benefits, relatively few people chose M-66 as a preferred course of travel. In an effort to help the cause, the Michigan legislature passed Public Act 170 of 1959 officially declaring the road from Indiana to Kalkaska to be the Green Arrow Route (in 2001, by virtue of PA 142, the legislature abreviated the length to run from Kalkaska south to about the northern border of Calhoun County, a deed reiterated by PA 138 of 2004). The degree to which this gesture succeeded in highlighting M-66 can be gauged from the fact that probably no one reading these words has ever heard of this designation.

Longfellow wrote, "I shot an arrow into the air, it fell to earth I knew not where." Some individuals back in the late 1950s tried to launch a green arrow route that would shoot travelers in a direct line from the Indiana Toll Road north to the Straits of Mackinaw. This airy idea eventually fell to earth, and people looking for evidence of it today can search I know not where.

Coordinates: F-N/9-10

GREEN DRIVE

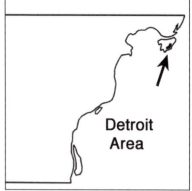

Detroit Area

At the mouth of the St. Clair River there is a delta comprised of a number of islands. This natural formation was created by the silt suspended in the waters leaving Lake Huron, particles which precipitated out when the stream load reached the settling basin we know as Lake St. Clair.

For years this semi-aquatic habitat was a popular place for fishing and hunting, as its diverse environment was home to a vast array of wildlife. But by the late nineteenth century this pleasant mixture of land and water was beginning to attract people aiming for pleasure and relaxation as well as at animals.

Eventually, all along the three main channels crossing the St. Clair Flats (as the delta is called) there began to appear a variety of structures like clubhouses, hotels, vacation complexes, marinas, cottages, and grand private residences, all catering to those who wished to recreate in what came to be called "America's Little Venice" because of its many liquid streets. The lands once home to bullfrogs, ducks and muskrats gradually became one of the premier resort locations in the country.

Initially, visitors to this summer playground reached their destinations on one of the many excursion boats that made daily round trips from Detroit to the Flats. Those who wanted to access the many islands in winter would just walk or drive sleighs over the ice. Later, when automobiles became common, a ferry boat service was established near Algonac so motorists could actually take their vehicles a short distance into this popular complex of earth and water by following some old wagon paths.

As increasing numbers of visitors drove cars into the Flats, the region's primitive access routes became overtaxed and unsuitable for the traffic load they had to bear. Seeking to address this problem, in March of 1926 a group of delta land owners met in Detroit to plan for the building of an improved road. Known as the Green Drive Committee (after one of its members, William H. Green Jr.), the group agreed to levy an assessment on all property holders along the South Channel and then commenced highway construction in July of 1927. The ensuing route was kept as a private road until all expenses had been paid, at which time it was turned over to the state and designated as trunk line M-154 in January of 1931.

The person whose name is saluted by the road was born 3 July 1863 in the Corktown section of Detroit. After being educated in the city's public schools, Green served as a deputy sheriff from 1901 to 1905 before moving on to the position of chief clerk to the County Auditor. Eventually seeking higher office, he convinced local voters to elect him as their County Treasurer from 1917 to 1921. Thereafter, until his retirement early in 1935, he served as Wayne County Auditor.

In addition to his role as public servant, William H. Green, Jr., acted as President of the St. Clair Flats Improvement Association. He was chosen to fill this post in part because, according to the newspapers of the time, he "was one of the first Detroiters to have a summer home at St. Clair Flats." In his obituary notice on the day of his death--2 August 1941-- the Detroit Free Press noted that the man whom Green Drive honors had been "instrumental in getting electric lights and good roads at the Flats."

Coordinates: L/14

GROESBECK HIGHWAY

Detroit Area

For about a century, anyone traveling by land between Detroit and Mount Clemens had to go via Gratiot Avenue (M-3). With the advent of the automobile, the amount of traffic eventually exceeded the carrying capacity of that road.

To relieve the congestion, the Macomb County Board of Supervisors decided to build a thoroughfare paralleling Gratiot about a mile to the west. Under authority of Resolution 15, passed 23 October 1925, this new route was to be called the Groesbeck Highway.

The proposed motorway was named in honor of the man who was then governor, Alexander Joseph Groesbeck. The christening of the road was also undoubtedly influenced by the fact that Groesbeck had been born in Macomb County on 7 November 1873 and received his common school education in Mount Clemens.

Upon graduation from high school, Groesbeck attended the University of Michigan law school, earning his degree in 1893. He subsequently established a highly successful legal practice in Detroit and became active in Republican politics.

In 1916 Groesbeck was elected state attorney general, serving in that capacity for four years. From that position he successfully ran for governor, a post he held from 1921 to 1926.

Though Macomb County sought to honor its favorite son with a road, finding the money with which to build it was proving to be difficult. To solve this problem and help ensure construction of the bypass, Groesbeck ostensibly interceded to have the route classified as a state financed trunk line.

Grading on the right-of-way began in 1926, but once Groesbeck was voted out of office at the end of the year, work on the enterprise pretty much ceased. Although everything was finished except the paving, nearly all of 1927 passed with no movement toward finishing the project.

Seeking to move things along, the state representative for Macomb County, Archie M. Reid, went to the State Administrative Board on 12 December 1927 and asked if attention could be given to completing the road. The Board was so impressed with his plea that it unanimously voted to name the highway after Reid and to proceed "at once" with the concluding phase of construction.

The paving of M-97 appears to have been done by 1930. Travelers along the route were "somewhat puzzled," however, as to the real name of the thoroughfare. Some signs said "Groesbeck Highway" and others said "Reid" or "Reed Hiway."

When asked about this confusing situation in 1934, the Macomb County Road Commissioner explained that the state was calling the road one name and the county another. "Those [Reid] signs were never official signs," he said. "So far as the Macomb County Road Commission was concerned, the road never was anything but Groesbeck Highway. We named it that, and we never changed it."

The matter of the road name may have been settled, but there was still some unfinished business with the highway. It dead-ended at the southern city limits of Mt. Clemens. Not until 1949 was the west belt line constructed around the town allowing M-97 traffic to reach its present terminus at Hall Road.

The final segment of Groesbeck Highway was inaugurated on 20 October 1949. This date was also chosen to formally dedicate the entire length of the 14-mile-long road.

On hand to participate in the ceremonies was the trunk line's namesake, Alexander Groesbeck.

Nearly a quarter of a century after he proposed the road, he was present to cut the ribbon at its official opening. Groesbeck died a few years later--on 10 March 1953--and was buried in Detroit, the point of origin for his memorial highway.

Coordinates: Southeastern Michigan Enlargement B-D/9-10

HAGGERTY ROAD

Detroit Area

Born in Greenfield Township, Wayne County, on 22 August 1866, as a lad he was a classmate of Henry Ford. The two youngsters sat on the same bench at school and were play chums throughout childhood. Later, as young adults, while Henry Ford pioneered with automobiles his boyhood pal, John Strong Haggerty, pioneered with the roads on which the self-propelled vehicles ran.

Haggerty was elected to the Wayne County Road Commission in 1907--its initial year of operation--a post he held for the next 27 years. In 1909 he convinced the county to build the first mile of concrete highway in the country on Woodward Avenue between Six-Mile and Seven-Mile roads. This experiment proved to be so successful that all across the nation governments began switching from brick and macadam for hard surfaces to cheaper, long-lasting concrete.

While Haggerty was known as an innovator, a good-roads enthusiast, and a major power in Wayne County government, he was equally famous as a businessman. In 1887 he started a brickyard near Michigan Avenue in Dearborn. The burgeoning growth of greater Detroit and the local popularity of brick as a building material helped to eventually make Haggerty a wealthy man. Even when sales of his products fell sharply during the Depression, he managed to remain professionally active furnishing brick to build Henry Ford's Greenfield Village.

In addition to practicing his trade, Haggerty found time to serve in a number of other capacities. He was a member of the Jackson Prison Board (1911-1912), on the Board of Directors of the Michigan Agricultural Society (1915-1925), Chairman of the Wayne County Republican Party (1920-1930), Michigan Secretary of State (1927-1930), and member of the State Civil Service Commission (1939-1940). Haggerty also devoted his time and money to helping the poor and needy, as during his life he adopted, reared and sent to college eighteen southeast-Michigan orphans.

Because of his many accomplishments and years of public service, when Wayne County was creating a major bypass route around Detroit in 1929, they decided to name it after Mr. Haggerty. The 58-mile-long highway ran from about Pontiac south to the Monroe County border. On account of its good quality and convenient location, the State Highway Department assigned this pavement--known then and now as Haggerty Road--the designation M-15 from 1930 to 1935.

Coordinates: Southeastern Michigan Enlargement C-G/4-5

HALL ROAD

Detroit Area

John Hall came to Michigan from New York state in 1836 and initially purchased 400 acres in east-central Macomb County. Hall's holdings were located in the extreme southeastern corner of Macomb Township, offering one mile of frontage along the southern and eastern borders of that administrative district in Section 36.

Hall was very astute in choosing his real estate, for not only was it on fertile soil but it was also very well situated within the regional transportation network. At the time of acquisition, Hall's property was transected by the famous Gratiot Road that went from Detroit to Port Huron.

About two decades later the Grand Trunk Railroad line between Detroit and Port Huron was also built through his farmstead (1859), giving him close access to two major forms of conveyance.

This mix of land communications was augmented in the early twentieth century when an electric interurban route was constructed through the old Hall homestead (1900). This traction line--later part of the Detroit United Railroad system and mainly designed to haul passengers on an express basis--had a station on the Hall estate. The last major addition to the roads serving the Hall property occurred in 1949 when Groesbeck Highway (M-97) was built up to the southern border of the family farm.

Thus, at one time or another there were two main roads and two railroad lines running south to north across or terminating at the Hall grounds. But there was only one east/west street that passed by the Hall address and intersected all of these routes, and not surprisingly this

major traffic artery was known as Hall Road in honor of the family.

Hall Road was no different than any other major county thoroughfare until 1916, when the state designated it trunk line M-59. The highway was chosen for this special status because it "gives Pontiac and Oakland County people a direct route to the lake [St. Clair] shore [and] to Mt. Clemens people it gives the direct route to Oakland County and its beautiful lake region."

Initially M-59 proceeded east out of Utica as far as the Romeo Plank Road, where it turned south and entered Mount Clemens along Cass Avenue. In 1931, however, the route was realigned to its present configuration north of town, finally passing by the original residence of the clan whose surname now marks the signposts along one of southeastern Michigan's busiest avenues.

Coordinates: Southeastern Michigan Enlargement B/9-10

THE HAMILTON WAY

"The Hamilton Way" sounds more like a technique or procedure to employ when engaging in some activity rather than the title for a highway. But if anyone wanted to do things Hamilton's way they might very well get a road named after them, as his method of conduct proved to be very successful.

The start of this tale begins in Waterboro, Maine, where Frank Hamilton was born on 20 November 1848. He was reared on a farm near this quiet New England town and attended country schools there before leaving at the age of 16 to work in a dry goods store. The experience he gained as a youth in this business ultimately lead him to a successful mercantile career as an adult.

With a good knowledge of the retail trade, Hamilton came to Traverse City, Michigan, in May of 1868 to serve as a salesman in the local store of Hannah, Lay & Company. Just five years later he left this position to team up with James Milliken (grandfather of our state's fortieth governor) and open his own firm of Hamilton, Milliken & Company.

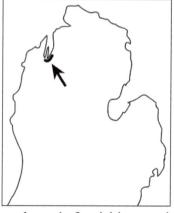

This partnership did very well over the years, eventually growing so big it was deemed best to divide the establishment. In 1892 the business was split into two separate firms giving Hamilton the clothing and men's furnishings and Mr. Milliken the dry-goods, carpets and cloak lines Hamilton continued to operate his store until 1921, when he sold the concern after 53 years of marketing goods in Traverse City.

During his more than a half-decade as an entrepreneur in town, Hamilton was active in a number of civic and commercial matters. He was, for instance, one of the organizers and first president of the Traverse City Business Men's Association (1885) and the Michigan Business Men's Association (1886), both ostensibly the first of their kind in the country. He was also director of the local First National Bank and a member of the Board of Trustees for the Dixie Highway Association.

In the realm of government, Hamilton served at various times as Traverse City councilman, mayor, and school board member, in addition to being treasurer of the local Northern Michigan Asylum. At the county level he was the first road commissioner and the body's chairman for its first twenty years (1909-1929), as well as a member of the advisory board to the State Highway Commission.

As can be seen from this biographical sketch, Hamilton was keenly interested in improving ground transportation across the northwestern Lower Peninsula. As early as the 1890s, most of the signboards about the region advertising his store included the phrase "Hurrah For Good Roads." Because of his strong and effective boosterism for better highways throughout the area, he eventually became known provin-

cially as the "Father of Good Roads."

In recognition for all that Hamilton had done to help develop motorways in the vicinity, the Traverse City Rotary Club (which, incidently, he helped to establish) proposed in November of 1920 that US-31 be named The Hamilton Way from about the downtown area north to the county line near Elk Rapids. A delegation from the fraternal organization promptly presented this idea to the County Board of Supervisors, and these public officials approved the concept by unanimous resolution on 14 April 1921.

His obituary notice, which appeared on page one of the Record-Eagle for 11 September 1940, said that Hamilton "was instrumental in securing the first graveled roads and later the first paving of rural roads in the state." With such accomplishments to his credit, it is unfortunate that today hardly anyone in Michigan remembers which way is the Hamilton Way.

Coordinates: G/9

HARTEL ROAD

The road between Grand Ledge and Potterville has existed almost as long as the two communities it connects. It's a straight north-south highway that follows the section lines, the survey coordinates that were usually used for establishing transportation routes west of the Appalachian Mountains.

For most of its life this artery of movement was informally known as the Potterville-Grand Ledge Road, unimaginatively named for the places that more or less defined its top and bottom. As traffic between the two settlements grew over the years, state government eventually took notice and declared it a trunk line highway in 1932. With this action, the route acquired the additional name of M-100.

Given its upgraded status, use of the motorway increased to the point that the stretch between Potterville and Grand Ledge had to be paved for the first time in 1940. Thus, what had started out as just two parallel ruts through the woods of pioneer Michigan had--in about eighty years--become a hardsurfaced thoroughfare with

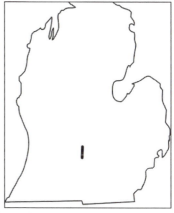

a descriptive name and a highway number. But this, it turned out, was not good enough.

Many of the roads in Eaton County had no names at all or had unofficial titles, like the Potterville-Grand Ledge route, that merely described the points they linked. Determined to correct this confusing or inadequate situation, local officials established a study group to look into the matter and come up with a solution.

While most committees seem to be rather ineffectual, this one actually left its mark on the landscape. It "spent much time and thought interviewing old settlers and in searching out old trails and historical events of local importance for commemoration." Having completed this phase of its project, the committee then made sure that "long-established road names were retained, while names of pioneer families and outstanding and widely known persons were given to roads having no such designation."

One of the families honored were the Hartels, who first came to the area around the time of the Civil War. They originally settled south of Potterville, but as the clan grew in numbers they eventually spread out over more of the vicinity. Because of their early arrival

in the county and their long tenure as residents of Benton Township, late in 1940 the committee decided to bestow the Hartel name upon the road that began near the original homestead and proceeded north to the town of Grand Ledge. And it has been thus ever since.

Coordinates: L/10

HASKELL L. NICHOLS MEMORIAL HIGHWAY

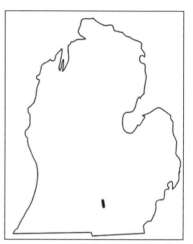

He was the longest-tenured state senator in Michigan history and, with 34 total years at the Capitol in Lansing, the second-longest serving lawmaker ever elected to the legislature.

The holder of these records is Haskell Linton Nichols, who was born at Homer, Michigan, on 28 July 1896. After being educated in the local schools, he received additional training by the Army in World War I, where he earned the rank of Second Lieutenant.

After the Armistice in Europe, Nichols entered the University of Michigan law school, from which he graduated in 1923. He subsequently moved 35 miles west to Jackson, where he practiced law until his death there on 30 April 1991.

Being interested in politics, Nichols eventually ran for public office, serving in the Michigan house of representatives from 1932 to 1942. He next moved on to the state senate, gaining election to that chamber from 1942 to 1966.

For all but two of his senate years, Nichols was chairman of the chamber's Highway Committee. This was the perfect assignment for the man, because he said he "loved high-

ways."

Nichols so strongly believed in improved streets that he once joked that he "had black-top in his veins and cement in his arteries." Another funny story was that--because Nichols worked so hard for his district and the cause of transportation--all roads in Michigan lead to Jackson.

After the death of Nichols, it was only fitting that some highway be designated in his honor. This was accomplished by Public Act 249 of 1992, which so marked a ten-mile section of trunk line near his home town.

The enabling legislation declared that US-127 from the northern border of Jackson County south to I-94 would be named in Nichol's memory. This thoughtful gesture and its appropriate signage was officially dedicated just north of Jackson on 14 January 1993, with family and dignitaries present.

Coordinates: M/11

HAYES ROAD

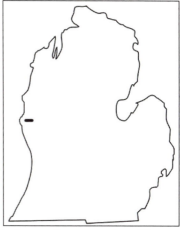

For nearly the first half of the twentieth century, identifying roads in Oceana County was a confusing proposition. Some roads were not named at all, while others had a wide range of titles along their lengths. Some regularity and uniformity was called for, and a formal proposal that this be done was made to county officials by the Consumers Power Company in 1947. After a committee was established to study this problem and recommend a solution, a systematic and organized system of road names was adopted in January of 1948.

Under the new arrangement, nearly all east/west roads in Oceana County were to honor U.S. Presidents. Starting at the north boundary of the county, the first street was named for George Washington and then matters proceeded southward in ascending chronological sequence up through Franklin D. Roosevelt. It was the good fortune of Rutherford Hayes that his name just happened to fall on the one east/west road in Oceana County that carried trunk line status (M-20), thus giving him a state memorial highway within Michigan.

Rutherford Birchard Hayes, the nineteenth president of the United States, was born 4 October 1822 in Delaware, Ohio. After being educated in a series of private schools, he graduated from the Harvard Law School in 1845 and subsequently established a law practice in Ohio. When the Civil War commenced in 1861, Hayes left his legal pursuits and accepted a commission as Major in the Ohio Volunteer Infantry. He distinguished himself in the military by being wounded four times and having four horses shot out from under him. Two months after the war ended Hayes resigned from the Army, having risen to the brevet rank of major general.

While fighting at the front, Hayes became a candidate for the House of Representatives. Though he did no campaigning, he won the election and took his seat in Congress after his discharge from service. Hayes remained in Washington D.C. until July of 1867, when he resigned to become governor of Ohio, a post which he held for three terms. Based upon his favorable record as the chief executive of a major Midwestern state, Hayes was chosen the Republican candidate for president in 1876. In what became the most disputed election in U.S. history, Hayes eventually won the contest by one vote over his opponent Samuel J. Tilden.

Having made a prior commitment to serve just one term, Hayes left our nation's capital in 1881 and retired from politics. He spent the rest of his years at his home in Fremont, Ohio, before being called to the great beyond on 17 January 1893. Today his estate, including his grave site and a memorial library, is open to the public on the outskirts of Fremont.

During his career as a public servant, Hayes achieved many laudable goals and received numerous commendations. Unfortunately, however, he will be remembered more for introducing the custom of Easter Egg rolling by children on the White House lawn than for having a memorial highway named for him in western Lower Michigan.

Coordinates: J/7-8

HIAWATHA ROAD

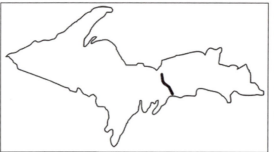

Nearly everyone has heard of "Hiawatha," and most people likely know that he is the main Indian character in a narrative poem written by Henry Wadsworth Longfellow in 1855. Beyond this, however, conventional wisdom pretty much ends. A review of the facts, therefore, is probably in order.

Hiawatha (meaning "he makes rivers") is believed to be an actual historical figure who was a tribal chieftain or medicine man in upstate New York. Around 1570 he persuaded five warring tribes--the Mohawk, Oneida, Onondaga, Cayuga, and Seneca--to make peace among themselves and form a confederacy of nations called the Iroquois. This union eventually became the most powerful Indian alliance on the North American continent.

Because of this accomplishment, Hiawatha was revered as a man of great power. After his death, as the story of his success was passed down to succeeding generations of Native Americans, his reputation grew to heroic proportions. Eventually the legend of Hiawatha appeared in the writings of Henry Rowe Schoolcraft, a Michigan man who collected and recorded the myths and sagas of Great Lakes Indians. When Longfellow read about this tale in one of Schoolcraft's books, he was inspired to write in verse a somewhat modified account of Hiawatha's story.

In his fictional "Song of Hiawatha," Longfellow makes his main character a young chief whose tribe lives in a forest near Lake Superior. Because the author relocates the action from upper New York state to the upper Midwest, there are today many features in northern Michigan honoring Hiawatha. As a case in point, in Schoolcraft County alone there is a

creek, national forest, former settlement and township bearing his name, and at one time there was even a "Hiawatha Road."

The present pavement between Manistique and Shingleton was initially proposed in 1878, when funds were first appropriated for its partial construction. However, the trail did not become a trunk line route until 1927 when the State Administrative Board authorized the Highway Department to take over the 33-mile stretch under the designation of M-94.

At that time there existed a small rural community about midway between Manistique and Shingleton called "Hiawatha." Since people traveling the length of the highway in either direction had to pass through this hamlet, the route became popularly known as the "Hiawatha Road."

It was in this isolated village that the new highway was formally dedicated with a "monster celebration" on 30 August 1927. About 400 people gathered at the Hiawatha Grange hall for speeches, a chicken dinner, and an evening of dancing as they marked the opening of an important connecting road between lakes Michigan and Superior.

But the presence of a state transportation artery could not save the little town that hosted its commemoration, and the settlement ceased to exist in the 1940s. With the disappearance of the community halfway along its course, the label "Hiawatha Road" gradually faded from vogue and eventually the route became known solely by its assigned number. Today, the only namesake road in the vicinity is just to the east in Mackinac County where much of route H-40 is called the "Hiawatha Trail."

Coordinates: C-D/7-8

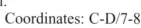

HOFFMAN ROAD

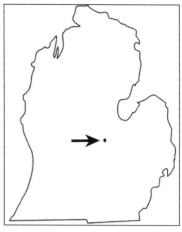

Present-day M-52 north of Owosso was one of the first trunk lines established in Michigan, its designation occurring around 1916. Though parts of this highway near Saginaw and Owosso were quickly improved, the back-country sections--particularly the stretch between Saint Charles and Oakley--were left as poor dirt roads.

One man who worked tirelessly to have the rural segments of the system upgraded was Jacob Bowman Hoffman. It was his belief that if all of northern M-52 was brought up to current standards it would allow farmers to more easily haul goods to and from markets and increase the amount of interaction between Saginaw and Owosso.

Stimulated by Hoffman's promotional efforts, in 1922 local citizens circulated petitions asking the Highway Department to "harden" M-52 in most of Saginaw County. This campaign to influence state government was successful, and late in that same year construction activities were started on the worst portions of the road.

By the end of 1924 all of northern M-52 had either been paved or turned into a good gravel highway. On 20 December 1924--the same day construction work on the trunk line was inspected and improved--the Saginaw County Road Commission paid tribute to Jacob Hoffman and his labors on behalf of M-52 by passing a resolution declaring that the division from Saint Charles to Oakley would be "hereafter known as the Hoffman Road."

Unfortunately, Mr. Hoffman was not present to receive or appreciate this gesture, for he had died on 4 March 1923. It was in posthumous recognition of the man's labors for

improved north/south transportation that the Board named a piece of the road in his honor.

Born on 2 February 1853 in Elmira, New York, Jacob Hoffman came to Saginaw County in 1893. He bought a farm on Ridge Road that he affectionately called "Hard Scrabble," and he developed and expanded this operation until he was one of the most prosperous residents of the region.

The leading citizen of Oakley, Mr. Hoffman was a major force in civic and political affairs. At the local level he variously served as village clerk and president, secretary of the Oakley Farm Bureau elevator, and community banker. On the broader scene he was supervisor of Brady Township for 24 years, director of the Saginaw County Agricultural Society, a member of the county fair board since its inception, and chairman of the county board of supervisors.

For these accomplishments alone Saginaw County would have been justified in designating a road in gratitude to Jacob Hoffman. But given his labors in the cause of bettering the northern extent of M-52, it is appropriate that a bit of that road would be named in his honor. Unfortunately, no evidence of this tribute remains in the community memory or on the contemporary transportation scene.

Coordinates: K/11

HOOSIER HIGHWAY

When the Upper Mississippi Valley was being settled there was a fad in nick-naming residents of the various states. The results of this practice are still with us today as we refer to Wisconsin badgers, Minnesota gophers, Iowa hawkeyes, and Ohio buckeyes.

All of these appellations are as understandable to contemporary Midwesterners as they were to the pioneers of yore. But what are we Wolverines to make of the word "Hoosier." Is it animal, vegetable or mineral?

The origins of the term "Hoosier" are uncertain, but it is a good bet that its derivation was not complimentary. First used on this continent in the South, the word was applied to a rough, uncouth, ignorant class of people. Other sources trace its lineage to old English where it was descriptive of a low, vulgar person.

A somewhat far-fetched but popular explanation of the word is that it began as a mocking reference to the accent of Indiana natives and their inquiring greeting to visitors knocking on their cabin doors, "Who's 'ere?"

Why should Michiganers care about any of this "Hoosier" business? Because on 15 October 1917 the Hoosier Highway was established, a route that went from Detroit south to El Paso, mainly for the benefit of "tourists desiring to go to Texas in the winter."

In Michigan, the Hoosier Highway ran west from Detroit to Saline along the course of present-day US-12. Beyond Saline the route passed

through Tecumseh, Adrian, and Morenci over what are now just secondary roads.

The symbol of the Hoosier Highway was a large red letter "H" on a white background. This design was painted on at least five telephone poles to the mile to guide wayfarers to their destinations.

In 1926 the U.S. Bureau of Public Roads began numbering trunk lines, a practice that eventually eliminated the need for most named highways and the special marks that each of them had to place along their routes.

Thereafter, instead of searching for the unique character of a particular trail association painted on roadside features, motorists could look for the distinctive shield of a standardized federal highway sign and just follow the number of the trunk line.

The introduction by the government of a uniform method of directional markers led to the disappearance of earlier means of designating courses of travel. But until the inauguration of the federal transportation system, the Hoosier Highway was the only named primary road in Michigan that paid honor to another state.

Coordinates: M-N/12-13

HOOVER DRIVE

Detroit Area

To most Americans, his name is associated with a large dam on the Colorado River not far from Las Vegas, Nevada. To many Europeans, he is remembered for his life-saving relief efforts during and after two world wars. To political scientists, he is primarily known as the benefactor of an Institution on War, Revolution, and Peace in central California. And to historians he is viewed as an expert administrator and the thirty-first President of the United States. Such are the diverse views of Herbert Clark Hoover.

Born 10 August 1874 in

West Branch, Iowa, Hoover was orphaned at the age of eight and raised by relatives who instilled in him a respect for education. This thirst for knowledge led him to enter Stanford University as a member of the newly-founded college's first freshman class. Graduating from this school in 1895 with a degree in geology, he went on to become an internationally known and highly successful mining engineer.

When World War I broke out, Hoover began donating his time and money to help feed the millions of people who were starving in Europe. After a break in this routine during 1917-1918 to serve as U.S. Food Administrator--helping to stimulate domestic crop production and promote resource conservation--he returned to his relief activities abroad until 1921, when he accepted the position of Secretary of Commerce.

After continuously discharging the duties of this Cabinet post through two administrations, Hoover ran for the Presidency in 1928 on the Republican ticket. Though he made only seven speeches during the campaign, he won the race by landslide proportions, making him this country's first chief executive born west of the Mississippi River. After one term in Washington, D.C., he ceased to hold elective office and gradually became a respected elder statesman.

When World War II began, Hoover once again lead efforts to care for the needy, a commitment that continued after the cessation of hostilities. For his lifetime efforts to distribute provisions and supplies to the suffering, he was made an hon-

orary citizen of Belgium (where every July 5 is celebrated as "Hoover Day"), Poland, Estonia, Finland, and 24 European cities. In addition, he was recognized with degrees by 87 colleges and universities around the globe and was the recipient of over 500 medals, awards and testimonials from all over the world.

For his professional accomplishments, Hoover was known as "The Great Engineer." For his leadership in wartime and famine relief he was hailed as "The Great Humanitarian." For his impressive work in the Commerce Department he was labeled "The Great Secretary." And for his efforts in old age to bring efficiency to the federal bureaucracy he was called "The Great Public Servant." This remarkable career came to an end on 20 October 1964, in New York City, when Hoover died after living longer following his departure from the White House than any other former President.

The President's connection with Michigan in the context of memorial highways occurred on 18 October 1929. In that month Hoover visited the Motor City as part of a ceremony paying tribute to the great inventor, Thomas Alva Edison. Seeking some means of also bestowing favor upon our nation's leader, the Detroit Common Council unanimously voted three days before his arrival to name a part of what is now route M-97 in his honor. And so it is that a portion of this trunk line in northern Wayne County is today called "Hoover Drive."

Coordinates: Southeastern Michigan Enlargement D/9

HURON COUNTY
MEMORIAL HIGHWAY

Huron County sort of forms the nail on Michigan's thumb. Following the circumference of this finger tip is trunk line M-25, one of the most scenic drives in the Lower Peninsula. Because of its beauty, such a road would make a wonderful tribute if someone wanted to establish a memorial highway. It is not surprising, therefore, that such a proposal was made in the past by residents of the area.

The people of Huron County have generously offered their youth in defense of this nation when its freedoms were deemed at risk. Of the 342 men it sent to fight in the Civil War, 42 made the ultimate sacrifice and were killed in action. Again in World War I when duty beckoned, 937 of its citizens answered the cry to battle, of whom 44 paid with their lives. As the clouds of war formed just prior to World War II and thoughts turned again to a possible call to arms, Huron County officials began thinking about a way to honor its veterans.

A committee formed of the Supervisors decided the best way to accomplish this noble goal was to declare the road arcing around the Thumb to be the Huron County Memorial Highway. This action would not only pay homage to local soldiers, sailors and marines, it would also have the added benefit of attracting tourists to the region. For the benefit of these recreational travelers, it was decided to also mark the historic spots along the 92-mile route.

Some of the points of interest to be highlighted were the summer home of President Garfield at Port Austin, the home of former governor and later United States Supreme Court Justice Frank Murphy, the Caseville campsite of

George Meade (subsequently Commander of the Union Army in the Civil War), the home of President William McKinley at Caseville, and the site of the former religious colony Ora et Labora near Bay Port.

By the time officials had finished making plans for the memorial highway, the Second World War was underway and there was, as a consequence, a scarcity of metal to use for making the desired road signs. Thus, in ironic fashion, global hostilities prevented Huron County from fulfilling its ambition to honor those from its jurisdiction who had served in battle.

Once the War was over and the surviving soldiers had returned home, people all across our state were eager to resume their normal lives. Unfortunately, as public focus shifted from combat to peace, the idea of a memorial shoreline highway in eastern Michigan gradually faded into obscurity. As a result, the contemplated road of remembrance was never established, depriving veterans of Huron County of a distinctive thumbprint.

Coordinates: I/13-14

HURON SHORE HIGHWAY

As early as 1858 the state began authorizing and supporting the construction of a road along the Lake Huron shore between Bay City and Mackinaw City. The product of this effort was of mixed quality, usually resulting in adequate stretches near settlements and little more than a crude trail in rural areas.

By 1913, the road connecting Saginaw Bay with the Straits of Mackinac was passable for automobiles over just two-thirds of its length. In an attempt to create a decent travel route along the entire distance, early in that year the Lake Huron Shore Good Roads Association was formed by representatives from the seven east-coast counties through which the highway passed.

This organization wanted to quickly improve the region's main thoroughfare to make long-distance movement easier for local citizens, attract car-driving summer tourists, and open up inaccessible parts of the district to prospective land buyers. The question was how to accomplish this goal with limited funds in the face of wide-spread needs.

The answer to this problem was found in Iowa, where earlier thousands of farmers had participated in the road-building equivalent of a barn raising and constructed 137 miles of highway in just one day. Hoping to duplicate this effort locally, it was decided to hold the first "good roads bee" in Michigan to finish the 250-mile water-edge route dubbed the Huron Shore Highway.

The entire enterprise was to be accomplished through volunteer labor, with over $25,000 in monetary contributions coming from public and private sources. In lieu of cash, some firms donated gravel, stone or other useful products, while the dominant railroad in the area offered reduced rates on transporting workers and supplies. Manufacturers of road-building implements lent a hand by offering prizes for those crews doing the best job and the most work.

Pledge sheets were circulated seeking support for the undertaking, and nearly 11,000 people enlisted to help the cause. Over 8,000 men agreed to provide one day of their life as laborers, 2,500 women signed up to make noon and evening meals for the workers, 3,000 teams of animals were pledged to pull wagons or graders, and hundreds of private vehicles were promised to carry urban residents from their homes to work sites in the country.

When the day of the great event arrived on 9 June 1913, the population of northeastern Michigan nearly turned out en masse to improve its most important artery. Some towns declared a holiday, many shops closed, and most business was suspended so people could participate in the pro bono project.

Workers reported at 6:30 a.m. wearing old clothes and carrying a shovel, pick, or other appropriate tool. From dawn to dusk they labored as their undertaking--having captured national attention--was monitored and docu-

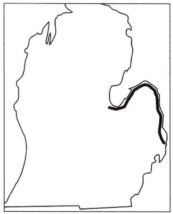

mented by a number of reporters, photographers, and even a movie crew.

By nightfall the entire course had at least been roughed out, though some finishing touches were necessary in spots to make the road fully useable. Unpaid crews continued to address these matters in following days, and by June 20 a "thru-route" had at last been constructed along the west coast of Lake Huron.

So successful was this venture that state government sought to duplicate it elsewhere around Michigan. Accordingly, for the next three years the governor issued proclamations declaring a specified date in June to be "Road Bee Day." The people in the northeastern Lower Peninsula participated in these annual events, but mainly did so to keep their famous shoreline route in good repair.

Ironically, the Huron Shore Highway was a victim of its own favorable publicity. Transportation promoters looked upon the route as a desirable component of a bigger picture, and by the Spring of 1917 it had officially become part of a route from Toledo to the Straits called the East Michigan Pike. Today, the EMP is ancient motoring history, but the old Huron Shore Highway lives on as the most northerly and picturesque part of modern US-23.

Coordinates: E-J/11-13

HURON SHORE PIKE

As early as 1844 the state legislature began passing laws for the building of road segments north from Port Huron and around the Thumb of Michigan over to the Saginaw River. These affairs were little more than dirt trails designed for local traffic, and few long-distance travelers ventured upon them.

After the turn of the last century people, mainly from the Detroit area, were increasingly attracted to the Lake Huron shore for recreational purposes. Private cottages, resorts, and summer colonies grew along the coast line, but the Thumb area was largely "avoided by tourists because of the uninviting shape in which the roads were generally found."

As early as 1911 there were calls for building an improved road skirting the lake shore from Port Huron to Bay City, but a serious effort to accomplish this goal did not begin until 1915. Incredible as it may seem, in that year more than 95% of the people between Port Austin and the St. Clair River signed a petition requesting the state to build a new road around the outer edge of the Thumb.

The hoped-for avenue would, it was said, eliminate the comparative isolation of many Thumb coastal communities and lead to the development of the region's many potential lakeside resting places. Vehicular access to the beautiful Huron shore line would also attract numerous sightseeing tourists, making the road one of the most scenic drives in the Midwest.

To help fulfill these ambitions, the Huron Shore Pike Association was formed on 17 May 1916. It faced a daunting task at the time of its creation, for of the 125 miles of coastal road between Port Huron and Bay City, only 27 miles were of an improved nature. All of the remainder had to be constructed or rebuilt.

To raise money and enthusiasm for the project, two months after its founding the Association made a publicity tour around the periphery of the Thumb. Reporters accompanying the expedition said that almost every farm en route "was decorated in honor of the occasion and crowds awaited along the roadside to give the boosters a greeting as they passed. In all the towns a rousing welcome was given those on the junket."

This promotional circuit of the Thumb's margin achieved its goal, for soon thereafter the Highway Department started surveying the route for the Huron Shore Pike and actual construction began on selected portions in 1917. Within a decade a good gravel road had been finished along most of the lake shore between Port Huron and the head of Saginaw Bay.

Once a highway had been built around the Thumb, the Huron Shore Pike Association went out of business and was replaced on 16 September 1929 by the Huron Shore Road Association. For while the Pike Association had succeeded in its goal of having a coastal route built, the Road Association was created for the purpose of having that motorway paved.

Ironically, it took nearly three times longer to get the Huron Shore Pike paved than it did to get it built, as the last stretch of hard surface was not completed until 1959. Since then the original dream of the region's good-roads buffs has come true, as each year thousands of vacationers and tourists travel M-25 giving thumbs up to the highway around Michigan's Thumb.

Coordinates: I-K/12-14

IRON BRIGADE
MEMORIAL HIGHWAY

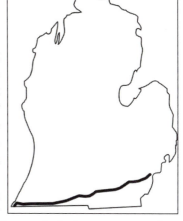

The 24th Michigan Infantry Regiment served in the Civil War. It was one of five regiments of soldiers from the Midwest that comprised the Iron Brigade.

This military unit got its nickname because, when in battle, its men stood their ground like they were made of iron. Perhaps on account of this bravery, the 24th Michigan Infantry lost more troops during the War than any other Union regiment.

The 24th Michigan was also known as "the Detroit and Wayne County Regiment," as 88% of its 1,030 men came from those two jurisdictions. The unit was mustered into federal service on 15 August 1862, and thereafter fought in nearly every major battle of the Civil War.

The most famous engagement for the 24th Michigan occurred at Gettysburg, where the Regiment helped slow the Confederate advance and allowed Federal forces to gain a position for victory. But this achievement was costly, for in just the first day of battle the unit lost 80% of its engaged force.

Subsequently reinforced, the 24th Michigan Infantry continued to fight until, near the War's end, it was withdrawn from the field and assigned to guard duty near Springfield, Illinois.

Because of its distinguished service record and high reputation, the 24th Michigan Infantry was given the privilege of being the military escort for Abraham Lincoln's funeral procession as it passed through his home town. Not long after this honor was discharged, the Regiment was mustered out of service at Detroit.

When the 24th Michigan Infantry had gone off to war, it traveled along present-day US-12. It would be fitting, thought some, if that road could somehow be used to commemorate this famous unit.

In 1994 the Michigan legislature gave its blessings to these sentiments in the form of House Concurrent Resolution 626. Consequently, US-12 from the Indiana border to Detroit was designated the Iron Brigade Memorial Highway.

Because the road honoring the Iron Brigade is so long, dedication ceremonies took place at two different times and places. The first occurred at New Buffalo on 9 October 1994, and the second at Detroit on 11 November 1995.

Michigan is not the only place where US-12 commemorates the Iron Brigade. Two other states--Wisconsin and Indiana--also contributed regiments to this unit. Since US-12 passes through their territories, the Hoosiers and Badgers have likewise named this route in the Iron Brigade's honor.

Coordinates: M-N/7-13

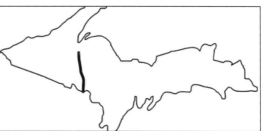

ISLE ROYALE TRAIL

As the largest island in Lake Superior, Michigan's Isle Royale is in the curious position of being much closer to the shores of Minnesota and Canada than it is to the nearest mainland portion of our state, the Keweenaw Peninsula. No matter from which jurisdiction one departs, however, the only way to reach the island is by seaplane or boat.

Covering 210 square miles of rugged terrain, the freshwater archipelago consists of one big island called Isle Royale that is about 45 miles long and nine miles across at its widest point. Surrounding the main island are over 200 adjacent islets that make the geographic feature both a hazard and an attraction for boaters.

When the French were led to the island by the Indians, the Europeans called it Isle Royale in honor of their King Louis XIV. With the passing of time, the island came into American hands in 1783 when Benjamin Franklin insisted during treaty negotiations with the British that it be included within the boundaries of the fledgling United States.

When Michigan became a state in 1837, Isle Royale was made part of her territory in partial compensation for yielding Toledo and an adjacent strip of land to Ohio. The Chippewa Indians surrendered their claim to the island under terms of a treaty in 1843.

Thereafter, the island was at various times exploited for its fish, timber, and copper resources. Despite this commercial impact and the occasional visit by tourists, Isle Royale remained pretty much a wilderness area into the early twentieth century. Thinking this condition worthy of preservation, in 1920 a writer for the Detroit News began promoting park status for the island.

A bill for this purpose was first introduced in Congress in 1922, and a long battle ensued over the merits of the idea. Finally, on 3 March 1931, a Public Law was passed incorporating the island into the national park system. Today, attracting only about 12,000 people per year, Isle Royale is the least visited national park in the contiguous United States.

After Isle Royale National Park was established, some people in the Upper Peninsula had grandiose (and false, it would turn out) impressions of the number of people who would want to visit the island. Many communities south of the Keweenaw Peninsula hoped to benefit from the great tourist traffic that was anticipated to pass enroute.

One such group of optimistic merchants belonged to the Crystal Falls Businessmen's Association. In January of 1932 these entrepreneurs organized themselves and others along US-141 to promote the road as the Isle Royale Trail. This highway, drawing travelers from such metropolitan centers as Chicago and Milwaukee, would be a shortcut to embarkation points to the island by saving up to 100 miles driving over competing routes.

Though interests promoting US-141 called that highway the Isle Royale Trail, they were never able to get official sanction for the title. Cities along competing US-41 and other routes objected to someone else having this popular name, and legislators in Michigan and Wisconsin were "besieged with letters and telegrams opposing such a designation" for any one of the several roads to the jumping-off points to the Park. In the end, one could say the Isle Royale Trail was the victim of a battle royale.

Coordinates: C-D/4

JACKSON COUNTY ROADSIDE MEMORIAL

Jackson County, like many other governmental bodies during and after World War II, felt moved to honor its sons and daughters who fought to preserve our liberties during that conflict. The only question was how best to express this gratitude?

By early 1945 a decision had been made to show appreciation to veterans by means of permanent memorial plantings. From the eastern edge of Jackson city limits east to the Washtenaw County line, one tree would be planted for each of the 2,108 county inhabitants serving in the armed forces.

The proposed landscaping was to be along both sides of route US-12 (now Michigan Avenue), with trees spaced 30 to 150 feet apart and

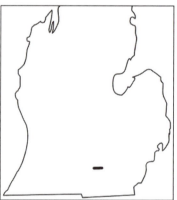

on a line 48 feet from the highway center for a distance of 12.6 miles.

To initiate this undertaking, a total of $5,000 was quickly raised from private sources for the purpose of buying suitable planting stock. About 400 pines, 500 elms, 600 maples, and 600 flowering crab trees were bought for creating the memorial highway.

Next--in a spirit of inter-governmental cooperation--the county road commission offered to truck in the trees from the nursery, the State Highway Department agreed to supervise their planting, and officials at Southern Michigan prison loaned the cause trusted inmates to provide the necessary labor.

Thanks to this generosity and good coordination, all of the planting was done by the end of May, 1945. Thereafter, time was spent working on an associated memorial park that included a tablet listing the names of 290 Jackson County residents who

were killed while serving in uniform.

By 16 June 1946, the project was finished and ready for dedication. On that day over 2,000 people showed up at the west end of the parkway to attend ceremonies commemorating the purpose of the effort and its completion.

Commissioner Charles M. Ziegler was on hand to accept the improvements on behalf of the citizens of Michigan. He pledged to "the people of Jackson County that the State Highway Department will meet its responsibility in seeing that this memorial is kept in proper care at all times."

In 1958, the Highway Department was forced to relocate the companion memorial park and honor roll, but some of the original trees and shrubs still remain in their set places along the route of Jackson County's Roadside Memorial.

Coordinates: M/11

JACOBETTI HIGHWAY

Most people would agree that anybody who spends forty years in the same job deserves some kind of recognition. Such was the case of Dominic Jacobetti, who served the people of the 109th District (mainly Marquette and Alger counties) as their State Representative for four decades.

First sent to the Michigan House in 1954, Jacobetti was elected to a record-setting 21 terms. He is Michigan's longest-serving legislator, and with term limits now in force he is guaranteed to remain so.

Born in Negaunee on 20 July 1920, Jacobetti grew up in that Lake Superior iron-mining town. In 1938 he graduated from St. Paul's Catholic High School, where he was captain of the basketball and football teams.

In 1940, Jacobetti went to work at the Athens Iron Mine in Negaunee. Exhibiting strong leadership qualities, his fellow miners eventually

elected him president of their United Steelworkers labor union, Local 4950.

After fifteen years as an iron ore miner and labor leader, Jacobetti decided to enter politics. Successful on his first try for public office, he took his seat in the Capitol at Lansing in January of 1955.

At that time, Michigan's transportation network was poorly developed by contemporary standards. There was no Mackinac Bridge across the Straits and no freeways to ease travel north. Consequently, with 400 miles separating him from his constituents, early in his law-making career Jacobetti was able to go home just once a month.

As land communications improved over the years, Jacobetti was able to more frequently visit his district. Eventually, things got to the point where he could return home on almost a weekly basis, a journey that had him spending many hours driving on route M-28.

Jacobetti's colleagues had these frequent trips in mind when they chose to honor his many accomplishments. Thinking of the numerous times he had commuted from Lansing to the Upper Peninsula and back, they passed House Resolution 506 of 1986 establishing the Jacobetti Highway along M-28 from route M-123 west to the far city limits of Negaunee.

According to Jacobetti's son,

there were no on-site ceremonies to mark the placement of roadside signs for this gesture nor was the stretch of road formally dedicated to its namesake after Jacobetti died on 28 November 1994. For the man from Negaunee did not want a fuss made over his achievements, preferring instead to direct attention to the problems of his constituents rather than personal glories of the past.

Coordinates: C/6-10

JAMES COUZENS HIGHWAY

As early as 1924, a movement began in southeastern Michigan to build a road from Detroit northwesterly through Owosso, Alma, Big Rapids and Baldwin to Ludington. The proposed cross-state route, designed to bisect the angle formed by Woodward and Grand River avenues, was appropriately called the Northwestern Highway.

This diagonal thoroughfare was built in 1929 as far north as 14 Mile Road, its terminus today. There, local opposition and reduced budgets due to the Depression brought an end to the construction project.

Other than widening to accommodate increased traffic, no significant modifications occurred to the Northwestern Highway until 9 November 1937. On that day, the Detroit City Council approved changing the name of the road within Wayne County to the James Couzens Highway.

The man being honored by this gesture was born in Chatham, Ontario, on 26 August 1872. At the age of 18 he came to Detroit to work for the Michigan Central Railroad, and he remained a resident of the town for the rest of his life.

In 1903, Couzens met Henry Ford just as the automobile inventor was starting the Ford Motor Company. Impressed with Couzens' abilities, Ford hired the man and over the next 13 years made him at various times corporate secretary, business manager, sales manager, general manager, treasurer, vice president, and director.

Couzens not only was a good worker for his employer, he was a good investor for his own interests. When he sold his share of Ford Motor Company stock to Henry in 1919, he received in return nearly $30,000,000.

Following his stint with Ford, Couzens went into government by serving as Commissioner of Detroit's Street Railways (1913-1915), Police Commissioner (1916-1918), Mayor (1919-1922), and United States Senator (1922-1936).

For this service, Couzens did not accept a penny. All of his salaries as a public official were donated to charity. Furthermore, it is estimated that he also gave away all of the money he received from Henry Ford, making him "the biggest public benefactor in the history of Michigan."

When James Couzens died on 22 October 1936, the citizens of Detroit expressed their gratitude for his philanthropy by naming one of their principal streets in his memory. This tribute grew in stature as the James Couzens Highway developed from a multi-lane commuter route into a major urban expressway.

The zenith of this community recognition occurred in 1964, when the official state road map briefly showed what was then I-696 between Wyoming Avenue and Eight Mile Road as the James Couzens Highway. But the Detroit Common Council changed the name of the trunk line to John C. Lodge Expressway, and Couzens High-way--now demoted to James Couzens Drive--became just a feeder route paralleling both sides of expressway M-10 in uptown Detroit.

Coordinates: Southeastern Michigan Enlargement D/7

JAMES G. O'HARA FREEWAY

Nick Ciaramitaro, Representative to the Michigan Legislature, is a patient and resourceful man. Were the case otherwise, there would probably not exist today a highway named after his former boss and mentor, James Grant O'Hara.

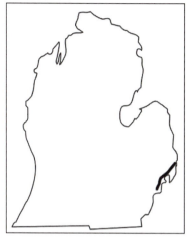

O'Hara, born in the District of Columbia on 8 November 1925, came to Detroit with his parents in 1939 and graduated from the University of Detroit High School in 1943. Immediately thereafter he joined the Army as an enlisted man, serving as a combat paratrooper in the Pacific Theater from 1943 to 1946.

After World War II, O'Hara earned bachelor and law degrees from the University of Michigan. He practiced law in Detroit and Macomb County until 1958, when he was elected Representative to Congress from the Twelfth District.

While serving his constituents in the Nation's Capitol, O'Hara became one of the architects of the Great Society programs. He also developed a reputation for supporting laws that protected the environment, civil rights, labor, consumer rights, and public education.

After eighteen years in Congress, O'Hara left Capitol Hill in 1977 to practice law in Alexandria, Virginia. He died at this home there on 13 March 1989, a victim of cancer.

As a former aide to James O'Hara, Nick Ciaramitaro knew better than most how his political role model had distinguished himself as a public servant. Ciaramitaro wanted some tangible way of recognizing this man's successful record personally and on behalf of the electorate in all or parts of St. Clair, Oakland, Macomb and Sanilac counties.

Since O'Hara's Michigan residence was in Utica, and since highway M-59 runs through Utica, in 1989 Ciaramitaro introduced a bill to name that trunk line in O'Hara's memory. A majority of legislators could not be found to support the measure, however, so it never became law.

Later, Ciaramitaro heard that O'Hara had helped to get federal funding for route I-94 when the east-Michigan portion was under construction. Since this road ran through part of O'Hara's legislative district, Ciaramitaro unsuccessfully introduced a bill in 1991 to get I-94 named in honor of the deceased congressman.

Realizing he needed to take a different approach to the problem, Ciaramitaro waited six years before acting again to pay tribute to his old friend. In 1997 he cleverly inserted a section into the Transportation Department budget which named "the portion of I-94 lying within both Macomb and St. Clair Counties as the James G. O'Hara freeway...."

Because Public Act 117 of 1997 allowed Ciaramitaro to honor a fellow lawmaker and associate, he did not want this gesture to cost the taxpayers a penny. Consequently, he wrote into the enabling statute a provision that required all O'Hara road signs and designators to be purchased with private funds.

Ciaramitaro and his supporters raised the nearly $10,000 required to buy and erect the markers denoting the O'Hara Freeway. The Representative, along with invited guests, dedicated the memorial highway on 16 October 1998 at the Port Huron Welcome Center.

Coordinates: K-L/14

JAMES M. PELTON FIREFIGHTERS MEMORIAL HIGHWAY

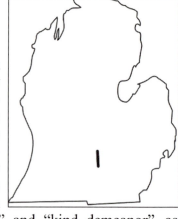

While on his way to a fire department meeting on 10 August 2001, James Pelton's car was hit by a vehicle that had run through a stop sign near Mason, Michigan. The impact of the collision cost Pelton his life and took from the general community a man variously described as being a "diligent worker," "tireless modernizer," and "innovative leader."

Born on 5 May 1943 in St. Johns, Clinton County, James Monroe Pelton later moved about thirty miles south to Mason where for 39 years he worked as a barber and volunteer fireman. He also earned certification as a fire inspector plus served as a member of the Local Emergency Planning Committee and was vice-chairperson of the Ingham County 911 Advisory Committee.

Pelton initiated construction of

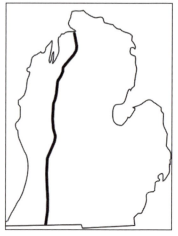

a new fire station and had recently been appointed Mason's first full-time fire chief when the auto accident resulted in his untimely demise. Wishing to honor this man with a "positive attitude" and "kind demeanor"--as well as commemorate his service to the community--the Legislature passed Public Act 195 of 2003 making all of trunk line US-127 in Ingham County the "James M. Pelton Firefighters Memorial Highway." This gesture was solemnized by dedicatory ceremonies at the Mason Fire Station on 14 May 2004.

Coordinates: L-M/11

JAMES WHITCOMB RILEY MEMORIAL HIGHWAY

In the summer of 1925, certain interests began to promote a road to connect Miami, Florida, with Petoskey, Michigan. The purpose was to establish a national highway by which people would travel to northern resorts in summer and southern resorts in winter.

The idea for the motorway originated in the public schools of Anderson, Indiana. The children there were ostensibly asked what kind of permanent memorial should be created for the homestate poet James Whitcomb Riley, and they suggested a highway in his honor connecting the nation's summer and winter playgrounds.

The Michigan portion of the trail, which essentially followed contemporary US-131, was marked off in August and September of 1926. To guide travelers, telephone poles all along the route were painted with white bands on which in orange letters were written the words "Riley Hi-way."

This activity, and that of promoting public use of the road, was funded by the sales of mem-

berships in the James Whitcomb Riley Association. Because of the potential benefit this highway could bring to Michigan, many people and groups in our state paid the $25 dues to join this organization.

The return on these investments was short-lived, for the Riley Highway and its sponsor were soon under attack. The cause of the problem was two-fold. First, the sponsors of the Riley Highway had selected a route that was already known as the Mackinaw Trail. Few Michiganers were willing to replace a meaningful and familiar road name for a new and foreign one.

Second, the Riley Highway promoters had failed to secure official acceptance of their endeavors. Public Act 410 of 1919 said it was illegal for any "association to delineate or mark any other routes or trails through the State of Michigan...unless the same shall be approved in writing by the State Highway Commissioner." Because this stipulation had not been followed, many in government were opposed to the project.

By December of 1926, this combination of factors had put an end to the Riley Highway in Michigan. With Michigan out of the equation, the entire enterprise unraveled and the Riley Association collapsed.

The man over whom all this fuss was being made had died about a decade earlier on 22 July 1916. A highly famous writer and lecturer, his name was to American poetry as Mark Twain's was to American prose.

Born in Greenfield, Indiana, on 7 October 1849, Riley grew up in the Hoosier state and came to know well the dialect and customs of its country folks. Working as a journalist, he began to write nostalgic poems for the common people about Indiana scenes and characters.

His verse quickly won him a national reputation, with people referring to him as the Burns of America. Some of his best known works were The Old Swimmin' Hole, When the Frost is on the Punkin, An Old Sweetheart of Mine, and Little Orphant Annie.

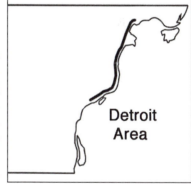

A measure of the man's ability can be gauged from the fact that few people in history have devoted their lives to poetry and made a fortune from it. Riley made lots of money from his work and his verses also earned him, for a brief time, a memorial highway in Michigan.

Coordinates: F-N/9-10

JEFFERSON AVENUE

American history is full of personalities who were outstanding figures in their time. One such individual was a leading architect of his era, his book collection formed the nucleus of the Library of Congress, he created our decimal system of coinage, founded the University of Virginia at Charlottesville, was fluent in Latin, Greek, French, Spanish and Italian, and has his likeness on the face of Mount Rushmore.

If more clues are needed to identify this man, he was the principal author of the Declaration of Independence, founder of what became the Democratic Party, first president to be inaugurated in Washington DC, buyer of Louisiana Territory and instigator of the Lewis and Clark Expedition that explored the purchase, and author of the "Manual of Parliamentary Practice" that is still used as the basis for procedure in the United States Senate.

This remarkable character was Thomas Jefferson, born at Shadwell, Virginia on 13 April 1743, the son of a wealthy landowner. After finishing college in 1762, he went on to study law and was subsequently admitted to the bar in 1767. He remained a practicing attorney until 1774, when the onset of the Revolutionary War closed the courts.

Aside from his private activities in the legal profession, Jefferson had an astounding career as a public servant. In seemingly quick succession he became a member of Virginia's representative body (1768-1778), governor of Virginia (1779-1781), member of Congress (1783-1784), minister to France (1785-1789), Secretary of State (1789-1793), Vice President (1797-1801), and third President of the United States (1801-1809).

Following his tenure as this nation's chief executive, Jefferson retired to his farm at Monticello where he conducted numerous experiments in scientific farming. He died on 4 July 1826, the fiftieth anniversary of the adoption of the Declaration of Independence.

It was while Jefferson was President that Michigan became a Territory in 1805. To help administer this new government, Jefferson appointed to office his good friend Augustus Woodward. When Woodward reached Detroit he found nothing but ruins, for the settlement had been completely destroyed by fire a few weeks earlier.

It was essential that the community be quickly rebuilt, and to help achieve this goal Woodward agreed to lay out an improved plan for the town. As he mapped on paper his vision of lots and streets, Woodward gave the name of his mentor--Jefferson--to the principal thoroughfare that followed the river from the city center north. Later, as Detroit grew, Jefferson Avenue grew with it, eventually reaching all the way to Mount Clemens and beyond.

Because it was a main route of travel along the Detroit River and Lake Saint Clair, in 1939 the State Highway Department declared most of Jefferson Avenue to be M-29 between Mount Clemens and the southern boundary of Macomb County. This trunk line status remained in effect until 1970, when the road named for Jefferson reverted back to being just a major artery for carrying local traffic. Today, the street remains a common thoroughfare for an uncommon man.

Coordinates: Southeastern Michigan Enlargement A-E/9-11

JEFFRIES EXPRESSWAY

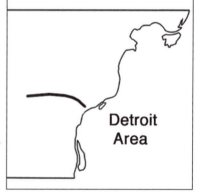

Detroit Area

As anyone who has driven in Detroit knows, all of the freeways are identified by number and name. The highway number is assigned by the federal government or the Michigan Department of Transportation. The highway name is bestowed by the Detroit Common Council or the state legislature.

In keeping with this practice, the mayor of Detroit reminded the Common Council that one of his predecessors--Edward J. Jeffries, Jr.--had created a "well-conceived plan for the construction of a network of expressways within the city of Detroit during the postwar years. The Common Council unanimously endorsed his proposal which marked the first step toward the building of Detroit's modern highways."

Because of Jeffries' efforts to improve transportation, continued the mayor, it seems "that in all equity one of Detroit's expressways should be named in his honor. Plans are now being prepared and construction will [soon] start on the Detroit section of the" I-96 trunk line. "Because this highway will span a large area of the city to which he contributed so much, we respectfully urge your Honorable Body to adopt a resolution to name this highway the Jeffries Expressway."

The Detroit Common Council quickly considered this proposal, and then on 14 April 1959 unanimously re-

solved "that the next expressway constructed in the City of Detroit be designated as the Jeffries Expressway in honor of the late Mayor Edward J. Jeffries, Jr."

Jeffries, born in Detroit 3 April 1900, graduated from Northwestern High School and then went on to the University of Michigan where he earned a law degree in 1923. Returning to Detroit, he began practicing law and engaging in politics.

Beginning in 1932, Jeffries was elected four consecutive times as city councilman and then four consecutive times as Mayor. While taking a break in Florida from his official duties, he died of a heart attack on 2 April 1950.

Jeffries was a highly popular politician. He viewed himself as the personal bodyguard of the downtrodden and the laboring person. In tribute to the man, the citizens of Detroit allowed his body to lie in state at City Hall with an honor guard of police and firemen.

The City Hall itself was draped in black, and all flags on municipal buildings were struck to half staff for 30

days. And as Jeffries' funeral service began at 2:30 p.m., all street cars and busses in the city stopped for one minute. No wonder they named a road in memory of the man.

The initial section of the Jeffries Expressway first carried traffic in July of 1971. The final leg of this route had its ribbon cut on 21 November 1977. With this act, the only unfinished section of I-96 in Michigan was completed and the last Detroit freeway was opened.

Coordinates: Southeastern Michigan Enlargement E/5-8

JOHN C. LODGE EXPRESSWAY

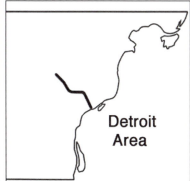

Detroit Area

The first superhighway in Detroit to intentionally recognize an individual was the John C. Lodge Expressway (also known as state trunk line M-10). This decision was announced on 26 January 1944 when "the Wayne County Road Commission submitted the plans for this project to the city and suggested it be named in honor of John Christian Lodge."

Lodge, who at the time was Council president, "warmly thanked [the] members of the Road Commission for naming the proposed highway" as a tribute to him. "Not only was it a fine thing to do," he quipped, "but gosh, I would be pretty happy if I thought I deserved half the honor."

What had Lodge done to get this recognition? During his career he had been a member of the commission that drafted the 1908 state constitution, a representative to the state legislature (1908-1909), Detroit alderman (1910-1918), Detroit councilman (1919-1927), mayor of Detroit (1928-1929), councilman again (1932-1947), and member of the county board of supervisors (1948-1950). He had, in fact, held elective office longer than anyone in city or state history.

Lodge's campaign style was quite unusual, if not unique. He refused to run for office in the conventional way, never making statements or speeches in his own behalf, disdaining all advertising and the usual trappings of a political contest, believing his record spoke for itself. "If the people want me, they'll elect me," he reasoned.

This civic and political leader was born in Detroit on 12 August 1862 and, after being educated in the local public schools, he graduated from the Michigan Military Academy at Orchard Lake in 1881.

In 1887 Lodge became a reporter for the Detroit Free Press, later serving as city editor from 1893 to 1896. His next job, from 1897 to 1905, was as chief clerk for the Wayne County auditors. His last position before entering politics was as secretary to the mayor from 1906 to 1907.

During his life of community service, Lodge became Detroit's most respected statesman and public conscience. So much did the people love him that, after his death on 6 February 1950, his body was allowed to lie in state at City Hall with a police and fireman honor guard. Memorial services were held for him in all 330 public schools, and at the hour of his funeral everyone in city government observed a minute of silence in his memory.

Construction started on the Lodge Expressway on 22 October 1947. When it came time to dedicate the opening of the road in January of 1953, council members found to their embarrassment that they had never officially designated the name. An ordinance was quickly drafted rectifying the oversight, and on January 20 the measure was unanimously passed by the governing authorities. John C. Lodge--the man who refused to own a car or drive one--at last had a freeway legitimately bearing his name.

Coordinates: Southeastern Michigan Enlargement D-E/7-8

JOSEPH H. MEAGHER MEMORIAL HIGHWAY

Few people reading this column will have heard of Joe Meagher. In part, that's due to his style. Associates said he had a "talent for being out of the limelight, but responsible for the action."

A former state legislator summed up Meagher's philosophy with the phrase, "It's easier to get things done if you don't care who gets the credit." Joe was the man who got things done.

Joseph Meagher's life began on 26 November 1925 in Bessemer, Michigan. After graduating from the local high school, he entered the U.S. military, serving with the Navy Amphibian Forces in the South Pacific.

After World War II, Meagher attended Michigan Technological University, where he received a bachelor's degree in civil engineering. These skills were soon put to work for the Ontonagon County Road Commission, which hired him on 1 April 1952.

For 36 years Meagher served as

an award-winning engineer/manager for the county road commission. In addition, during this time he was an important member of numerous other city, county, regional and state organizations.

Meagher left the employ of local government on 1 July 1988. Unfortunately, his retirement was brief, for he died of cancer on 17 February 1991.

Seeking to honor their lost colleague, on 12 June 1991 members of the Ontonagon County Road Commission petitioned the legislature to name part of a state highway in Meagher's honor. The response came about a year later as Senate Concurrent Resolution 286.

This document declared that "state trunk line M-38 from the Ontonagon village limits easterly to the Houghton County line" shall be named the Joseph H. Meagher Memorial Highway. In the presence of dignitaries and family members, the road was so dedicated on 29 May 1992.

Coordinates: B/3

JOY ROAD

On the north side of Mount Clemens there is a short east/west avenue named Joy Road. In May of 1941, officials in Lansing declared that 2.4 miles of this street would be designated trunk line M-160, apparently as a partial access route to Selfridge Field. Just four months later this designation was revoked, making this stretch of pavement perhaps the shortest-lived state highway in Michigan history.

The road is named after Henry Bourne Joy, a man born in Detroit on 23 November 1864. Schooled at the Michigan Military Academy, the Phillips Academy (Andover MA), and Yale University, Joy returned to Michigan in 1886 and began to make his presence felt in the world of commerce.

After starting out with the Peninsular [Railroad] Car Company, Joy became director of the Fort Street Union Depot Company (1889-1896) and

Detroit Area

then president of the Detroit Union Depot Company (1896-1907). Meanwhile, he organized and became director of the Peninsular Sugar Refining Company at Caro MI (1899-1906) and its successor, the Michigan Sugar Company (1906-1910).

One of Joy's biggest accomplishments was

building the Packard Motor Car Company plant in Detroit in 1903 and then becoming in quick succession its general manager (1903-1909), president (1909-1916), and chairman (1917). During this time he also served as director of the Federal Reserve Bank of Chicago (1913-1914) and helped found the modern-day Detroit Athletic Club (1915).

Another remarkable feat of Henry Joy was his mixing of business and commitment to his country. Twice he took time out from running his various enterprises to help our nation in time of war. In 1898 he served as chief boatswain's mate in the Spanish-American War and during 1917-1918 he was an officer in the U.S. Signal Corps, entering as a Captain and leaving as a Lieutenant Colonel.

The final highlight on Joy's resume was his organization of the Lincoln Highway Association in Detroit during June of 1913. This group had as its goal the building of a concrete road from New York to San Francisco as a memorial to our six-

teenth President. As director of the effort from 1913 to 1926 (except when on military duty), Joy and his associates succeeded in creating a great coast-to-coast national highway that became America's first main arterial interstate route.

While Joy lived mainly in Grosse Pointe Farms, he had a 100-acre recreational estate or "ranch" just north of Selfridge Field on the shores of Lake St. Clair. In fact, the land upon which the Selfridge base is built was originally known as Joy Aviation Field until the namesake Michigan capitalist sold most of the property to the United States government 1921.

Given his widespread entrepreneurial fame and connection to the area, it is not surprising that Macomb County would name a road in Joy's honor. This gesture of tribute occurred in 1917 when the main access highway was built from Mount Clemens east to the air base, remnants of a route which still exist to this day.

Coordinates: Southeastern Michigan Enlargement B/11

KALAMAZOO COUNTY MEMORIAL HIGHWAY

As the end of World War II became discernible in the spring of 1945, people on the home front began thinking of ways to honor those who had served on active duty. In Kalamazoo County there was strong sentiment for some kind of living memorial, rather than the statuary or buildings that were so often used as tributes for the veterans of World War I.

In keeping with these views, fifteen garden clubs in the greater Kalamazoo area jointly proposed that route US-12 between Kalamazoo and Oshtemo be made into a memorial highway. They suggested that the four-mile stretch of road be beautified with trees and flowering shrubs in recognition of the county's soldiers.

This concept was given supremacy over any competing ideas when it was endorsed by State Highway Commission Charles M. Ziegler. He even assigned his agency's landscape architect to design the parkway and supervise the planting of

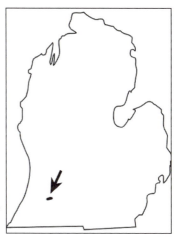

appropriate flora.

In negotiations between the two parties, Ziegler committed the Highway Department to acquiring and planting the vegetation, and even assuming some of the subsequent maintenance expenses. In return, the garden clubs had to reimburse the agency for the costs of its labor.

To raise the necessary money, the collective garden clubs acquired funds through solicitations and by holding teas, flower exhibitions, and fashion shows. Finally, two years after they started, the sponsors managed to earn the $5,000 needed for the project.

Several hundred trees and shrubs were planted with these dollars, turning the western approaches of Kalamazoo into a tranquil land-scaped drive "symbolical of the peace which all people desire." The completed enterprise was dedicated on 29 June 1947, at which time the memorial was formally accepted by the Highway Department.

In the ensuing half-century the Kalamazoo to Oshtemo road has been widened and largely developed by commercial interests, leaving few if any of the original plantings in place. But although time has changed or removed the memorial trees and shrubs, the accomplishments they were meant to honor remain everlasting.

Coordinates: M/9

KALAMAZOO-DEERING TRAIL

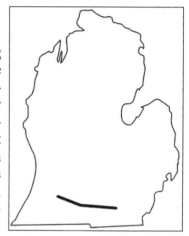

In April of 1921, the Adrian Daily Telegram editorialized in favor of naming rather than numbering roads. "What a joy it would be," opined the newspaper, "if we were to take from our state trunk lines their dreary, uninviting, thumb index numbers copied from the files of the state highway department and affix instead the names of our war units, our heroes, our governors, and our statesmen."

The editor went on to explain that "the highway department, facing the necessity of listing and cataloguing its projects, has given numbers to the various improved roads. But [road labels like route or] Trunk line 27 means nothing to the layman and they never will if he can help it. No one wants to remember them or use them in his conversation."

Perhaps following the sentiments in this column, less than one month later representatives from local chambers of commerce met to form the Kalamazoo-Deering Trail. This motorway was to follow the course of an old Indian track that ran east to west across the south-central part of the Lower Peninsula.

This group of promoters had heard that present-day US-223 was about to be built from Toledo to Adrian. Wishing to entice drivers using the new road to venture further into Michigan, the businessmen decided to create a named highway for travelers to follow westward from Lenawee County.

The course taken by the Kalamazoo-Deering Trail--while perhaps important to the Native Americans--was not nearly so significant to their European successors and thus much of the footpath was never incorporated into the state trunk line system. Starting at Adrian, the route approximately followed contemporary US-223 to its northern end, US-12 west to Moscow, then secondary roads through Burlington, Athens and Vicksburg to Kalamazoo.

Since there were alternative routes between Adrian and Kalamazoo vying for drivers, the backers of the Kalamazoo-Deering Trail decided they would gain a competitive edge through the "establishment of camp sites at many of the pretty places along the trail. Shelters could be erected in many spots near the towns which are ideal for camps. Tables could be arranged near running streams and everything could be provided for the convenience of the traveler. This would be a further inducement for them to follow the route."

But the presence of all these amenities could not save the Kalamazoo-Deering Trail from the fact that it was poorly positioned for the needs of automobilists. Primarily located out of mainstream travel, the road had practically no chance of success. Evidence that this was so can be drawn from the fact that probably no one reading this vignette has ever heard of the highway until now. If the phrase "Kalamazoo-Deering Trail" is spoken today, it is in reference to its use by Michigan Indians and not by motor vehicles.

Coordinates: M-N/9-12

KEITH DEACON
MEMORIAL HIGHWAY

Detroit Area

Donald Keith Deacon was born on 19 January 1927 near Kingsville, Ontario, and raised in that community. Fortunately for southeastern Michigan, in 1956 he left Canada and came to Detroit to work for the Manufacturers National Bank. He spent the remainder of his career with this institution, retiring in 1990 as second vice president.

Meanwhile, Deacon led a second life as a government official. Initially, he served on the charter commission for the city of Farmington Hills (1973). Then, in rapid succession he was a member of the city's council (1973-1979), mayor pro-tem (1975-1976, 1979), mayor (1976-1977), member of the local economic development corporation (1979-1996), election precinct worker (1990-1996), and member of the building authority (1993-1996).

This one-man municipal superman was clearly concerned about public service in general and, as a civic leader, improving the life of his fellow citizens. But he took particular interest in the roads of his jurisdiction, especially seeking solutions to the vehicle congestion that troubled his community.

At the top of his priority list was improving conditions at the highway M-5/Grand River Avenue interchange. This confluence of routes was so badly tied up with traffic that locals took to calling it the "dysfunction junction." The lost time and stalled movement caused by this problem was adversely affecting the economic development of the Farmington Hills area, and Deacon resolved to correct the problem.

He first sought money from conventional transportation sources to deal with the matter. When this failed, he helped get over a million dollars in federal demonstration grants to initiate remedial action. These funds, coupled with other sources of revenue, finally managed to underwrite construction that untangled the gridlock affecting part of highway M-5.

When Deacon died on 12 February 1996, people remembered his struggles to improve driving conditions in and around Farmington Hills. It would be a fitting tribute to this man, they reasoned, if the road he helped to free from gridlock was named in his honor. The city council passed a resolution in support of this idea, and local lawmakers introduced a bill in Lansing to give official status to these sentiments.

After due deliberation, the Michigan legislature passed Public Act 12 of 1999 designating "the part of highway M-5 located in the area lying between the interchange of highways I-96, I-696 and I-275 and 8 Mile Road in the city of Farmington Hills and the city of Farmington as the 'Keith Deacon Memorial Highway'." With appropriate ceremony, this deserving gesture of recognition was dedicated on 9 June 1999 at the site of the recently improved free-flowing trunk line artery.

Coordinates: Southeastern Michigan Enlargement C/5

KEVIN SHERWOOD
MEMORIAL HIGHWAY

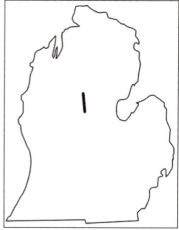

The subject who inspired this road of remembrance was born in Midland, Michigan, on 3 May 1966 and as an adult he became a career officer with the Clare County Sheriff's Department. On 9 October 2003--after serving nine years as a policeman--Sherwood was fatally injured while on patrol near the Hatton Road overpass when his car was hit head-on by a drunk driver going the wrong way on US-127. As the first Clare County deputy ever killed in the line of duty, it was proposed to honor Sherwood by naming a stretch

of the expressway between Clare and Harrison in his memory. This wish was accommodated by the Legislature which, in 2004, passed Public Act 147 declaring that "the portion of highway US-127 in Clare County shall be known as the 'Kevin Sherwood Memorial Highway'," This tribute had not yet been dedicated at the time this book went to press.

Coordinates: I/10

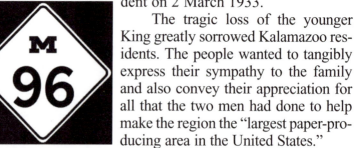

KING HIGHWAY

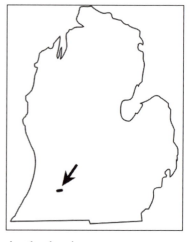

Heading east out of Kalamazoo on M-96 is King Highway. Does this name signify an honor to royalty or a tribute to the road's grand scope? In this case the facts are not so romantic. The name is simply a town's way of thanking two men for their betterment of the community.

The story begins with John Francis King, who was born in Allegheny County, Pennsylvania, in 1859. As an adult, he worked in various paper mills around the country where he developed an expertise in the craft.

In 1885 his path led to Kalamazoo, where he was employed by the Kalamazoo Paper Company. In service to this firm, his skills and assets grew to the point that by 1902 he was able to organize a new corporation called the King Paper Company.

John King managed this plant until 1915, when he left to create another addition to Kalamazoo's industrial complex, the Rex Paper Company. Through the development of these businesses--and through his many innovations in papermaking machinery and methods--he became one of the best known professionals in his field.

When John King died on 13 March 1922, he was replaced at the Rex Paper Company by his son, Merrill. Born in Otsego, Michigan, on 21 May 1890, Merrill Bryant King had been groomed to succeed his father in the business.

Merrill had been vice-president of the Rex Paper Company since its inception, so when circumstances required him to assume the director's role he comfortably handled the responsibilities. He remained president and general manager of the firm until his untimely death in a plane accident on 2 March 1933.

The tragic loss of the younger King greatly sorrowed Kalamazoo residents. The people wanted to tangibly express their sympathy to the family and also convey their appreciation for all that the two men had done to help make the region the "largest paper-producing area in the United States."

A way to accomplish both goals was found on 20 May 1935. On that day, the Kalamazoo City Council unanimously adopted a resolution naming part of what was then US-12 within the eastern municipal limits King Highway in honor of John and Merrill.

In part because of these two men, more paper was made in Kalamazoo than any other city in the world. Fully one-half of the town's labor force was employed in paper and allied industries. It was appropriate, therefore, that in gratitude the city should declare one of its major trunk lines fit for a King.

Coordinates: Kalamazoo Inset

KING'S INTERNATIONAL HIGHWAY

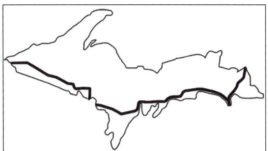

Why, readers might logically ask, would Michigan (or any state in the Union) have a highway in tribute to a King? After all, this country fought the Revolutionary War in an effort to be free of monarchs. While the answer lies in geography, not history, it is necessary to go back in time for an explanation.

By 1920, the United States had seven Atlantic-to-Pacific roads. The Canadians had none. To partially redress this imbalance, our friends north of the border decided to construct a highway from Halifax to Vancouver (later, St. John's became the eastern terminus). When finished, it would be the longest national road in the world.

In 1920, the path of the newly-conceived transcontinental trail was laid out along the southern border of Canada. Because there was no road north of Lake Superior or any prospect of building one in the near future, part of this ocean-to-ocean trunk line had to be routed through the Upper Peninsula of Michigan.

Those Canadians who wanted to travel coast-to-coast wholly within their country had to put their vehicles on boats or railroad cars at Sault Ste. Marie, Ontario, and ship them to present-day Thunder Bay. Anyone wishing to drive the distance was forced to take a diversionary trip into Michigan.

So it came to pass that the King's International Highway appears on early motoring maps of our state.

Though the course of this road varied over time with the development of Michigan's transportation network, in essence it followed contemporary US-2.

For nearly forty years the Upper Peninsula hosted travelers on the King's International Highway. Then, in an effort to close what had become known as "The Gap," the Canadian government began a concerted effort to build a road through the wild terrain north of Lake Superior.

After the surveyors had marked the best route, building crews began construction along the 165-mile missing link. In many cases, because of the remote nature of the region, men and their supplies had to be brought to the work sites by boat or airplane.

The laborers toiled year round, blasting through 40 miles of rock, bridging 25 rivers, and surmounting elevations of up to 1,600 feet. Finally, four years after commencing the project, the Highway was finished and opened to traffic on 17 September 1960.

By then, the enterprise had taken on a new name. No longer was it called the King's International Highway. A more descriptive and familiar title had taken its place. The road signs between Halifax and Vancouver said "Trans-Canada Highway", and Michigan lost the only foreign memorial highway it ever had.

Coordinates: C-D/1-11

KOREAN WAR VETERANS
MEMORIAL HIGHWAY

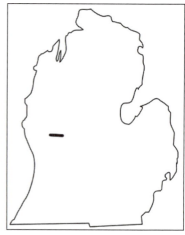

Japan gained control of Korea in 1895 and made it a part of "the land of the rising sun" in 1910. As the defeat of Japan became more certain during the course of World War II, the Allies decided that at the conclusion of hostilities Korea would be made a free and independent country.

When the second great world conflict finally ended in 1945, it was agreed that the Soviet Union would accept the surrender of Japanese troops north of the 38th parallel in Korea and that the United States would accept the capitulation of soldiers south of that line. Though this horizontal plane of latitude was supposed to be a temporary military demarcation boundary, the Soviets soon made it into a permanent political border.

Not long after disarming the Japanese forces within its assigned zone of authority, the U.S.S.R. closed off its sector, established a puppet communist government, and began building a large North Korean army. Once this military force had been fully formed and trained, it launched a surprise invasion of South Korea on 25 June 1950.

The recently-formed United Nations, reacting to this aggression, passed a resolution encouraging its members to "furnish such assistance to the Republic of Korea as may be necessary to repel the armed attack." In response, sixteen countries sent troops to stem the aggression and 41 governments sent military equipment and other supplies. This multinational force, representing the United Nation's first military action, was led by U.S. general Douglas McArthur.

At first this "police action" went well for the UN contingent as the North Korean aggressors were fairly quickly thrown back. However, when the People's Republic of China entered the war on North Korea's side in November of 1950, the level of combat greatly increased. The two opposing forces remained essentially stalemated until 27 July 1953, when an armistice was signed making the battle lines the boundary line between North and South Korea.

The Korean War not only witnessed the first combat use of helicopters and the first battles between jet aircraft, it also saw an appalling sacrifice of human life. The Communist side is believed to have had 1,600,000 troops killed, wounded, or missing while in South Korea alone about a million civilians lost their lives. For the United States, approximately 33,600 soldiers were killed in action, about 103,000 were wounded, and over 10,000 were made prisoners of war during 37 months of fighting.

A half-century after the onset of the Korean War, the state legislature looked for some way to honor the approximately 200,000 Michigan servicemen and women who participated in that conflict and the 1,456 citizens of our state who lost their lives during the period of hostilities. They chose to do this by passing House Bill 5996 of 2000, which designated a portion of M-59 in Livingston County as the "Korean War 50th Anniversary Memorial Highway." However, this well-intentioned gesture was vetoed by the Governor on 27 December 2000 because trunk line M-59 had already been named by a previous legislature in honor of Vietnam veterans.

Not to be deterred, some former Korean War soldiers tried again to get a state trunk line named in recognition of the those Americans who served in that Southeast Asian combat. This time picking a road that had not been preempted by some other tribute, their effort was rewarded by the passage of Public Act 563 of 2002 which declared "that portion of highway M-82 beginning at the city of Newaygo in Newaygo County and extending east to Howard City in Montcalm County shall be named the "Korean War Veterans Memorial Highway."

There is one other Korean War Veterans Memorial Highway in

Michigan that merits mention here for the sake of thoroughness, even though it is not on a state or federal trunk line. On 10 January 2000, the Troy City Council passed a resolution making part of Big Beaver Road a motorway of commendation to those men and women who served in Korea during the early 1950s. Though street signs were subsequently erected to commemoriate this honor, there were no dedication ceremonies to mark the occasion.

Coordinates: J/8-9

LACROIX ROAD

For decades, the western bank of the St. Clair River south of Algonac has been a recreational paradise. All along the Michigan side of the South Channel there are marvelous private homes, summer cottages, and resorts catering to the desires of those who wish to get away from it all and relax in a beautiful environment. Much of the credit for developing this extensive vacation retreat goes to an early settler in the Harsen's Island area, William A. Lacroix (pronounced LaCroy).

Lacroix was born nearby in Cottrellville on 25 November, 1846. As a young adult, he operated a successful lumber business just upstream in Marysville, a contemporary suburb of Port Huron. To assist in this trade, Lacroix owned several vessels for hauling cut timber, craft that he was actually qualified to operate as a licensed ship's captain.

Eventually, Lacroix tired of this profession and became a general contractor. In this capacity he helped to construct part of the ship canal that the U.S. government authorized as an aid to navigation through the St. Clair River delta. When this project was finished, he continued to work in extreme southeastern St. Clair County installing pilings and digging channels along with building roads, docks, and erecting various private structures and public facilities.

By the early 1880s, Lacroix had settled along the lower reaches of the St. Clair River opposite the Indian Reserve in Lambton County, Ontario. In 1888 he subdivided part of his property there, creating at that time a commercial site known as Sans Souci (French meaning "without care" on account of its pleasant surroundings).

This small trading center acquired special status on April 24, 1900, when it became the first and only post office on all of Harsen's Island.

To serve this young and growing community, Lacroix built a store there in 1898 with his residence located on the second level above. This shop sold a variety of goods in addition to serving meals throughout most of the day. So successful was this endeavor that by 1905 Lacroix was able to afford a luxurious new three-story home complete with marble counter tops, indoor plumbing, plus hot and cold running water. The large former one-family dwelling is still standing a hundred years later, known now as the Ship 'n' Shore Inn.

When William Lacroix died on 1 May 1922, the Detroit News said that he had "done more than any other man to make Harsen's Island what it is today." The memory of this active man is preserved in contemporary times by Lacroix Road, a route that he laid out in 1888 when he first platted his property at Sans Souci. In January of 1931, the State Highway Department gave the route official status as trunk line M-154, a designation it still carries in the twenty-first century. It is unfortunate, but no sign of intentional disrespect, that most local residents identify the pavement by these three digits rather than by the name of the pioneering person who first created the road.

Coordinates: L/14

LAKE MICHIGAN DRIVE

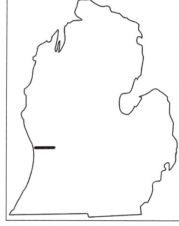

Lake Michigan Drive. The very words conjure up an image of a road wending its way through tumbled dunes adorned with verdant foliage. The mind's eye can even see beyond the undulating foreground the distant shimmering waters and beckoning beaches of our third largest Great Lake.

With mention of the highway one can almost smell the invigorating scent of lake air, feel the refreshing on-shore breeze cool a heated face, and hear the calls of seagulls who seem to use the coastal atmosphere as their playground. Rounding out the picture summoned forth by this name are sunset clouds of gold pierced by many-hued shafts of light that slowly sink beyond the gentle waves at the end of a summer day.

Unfortunately, these images would be inappropriate because Lake Michigan Drive does not go along the flanks of its namesake as one would logically surmise from its title. Instead, the highway was christened because it was the route that many people in the Grand Rapids area used if they wanted to drive TO Lake Michigan.

The existence of this road goes back many years when it served to accommodate local traffic under the name of West Bridge Street. Its status was elevated in January of 1927 when government officials decided to make it part of the state trunk line system, known today as M-45.

This designation did not, in and of itself, make the route a major transportation artery. To reach this level of use the road would first have to be paved and widened. In an effort to obtain these improvements, 200 residents from Kent and Ottawa counties

went to Lansing in April of 1927 to plead their case.

Leaders of this delegation noted that tourist traffic on the area's other main roads was so congested that a relief outlet was necessary, a function that could be filled by a 25-mile, straight shot to Lake Michigan. To help the prospects for their case, the petitioners convinced most of the property owners along the route to donate the land needed for a 100 foot right-of-way.

The arguments and incentives presented at the meeting were successful, and so the State Highway Department soon commenced work on upgrading the east-west thoroughfare. Construction proceeded from both ends, with much of the work provided by up to 80 convicts from the Ionia Reformatory who each earned ten cents per hour for their labors.

The project was sufficiently advanced to be dedicated on 29 August 1928 at Allendale, although the formal opening of the road did not occur until 15 November 1928 when its passage through John Ball Park was finished in Grand Rapids. The following month the name of the route was officially changed to Lake Michigan Drive, and so occurred the final act in creating what was described as West Michigan's first "superhighway."

Coordinates: L/8

LAKES & RIVER DRIVE

In late April of 1917, the Lake and River Drive Association was formed in Algonac. The purpose of this organization was not only to improve the road network in extreme eastern Macomb and St. Clair counties, but also to attract more money-spending tourists to the littoral areas of these two jurisdictions.

Beginning in 1918, Rand McNally showed this named route on its highway maps as a line extending from Detroit north along the intervening shores to Grindstone City at the tip of the Thumb. In truth, the road along the coast of Lake Huron was not well developed at this time, so subsequent editions (through 1922) of the Chicago firm's cartographic travel aids wisely depicted the Lakes & River Drive running from the Motor City north to just Port Huron.

It is strange that the title of this route would consistently use "River" in the singular, since the path of the motorway followed the Detroit and St. Clair Rivers. The two water bodies lending their names to the avenue were Lakes St. Clair and Huron. However, when the maximum extent of the highway was truncated back to Port Huron from Grindstone City, then the course of the road skirted only Lake St. Clair. Thus, to be accurate the appellation of the designated thoroughfare should

have been "Lake & Rivers Drive," the reverse of its actual name as represented by Rand McNally. Perhaps this confusing inaccuracy partially lead to the trail's demise.

As eventually laid out, the Lakes & River Drive extended north from the Motor City along Jefferson Avenue or parallel streets to Mount Clemens. At this point, tracing the path of Gratiot Avenue, the artery went on to Chesterfield, New Haven and Richmond before turning directly east and running into the town of St. Clair. From there the road pretty much hugged the river before terminating in Port Huron.

Lakes
& River

Readers may wonder why the designated highway didn't follow all of contemporary M-29 in keeping with its claim to be a "Lakes & River Drive." The answer lies in the fact that the shore-skirting road did not finally assume its present waterside configuration until 1923, not coincidentally the first year that the old inland route was removed from Rand McNally's maps.

Coordinates: K-M/14

LaPLAISANCE BAY TURNPIKE

As commerce developed on the eastern Great Lakes in the early 1800s, it was deemed necessary to create a harbor at the western end of Lake Erie. With present-day Monroe being the only settlement of note in the area at that time, in 1826 Congress authorized the survey of what was then the community's port at LaPlaisance Bay (The Pleasant Bay), a shoreline indentation a few miles south of town.

Following the nautical survey, between 1828 and 1830 breakwaters were put in at the site, a lighthouse built, wharves constructed, and an anchorage made for the little fleet that served southeastern Michigan. All that was lacking was a road by which products could be moved from

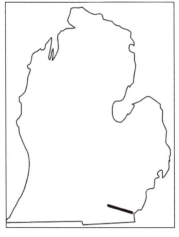

the ships to inland markets.

Congress took care of this deficiency on 4 July 1832, when it authorized the construction of a road from contemporary Monroe northwest to Cambridge Junction. The route was surveyed later that year and groundwork began in 1833 with Frenchmen from the River Raisin area providing most of the labor.

By the fall of 1834 the enterprise was finished as far as Tecumseh with the balance of the way indicated by blaze marks. But the established route further inland was difficult to follow, and to some pioneers struggling to push beyond the frontier the path seemed to just disappear up a tree.

Fortunately, this ambiguous course was corrected by the summer of 1835, when this track to the interior was completed at a total cost of $40,000. Since the road connected the hinterlands with a point on the Lake Erie shore, it was named after its destination the LaPlaisance Bay Turnpike.

The word "Turnpike" implies that there were turnstiles or gates at intervals across the road at which people were forced to pay tolls for using the highway. However, historical evidence indicates that movement along the thoroughfare was free until 1849, when the legislature granted at least part of the route to a plank road company that could charge travelers a fee.

As the years passed and LaPlaisance Bay lost its maritime and commercial significance, people gradually ceased to associate its name with the road that lead to its shores. Since Monroe was the destination or point of departure for most people using the route, by the turn of the last century the highway had become commonly known as the Monroe Pike.

By either name the road can be said to have had its dedication on 11 September 1922. It was on that day that hundreds of people came to Cambridge Junction to witness the unveiling of a bronze tablet on a boulder marking the point where the LaPlaisance Bay Pike met the famous Detroit to Chicago Trail. This gesture of respect for the LaPlaisance Bay Pike was repeated at a ceremony nearby on 1 August 1929 and later in Tecumseh at the erection of an historical marker in 1966. Despite all of this official recognition, the road's fame was fleeting for we know the highway today by its more prosaic identity, trunk line M-50.

Coordinates: N/12-13

LASALLE TRAIL

To some people the word "LaSalle" is the name of a car produced by the Cadillac Division of General Motors from 1927 to 1940. To others it is associated with a city and county in north-central Illinois or a major street in downtown Chicago. But to most people in Michigan it brings to mind a famous European explorer who played an important role in the history of the Midwest.

Rene Robert Cavelier Sieur de LaSalle was born 21 November 1642 in Rouen, France, and educated in that town to the college level. Thinking his prospects for success rather limited in his native land, in 1666 he came to the New World for adventure and fortune.

LaSalle began his life in North America as a fur trader near Montreal. Before long, however, he succumbed to a desire to discover passages and places that would benefit him and his mother country (probably in that order). This meant

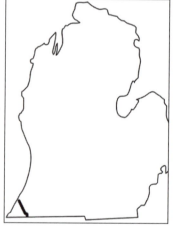

wandering about the Great Lakes region in search of riches, possible conquests, or profitable avenues of commerce.

One of LaSalle's biggest expeditions occurred in 1679. He built the first sailing vessel on the Great Lakes near present-day Buffalo and voyaged from there to Green Bay to pick up stockpiled furs. Then, taking to canoes, he and his party paddled south to the mouth of the St. Joseph River where he built Fort Miami near the location of contemporary Benton Harbor, Michigan.

Once established at what was then a highly strategic place, LaSalle proceeded up the St. Joseph to what is now South Bend, Indiana, where he portaged over to the watershed of the Kankakee River. Following the flow of this stream he eventually came to the site of present-day Peoria, Illinois, where he constructed another post from which to operate.

Finding himself short of supplies at this point in his travels, LaSalle decided to return to his home near what is now Kingston, Ontario, to re-equip. Since it was late winter of 1680 and the streams were frozen, he walked from Peoria across the southern Lower Peninsula to the eastern end of Lake Ontario, more than 1,000 miles in just 65 days.

Two years later LaSalle was ready to sally forth again. More or less picking up where he had left off, in 1682 he became the first European (and possibly the first person ever) to descend the Mississippi to its mouth. There, at the terminus of the continent's greatest river, he claimed the entire drainage basin for France and named the territory Louisiana after his King, Louis XIV.

Accomplishments of this nature deserve to be recognized in some fashion, and one appropriate way is through the creation of a memorial highway. With this thought in mind,

the Lions Club of South Bend, Indiana, proposed around 1932 that a special scenic road be marked off in recognition of LaSalle's discoveries and his brief connection with the local area.

The contemplated motorway was designed to run (in approximate terms) from the portage to the Kankakee River in South Bend north along trunk line M-51 to Niles. From there the route went west to Buchanan, north to Berrien Springs, and then northwest along old US-31 to the town of St. Joseph, terminating at the stone monument to LaSalle that is situated there along the bluff at the Lake Michigan shore.

Since the concept and energy for this memorial parkway originated in Indiana, it is not surprising that some portions of this trail of tribute were designated by signs in Hoosierland as early as 1937. However, enthusiasm for the enterprise never seems to have caught on in Michigan, causing the road honoring the Frenchman to be unmarked and forgotten in the Lower Peninsula where LaSalle built what may have been the first fort and made his epic trans-state journey by foot in 1680 across the wrist of the mitten.

Coordinates: N/7

LEIF ERICKSON HIGHWAY

Michigan has a few memorial highways that pay tribute to individuals who were likely never in this state. One of these persons is Leif Erickson, after whom M-95 has been named in the Upper Peninsula.

This road generally connects Kingsford (US-2) and Champion (US-41). Along its route, just 4.5 miles south of Republic, there is a Leif Erickson memorial roadside park where a marker can be found celebrating the great Scandinavian explorer.

This memorial highway is the product of efforts by the Norse Civic Association of Detroit. The members of this group wanted some public recognition for the man they and many others be-

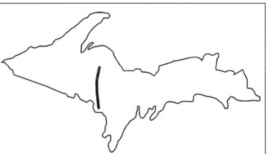

lieve to be the first European to set foot on North American soil.

Erickson, of course, was the famous Viking mariner who, according to ancient Icelandic sagas, sailed west from Scandivavian colonies in Greenland about 1000 A.D. and discovered a transatlantic country he called Vineland or Wineland because of the abundant grapes found there.

After the members of the Norse Civic Association brought this historic event to the attention of the State Highway Commissioner, Charles M. Ziegler announced on 28 April 1951 that under his authority trunk line M-95 would be known as the Leif Erickson Highway.

About 1.5 years later, on Leif Erickson Day 11 October 1952, the newly christened road was dedicated. Among the 200 people at the ceremony were diplomats from Denmark, Finland, Norway, and Sweden.

Highway Commissioner Ziegler, the main speaker at the occasion, said he had chosen to name M-95 after Erickson for two reasons. "First, it was an opportunity for me to recognize and compliment the large group of fine American citizens of Scandinavian ancestry who have contributed so much to the cultural and economic progress of our State and country." "Second," continued Mr. Ziegler, "I concur in your desire for recognition of the importance of Leif

Erickson's exploits to Michigan."

There is some doubt as to whether or not the State Highway Commissioner was authorized to unilaterally name roads in Michigan. To eliminate any doubt as to the legitimacy of this designation, in 2001 the Legislature passed Public Act 142 which unambigiously gave the road official status.

Though the path that Leif Erickson took in his wanderings about North America is largely unknown, and probably did not include the Great Lakes region, finding his route in Michigan will now be as easy as looking at our official state highway map.

Coordinates: C-D/4-5

LIBERTY HIGHWAY

During World War I there were Liberty Bonds, Liberty Loans, and Liberty Motors (the name given to Ford airplane engines). Sauerkraut and hamburger (both German names) respectively became Liberty Cabbage and Liberty Steak. Even Armistice Day or Veterans Day (November 11) was originally called Liberty Day. Not surprisingly, there was also a Liberty Highway.

The first mention of this road was in August of 1918, when it was promoted as a motorway of tribute stretching from the big Army induction center at Battle Creek's Camp Custer northeast to Bay City. This special drive was to be in "honor of the soldiers who have gone to the front in the war with Germany." The title "Liberty" was chosen because it was a "name that will always keep green the memory of our splendid soldiers and sailors who are offering their lives that freedom may survive."

As the War drew to a close, the scope of the proposed Liberty Highway increased. As envisioned in revised form, the expanded road began at New Buffalo and followed the approximate route of I-94 east to about Marshall where it diverted to I-69 and continued on to Port Huron. The original portion of the Highway remained in the scheme, generally taking M-66 north from Battle Creek to M-78, M-78 to I-69, I-69 northeast to M-52, M-52

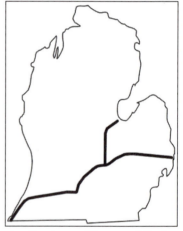

to M-46, M-46 to M-13, and M-13 to Bay City.

Thus, there was created at least on paper "a memorial to the men who will have fought and won the battle for liberty" stretching across the state from Lake Michigan to Saginaw Bay and Lake Huron. This concept received initial popular support because, as "a great paved highway carrying the traffic and serving the needs and ambitions of the new social condition which is to be born out of this war," the plan had sentimental and practical value.

Those individuals who were backing the Liberty Highway suggested that big boulders be placed along the route to display the military record of each city, township and county through which it passed. These large stones would be "set up by the side of the road bearing a memorial plate of uniform design" which would convey for each governmental unit the number of sons sent to war and the number killed in service. In this way the cross-state avenue of recognition would have "on its borders, in permanent view of the thousands who would travel its course for generations to come, ...the memorial records of the men who fought the great fight."

While this notion may have had merit, there is no evidence of any inscribed rocks being placed along the Liberty Highway. The record does show, however, that in December of 1922 Kalamazoo County planted 110 walnut trees along its segment of the road, one for each resident lost in the conflict. This act must have been impressive or touching, for not long thereafter the Liberty Highway Association expressed a desire to plant 100,000 more trees along the right-of-way.

Unfortunately, this linear forest was never put in the ground. For by then World War I was nearly five years in the past, the country was absorbed in enjoying the Roaring Twenties, and public attention was diverted to things more pleasurable than remembering a tribute to the senseless death of thousands of soldiers. So as America celebrated its temporary liberty from war and worry, the name "Liberty Highway" slowly disappeared from the Michigan transportation scene. It is ironic that today we remember those who died for this country but have forgotten the road that saluted their sacrifice.

Coordinates: J-N/7-14

LOGAN STREET

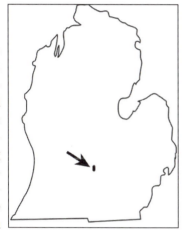

A number of Michigan towns--among them being Ann Arbor, Battle Creek, Detroit, Grand Rapids, Kalamazoo and Lansing--have streets called "Logan." If one were to look into the origins of these names they would probably find that nearly all of them pay homage to the same person, John Alexander Logan.

General Logan was never a resident of our two peninsulas, never fought a battle on our territory, and is not recognized as a commander of Michigan troops. However, it was on account of him that one of the most influential associations in our state's history was founded in the nineteenth century and why today we have a national holiday in May.

The story begins on 9 February 1826 when Logan was born in rural Jackson County, Illinois. Not long after reaching the age of majority, he enlisted in the Mexican War as a private and, through outstanding performance, quickly rose to the rank of second lieutenant in the First Illinois Infantry.

Following his discharge from military service, Logan entered politics. In succession over the next decade or so he was elected or appointed Clerk of Jackson County Illinois (1847), member of the Illinois House of Representatives (1852-1857), Prosecuting Attorney for the Third Judicial District of Illinois (1853-1857), and Congressman from his district in Illinois (1859-1861).

When the Civil War commenced in 1861, Logan resigned his seat at the nation's Capitol in Washington DC and returned to his home base where he accomplished the amazing feat of raising an entire regiment of volunteer soldiers to fight for the Union cause. For this act he was given command of the Illinois unit along with a Colonel's commission. Through meritorious conduct in the field during the remainder of the War, Logan eventually attained the rank of Major General.

Following the conclusion of hostilities, Logan returned to public service as representative to Congress from his old district in Illinois (1867-1871). During the rest of his career he was one of his home state's two U.S. senators (1871-1886), and in 1884 he was the vice-presidential candidate on the Republican Party's national ticket.

None of these accomplishments, impressive as they are, would prompt Michigan towns to name their streets in honor of Logan. Instead, such recognition is attributable to two of his other accomplishments: in 1865 he helped to found the powerful organization called the Grand Army of the Republic and in 1868 he inaugurated the observance of Memorial Day, originally the custom of decorating soldiers' graves with flowers every May 30th.

For this reason, in the 1860s (the best estimate is 1864) Lansing christened what became its longest street in tribute to General Logan. When the town council changed the road's name in 1994 to "Martin Luther King Jr. Boulevard," the old Civil War officer was left without suitable recognition. To rectify this matter, House Bill 5971 of 1996 and House Bill 4713 of 1997 was introduced in our state legislature

for the purpose of designating trunk line M-99 the "General John A. Logan Memorial Highway." Unfortunately, by this late date Logan was viewed by most people as just an obscure character in ancient North American history, and so no support could ever be mustered for passing a law to restore the honor that Michigan's Capital City once gave to a man who taught a nation to honor its dead.

Coordinates: L-N/10-11

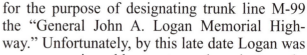

LUCE ROAD

Up until about World War II, many of the roads in Michigan were not uniformly identified. A given highway could have many names along its length, most determined by local residents rather than some broader authority. This situation created problems for utilities like the Consumers Power Company, which had difficulty providing electric service to rural accounts when their customers' homes were along routes that had no official titles or residential street numbers.

In an effort to address this situation in Gratiot County, in January of 1942 Consumers Power asked the governing Board of Supervisors to name all of the roads within their jurisdiction. A committee was formed to consider this matter, and this body decided to designate all highways running east and west after U.S. presidents and those routes oriented north and south after Michigan governors. This concept was presented to the county's leaders on 17 April 1942, and they unanimously accepted the proposal on the same day.

As devised, the identification system started with the earliest governors on the eastern side of the county and worked up the order of gubernatorial succession toward the west. As fate would have it, when laid out the most northerly four miles of Luce Road coincided with trunk line US-27. This pairing of name and number continued until 1961, when the course of

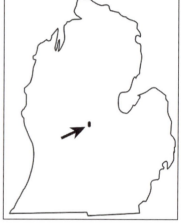

US-27 was officially shifted to a new limited access corridor just to the east of its old alignment, thus putting an end to Luce Road as a federal memorial highway.

The namesake of this pavedway, Cyrus Gray Luce, was born in Windsor, Ohio, on 2 July 1824. After receiving an education typical for that period, he spent seven years as a young man working in his father's woolen mill. With the money he had saved from these labors, in 1849 Luce purchased a farm in Branch County and permanently moved to Michigan.

Luce did well in his new environment, as within three years of his arrival he was elected to the township board of supervisors (1852-1863). He subsequently was appointed or elected to such posts as state representative (1854-1855), Branch County Treasurer (1858-1862), state senator (1865-1868), delegate to the state constitutional convention (1867), state oil inspector (1879-1883), member of the state board of agriculture (1885-1887), and governor (1887-1891).

Luce took his responsibilities seriously, as evidenced by the fact that he was the first governor to actually live in Lansing during his tenure so he

could stay close to his work. After two terms in office Luce's energies were spent, so he left the world of politics for the comforts of his farm near Gilead. He died in Coldwater on 18 March 1905, probably never anticipating that at some future day, in tribute to his public service, there would be for nearly twenty years a federal highway bearing his name.

Coordinates: J/11

MACKINAW SCENIC
SHORTWAY ROUTE

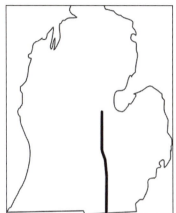

Until the second quarter of the Twentieth Century, most highways in the United States were known by name. This situation was acceptable for slow-paced times with relatively little traffic. But as motorized vehicles became more prevalent and the speed of movement increased, a better system of road identification became necessary.

In 1925 the American Association of Highway Officials met to solve the problem by devising the federal trunk line numbering system that we are familiar with today. The Michigan legislature accepted this scheme by Public Act 318 of 1927, giving the Highway Commissioner sole authority over route signage along the state's roads.

The directors in charge of the government agency responsible for highways were quite strict in limiting route markers along the public thoroughfares, and particularly in permitting such designations on the official state road maps. In fact, prior to 1992 when the Great Lakes Circle Tour logo first appeared on Michigan's annual aid to drivers, only one exception had been granted to the policy of keeping the state transportation map free of symbols for named roads.

The sole case of special consideration first appeared on the 1939 highway map as a block "M" within a circle, and it remained there through 1942. This emblem was placed adjacent to a series of roads that ran north and south in a nearly straight line between highways US-23 and US-127.

The letter "M" represented the Mackinaw Scenic Shortway Route, a path that promoters claimed was a quicker way for those traveling to the Straits because it avoided the congestion of major urban centers. It started on the Ohio boundary at Morenci, and by following what today are mainly secondary roads it continued on up through Rome Center, Onsted, Brooklyn, and Grass Lake to Stockbridge. There it followed the present course of M-52 to Owosso, from which point it proceeded nearly straight north through Hemlock to Midland, its terminus.

The idea for this shortcut to the north began in February of 1938 and it was soon endorsed by a number of village councils, road commissions and chambers of commerce along the way. Various individuals and organizations in close proximity to the route raised money to help support the cause, most of which was spent on road signs and billboard advertising.

The official identifying symbol of the highway was a black "M" on a white background circumscribed by a red border. The route was marked with hundreds of small signs bearing this logo, while placards of a similar nature were put in the windows of neighborhood businesses as part of the promotional campaign.

But all of these efforts were for naught, as the push on behalf of the alternate road north was interrupted by America's arms buildup just before World War II. In August of 1941 the federal government declared competing routes US-27/US-127 to be part of the national Strategic Military Highway Network, making them essential for the defense effort and qualifying them for millions of dollars in federal road funds.

The ensuing improvements made these two routes some of the most popular avenues to the Straits, which is why no one any longer remembers the Mackinaw Scenic Shortway Route.

Coordinates: J-N/11-12

MACKINAW TRAIL

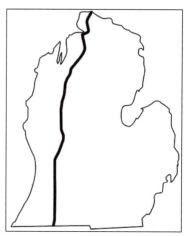

Mackinaw, or Mackinac, is one of the most famous terms in Michigan. The Indian word for "turtle," this name has been given to a village, city, township, county, straits, island, fort, bridge, lake, state forest, and state park plus a specific type of coat, boat, and blanket.

With such widespread use of the word, it is not surprising that it has also been applied to a road. But since two routes can lay claim to this honor, some explanation is in order for the benefit of readers.

The original Mackinaw Trail was an Indian path that ran from Saginaw north through the interior to present-day Mackinaw City, then across the Straits and on to Sault Ste. Marie. Most of this distance was surveyed for a road in 1835, but it was not until decades later that it was actually made passable for vehicular travel.

Though generally not known as the Mackinaw Trail today, evidence of this route's previous name can still be found on road signs in parts of Saginaw, Bay, Cheboygan, and Mackinac counties.

The contemporary Mackinaw Trail scarcely comes near the old track. For while the former course connected Saginaw Bay with the Soo, the present route runs from around Niles north to the Straits.

This transfer of a name from the eastern to the western part of the state all began at Cadillac in October of 1915. It was then and there that the Mackinaw Trail Association was formed for the purpose of developing a modern highway from Grand Rapids to Mackinaw City.

The concept for this road stemmed in part from traffic congestion along what is today highway US-31. With so many people driving that trunkline for tourist and sightseeing purposes, an alternate interior route for higher-speed travel was seen as

necessary.

To encourage use of what is today US-131, the Association dubbed this diversionary course the Mackinaw Trail. In devising a symbol for the route that motorists could follow on sign boards, the group adopted the Mackinaw Trout, the same logo used by the Grand Rapids & Indiana, the railroad that paralleled the highway.

As the number of cars traveling US-131 grew, the Association sought the government's blessing for its cause. In 1929 it convinced members of the Michigan House of Representatives to officially designate it the Mackinaw Trail, but the measure ultimately died in the Senate.

With the opening of the Mackinaw Bridge in 1957, state interest was focused on the old Indian word. Attempting to capitalize upon this situation, the legislature was once again asked by promoters to bless their naming of the road. The result was Public Act 170 of 1959, a statute declaring US-131 from Indiana to Petoskey, and US-31 from Petoskey to the Straits, the Mackinaw Trail.

Some alterations to this status occurred in 2001 when the Legislature passed Public Act 142. This piece of lawmaking essentially left the course of the Trail intact but it officially modified the name of the road from "Mackinaw" to "Mackinac." While the slight change in spelling may have affected how some travelers pronounced the word, it certainly did not detract in any way from the pleasure they experienced from the drive.

The latest chapter in this route's saga occurred in 2004 under color of Public Act 138. This statute declared that the portion of trunk line US-131 from Kalkaska to Petoskey, and the segment of US-31 from Petoskey north to the Straits, would henceforth be known as the "Green Arrow Route-Mackinac Trail." Some people subsequently questioned the wisdom of having a compound road name whose signboards will be nearly as long as the highway itself.

Coordinates: F-N/9-10

MANITOU TRAIL

The Algonquin Indians of the Great Lakes region worshipped or venerated forces with supernatural powers. These gods or spirits were called Manitous, and as such they were objects of religious awe and reverence. These masters of life--if appealed to or appeased--could make the hunt successful, the warrior strong in battle, and the perilous journey safe.

Since such deities played a major role in ancient Indian culture, it is not surprising that references to them would appear in the territories once inhabited by indigenous peoples. Here in Michigan, for example, there is Manitou Island off Keweenaw Point, Lake Manitou (Leelanau, Oakland and Shiawassee counties), Manitou Passage (in eastern Lake Michigan), Manitou Payment Point (Mackinac County), the village of Manitou Beach (Lenawee County), plus a township and a former county (1855-1895).

By far the most famous landforms carrying the Manitou name are the North and South Manitou Islands just west of Leland. According to Indian lore, these large glacial remnants in Lake Michigan represent two drowned cubs who tried to follow their mother (Sleeping Bear) on a swim from the Wisconsin shore east to the Empire Dunes complex. As an aside, it is also worth noting here Manitoulin Island in northern Lake Huron. Though not within Michigan's borders, this largest freshwater island in the world is just on our doorstep.

In addition to all of these physical and cultural features named Manitou, there was also a long stretch of pavement possessing this title. The story of this christening goes back to 1913, when trunk line M-22 became the first state highway established in Benzie, Leelanau and Manistee counties. Despite its early presence on the

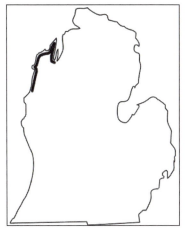

transportation scene, route M-22 was not heavily used because most drivers seemed to prefer riding on the nearby alternative US-31.

In an effort to attract more vehicles to the Lake Michigan shoreline drive, the M-22 Association was founded in February of 1953. The purpose of this organization was to increase traffic along the coastal road by publicizing its virtues through advertising and other promotional activities.

Before touting the benefits of a spin in the family car along M-22, the route's backers figured they first needed a "catchy" name for the highway. The Association ran a contest to find the best title for the road, and on 15 April 1953 its board of directors chose "Manitou Trail" out of more than 500 entries.

Almost immediately special brochures were printed up and placemats produced boosting travel on scenic M-22. And for a number of years thereafter advertisements could also be seen in various venues in favor of the winding vehicular path along the northwestern Lower Peninsula shore. But before the old Indian name could become popular with the motoring public, the assets of the Association became unequal to the task of championing a road off the beaten path. The sponsoring group eventually dissolved due to funding problems and the Manitou Trail found itself beyond the help of even the great spirit gods of the Native Americans.

Coordinates: F-H/8-9

MARSHALL'S TERRITORIAL ROAD

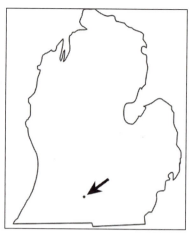

First settled in 1830 and platted in 1831, Marshall developed so quickly that in just five years it qualified for village status. Its rapid early growth was furthered by its location along the main Territorial road running west out of Detroit, its standing as the seat of Calhoun County, and its role as a service center to the Michigan Central Railroad.

Marshall, certainly in the nineteenth century, was noted as a community of numerous prosperous and prominent people. Because of their wealth and position in society, many of these individuals built residences of size and design that reflected their station in life. As a result, today "the architectural excellence of Marshall's homes is known through the Midwest."

The fame of the city's population, residences and businesses can be seen in the fact that there are twenty-eight historical markers along the 1.2-mile long central business district, of which fourteen have received official state sanction. In part because of this concentration of human and structural heritage, in 1991 the federal government declared much of downtown Marshall to be a National Historic Landmark District.

When Michigan began to seek out and highlight its Heritage Highways, the fourteen-block commercial strip along the old east/west Territorial Road through Marshall seemed like a natural candidate. Among other things, this stretch of pavement included the National House Inn (the state's oldest operating inn, built in 1835), the founding site of the Brotherhood of Locomotive Engineers (1863), and the interesting American Museum of Magic and the U.S. Postal Museum.

After carefully studying the matter for nearly five years, the Michigan Department of Transportation decided to promote and preserve Marshall's historical and cultural assets by including most of the old town along Michigan Avenue in the Heritage Highway program. This action, it was felt, would help showcase the community between East Drive and Cherry Street "and serve as a reminder of its rich legacy."

The addition of Marshall to the register of Michigan's Heritage Highways occurred in August of 2000 and the appointment was dedicated on 11 January 2001 with fitting ceremonies at the Honolulu House, one of the distinctive dwellings unique to the town. In response to the wishes of the local Chamber of Commerce, the name "Marshall's Territorial Road" was bestowed upon the newly designated motorway, making Business Loop I-94 the only Heritage route along an Interstate business connecting link.

Coordinates: M/10

MARTIN LUTHER KING JR. BOULEVARD (LANSING)

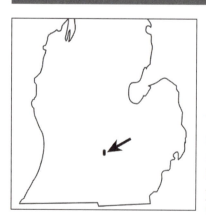

After Martin Luther King, Jr., was assassinated in 1968, many communities throughout the country designated streets, parks and statues in his honor. One exception to this practice was Michigan's Capitol City.

Wishing to redress this oversight, early in 1986 members of the Pastor's Conference of Lansing suggested that the name of the city's longest street--Logan--be changed to Martin Luther King, Jr., Boulevard.

Because of the large number

of people and businesses affected by this idea, the proposal was not well received. Not wishing to adversely impact unsupportive city residents, the Pastor's Conference looked for alternatives.

In October of 1988, twenty years after King's death, the Pastor's Conference members recommended changing Lansing's "Allegan" Street to "Martin Luther King" Street. This street was chosen because it was shorter than Logan and it passed through the black community.

This overture was also rejected, because it would alter part of Lansing's heritage. When the city was originally platted in 1847, its east-west streets were named after various counties in the state. Eliminating "Allegan" would inappropriately disrupt that historic pattern.

Next it was suggested naming the Capitol Loop after King, a route designed to guide visitors through the state Capitol complex. But this concept was also nixed because special signs for the circuit had already been made and were about to be installed.

By early 1989 the focus of a King memorial had once again returned to Logan Street. And again people objected to the plan because of its cost ($32,000 to replace signs) and the fact than it would erase a tribute to another

American hero, General John A. Logan of Civil War fame.

Just as this impasse was about to divide the city, a rather ingenious compromise was offered to defuse the situation. The mayor recommended that Logan Street bear two names, and residents would be free to use either King or Logan as they wished.

On 24 April 1989, the city council unanimously adopted this proposal and the name-sharing concept became official. By late August King signs were in place, and the street of contention had a dual name.

Despite its ability to temporarily calm tensions, co-naming the street was really not a long-term solution to the problem. Consequently, early in 1992 the Pastor's Conference returned to the city council and asked that the dual identity be dropped in favor of a single designation for King.

This matter was debated for more than two years before the council, on 28 March 1994, finally agreed to scrap the shared billing in favor of a solo King Boulevard. And in this way all of M-99 in Lansing became a memorial highway.

Coordinates: Lansing Inset

MARTIN LUTHER KING MEMORIAL HIGHWAY (BATTLE CREEK)

From time-to-time, we hear someone referred to as a person who is so well known they need no introduction. Though Dr. Martin Luther King, Jr., is such an individual, it is not inappropriate to briefly review his life.

Born in Atlanta, Georgia, on 15 January 1929, King was the son and grandson of Baptist ministers. This background probably influenced him to seek advanced education in theology, a formal academic quest which ended with a Ph.D. at Boston University in 1955.

Following his ordination as a minister of the gospel, King accepted a pastorship in Montgomery, Alabama. Soon thereafter, he led a victorious protest against a local public transit system which required all blacks to sit in the rear of

its buses.

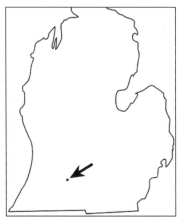

This accomplishment, through nonviolent means, launched King on a nationwide effort to confront and eliminate segregation, prejudice and injustice. So successful were his non-hostile labors towards these goals that in 1964 he was awarded the Nobel Peace Prize.

King continued to employ passive resistance and non-combative techniques to promote civil rights, equality, and non-discrimination throughout America. His efforts in this cause

MICHIGAN
141

were stopped on 4 April 1968 when he was assassinated in Memphis, Tennessee.

Because of King's many accomplishments and noble dreams for this country, a movement arose in Battle Creek to designate some appropriate road in honor of the man. This idea was endorsed by the local NAACP, the Urban League, and the Battle Creek City Commission.

After discussing the matter, these groups decided to name part of Skyline Drive for the civil rights leader. This stretch of freeway was chosen primarily because its adoption would not entail any new address changes for businesses or homeowners.

Because the selected road was a

state highway, however, it was necessary to get approval from Lansing before any final action could be taken. The required permission came in the form of House Concurrent Resolution 34 of 1991, through which the Legislature officially created the Martin Luther King Memorial Highway.

According to this document, the road of remembrance was to include M-66 and I-194 from Columbia Avenue north to M-96 and the I-94 Business Loop. With proper government sanction obtained, the citizens of Battle Creek dedicated their tribute to Martin Luther King on 5 August 1991.

Coordinates: Battle Creek Inset

MASON DRIVE

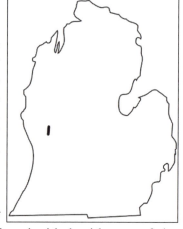

There is a main thoroughfare running south out of the town of Newaygo for about nine miles known as Mason Drive. This road does not honor brick layers or members of the fraternal organization called Free & Accepted Masons. Rather, the highway pays tribute to the youngest chief executive ever elected in Michigan history and the first governor of our state, Stevens Thomson Mason.

This is not the only tribute to this young politician, as at least two towns, a township, a county, a residential hall at Michigan State University, and a major state government office building in Lansing also bear his name. But to understand how part of trunk line M-37 came to honor his memory one must first know something about the man.

Born in Leesburg, Virginia, on 22 October 1811, Stevens was raised in Kentucky before coming to Michigan with his parents in 1830 when his father was appointed Territorial Secretary. When the elder Mason resigned in 1831 to move from Detroit to Texas, President Andrew Jackson named the nineteen-year-old son to fill the vacancy.

Stevens performed well as Territorial Secretary until 6 July 1834, when the death of then-Governor Porter made him--under the rules of succession--ex-officio governor of Michigan.

Mason served so ably in this capacity that the citizens elected him to his own term in office in 1835 at the tender age of 24 and to a second term in 1837.

Mason's second success at the polls was a sort of Pyrrhic victory, for it coincided with one of the worst economic depressions in American history. As conditions worsened during the Panic of 1837, it is not surprising that people began to hold public officials accountable for some of their woes. Realizing that his low popularity would prevent him from winning at the ballot box again, Mason retired from politics and moved to New York City where he practiced law until his premature death from pneumonia on 4 January 1843.

As time passed, people came to view Mason's tenure in office more objectively and gained a fuller appreciation of his contributions to our state's history. Seeking to posthumously give the man his due, in 1905 the Michigan legislature authorized the removal of Mason's body from its New York City resting place and his reinterment at Capital Square in Detroit. The spot is marked today by a life-size likeness of the "boy governor," the statue cast in bronze from some melted down cannon from old Fort Michilimackinac.

Fast-winding forward four decades, in 1945 the Consumers Power Company asked Newaygo County officials to systematically and comprehensively name their roads so the utility firm's workers could more easily find the homes of its rural customers. Consumers Power recommended that all north/south roads in the western half of the county be named for Michigan governors, an idea

that received local government approval on 21 December 1945. Since the plan called for generally listing the former governors in chronological order from east to west, Mason's name went on the first road down the middle of the county. And as part of this road happened to be route M-37, good fortune gave Mason his claim to a memorial highway in this state. This was certainly fitting recognition for a man who lived among us for just a decade but served as one of our early leaders for eight of those years.

Coordinates: J-K/8

MATT MCNEELY BOULEVARD

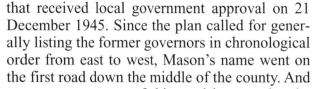

Detroit Area

He was the longest serving Speaker Pro Tempore in the history of the Michigan House of Representatives, the first black legislator elected to a leadership position in that body, plus co-founder and first president of the National Black Caucus of State Legislators.

The subject is Matthew McNeely, a man born in Millen, Georgia on 11 May 1920 and eventual immigrant to Detroit in 1938. Like many newcomers from the South, McNeely found work in an auto factory, evolving in his job to become education director of Local 306 of the UAW.

McNeely's communication and interpersonal skills made him a rising figure in the downriver area of Detroit, talents which ultimately led him into politics. He was first elected to the House of Representatives in 1964 and continued holding his Third District seat until 1986. During the first two terms of his 22-year career he was Associate Speaker Pro Tem and during the last 18 years he was Speaker Pro Tem.

McNeely excelled in his capacity as leader, a fact which led to House Resolution 779 of 1986 lauding him for his exemplary service. This tribute was reinforced the following year when House Resolution 11 of 1987 conferred upon him the permanent title of "Speaker Pro Tem Emeritus."

The last gesture of gratitude for his many years of public service came in 1997, when the legislature passed Public Act 14 declaring that part of highway M-85 between Outer Drive and I-75 to be the Matt McNeely Boulevard. This recognition was supported by the mayor of Detroit who issued a proclamation officially co-naming part of South Fort Street for the former representative.

Only 116 people have a Michigan state or federal road named in their honor, so this expression of gratitude for tending to the political needs his fellow citizens was the capstone of long and productive life. It was with justifiable pride that Matt McNeely joined his many friends in dedicating "his" road on 25 July 1997.

Coordinates: Southeastern Michigan Enlargement F/8

MEMORIAL DRIVE (IRON MOUNTAIN)

The Kiwanis Club--a civic group known to just about everyone in North America--was founded in Detroit, Michigan, on 21 January 1915. Its name is derived from an Indian word that means, roughly translated, "we get together." The association's approximately 600,000 members, organized into about 8,400 chapters world-wide, are business and professional men and women who engage in a wide variety of community service projects.

In October of 1922, the Kiwanis Magazine offered a suggestion as to how its members might benefit their respective towns. The monthly journal reminded its readers that Armistice Day is "fresh in the minds of thousands in our midst who actually took part in the struggle [of World War I]. Kiwanians, there are men who lost their sons and men who lost their buddies [in this conflict]. November 11 is the anniversary of that day on which possibly you realized most keenly the loss of your son, for he was not to return. Others of you lost your buddies and on that day you are most conscious that they could not come back with you. Are you going to let this day pass by unnoticed?"

"Wouldn't it be fitting," the periodical asked, "to plant trees in your parks or along your highways in memory of those men who gave up their lives? As we pass those trees in years to come, we will bow our heads in solemn reverence and say a few words of prayer for our fallen heroes. You can realize how the simple act of planting a tree will make your home town mean more to you. Why not present this to your club? Find out if your fellow members think well of the plan. Have your members don overalls and do the planting themselves."

Though it required nearly a decade, the Kiwanians in Iron Mountain finally took this message to heart. On Memorial Day of 1931 they consecrated the portion of route US-2 between their town and Quinnesec as a Memorial Drive to the deceased veterans of Dickinson County. Standing at the side of this road of remembrance with representatives from various veterans' organizations, the members of the local Kiwanis Club "gathered to dedicate Memorial Drive as a token [of] our love and loyalty to the men of this county who sacrificed their lives in defense of our stars and stripes."

In addition to a named highway and words of tribute, the sponsors elected to establish a living token of community appreciation in the form of memorial trees. There was one sapling planted for each honored soldier, the trees placed on both sides of the highway thirty feet back from the right-of-way and thirty-five feet apart. According to plan, "each tree in the drive will be named and dedicated to one of our departed comrades" with an attached metal tag identifying the departed veteran by name, rank, unit, and date of death.

Over one hundred trees were set out along the flanks of Memorial Drive, all of them either cherry or apple. The Kiwanians said they made this choice for two reasons. "First, these trees bear fruit, and as they bear fruit we hope that the principle for which these honored dead have fought will bear fruit to the end that we may enjoy a lasting and honorable peace among all nations of the world. Second, these trees have blossoms, so that in the springtime you will drive through a lane of fragrant flowers and in the fall through a lane of sparkling, ripening fruit."

Alas, the hoped-for peace was not to be, for just ten years later World War II began for America. Regrettably, the trees are now all gone, destroyed by the ravages of time, ensuing roadside development, and the need to increase the width of the federal highway. And the Memorial Drive title is long forgotten by nearly all residents of the region, with only the pages of this book preserving the honors once bestowed by a grateful community.

Coordinates: D/4-5

MEMORIAL DRIVE
(NORTH MUSKEGON)

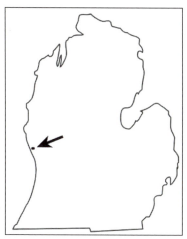

In the summer of 1920 a proposal was made to build a road to serve the north shore of Muskegon Lake. Some streets already existed along the waterfront in the town of North Muskegon, but now a call was being made to improve the transportation network westward to Lake Michigan.

Within a year the scheme had gained the necessary support, and with assistance from state government coffers construction activities were commenced. The plan was to in essence extend Ruddiman Avenue, the main street of North Muskegon, on out to what is today Muskegon State Park.

As work on the project proceeded in mid-1921, certain parties suggested that the new road be made a memorial to those Muskegon County combatants who were killed in World War I. The concept included the planting of about a hundred trees along the route (one for each serviceman who died in the conflict), with name plates in front of each tree to indicate the soldier being honored.

The officials responsible for approving such things readily endorsed the idea and recommended the name of North Shore Memorial Highway. However, by the time the North Muskegon city council considered the matter on 17 November 1921, they unanimously chose the name Memorial Drive instead.

Though a thoughtful gesture to departed veterans, this was not a universally popular action. The problem was not that many people wanted the more elaborate title for the road, it's that many residents wanted no change at all. The ordinance eliminated the name of Ruddiman Avenue, and a large segment of the citizenry felt this was an affront to a local pioneer.

George Ruddiman, one of the first white settlers of greater Muskegon, was born in Aberdeen, Scotland, on 29 September 1815. He set out for America in 1833, and by April of 1840 his path had led to Muskegon. George ended up in the lumber business, a local enterprise that he operated with his brother, John. He must have also dabbled in agriculture, for he claimed to have "introduced fruit growing in western Michigan."

It is understandable that some townsfolk would want to preserve a name so important to their history. An opportunity to restore the Ruddiman name to its perceived rightful place came in 1923, when talk began about building a memorial causeway at the head of Muskegon Lake. If another tribute to area veterans was in the works, then politicians felt it might be safe to abbreviate the existing one. Accordingly, on December 3 the North Muskegon city council voted to eliminate Memorial Drive from its jurisdiction and return Ruddiman Avenue to the signposts.

Memorial Drive remained the name of the road west of North Muskegon. It took on state trunk line status in 1932 when it was declared M-148 by the Highway Department. Within a year it had acquired a new number, M-20, a designation it retained until 1962 when its identity was once again changed to M-213. Its status as a state route ended in 1971, but the road still stands today among the many Michigan highways paying homage to the deeds of our military heroes.

Coordinates: Muskegon Inset

MEMORIAL HIGHWAY (ISHPEMING-NEGAUNEE)

As early as August of 1918--months before World War I ended--the journal <u>American Forestry</u> was encouraging the creation of roads of remembrance for those who answered the call to arms of our country. The magazine suggested communities establish "liberty highways" or "memorial drives" lined with "Victory Oaks" consecrated to our fallen warriors.

The idea was to plant one tree for every serviceman who sacrificed his life in the great conflict. This act was to be a civic ceremony, with the relatives of each hero participating. On or beneath the trees were envisioned individual bronze markers inscribed with the soldiers' names and military records.

The editors of <u>American Forestry</u> felt the debt this nation owed to its men in uniform who died for liberty could be partially paid by erecting living memorials in their honor. "The trees will be," they said, "in their very greenness and robust strength, reminders of the youths who gave their vigor to win the big war."

Former president William Howard Taft threw his weight behind the road-of-remembrance movement when he stated that "one fitting and appropriate memorial to our soldier dead would be rows of fine trees planted along the great through highways of the various states. They will stand there for many generations to come and keep fresh in the minds of all passers-by the heroic deeds of those young Americans who gave their lives that freedom and justice and truth might not perish from the earth."

Taking this advise to heart, the Women's Service Club of Ishpeming

started a movement to plant one tree for each of the twenty local men killed in the War. In support of this effort, the Land Department of the Cleveland-Cliffs Iron Company donated twenty rock elms and volunteered to put them in the ground at any specified site.

The promoters of the tribute decided to place the memorial trees along both sides of the main state highway between Ishpeming and Negaunee (then known as M-15) spaced one hundred feet apart. Near the common boundary between the two towns, these trees were planted and dedicated in early November of 1920.

Brass name plates identifying each soldier were provided by the American Forestry Association. Rather than attaching these tags to the saplings, the community fixed them to large concrete blocks which were permanently set two feet into the earth in front of the memorial trees.

In the years that followed, the elms died of disease, the state trunk line became County Road 480, and the local populace slowly forgot about the tribute they had established after the First World War. In May of 1981, a reporter for the Marquette <u>Mining Journal</u> found this hallowed ground overrun with weeds, some of the concrete blocks broken, and many of the soldiers' name plates removed.

Upon receipt of this news, community volunteers quickly cleaned up the site and made it presentable once more. But even if this stretch of memorial highway should again become overlooked by caretakers, the actions of the men it honors will remain unforgotten in the annals of history.

Coordinates: C/5

MEMORIAL ROAD (HOUGHTON)

When this nation asked for soldiers to serve in World War I, Houghton gave generously of its young manhood. Duty called, and numerous citizens of this Upper Peninsula town heard and answered.

Of the many khaki-clad residents of Houghton who were sent abroad in humanity's cause, sixteen gave all that liberty and justice might prevail. For these individuals, the community felt it should create "an enduring record of the valor, heroism and sacrifice of our boys."

They method by which this wish would be accomplished was determined in July of 1921 when the local American Legion post decided to plant sixteen elm trees in memory of Houghton's dead warriors. Trees were selected because they were seen as living shrines that would perpetuate the memory of the lost soldiers and emphasize the significance of their sacrifice.

While the oratory and music that celebrated war's end had passed, the memorial trees would remain erect as lasting expressions of Houghton's feelings for its sons who did not return. A tribute to its hometown heroes, the elms would permanently show that the community remembers those who paid the ultimate price in defense of freedom.

Sheldon Street, west of the bridge connecting Houghton and Hancock, was chosen as the site for this local expression of gratitude. The Le-

gionnaires planted one-year-old trees on the north side of this road forty feet apart and four feet from the curb line.

Around each tree was built a six-foot-square concrete box and the enclosed space was filled with flowers. Then, in front of each tree was placed a concrete block bearing a bronze plate inscribed with the veteran's name and his date of death.

When the city council members saw the results of this labor, they were so impressed that on October 31 they passed a resolution changing the name of West Sheldon Street to Memorial Road. This action became official at 11:00 a.m. on 11 November 1921, the same time the memorial trees were dedicated by appropriate public ceremonies.

Thus, it was also at this moment that most of highway M-26 in Houghton became a street of remembrance. Unfortunately, the name of the Memorial road is all that is left today as evidence of its intended purpose.

Any trees that survived the Dutch Elm Disease were removed when the width of the state highway was widened from two lanes to four. And the personalized bronze and concrete tablets were removed to the Houghton City Garage, from which they were subsequently passed on to the families of the deceased or simply disappeared over time.

Coordinates: A/4

MEMORIAL ROW (ALMA-ST. LOUIS)

On 12 November 1918--the day after the armistice was signed ending World War I--the American Forestry Association suggested that our nation plant trees in honor of America's servicemen and women. These leafy sentinels would stand as memorials for the dead and as tributes to the ideals for which all in the armed forces fought.

But, according to the foresters, planting a tree would do more than just commemorate the past brave deeds of those in the military. Such an act would also demonstrate a desire to improve the present and the hope for a better future. And these noble visions, too, are tributes to the soldiers who helped preserve our faith that this verdant country now and hereafter is worth caring, fighting, and dying for.

Those who planted saplings by which to remember our soldiers would, it was said, get many things in return. In time the trees would add a touch of beauty to barren ground or liven a dull landscape. They would offer comforting shade under their green canopy in summer, stand as a buffer against the sting of winter's snow, and provide protection from the wind in all seasons.

Eventually, the branches and foliage of memorial trees would protect and enrich the earth upon which they stood. They would afford shelter to a wealth of wildlife, and their fruit would be a source of sustenance to man and beast alike. And at the end of life they would become a thing of utility, providing the basis for a wide variety of wood products.

It was with these benefits in mind that in June of 1923 members of the Alma Civic Improvement League decided to plant 280 elms along both sides of the three-mile highway connecting their town with nearby Saint Louis. The project was designed to recognize those citizens from the community who took part in World War I.

Money for the enterprise was raised through donations and from the sale of $1.00 cookbooks created by the women of the League. The organization's efforts were rewarded on Arbor Day (May 2) of 1924 when the first trees were planted and the undertaking dedicated. A grand parade marked the occasion, stores in town closed for part of the day so everyone could join the celebration, and the mayor formally accepted the project on behalf of the city's residents.

Today, outside of old newspaper columns, there is no evidence these actions occurred. What at the time was highway M-46 and then later M-177 has not been a state trunk line since 1939, the road being known by contemporaries simply as Michigan Avenue. And the original trees all succumbed to the elements or Dutch Elm Disease, destroying the hard work of those who created a Memorial Row on behalf of local veterans.

Coordinates: J/11

MEMORY LANE (BARAGA)

Almost since its inception, the agency known today as the Michigan Department of Transportation has required more than just civil engineers to build its highways. Members of other professions have also contributed

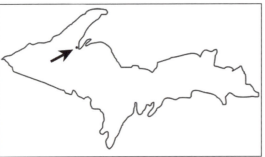

to the construction and maintenance of the public trunk line system.

This need to employ people representing a wide range of skills stems from the fact that roads are more than just ribbons of concrete or asphalt. They are also linear landscapes in need of planning, development, and ongoing care.

For example, when new highways are being designed, efforts must be taken to ensure that as much desirable existing growth is preserved along the right-of-way as possible. After all of the grading is finished, it is necessary to prevent surface erosion by establishing ground cover on exposed surfaces.

In barren or unsightly places, vegetation will commonly be planted in an effort to beautify a stretch of road that otherwise might be an eyesore. Also in these open areas, rows of conifers will often be established because they form snow barriers that help prevent drifting.

Once a thoroughfare has been built, specialists will--when and where appropriate--develop scenic turnouts, attractive rest areas, parking facilities, and roadside picnic grounds for the benefit of motorists. These and other amenities for travelers together require almost constant attention by groundskeepers and horticulturists.

To plan and supervise these kinds of developments, the old Highway Department hired a landscape engineer in 1921. In 1927 he was joined by a forester, who was permanently put on the payroll to help deal with tree planting for the purposes of utility and beautification.

This team of professionals was significantly increased in the 1930s when National Recovery Highway grants, issued by the federal government, required that one percent of the funds received by each state be used for trunk line landscaping. One form of improvement that qualified for this aid was the roadside memorial planting.

In October of 1946, one of the Highway Department's foresters visited Baraga and suggested to the lo-

cal Lions Club that it plant trees along both sides of a stretch of US-41 as "a living memorial to the men and women who have served the country in World Wars I and II." This challenge was accepted by the members, and in the summer of 1947 they set out over a hundred red maples along the shore of Keweenaw Bay from Baraga State Park to a point just north of town.

These dual rows of paralleling trees, comprising what was then called Memory Lane, have now all disappeared as the elements and developers have taken their toll. But the achievements of the people honored by the road remain alive in the annals of history, a record that will outlast any living creation of man or nature.

Coordinates: B/4

MEMORY LANE (BESSEMER)

In 1944, anticipating the successful outcome of the battle by the Allies against the Axis Powers, the North American Commission of the American Legion issued a report on Living War Memorials. This

document observed that "thousands of communities in every section of the country are planning to build memorials within the next two or three years in commemoration of those heroic men and women who gave so much in the two World Wars. The establishment of such memorials will ever serve as a reminder to the living that those who died in defense of their country paid the supreme sacrifice that our nation might live and our liberties be preserved."

"For these memorials," suggested the authors, "let us not erect victory arches, shafts, or sculptured monuments. Let us instead build schools, hospitals, playgrounds, recreation centers, [and memorial highways] which will serve the life of the whole community. Let us dedicate these memorials to our valiant dead. But let us also dedicate them to the living--and to the promise of the future."

In offering guidelines for this type of tribute, the Legion recommended that "living memorials, whether in the form of structures or areas, should serve the greatest possible number of people..., be located to serve best all the people in the community, perpetuate the memory of these who gave their lives to their country, honor those men and women who served their country in the armed forces, [and] have facilities which will serve the entire community, young and old, for twelve months of the year."

Perhaps working from this manual, the Bessemer Woman's Club decided early in 1949 to create a permanent living memorial to those men and women of Bessemer City and Township who served in the armed forces of the United States in past wars. Their form of recognition was a Memory Lane comprising 2.3 miles of US-2 running east from Bessemer toward Ramsay.

Not content to just name a stretch of highway, the Woman's Club elected to turn the designated road into a landscaped parkway by planting along its margins 140 elms backed by 1,840 units of evergreens, flowering trees and shrubs. This touch was chosen because it was felt "the living tree, a symbol of peace, hope and faith, is a fitting memorial to perpetuate the sacrifices of those who fought to preserve peace."

Moneys to underwrite the costs of this project were raised through voluntary private donations. The planning and design of the landscaping--along with the extensive labor of putting the purchased vegetation in the ground--was performed free of charge by the State Highway Department un-

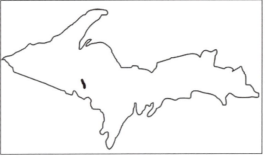

der orders of Commissioner Charles M. Ziegler, who officially endorsed the project.

This entire enterprise was solemnized on Memorial Day, 1949, at a point midway along the designated route. On that May 30th literally thousands of people in the region turned out to show dead and living American military veterans "the gratitude of a citizenry for their sacrifices in behalf of preserving the dignity of man."

Coordinates: C/1

MEMORY LANE (CRYSTAL FALLS)

At its national convention in November of 1921, the American Legion endorsed "the memorialization of highways by tree planting." This sentiment was further promoted in an article appearing in the March, 1922 issue of the Legion's weekly magazine.

Michigan. We therefore heartily...urge Legion posts all over the state to encourage similar memorial activities." These sentiments were unanimously adopted by the full membership at the state convention in August of 1923.

According to the story that was published in the official house organ, the Legion felt that "upon every road there should be living memorials to those who had served and those who had died in the [First World] War." To help realize this goal, "in every part of the country posts of the American Legion and other organizations have begun the planting of tree memorials."

"On Arbor, Memorial and Armistice Days this year," the piece continued, "thousands of memorial trees are to be planted and dedicated by Legion posts. The tree-planting idea that has been most evidenced is that of dedicating rows of trees along highways, each named for an individual soldier of the World War, living or dead."

Throwing its support behind this movement was the Michigan Department of the Legion. In July of 1923 the group's Executive Committee passed a resolution noting that "the American Legion of Michigan has repeatedly endorsed the creation and beautifying of memorial highways in

Taking this counsel to heart were the Legionnaires of the Louis Bowman Post in the town of Crystal Falls. Wishing to do their part in paying tribute to their fallen comrades in arms, the members of this body decided to turn US-141 between Amasa and M-69 into a Memory Lane.

The veterans accomplished their mission by planting a line of handsome pine trees along the route during the Spring of 1931. On May 30 of that year the enterprise was dedicated in the presence of a representative from the State Highway Department, who officially recognized the road "as a perpetual memorial to those who have given their lives in the service of their country."

For their part, the local Legionnaires pledged to keep their Memory Lane looking presentable.

The post commander, in making this commitment and explaining its purpose, said it was desired "that these beautiful pines should be a lasting memorial for the treasured memories of our hero dead."

At the same time Memory Lane was being dedicated, a stone monument was erected at the junction of highways US-2 and US-141 to commemorate the soldiers of all wars and serve as an entrance marker to the memorial highway. Today, the monument still exists but the road of remembrance that it signified has been all but forgotten. Fortunately, the achievements of those individuals the Lane honors have been preserved in the annals of history if not in the minds of those now living.

Coordinates: D/4

MEMORY LANE (ESCANABA)

With the conclusion of World War I, many communities considered establishing trees of gratitude to their citizens who answered the call to defend the cause of freedom. These living horticultural tributes were deemed to be a fitting reaction to the conclusion of a struggle that inflicted so much death and destruction.

Choosing trees to serve as memorials, rather than selecting inanimate objects, entailed some risk in Michigan, as the saplings could always succumb to such regional afflictions as chestnut blight, Dutch elm disease, or white pine blister rust. The highly variable environment, too, could destroy arboreal remembrances through the effects of drought, flood, extreme temperatures or wind.

Many cities, recognizing that it was difficult to create a permanent token of appreciation from things that could be easily claimed by the elements, elected to honor their military heroes with traditional markers and monuments. But Escanaba residents, perhaps being a bit bolder, decided they could minimize the risks to living memorials by picking vigorous native species that had proven they could thrive in that kind of habitat.

Activated by this logic, on 27 April 1929 members of the local American Legion post began setting out nearly 200 trees along US-2 and US-41 on the western approach to the city. The plantings, mainly eight-year-old maples and six-year-old white elms, were placed sixty feet apart along both sides of the highway for a distance of over a mile.

The Legionnaires were acting on behalf of all World War I veterans, but they did allow others to buy trees in the name of specific soldiers. The charge for each purchase was $2.80, and many clubs, businesses and persons took advantage of this opportunity to perpetuate the memory of an associate, employee, or loved one.

The response to this offer was so great that it generated more requests than could be handled the first year. Consequently, the program was continued in the spring of 1930 when another 150 trees were placed along what had become known as Memory Lane.

The American Legion members dutifully watered and cared for the trees, nurturing them along to the day when their branches would interlace to form a beautiful green tunnel along the city's main western thoroughfare. And the supporting trunks, it was hoped, standing erect like stately wooden soldiers, would bring to mind the pride and strength with which the residents of Escanaba fought for freedom and the honor they bestowed upon those who served that cause.

Unfortunately, despite the best efforts of the local Legionnaires, their efforts to protect and preserve the trees came to naught. For disease, and progress in the form of highway expansion and land development, eventually removed the fruits of their labors. Today, about the only remnant of this noble effort seventy years ago is a business west of town called the Memory Lane Motel.

Coordinates: E/6

MEMORY MILE

As World War II drew to a close in the summer of 1945, members of the Litchfield Garden Club met to consider how the community could honor those local soldiers who died defending freedom.

After discussing a number of options, it was decided that a memorial should be created of roadside plantings along a mile of route M-99 from town to the village cemetery. Because of the length of this project, the tribute was called the Memory Mile.

Part of the funding for this enterprise came from the village council, with the remainder being donated by private individuals along with support from various civic, service and fraternal organizations. The State Highway Department, in an effort to help a noble cause, agreed to supervise the plantings and maintain them free of charge.

For more than a year the 700 citizens of Litchfield carefully landscaped the flanks of the M-99 Memory Mile. In addition, they incorporated into the design a beautiful wayside park with a fishing pond, picnic tables, and outdoor fireplaces made of "memory stones."

In the center of this scenic setting was placed a large tablet listing the names of those ten men from the vicinity who "gave their all in World War II." Because of the area's low popula-

tion base, this number meant that 5% of Litchfield's total enrollment was killed in action, "the highest for any of the similar monuments erected throughout the nation."

The living memorial to these soldiers was dedicated on 8 September 1946 when over a thousand local residents and guests turned out in tribute to veterans and in celebration of the finished project.

On this occasion, Highway Commissioner Charles M. Ziegler accepted the deed to the park on behalf of the State and made a pledge that his Department would properly care for the horticultural labors of the Litchfield community along M-99.

In giving recognition to the sacrifices of deceased soldiers, the Litchfield Garden Club in turn received tribute. For their work in creating the beautiful Memory Mile, the 15 members of the group were collectively given a national award of meritorious effort in 1947.

Coordinates: N/10

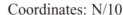

MERIDIAN ROAD

In order to precisely identify the position of every piece of property in Michigan, it was necessary to create a grid system by which to establish coordinates. We have all used this method of location, as it's the same one employed to find a place on the state road map that has letters in alphabetical order down the side and numbers in ascending order along the bottom.

When attempting to track down a particular town on the map, one simply finds the city's name in the accompanying index of places and obtains its number/letter code. Then, by going up

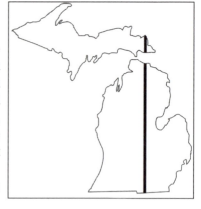

from the designated number on the bottom and in from the assigned letter on the side, one can find the desired place at approximately where the two lines meet.

A similar approach is taken when seeking a specific parcel of land in the Upper and Lower peninsulas. The main difference is that the two controlling axes are not at the bottom and side of Michigan, as on the road map, but in the interior of state. The horizontal coordinate for land location is called the base line and the vertical coordinate is known as the principal meridian.

In Michigan, the principal meridian runs straight north from near Munson on the Ohio border 334 miles to Sault Ste. Marie. Laid out by nine different surveyors between 1815 and 1840, it forms the standard reference line to which all real estate is tied under our rectangular survey system.

As early as 1840 roads were being built along the meridian line in the Lower Peninsula. But not until about 1893 did a movement arise to construct a highway along the entire length of the meridian to form an avenue "straight as the crow flies" from south to north and thus connect Michigan top to bottom.

This scheme remained just a dream until January of 1913, when the Roscommon Board of Supervisors passed a resolution in support of the concept and began lobbying for its construction. This effort paid off a few months later when the legislature passed public act 334 approving a state meridian road north of present-day M-46.

Boosters of the meridian route were delighted to have a highway bisecting the Lower Peninsula. It would open up unde-

veloped areas in the north, induce immigration, help fill vacant lands, and create a transportation backbone that would spawn other roads creating an interconnecting network.

Opponents of the idea countered by saying that the straight-line road would present many engineering problems as it allowed no deviation from a set path. Most telling, however, was the observation that the highway was not built from town to town--where people actually wanted to go--but instead was pushed through mainly unsettled land with little promise or value.

The arguments against a meridian trunk line eventually carried the day and most of the enterprise was ultimately abandoned. Today, all of the counties adjacent to the principal meridian have a "Meridian Road" except Cheboygan, Ogemaw and Roscommon.

However, the portions of the meridian that are designated state or federal highways are much more limited, with such segments confined to US-127 from the Ohio border north to Hudson,

US-127 from Jackson south to the county boundary, M-30 north of US-10 in Midland and Gladwin counties, and M-129 in Mackinac and Chippewa counties. So, aside from these few stretches of concrete, the effort to build a road straight up the meridian went straight down the tubes.

Coordinates: C-N/11

MICHIGAMME TRAIL

"Michigamme" is an Indian word that essentially means "large body of water." Michigan has a Michigamme lake, river, state forest, township and village. It nearly had a trail by that name also, and therein (as the saying goes) lies a story.

Around 1963 the Pentwater Chamber of Commerce began promoting an idea for a scenic byway along the western shore of the Lower Peninsula extending 470 miles from New Buffalo to Mackinaw City. Designed to follow established state and county roads running parallel to the region's main north/south trunk line, US-31, this route was expected to attract those who pre-

ferred to avoid the fast-paced expressways in favor of leisurely travel.

The proposed trail was to wind through fourteen counties, leading to or passing by various historic features, quiet small towns, quaint

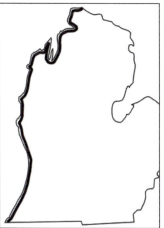

resort colonies, traditional farms with fruit-laden orchards, charming inland lakes, and majestic shoreline sand dunes. Along the way were numerous turnout spots for brief rests, scenic views, picnics, or the purchase of roadside produce.

Since the course of this drive to simpler times and places was designed to be out of the mainstream, its track was rather convoluted. Starting at the northern border of Indiana, the route followed former US-12 to Benton Harbor. From there it took old US-31 to Holland, at which point it went onto secondary roads up to Grand Haven. At Grand Haven it picked up US-31 as far as the Muskegon causeway, where it hugged the north shore of Muskegon Lake west to the state park and then ran up along Lake Michigan to Montague.

From Montague the trail continued to Pentwater along county road B-15, and then on to Ludington using backroads. At Ludington traffic again got on US-31, taking it as far as Manistee, at which point a diversion was made onto M-22 which was followed to its termination at Traverse City. Here US-31 was once more resorted to as far as Bay View, where a detour was made to M-119 and a destination of Cross Village. At this old Indian town the Michigamme Trail diverted onto county road C-66 east to Levering, where US-31 was again encountered and pursued to the end at Mackinaw City.

The path of this drive through a slower and more traditional Michigan was to be marked at no expense to the taxpayers by the various businesses and organizations supporting the concept. The rectangular signs chosen to guide motorists along this route to yesteryear displayed an American Indian in full headdress on the left with the name of the route on the right. All that was needed was approval of the State Highway Department to erect these markers along the appropriate roadsides and the Michigamme Trail would become a reality.

While state government may have been in favor of the Michigamme Trail, by July of 1965 it decided it was unable to give official blessing to such a notion. The reason for this rejection was supposedly because federal guidelines prohibited the erection of unapproved or non-conforming signs along national highways, in this case segments of US-31. With their identifying marker ostensibly banned from crucial parts of their chosen path, the backers of a casual tourist route along Lake Michigan's eastern shore saw their prospects for success go right in the drink.

Coordinates: E-N/7-10

MICHIGAN AVENUE

Is it acceptable to name a memorial highway after yourself? It had better be, or we Wolverines are in trouble for christening Michigan Avenue "after the great state which the highway serves."

The idea for such a road apparently started in Jackson, which proposed through its newspaper in 1922 that all towns on the main route between Detroit and Chicago (then depicted on travel maps as the Michigan-Detroit-Chicago Highway) collectively change the names of their principal east/west thoroughfares to create the longest street in the country.

Since Chicago and Detroit each had Michigan Avenues, it was suggested that communities along the main artery linking these two major cities adopt the same title for their stretches of the connecting road. Thus the highway would become Michigan Avenue end-to-end, greatly sim-

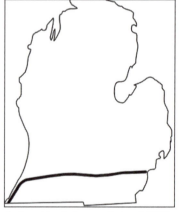

plifying matters for travelers by establishing a common name for 292 miles of pavedway.

Originally an Indian path known as the St. Joseph Trail, the route in question was established as an unnamed territorial road in 1829. Since it did not have a specific identify, most settlements along the way dubbed the road "Main Street" within their jurisdictions.

This moniker sufficed until 1920 when Sinclair Lewis wrote his critical book entitled "Main Street," and then the name took on pejorative connotations. Believing that their "Main Streets" marked them as one-horse towns and relics of the past, most major Michigan communities in the second tier of counties began heeding the advice of Jackson's newspaper to upgrade their image.

The first city to change the name of its main street to "Michigan Avenue" was Albion, followed in quick succession by Jackson and Marshall in 1924. Battle Creek joined the movement in 1928, and a year later Kalamazoo got in on the act.

Giving a continuous name to a cross-state highway may have made it easier to follow, but it also increased congestion along its course. With 50% of Michigan's population living within ten miles of the road, the volume of traffic it had to bear soon exceeded its carrying capacity.

To help solve this problem, the Michigan Avenue Highway Association was formed in January of 1929. This organization was led by Dr. John Harvey Kellogg of Battle Creek, a name associated with the famous brand of breakfast cereals.

The purpose of the group was to develop Michigan Avenue into the first transstate superhighway. The degree of their success can be gauged from the fact that route I-94, the modern substitute for Michigan Avenue that parallels its length, is today the second most heavily traveled trunkline system in the state.

Coordinates: M-N/7-13

MICHIGAN PIKE

Almost from the moment the automobile was marketed for the masses there was a sentiment in favor of having "an all-Michigan pike circling the Lower Peninsula" along the margins of the Great Lakes. As early as 1915 the Detroit Board of Commerce was promoting the creation of such a drive starting out just north of Toledo, running up to the Straits, and then back down the western coast to New Buffalo.

This 800-mile trek skirting the borders of Lakes Erie, St. Clair, Huron and Michigan was seen as the grand combination of two other roads in our state, the West Michigan Pike generally following contemporary US-31 and its counterpart along the other side, the East Michigan Pike, which approximated current US-23. The twin north-south trunk lines--which met at Mackinaw City--if traveled from beginning to end, would form a continuous thoroughfare circumscribing the shores of our "Water Wonderland."

Such a trip would be an attraction for tourists who are naturally drawn to the meeting place of beach and surf or the beautiful sights that usually accompany a visit to Michigan's freshwater seas. Vacationers, it was felt, would also react favorably to the adventure of "motoring the mitten" or tracing with their cars the "outline of the hand" of the Southern Peninsula.

To play up some of these features, by 1923

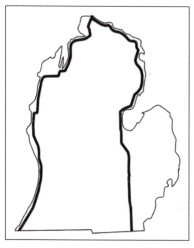

the coast-hugging highway had been nicknamed the 'Michigan Scenic Route." However, applying additional terms to distinguish the combined East and West pikes was rather risky as it could create confusion in the minds of potential users. The identity of the original concept was further blurred that year when the Great Lakes Tours Association christened a somewhat similar circuit for its members the "Michigan Trail."

All of these changes began to take their toll, and by 1926 the name of the Michigan Pike had completely disappeared in favor of the more pretentious title "Michigan Grand Boulevard." This phrase--probably dreamed up by some imaginative public relations specialist--not only forfeited the good will established by the old name but also misled people by trying to oversell the product as some broad, tree-lined avenue.

By now the damage to the cause was irreparable, for after 1926 the labels "Michigan Pike" or "Michigan Grand Boulevard" are not seen again. The long waterline drive that the words once represented essentially remained un-designated until 1988-1989, when roads that had years before been called the East Michigan Pike and West Michigan Pike were once again united under the umbrella label of the Great Lakes Circle Tour that most people are familiar with today.

Coordinates: E-N/7-13

MICHIGAN POLAR-EQUATOR TRAIL

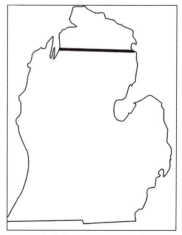

On 13 January 1965, there was established at the Michigan State University Museum an organization called the Michigan Polar-Equator Club. This body was comprised of outdoorsmen who wished to create an "association which would allow for better communication between persons with adventuresome avocations."

The membership included a wide variety of individuals ranging from big game hunters, fishermen, nature photographers and natural science professors to world travelers, authors, and conservationists. The goals of the group--aside from the enjoyment one another's company--were to encourage wildlife preservation, a better appreciation of our world's plant and animal life, wise natural resource management, the scientific study of our environment, and improved international understanding.

Because those seeking admission to the Club were required to have crossed the equator or the arctic circle, the members decided to commemorate a spot roughly midway between these two extremes: the 45th parallel of latitude. This circumglobal line bisects the Northern Hemisphere and the state of Michigan, running across the top knuckle of the Lower Peninsula mitten. It is the imaginary line halfway between the Equator and the North Pole.

The Club decided to take this little-known geographic fact and parlay it into a marked east-west automobile trail from Lake Huron to Lake Michigan. The idea was to stitch together a vehicular route of existing roads that followed as closely as possible the traverse of the 45th parallel across Leelanau, Antrim, Otsego, Montmorency, and Alpena counties.

Work on this enterprise began in June of 1970. Volunteers from the Polar-Equator Club first determined which path the trail should take and began gathering information on the historical, biological, geological and scenic attributes of the route. Then they created a suitable logo for identifying the route at one-mile intervals along its entire 139-mile length. The marker produced was a red, white and blue reflectorized disc bearing a symbolic map of the world. Positioned in front of this cartographic design was the image of a French voyageur, representing a mythical character known as the Great Lakes American Frontiersman.

With the plans for their project carefully made and organized, members of the Club turned to the Michigan legislature for support. The desired endorsement came in the form of Senate Concurrent Resolution 12 of 1971, which bestowed official blessings upon this endeavor. Once the imprimatur of the state was upon this undertaking, the various county boards of commissioners in turn gave their approval and the necessary government authorization was thus achieved.

The Polar-Equator Club arranged with Michigan's Prison Industries to have its road signs and metal posts manufactured, and by late summer of 1972 the members had installed these markers at regular intervals along the designated route. By the following year the Club had prepared at its own expense a forty-page guidebook to the Trail and was graciously offering the brochure free of charge to all interested parties.

The initial public reaction to the Trail was positive, and many people traveled along all or parts of its length which included segments of trunk lines M-32, M-33, M-65, M-66, and US-23. The popularity of the drive was such that by 1994 it was necessary for the Club to publish a revised edition of its guidebook to the motorway.

But despite these encouraging signs, the Michigan Polar-Equator Trail was in serious trouble. Many of the specially-created road markers were annually stolen, shot up during hunting season, or hit by wayward vehicles, requiring the Club to continuously spend thousands of dollars in replacement and repair costs. The membership could not afford this large expense year after year, and when no other organization could be found to help shoulder the financial burden the maintenance of the Trail was abandoned.

Because of the prolonged drain on its treasury, and also due in part to the forsaking of its pet project, the

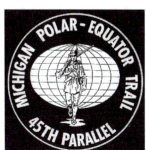

Club soon lost its vitality and was disbanded by its remaining members in 2000. Today, just a few years after the cross-state byway lost its sponsor, the staffs of the regional tourist bureaus in the northern Lower Peninsula tell callers they are not familiar with the Michigan Polar-Equator Trail.

People in the vicinity of the 45th parallel used to joke that "when you're here you're halfway there," meaning equidistant between the ice-covered top of the earth and its maximum tropical girth. Now, apparently, with the Michigan Polar-Equator Trail being so quickly lost to memory, one cannot even get behind the wheel of their car and be "here" any more.

Coordinates: F-G/9-12

MICHIGAN TRAIL

During the 1920s, an organization called the Great Lakes Tours Association published brochures promoting two trips in Canada and the American Midwest. The sponsors of these tours were almost entirely representatives of the travel business who owned or operated hostelries catering to the tourist trade along the path of the recommended routes.

One of these endorsed motoring jaunts was over a route called the "Michigan Trail" that, with only moderate exaggeration, included just about every major trunk line at that time in the Lower Peninsula and covered over a thousand miles of state highways.

The designated circuit began at Toledo, characterized as "the gateway to Michigan." From this northern Ohio town the route closely followed contemporary I-75 to Detroit. Once having reached yesteryear's version of the Motor City, the automobilist had the choice of taking the former equivalent of I-94 to New Buffalo, I-96 to Grand Rapids, I-75 to the Straits, or I-94 to Port Huron.

For a time there was another cross-state segment emanating west from Port Huron. This route matched or paralleled current I-69 between Port Huron and Flint, I-75 between Flint and Saginaw, M-46 between Saginaw and St. Louis, US-27 between St. Louis and Mount Pleasant,

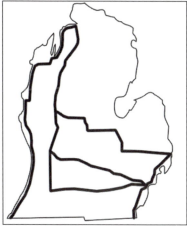

and M-20 between Mount Pleasant and Big Rapids.

Apparently possessing no sense of scale or proportion, the designers of the Michigan Trail also added to their network US-131 from Kalamazoo to Petoskey. Not content to end there, they concluded their grand tour by incorporating into their scheme US-31 from Mackinaw City to St. Joseph and US-23 from Bay City to the Straits.

It will not surprise the reader to learn that the itinerary laid out by the Great Lakes Tours Association did not catch on as a named highway. The route was much too long and diffuse, qualities that prevented it from establishing its own identity. Furthermore, a number of the trunk lines included in the mix already had names assigned to them, and these titles could not be supplanted by the amorphous and unwieldy spider web of roads collectively called the Michigan Trail.

Today, one can find in the holdings of historical societies and in the rare book rooms of libraries around the state literature touting the pleasures of driving the Michigan Trail. But one will search in vain for any stretch of pavement christened with that name because its backers lacked focus and established not a Trail but in essence a transportation network. By trying to do too much or please too many people they effectively led their followers on a confusing ride and doomed their road to a short life.

Coordinates: F-N/7-14

MICHIGAN-ERIE HIGHWAY

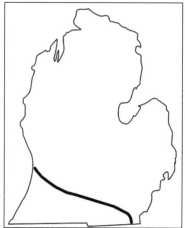

Most of the roads in Michigan run east and west or north and south following the survey lines. The exceptions are mainly those highways built along the paths of old Indian trails, the shores of the Great Lakes, and federally numbered routes. But a few state transportation arteries cut obliquely across our two peninsulas, and one of them was variously called by those along its course the Michigan-Erie Highway, the Erie Highway, or the Holland-Toledo diagonal.

Agitation for a federal east/west trunk line crossing southern Lower Michigan on an "air line" or fairly straight track began in May of 1934. The proposed highway closely followed US-223 from Toledo to Somerset, US-12 from Somerset to Moscow, back roads from Moscow to Marshall, I-94 from Marshall to Battle Creek, M-89 from Battle Creek to Allegan, and M-40 from Allegan to Holland.

Six months after this idea was floated, a support group was formed and it decided to call the desired route the Michigan-Erie Highway because it connected both of the Great Lakes bearing these names. The emphasis on freshwater also denoted a hope by the backers that the creation of such an angling thoroughfare would help draw motorists to the coastline attractions at either end of the road.

The biggest handicap facing this scheme was the lack of a first-class pavement between Moscow and Marshall. In an effort to solve this problem, the State Highway Department sought to buy the old Michigan Central railroad grade that ran between these two towns. The cost of this right-of-way proved to be too expensive, however, and so the missing transportation link in the middle of the Michigan-Erie Highway was never built.

For a time there was still some hope that the national government would step in and, under the auspices of the WPA or some other Depression-Era program, build a road through the gap in the envisioned federal highway. But the US funding cavalry never rode to the rescue of the scheme, and after a few years the shore-to-shore enterprise was abandoned.

Actually, the public's favorite whipping boys--Capitol Hill and the bureaucracy in Washington D.C.--were technically not at fault for the failure of the Michigan-Erie Highway. Responsibility for the proposed road's demise can more accurately be attributed to the beleaguered taxpayers of this state.

At the time the Michigan-Erie Highway was being considered, a nationwide formula was in place that said the length of federal roads in any state were limited to just 7% of a state's total trunk line mileage. In the middle 1930s, Michigan had its maximum allotment of federal highway mileage and was financially unable to add to the length of its state trunk line system. Thus, because of empty coffers in Lansing during the Great Depression, you can drive today from Toledo to Holland but (except for the stretch of US-223) not on the surface of a direct-route federal highway.

Coordinates: L-N/8-13

MILLER ROAD

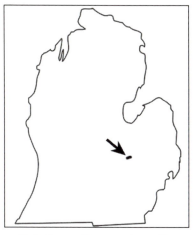

Adam Miller, born in Germany, came to America in 1795 to make a new start in life and seek his fortune in the "land of opportunity." He commenced farming in Livingston County, New York, but gradually concluded that agricultural pursuits would be more promising in the virgin territories of the western Great Lakes region.

Heeding the wanderlust that infected many other sodbusters of that time, Miller came to Michigan in June of 1836 and selected some acreage in Clayton Township, Genesee County. Having entered and paid for his claim at the Land Office, Miller went back to the Empire State, gathered up his family, and returned with them a few months later to the village of Flint. While his wife temporarily remained behind in this outpost of civilization, Miller and his three sons chopped a road from the Genesee county seat west-southwest to his new homestead.

When the access route was finished, Miller and his sons built a dwelling for themselves and, that autumn, Mrs. Miller joined her family as the first settlers in the township. The place where they lived was called "Miller Settlement" by others in the area and the path to their residence not surprisingly became "Miller's Road" or "Miller Road."

As other immigrants came to Clayton Township, some congregated around the Miller home forming a sort of hamlet. By 1843, the population of this assembly had grown to the point that the community was given a post office. The name bestowed upon this village was "Swartz [German for Black] Creek," the same as a small stream in the vicinity. Despite this change in titles, old habits apparently died hard. When, under Act

165 of 1848, the Michigan Legislature authorized the construction of a state road between Flint and Lansing, it stipulated that the public highway pass through "Miller Settlement."

This connecting link from the most southerly loop of the Flint River to the Capital of Michigan was built as authorized in the 1800s, but it was not officially brought into the state trunk line system until the summer of 1931 when it was given the designation M-78. Much of the Genesee County portion of this old highway retained this identifying label until November of 1970, not long after I-69 was finished west of Flint, and at that point Miller Road ceased to be a numbered transportation artery.

Today, Miller Road is still a path people take from downtown Flint to the west-central border of Genesee County. However, it has developed from a wagon track in the wilderness of pioneer Michigan to a vehicular conduit between an urban center and some of its neighboring "bedroom" communities along the I-69 corridor. Through this 165-year evolution, the thoroughfare has gone from being a primitive trail to a state highway and now a major service drive. During all of this time and these changes, the route has remarkably kept its original christening of Miller Road, a name apparently as hardy as those who first brought it to the region.

Coordinates: Flint Inset

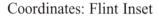

MONROE HISTORIC HERITAGE ROUTE

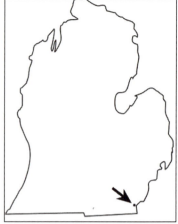

Michigan has a number of roadside buildings, objects, sites and districts that manifest our rich cultural heritage. They combine to create the distinguishing characteristics of a community or help make up the uniqueness of a place.

Members of the legislature believed these special things and qualities should be preserved, highlighted, and made accessible to the traveling public. The best way to achieve this ambition, reasoned lawmakers, was to identify these unique features and then ensure they were made known to motorists by signs, promotional literature, and symbols on the official state highway map.

A program to accomplish this goal was implemented by the passage of Public Act 69 of 1993. This law set up a means by which local governments could obtain state help in highlighting their historic resources adjacent to any route number that started with an "M", a "US", or an "I."

The terms of the statute required applicants to not only find and describe their most treasured roadside remnants of the past, but also make a commitment to restore, preserve, and maintain them according to certain high standards. In return, successful candidates for a heritage route designation would receive a prized opportunity to attract visitors, enhance the local image, and further develop pride in their community.

Learning of this new law, in November of 1993 the city of Monroe formed a committee to determine how the town could take advantage of the opportunity offered by the legislation.

The group inventoried local assets, integrated them into a coherent plan, and soon became the first city in the state to apply for a heritage route designation.

What the committee discovered in the course of its work was that Monroe was the second oldest town in the Lower Peninsula, yielding in age only to Detroit. Representing this rich past were about forty historic sites scattered along two miles of M-125 running through town. These landmarks ranged from an old statue, a bridge, and cemeteries to antique structures like churches, businesses and homes.

The conclusion was that Monroe had a lot to show for its two centuries of life, and this finding served to heighten awareness of the town's tangible traditions. Determined to highlight and save these community attractions, the committee sought the state's blessing in accomplishing this goal.

On 2 February 1996, Monroe became the

first city in Michigan to win approval for an historic heritage route. This designation was dedicated ten weeks later, and on that occasion residents of the city also celebrated the work of their ancestors by pledging to recognize and protect these rare trunk line attributes.

Coordinates: Monroe Inset

MONROE ROAD

In 1817 President James Monroe became our nation's first chief executive to visit Michigan. One of his stops in this journey to the American frontier was at a community called Frenchtown, the third permanent settlement in our state and the site of its second post office (after De-troit). The citizens of this village were so honored by the presence of this dignitary that they elected to name the place after him, a decision which gave rise to the city we know today as "Monroe."

Fifth President of the United States, James Monroe was born in Westmoreland County, Virginia, on 28 April 1758. At the young age of 18, in 1776, he was commissioned a lieutenant in a Virginia regiment of the Continental line. Rising to the rank of major, Monroe was wounded in action at Trenton and he subsequently resigned from the Army in 1778.

After studying law under Thomas Jefferson, Monroe began a long public career in 1782 by successfully running for a seat in the Virginia Assembly. Following this political achievement, he served as one of Virginia's representatives to the Confederation Congress (1783-1786). Then, during the years 1787-1788, he returned to the Virginia House of Delegates before accepting his state's appointment to the U.S. Senate in 1790. Monroe left our nation's highest deliberative body during 1794-1796 to become minister to France, and then returned to America to serve as governor of Virginia from 1799 to 1802.

In 1803, Monroe began a five-year stint with Uncle Sam's diplomatic service, the highlight of which was helping to negotiate the sale of the extensive Louisiana Territory from France for just $15,000,000. By 1810 he was back serving in the Virginia legislature, advancing to that state's governor's office the following year. Monroe's talents, however, were too valuable to confine to the local level, so he was soon brought into the federal government as Secretary of State (1811-1817) and, concurrently, Secretary of War (1814-1815).

All of this political experience made Monroe a well-known states-

man, a fact which helped him win the presidential elections of 1816 and 1820. So successful was he at running the country that his administration has popularly been called "the era of good feeling." After completing his second term in 1825, Monroe retired from public office, serving only as Regent of the University of Virginia. This man who had helped give birth to a nation died in New York City on July 4, 1831.

Many historians believe that Monroe's greatest accomplishments as president were in the field of foreign affairs. His highlights in this field were limiting naval forces on the Great Lakes (Rush-Bagot Agreement of 1817), establishing the 49th parallel of latitude as the boundary between the U.S. and Canada from Lake of the Woods (Minnesota) west to the Rocky Mountains (1818), acquiring Florida from Spain for $5,000,000 (1819), and establishing the famous Monroe Doctrine which declared the Western Hemisphere closed to future European colonization (1823).

When, in April of 1942, the leaders of Gratiot County decided to name their east/west roads in honor of America's former presidents, they sequentially listed our nation's highest officials from top to bottom within their political boundaries. As luck would have it, in the order of succession the name of James Monroe fell upon route M-46, giving him a place in the inventory of Michigan's memorial highways.

Coordinates: J/10-11

MOSES J. JONES PARKWAY

There may be just one memorial highway in Michigan that was ever established on paper prior to its actual creation. This exception to the rule is called the Moses J. Jones Parkway, and it is located in Muskegon.

The road is named after Moses Jacob Jones, who was born in Montgomery County, Alabama, around 1898. Drawn to religion as an adult, Jones preached at churches in or near Pittsburgh, Grand Rapids, and Hammond, Indiana.

In 1936, Jones came to Michigan as pastor of the John Wesley AME Zion Church. His serv-

ice to this congregation continued for 36 years, until his retirement from the pulpit in 1972 as dean of local clergy.

During the time Reverend Jones practiced his craft, he helped to found

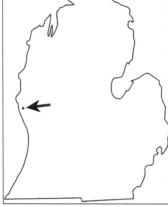

the Muskegon Urban League, established the annual city-wide biracial Goodwill Dinner, and did mission work in more than 100 countries.

Reverend Jones had given much to his community. As he neared the end of his life in 1989, the citizens of Muskegon sought some way of expressing their appreciation for all that the popular minister had done.

The initial proposal was to rename after him the street upon which Reverend Jones lived. While local residents had no objection to honoring their distinguished neighbor, they did balk at a change in their address.

So, new ideas were presented on how to recognize "a legendary figure in Muskegon's history." Some of the suggestions included renaming other streets, a senior citizen center, a community building, or even city hall after Reverend Jones.

While these options were being debated, Moses J. Jones died at his home on 20 May 1989. Just three days after his death, the Muskegon City Commission voted to simultaneously

name and dedicate a northern stretch of Seaway Drive from Spring Street to Getty Street in his honor.

The city officials did not want this gesture to look like a sudden response to Jones' death, since the they had been studying a tribute to him for nearly five months. Therefore, the Commission agreed to make its decision retroactive to 1 May 1989 so future observers would not interpret "his passing as a part of the justification" for the city's action.

The street renamed in Jones' memory was also known as Business Route US-31, a highway over which the State of Michigan had some jurisdiction. So the legality of his tribute would never be questioned, in November of 1989 the Legislature passed House Concurrent Resolution 425 officially establishing the Moses J. Jones Parkway.

Coordinates: Muskegon Inset

MUSKEGON COUNTY MEMORIAL CAUSEWAY

Shortly after the end of World War I, the town of Muskegon erected a temporary memorial arch in tribute to its citizens who answered their country's call to arms. The structure was mainly a symbol of a city's thanks and welcome, with a more permanent monument to come later when time and money allowed.

In 1925, the community decided that its enduring shrine to "all ex-service men and women" would be a beautiful park built between the two arms of a proposed dual highway connecting Muskegon and North Muskegon. The interior of the planned boulevard would be landscaped in such a way that its appearance would pay honor to those who wore this nation's military uniforms.

The two parallel drives were to be created by building a causeway at the head of Muskegon Lake. Since some major water channels flowed through this area of lowlands and marshes, fixed bridges would be constructed to carry traffic across the principal streams that formed the flats in the Muskegon River delta.

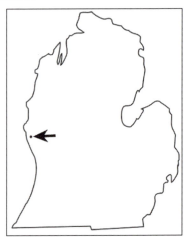

Because some of these channels were technically navigable waterways, the federal government would not allow any bridges to impede travel on them until thorough analyses had been conducted. Consequently, even though the Muskegon County Board of Commissioners approved the road in 1926 and the accompanying memorial park in 1927, it was not until a few years later that the U.S. Corps of Army Corps of Engineers finished evaluating the impact of the project on shipping.

Once specialists determined that fixed spans would not pose a threat to navigation, work on the causeway began. The eastern double-drive was finished first in the summer of 1931 and the western two-lane segment reached completion one year later.

With the twin roads across the swamplands in place, it was time to turn attention to developing the intervening space into a memorial park. Local residents on relief were recruited as laborers for the job when it won designation as a federal WPA project.

The area between the two branches of the causeway totaled around 50 acres. About a third of this nearly 300-foot-wide tract was left as water in the form of lagoons, reflecting pools, and a fountain illuminated with colored lights. The remaining portion was carefully landscaped with trees, evergreens, shrubs, and flowers. In recognition of sacrifices made in defense of liberty, a limestone shaft was added bearing two bronze plaques listing the names of 104 Muskegon-area youths who lost their lives in World War I.

Thus, a former tract of marsh covered with reeds and rubbish and once derisively called Muskegon's muskrat farm was transformed into a west-shore landmark known as "Michigan's most beautiful mile." Through cooperative action, members of a community created a monument to their dead and an inspiration to the living.

On 11 November 1934--the sixteenth anniversary of the armistice

signing that ended World War I--10,000 spectators assembled at the site to dedicate the Muskegon County causeway and memorial park. Today, many years later, people driving M-120 can still visit and enjoy this special public place that continues to serve the multiple purposes for which it was created.

But those who come to the elevated road that crosses the waters near the mouth of the Muskgon River will find one thing different about the drive: it now has a slightly different name. The Michigan Legislature, speaking through Public Act 142 of 2001, declared that "highway M-120 in Muskegon County beginning at the intersection of highway M-120, Lake Avenue and Whitehall Road, and extending south for one mile shall be known as the 'Veteran's Memorial Causeway'."

While it is not the purpose of this study to include memorial bridges, this section would be incomplete without reference to the fact that the Michigan Legislature, by virtue of Public Act 256 of 1998, designated the two bridges over Cedar Creek within the connecting causeway the Veterans Memorial Bridges.

Coordinates: Muskegon Inset

94th COMBAT INFANTRY DIVISION MEMORIAL HIGHWAY

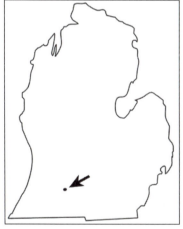

The 94th Combat Infantry Division was activated at Fort Custer near Battle Creek, Michigan, on 15 September 1942. After months of training at various other camps around the United States, the outfit left New York City harbor for the European theater on 6 August 1944.

Eventually landing in France one month later, the 94th Division became a part of General George S. Patton's Third Army. For 209 days the infantry unit remained engaged against Nazi troops, suffering in the process a casualty rate of 74% (4,789 soldiers wounded and 1,156 killed in action).

The 94th Division fought its way into Germany on 8 January 1945, and by the end of hostilities it had captured hundreds of miles of territory and 26,638 of the enemy. After the Fascists had surrendered, the Division assumed occupation duties for six months around Dusseldorf and in Czechoslovakia in support of temporary military governments.

Because of its outstanding performance in World War II, by the end of 2001 five states had designated parts of their transportation systems in honor of the 94th Infantry Division (Colorado, Connecticut, New Jersey, New York, and Pennsylvania). Since the unit had been organized at Battle Creek--and since the interstate highway passing through that town bore the same number as the Division--it seemed only fitting that Michigan also name a portion of its freeway network in tribute to the men of the 94th.

Acting upon this logic, the Michigan Legislature passed Public Act 305 of 2002 which made I-94 from exit 92 east to trunk line M-66 the "94th Combat Infantry Division Memorial High-way." This expression of appreciation to the freedom fighters of that outfit was dedicated with appropriate roadside ceremonies on 28 September 2002. About a hundred people gathered at the rest stop along the designated six-mile stretch of expressway to pay homage to the veterans of this unit and their distinguished record in the European Theater from 1942 to 1946.

Coordinates: Battle Creek Inset.

OHIO-INDIANA-MICHIGAN WAY

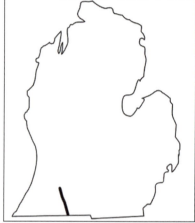

Near the end of World War I, a named route was established running south out of Kalamazoo to the Michigan border and beyond. This designated motorway passed through Vicksburg, Mendon, Nottawa, and Sturgis before heading on down to its terminus at Richmond, Indiana. Though the transportation network of that era perceived this course as a main thoroughfare for vehicles, today most of this route in the Wolverine State is comprised of secondary roads rather than numbered arteries.

The O.I.M. Way, as it was popularly known by name and signage, was born in August of 1918 when John Garrett Brink--an employee of the famous Chicago map-making firm of Rand McNally & Company--laid out and marked the highway as part of the concern's "Blazed Trails" program. Under this enterprise, which lasted from 1908 to 1926, Rand McNally helped to plan and identify local and regional routes across the country for the benefit of the traveling public. These roads were then included on the maps published by Rand McNally for mo-torists, making them the most up-to-date cartographic sources for drivers to follow.

Unfortunately, the Lower Peninsula portion of the O.I.M. Way was poorly chosen, as relatively few vehicles followed its path and state officials never saw fit to favor it with trunk line status. Consequently, the named highway had a brief life span and within just a few years evidence of its existence permanently disappeared from the literature used by travelers. Hardly anyone today has heard of the Ohio-Indiana-Michigan Way, but its short story will at least be preserved for years to come between the covers of this book.

Coordinates: M-N/9

OLDS FREEWAY

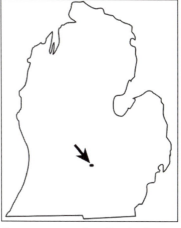

In September of 1966, not long after it was decided to build I-496 through Lansing, the City Council unanimously voted to name the new road after Ralph W. Crego. This man had served as a council member for 8 years and then as mayor of the town for nearly 18 years, longer than any person in Lansing history.

The Historical Society of Greater Lansing disagreed with this decision, proposing instead the "R.E. Olds Expressway." The Society said this name would be more appropriate because the freeway will "engulf the R.E. Olds property" which is in the right-of-way, and it will be a good way of "recognizing the contributions of R.E. Olds to the industries of the city."

Since the Council had already acted on its choice, the Historical Society needed to find some other means of accomplishing its goal. The alternative approach appeared in February of 1970 as House Resolution 48 in the Michigan legislature.

This measure was created for the purpose of designating I-496 the "R.E. Olds Expressway." Realizing the resolution would pass, and realizing they had been out maneuvered, the Lansing City Council began to take remedial action.

First, the Council conveniently discovered that its act to name I-496 for Crego had not been "formally adopted." This left the members free to name a city park for Crego, instead.

Then, in October of 1970, the Council unanimously decided to designate I-496 the "Oldsmobile Expressway." At about the same time, the state legislature approved House Resolution 48 making I-496 the "R.E. Olds Expressway." Now the road had two official names, one for a vehicle and one for a person.

When the City Council found out about this embarrassing situation, it was miffed. The state representative who sponsored the competing language at the Capitol was "sharply criticized" by the Council members "for introducing the R.E. Olds resolution without first consulting" them.

The conflict was resolved when the legislator intercepted the approved resolution before it could be sent to the State Highway Department for action. Thus, when I-496 was opened and dedicated on 18 December 1970, it was christened the "Oldsmobile Expressway."

This moniker troubled some, for it honored just the car and not also the man. The chance to take remedial action for this oversight came in 1972, when Oldsmobile celebrated its 75th anniversary.

In recognition of this special occasion, Senate Concurrent Resolution 345 was introduced in the legislature for the purpose of changing the name of Lansing's cross-town artery to something that was broader in scope. This more comprehensive language was quickly approved, and on 21 August 1972 new signs went up declaring I-496 within Lansing's city boundaries to be the "Olds Freeway."

Coordinates: Lansing Inset

107th ENGINEERS MEMORIAL ROAD

Asubstantial number of Michigan's dedicated highways relate to servicemen and women in some way. A good example in the Upper Peninsula is short highway M-107, established in 1935 as an access route to the Porcupine Mountains in Ontonagon County. These picturesque heights are said to be the highest lands "between the Black Hills and the Adirondacks."

This scenic road runs from Silver City west to the Porcupine Mountains Wilderness State Park and its beautiful Lake of the Clouds. The trunk line was chosen to honor the 107th Engineer Combat Battalion because the two entities share the same number in their titles and the military unit originated in 1881 at nearby Calumet.

Comprised of companies from Escanaba, Manistique, Marquette, Calumet and Ishpeming, the 107th Engineers saw combat in the Spanish-American War, World War I, and World War II. While on active duty, the 107th Engineers earned 13 battle streamers to carry on their unit's colors.

On account of the feats that merited these decorations, Highway Commissioner Charles M. Ziegler decided to designate a state road in the battalion's honor. This mission

was accomplished on 13 June 1954 when approximately 1,200 people convened at a lakeside turnout about midway along the route of M-107. There, at a special ceremony, the highway was dedicated to one of the longest serving military organizations in all of northern Michigan.

To commemorate the occasion, a three-ton boulder was selected from the Norwich Mine location and taken to the roadside parking area about four miles west of Silver City. The massive rock was placed on a concrete base and a suitably inscribed bronze plaque attached as a permanent monument to the 107th and its memorial highway.

The stone and metal marker still stands today in a beautiful setting near Lake Superior. It is a testimonial of thanks from a grateful public to those who gave up their yesterdays that we may enjoy the fruits of freedom today and tomorrow.

Also still standing is the road sign designating route M-107 as a trail of tribute. This notification to the public now carries greater authority, though, because in 2001 the Michigan Legislature weighed in and professed via Act 142 the state's recognition of the 107th Engineers by officially naming a picturesque drive in their honor.

Coordinates B/2

117th QUARTERMASTER BATTALION HIGHWAY

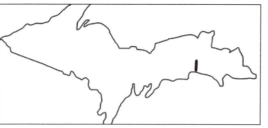

The 117th Quartermaster Battalion of the Michigan Army National Guard was activated on 1 March 1987. Headquartered in Kingsford near Iron Mountain in Dickinson County, it also had companies in Munising, Marquette, and Manistique.

This was a petroleum supply and transportation unit whose mission was to provide fuel to various elements of the corps to which it was as-

signed. The petroleum, oil and lubricants--along with direct maintenance support--was to be provided to front line combat units.

Though the 117th performed its duties well and was one of the top outfits in the Upper Peninsula, the Pentagon decided to deactivate the unit on 31 August 1992. The Battalion was reorganized as the 225th Quartermaster Battalion and reassigned to Detroit.

The ranking officer in the disbanded Battalion, Colonel James Jajich, felt his former troop should be recognized in some way for the outstanding job it had done during its unfortunately brief five-year existence. The best way to honor its memory, he felt, was to designate trunk line M-117 in Luce and Mackinac counties on behalf of the defunct military organization he once led.

M-117 was established along its present alignment in 1949 as a connector between highways US-2 and M-28. Noting that the route number of this linking pavement was the same as that of his decommissioned unit, the Colonel asked the Legislature to name the road after his former command.

This request was translated into House Resolution 148 of 1993. When

the final version of this measure was finally approved on May 26 of that year, it did not order the naming of trunk line M-117 for the 117th Quartermaster Battalion but simply urged to Department of Transportation of do so.

When given the option of whether or not to undertake this kind of action, MDOT generally does not fabricate and erect the appropriate signs unless it is fully compensated for the work in advance by private funds. Since Colonel Jajich was unable to come up with the approximately $1,500 necessary to pay for making and placing the signs, his goal of having a highway recognize the force he once controlled remains just a dream.

Coordinates C-D/9

126th INFANTRY MEMORIAL BOULEVARD

On 12 July 1855 a small band of Grand Rapids men joined together to form a military body called the Grand Rapids Light Guard. This local military unit remained largely ceremonial in nature until the Civil War, when it became activated as a component of the 3rd Michigan Infantry Regiment.

After the War Between the States, the Grand Rapids volunteers returned to peacetime duty as civilian soldiers. They were not called upon again to service until 1898, when they were brought into the Spanish-American War as part of the 32nd Michigan Infantry Regiment.

When service in Cuba was over, this Grand Rapids militia group assumed its regular activities as an on-call national guard unit. The citizens comprising this outfit remained in a stand-down mode until 1915, when they were mobilized to fight "Pancho" Villa in what became known as the Mexican Border Campaign.

Scarcely had this action been completed when the men were ordered to take up arms in World War I as part of the 126th U.S. Infantry Regiment, 32nd Division. As one of the first American units to reach the European theater of operations, it distinguished itself fighting the

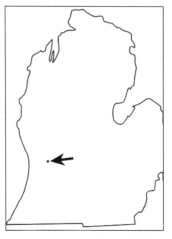

Germans during 1917-1918.

The last period of active duty for the Grand Rapids contingent was during World War II. It was part of the first ground force to engage Japan, and by war's end it had "served the most combat time ever by a United States Army regiment (654 days)."

With victory in the South Pacific, the men of the Grand Rapids regiment returned home to what has now become 52 years of demobilization. This peace was bought at a high price, however, for during its history the unit has "incurred well over 1,000 causalities."

In 1965, the headquarters of the 126th Infantry Regiment was moved from its home town of Grand Rapids. The association was relocated to the Grand Valley Armory on 44th Street in nearby Wyoming, Michigan.

After living at its new address for 25 years, the organization thought its host city might be interested in recognizing the "deeds and sacrifices of many generations of armed volunteers from West Michigan." To see if such was the case, the unit asked the Wyoming City Council to designate 44th Street as the "126th Infantry Memorial Boulevard."

After briefly deliberating the matter, the Council members agreed to bestow this honorary title upon the 3.5-mile stretch of 44th Street that falls within the city limits. Soon thereafter four signs along the route bearing the 126th regimental crest were erected as testimonials to this resolution, and on 12 July 1991 the commemorative gesture was dedicated.

Coordinates: Grand Rapids Inset Map

OSCAR G. JOHNSON MEMORIAL HIGHWAY

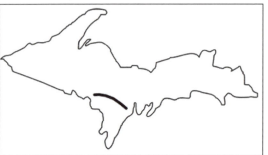

During World War II, the Congressional Medal of Honor was bestowed upon 463 American soldiers. One of these recipients was Oscar Godfrey Johnson, ostensibly the only Upper Peninsula resident ever to earn our country's highest award for exceptional bravery beyond the call of duty in combat.

Born 25 March 1921 in Foster City, Michigan, as a young man Johnson left the Upper Peninsula to join the U.S. Army, eventually serving in Europe with Company B of the 363d Infantry, 91st Infantry Division. While on active duty with his unit during the Second World War, Johnson performed his heroic acts on September 16-18, 1944, in the fight for Monticelli Ridge in the Apennines Mountains near Scarperia, Italy.

Johnson's unit--during an autumn campaign in Florence Province--came under attack from five companies of a German paratrooper regiment. As the battle between the Axis and Allied forces raged over the rugged terrain, Company B lost 168 of its 205 members.

Private Johnson's post in this conflict was along the left flank, where the action was so furious that he soon became the last man in his squad not killed or wounded. As the lone defender of his position, Johnson repelled six enemy attacks while

killing 20 Nazi soldiers, capturing 25 others, and rescuing two American servicemen during a two-day siege. Understandably, this performance qualified Johnson for America's premier military honor.

Following the War, Johnson returned to help his father on the family dairy farm near Foster City. Later, he went south and found work close to Lansing where for 30 years he served in the National Guard as foreman of a vehicle maintenance shop. After his retirement in 1980, he relocated to Kingsford in the Upper Peninsula where he lived as a celebrated citizen until his death in Dickinson County on 13 May 1998.

Because of his nativity in, and his long connection with, the central Northern Peninsula, many residents of that region wanted to recognize their local hero in some fashion after his passing. The method deemed most appropriate was a memorial highway, so Michigan lawmakers passed Public Act 2 of 2002 declaring route M-69 from about Randville east to its termination at US-2 as a trunk line in memory of one of our state's most gallant soldiers. This legislative tribute was dedicated on 6 July 2002 with concurrent ceremonies at both ends of route M-69.

Coordinates: D/5-6

PAN AMERICAN HIGHWAY

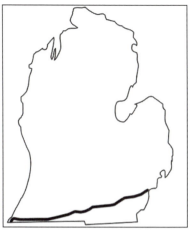

The Pan American Highway is a name familiar around the world as one of mankind's greatest engineering feats. This nearly 30,000-mile system of roads extends from the US/Mexican border south to the tip of Chile.

There is no individual road that can be identified as the Pan American Highway. The original concept has expanded and alternate routes have been added so that today it is a network of motorways linking nearly all of the nations in the Western Hemisphere.

Along its most notherly reaches, the Pan American Highway has four US terminals. One of these gateways is at Nogales, Arizona, while the other portals are located in the Texas towns of Eagle Pass, El Paso, and Laredo.

While all of this is well and good, readers may reasonably wonder what a Latin American trunk line has to do with the highways of Michigan. To answer this question it is necessary to briefly go back in history to the time when the great Pan American route was conceived.

The Pan American Highway was first seriously proposed in 1923 at the Fifth International Conference of American States. At this meeting it was suggested that a conference be held to study the feasibility of constructing a highway through the Americas. This resulted in the First Pan American Highway Congress, held in 1925.

Not surprisingly, the members of this body decided that a highway connecting the countries of the New World was desirable and possible. Responding to this news, in January of 1927 Wayne County representative Clarence J. McLeod introduced House Bill 15669 in Congress for establishing a commission to promote the Pan American Highway and formally fix its route.

The Michigan politician and a consulting engineer both recommended that the US portion of the inter-American road go from Detroit west along contemporary US-12 to New Buffalo and then on to Laredo, Texas. Though McLeod's bill did not become law, in 1928 he introduced and got passed Congressional House Joint Resolution 259 which authorized government assistance in building a highway "which will reach from Detroit, Mich., to the Mexican border and on to the capitals of the 17 Republics of Central and South America" (Canada, not being a "Republic," was initially excluded from the scope of the Pan American enterprise).

Just as it looked like Detroit would be the northern terminus for this country's segment of the Pan American Highway, Congress decided in 1929 that no single US thoroughfare would receive this name. To bestow this designation upon one route would upset too many competing interests, so it was decided that all roads in our national transportation network would be part of the Pan American system.

This decision was supported by the American Association of State Highway Officials, which advocated identifying roads by number rather than by name. In keeping with this position, the organization agreed that "no one route [in the US] be selected...as the Pan American Highway."

Detroit did not take well to loosing a chance to be the threshold for an important international artery. As late as 1935 local newspapers were still proclaiming that the town was on the Pan American route. But reality eventually set in, and today the Motor City is more interested in manufacturing cars for people to drive on the Pan American Highway than it is in being just another mile-marker along that road.

Coordinates: M/13

PARADISE TRAIL

Route M-37 runs 219 miles from Battle Creek up to the tip of the Old Mission Peninsula. In is southern extent, it was one of the earliest trunk lines created by the Highway Department, making its debut in 1913. Within a few years the road had been extended from the Cereal City as far north as Newaygo County, but then the rate of development slowed down considerably.

By 1927, the northward progress of M-37 had stalled out around the middle of Lake County. In an effort to get things moving again, a meeting was held in Baldwin on 28 November 1927. There an organization called the Grand Rapids-Leelanau Association resolved to actively promote finishing the highway as a direct route from the populous south to the waters of Grand Traverse Bay.

In an effort to bring attention to the road as a course of travel and an object of state funding, the Association named the highway the "Paradise Trail." While the group did not indicate where Paradise began and ended, the heavenly reference was to the divine scenic and recreational delights that awaited any wayfarer covering the distance between the Furniture City and the Traverse City region.

Realizing that the success of their project would be dependent upon more than just hype, the Association members touted the highway as a relief route to the flanking congested thoroughfares US-31 and US-131. They also helped their cause by convincing a number of

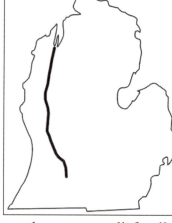

people to donate their land to the state as right-of-way for the proposed road.

Slowly this campaign began to produce results, and by 1930 the adopted highway was advancing north from Baldwin with help from crews of men on the county relief rolls working for their public assistance. The Association convinced the state to designate the last section of M-37 in 1933, but the trunk line was not finally completed until twenty years later.

By then, the original name of the road had been forgotten in favor of a less romantic but highly effective route number. In reality, though, passing off the highway as the path to Paradise was a difficult sell. With place names along the way like Dead Creek, Hardscrabble, Hodenpyle Backwater, Mesick, Slagle Creek and Wagonwheel, it was hard to convince people they were on their way to the promised land.

In response, those who created the idea of "Paradise Trail" would say they were not guilty of false advertising. For about midway between the two ends of the named road, about ten miles east of Baldwin, is the settlement of Nirvana. So long as that town exists, M-37 will indeed be a trail to Paradise in fact if not in title.

Coordinates: G-M/8-9

PAUL B. HENRY FREEWAY

As Michigan's transportation network developed, nearly all roads were of a point-to-point nature, connecting one settlement with another. These avenues of movement almost always passed through the centers of towns, which were often the destinations of travelers.

With the invention and subsequent mass production of the automobile, more and more vehicles crowded onto municipal streets creating massive congestion. This was the situation in downtown Grand Rapids, which by the mid-1920s was swarming with trucks and cars either entering and leaving the city on business or passing through along major urban arteries.

In an attempt to resolve this problem, in 1928 the State Highway Department agreed to build a 40-mile beltline completely around Grand Rapids. The southern segment of this bypass went from Cascade on the east to Grandville on the west and is today known as part of highway M-11 (28th Street). Construction on this enterprise was commenced almost immediately, and by 1934 most of the encircling ring was finished (the northern portion was never built).

This circumference highway served to adequately accommodate local traffic until the 1980s, when growth in the area--particularly south of Grand Rapids--made it clear that a bypass of the original beltline was necessary. One of the individuals who strongly supported this idea, and who worked to get federal funding for a study of the proposed project, was Paul Brentwood Henry.

Born in Chicago 9 July 1942, Paul Henry soon left the Midwest and was educated at Pasadena (CA) High School, Wheaton College, and Duke University. After earning a doctorate in political science at the latter institution, in 1970 Henry took up residence in Grand Rapids as a professor at Calvin College.

Quickly making his mark in southwestern Michigan, Henry accepted an appointment to the State Board of Education from 1975-1978, was elected to the state House of Representatives from 1979-1982, and served in the state Senate during the 1983-1984 session. In 1985 he won the contest to represent the people of Kent and Ottawa counties in the United States Congress.

Henry performed well as a public servant, winning reelections by record margins of up to 75% of the vote. But the career of this popular politician was prematurely ended on 31 July 1993 when he died at the age of 51 after an unsuccessful nine-month battle with brain cancer.

The affection for this talented man was national in scope, with well over a thousand people attending his last rites in Grand Rapids. Sixty members of Congress with their staffs flew in from Washington to attend the televised memorial service, a number so great it took three large passenger planes to accommodate them.

While the great turnout at Henry's funeral showed respect for a beloved public figure, the community sought to offer some more enduring form of recognition. An opportunity to realize this ambition occurred when construction started late in 1997 on the long-awaited interstate-type bypass south of Grand Rapids.

With Henry's early support of the highway in mind, the Michigan legislature passed Public Act 399 of 1998 designating the new $420 million road the Paul B. Henry Freeway. Thus, when completed in the year 2005, the twenty-mile route connecting I-96 on the east with I-196 on the west will serve as a tribute to one of the area's most respected politicians.

Coordinates: L/9

PEARL HARBOR MEMORIAL HIGHWAY

Pearl Harbor--named for the pearl oysters that once grew there--is an inlet on the southern coast of the island of Oahu, Hawaii. Six miles west of Honolulu, this natural marine shelter has ten square miles of navigable water, a fairly uniform depth of from 50 to 60 feet, and hundreds of good anchorages.

The harbor was first leased by the United States under a treaty signed in 1887. Not until 1908, however, was it actually used as a naval station. Over time it became a first class military base, eventually serving as headquarters for the entire U.S. Pacific fleet.

Though a hub of maritime activity, Pearl Harbor was unknown to most Americans until the morning of 7 December 1941, when Japan launched a surprise aerial assault upon the base. This attack sunk or severely damaged 19 of our fighting ships, eliminated more than 170 of our aircraft, and caused over 3,000 casualties. The destruction of the battleship Arizona, along with over a thousand of its crew members, was reportedly the greatest loss of lives on a single ship in U.S. Navy history.

This unprovoked aggression temporarily crippled America's Pacific fleet and marked the entry of our nation into World War II, a conflict which raged on for nearly four years after this incident. During the ensuing hostilities, "Remember Pearl Harbor!" became the rallying cry for Uncle Sam's sailors and soldiers as they sought to avenge what then-President Roosevelt characterized as "a day that shall live in infamy."

In 1958, some of the servicemen who had personally witnessed the Japanese attack on Hawaii formed the Pearl Harbor Survivors Association. In addition to encouraging the fraternization of these veterans, the organization sought to commemorate this momentous historical event and honor "the thousands of U.S. citizens who died or were wounded in that attack."

In keeping with the part of its mission that involved paying tribute, late in the year 2000--as the 59th anniversary of the Pearl Harbor raid approached--members of this group asked that a thirty-mile stretch of I-69 in Shiawassee and Genesee counties be named the "Pearl Harbor Memorial Highway." To accommodate this wish, the Michigan Legislature quickly passed House Bill 6139 making this designation official.

Unfortunately, the measure failed to receive the governor's signature before year's end, and so the attempted recognition never became law because of a pocket veto. Not to be deterred, the Legislature tried again in its next session and this time succeeded in passing the desired commendation in the form of Public Act 56 of 2001. This accomplishment was dedicated at the Swartz Creek rest stop along I-69 on 17 December 2001.

Coordinates:K-L/11-12

PERE MARQUETTE MEMORIAL HIGHWAY

Michigan has a Marquette city, township, county, mountain, and island. It also has a Pere (Father) Marquette river, lake, state forest, former railroad, and national memorial at St. Ignace.

Clearly, someone named Marquette played a significant role in our state's past. Since few people today know much about this person whose memory dots our landscape, a brief biographical sketch is in order.

Jacques Marquette, though a Michigan adopted son, was born in Laon, France, on 1 June 1637. He entered the religious order Society of Jesus at age 17 and was ordained a priest in 1666.

In September of that same year he arrived at Quebec to begin training as a missionary. For two years he studied Native American ways and languages in preparation for his service to the Indians.

In 1668 Marquette began work among the Ottawa Indians at Sault Sainte Marie, in essence founding the settlement. Three years later he established another mission at St. Ignace, giving that community a beginning date of 1671.

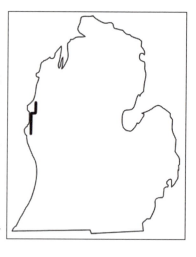

In December of 1672, Louis Joliet arrived at St. Ignace with instructions for Marquette to join him in exploring the yet unseen Mississippi River. Six months later the men with five companions set out in two canoes with the goal of traveling the great river to its source.

As the first white men to visit the upper Mississippi drainage basin, they took notes on the character of the region, described its people, and laid claim to all the land and water they discovered in the name of Louis XIV, King of France.

Marquette and his companions did not go all the way to the Gulf of Mexico. When they reached southern Arkansas, Indians told them about other Europeans downstream. Fearing capture by the Spaniards, the adventurous group turned back north.

On the homeward leg of the expedition, Marquette may have promised some Illinois Indians that he would return and instruct them in the Catholic faith. To keep this apparent commitment, in 1674 he left what is now Wisconsin for the contemporary town of LaSalle.

Marquette and his two assistants got a late start on their journey to the Illinois River. Caught by the advanced season, they were forced to overwinter at the present site of Chicago, becoming the first white men to live there.

In the Spring of 1675, Marquette finally reached the Illinois Indians. Dysentery had so debilitated him, however, that after just three weeks with the natives he decided to return to

his mission at Sault Sainte Marie.

Canoeing along the east shore of Lake Michigan, Marquette and his attendants were able to get as far as present-day Ludington before his deteriorating health forced the party to land. There the cleric died and was buried on 18 May 1675. A few years later his remains were recovered by the Indians and placed in the chapel at St. Ignace.

In recognition of Father Marquette's many accomplishments, his service to humanity and his connections to Michigan, in 1954 the state legislature passed Public Act 93 declaring route US-31 in Mason and Oceana counties to be the Pere Marquette Memorial Highway (updated by PA 142 of 2001).

On 18 May 1954, a number of people gathered at the Kibbey Creek roadside park south of Ludington for the dedication of the Pere Marquette Memorial Highway. Though the former trunk line has now been replaced by a modern US-31 freeway, at least in Mason County part of the old route is still known as Pere Marquette Road.

Coordinates: I-J/7-8

PHILIP A. HART
MEMORIAL HIGHWAY

Philip Aloysius Hart was one of Michigan's more outstanding contributions to national politics. Serving in the United States Congress from 1959 thru 1976, this highly respected gentleman was often referred to as "the conscience of the Senate."

During his tenure in our Nation's Capitol, Hart was instrumental in writing and passing civil rights, antitrust, and consumer protection legislation. So impressive was his mark upon the upper chamber that his colleagues named one-third of the Senate office building in his honor.

Back home, Hart was also known and appreciated for his work in creating two national lakeshores: Pictured Rocks (1966) and Sleeping Bear Dunes (1970). Elsewhere on the local scene, he was a director of the Detroit Baseball Compa-

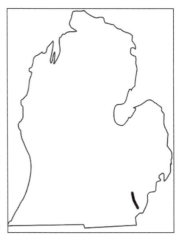

ny (owners of the Tigers) and the Detroit Football Company (owners of the Lions) during the period from about 1947 to 1957.

Born at Bryn Mawr, Pennsylvania, on 10 December 1912, Hart received his preliminary education at parochial schools in Philadelphia. Later he received a bachelor's degree from Georgetown University before graduating from the law school at the University of Michigan in 1937.

After being admitted to the bar, Hart practiced law with a Detroit firm until World War II began in 1941. He joined the Army at that time as a 2nd Lieutenant and in a few years rose to the rank of Lieutenant Colonel in the 4th Infantry Division.

Hart was wounded at Utah Beach, Normandy, on D-Day, 6 June 1944. He rejoined his unit in December of 1944 just in time to fight at the Battle of the Bulge. Hart was discharged from the service in 1946 with the Croix de Guerre (France), Bronze Star, and Purple Heart.

After the War, Hart returned to Detroit where he resumed practicing law from 1946 to 1950. In 1949 he was appointed a Michigan Corporations and Securities Commissioner, a post he held until 1951.

Liking the taste of public service, Hart went on to be director of the Michigan Office of Price Stabilization (1951-1952), a federal attorney (1952-1953), legal advisor to Governor G.

Mennen Williams (1953-1954), and Lieutenant Governor of Michigan (1955-1958). In 1958 Hart was elected to the United States Senate, a seat he continued to hold until his death on 26 December 1976.

Not long after his passing, members of the Michigan legislature sought to honor Hart's memory with some kind of appropriate gesture. The method they chose was to assign his name to a major trunk line road near his political base in the southeastern part of the state.

Accordingly, Senate Concurrent Resolution 307 of 1977 was passed by the lawmakers in Lansing declaring I-275 from Monroe north to route I-96 the Philip A. Hart Memorial Highway. There is no evidence that a dedication ceremony was ever held to commemorate this event.

Coordinates: M-N/13

PIONEER TRAIL

A large proportion of the early settlers destined for Michigan arrived through the gateway at Detroit. Once they had equipped themselves for a journey to the interior, many of these newcomers proceeded directly west along what was then variously called the Saint Joseph Road or the Territorial Road and referred to today as I-94.

This avenue of access, opened as far as Jackson by 1830, was initially little more than a name and some blaze marks on adjacent trees. In fact, the few vanguard travelers along the highway claimed that the wagon tracks of pioneers were about the only improvements that had been made to the route.

But by 1831 the condition of this former Indian trail was more favorable, and thousands of pioneers began teeming along its way enroute to homesteads on the fringe of civilization. In that year the amount of travel over the road was said to be "enormous," and about 100,000 acres of land were purchased by settlers in the region penetrated by the highway.

By 1832 even more humanity was flooding in along the recently opened road as, people de-

clared with some possible exaggeration, "covered wagons literally whitened its entire length." Patronage was so heavy at the relatively few inns and taverns serving the route that, according to some 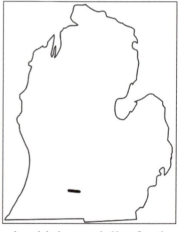 wags, "travelers offered as high as a dollar for the privilege of leaning against a post."

As bad as this congestion was, it probably worsened in 1834 when the first stage coach line began carrying passengers along the route from Detroit west to the contemporary town of St. Joseph. In the same year a steamboat was put into service ferrying people from St. Joseph on to Chicago.

This great influx and passage of pioneers stayed highly active until 1838, when a severe national economic depression temporarily reduced the rate of immigration. Movement, though decreased, continued along this artery of adventure until a paralleling railroad was finished in 1849, and thereafter the significance of the cross-state route remained diminished until the advent of the automobile.

By the turn of the twentieth century, few people remembered the important role the old Territorial Road played in populating Michigan. To remind citizens how significant the route was to the formation of our state, just before World War I every county along its course except Wayne erected historical monuments in its honor.

The citizens of one county went even further. Under the auspices of the Calhoun County Historical Society, in 1922 the stretch of highway between Albion and Battle Creek was named the Pioneer Trail. Since the road by then was a state trunk line, this desig-

nation was reportedly approved by the Highway Commissioner.

Today, it is still possible to ride along many parts of the old Territorial Road by following Michigan Avenue. One can drive on the now-paved former Indian trail, rolling smoothly over a surface that makes it difficult to imagine the ruts, bumps and mud that hampered travelers of yore. While motoring on these quiet stretches of mainly rural highway, one gets a sense of slipping back to a time when life was not geared so high. By leaving the rush of the present for these segments of country byway we can perhaps get a vague sense of what it was like to be a migrant on the Pioneer Trail.

Coordinates: M/10

PONTIAC TRAIL

Michigan has a number of communities honoring Indian leaders, among them being Kewadin, Mecosta, Newaygo, Okemos, Petoskey, Pokagon, and White Pigeon. But paramount among this genre of place names is Chief Pontiac, who has a city, a township, and an automobile attesting to his fame.

The man receiving this homage was born around 1720, the son of a Chippewa mother and an Ottawa father. He was raised in the vicinity of what is today northern Ohio and southern Michigan, becoming in adulthood an Ottawa war chief with residence near Detroit.

As the French and British struggled for control of North America, Pontiac sided with the Gallic fleur-de-lis (lily) against the English rose. When the banner of the Union Jack prevailed in this contest, Pontiac realized that in due time the lands of the Indians would be occupied by white settlers who would want to displace his tawny brothers as owners of the domain west of the Allegheny Mountains.

Deciding to act while the odds were still in his favor, Pontiac used his great powers of persuasion to form an unprecedented alliance of Native American tribes stretching from the Great Lakes to the Gulf of Mexico. The purpose of this union was to launch a coordinated revolt against

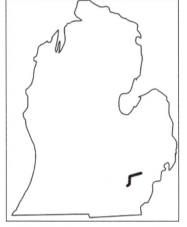

the English and expel them from Indian territory before the Red Coats were too strong to defeat in battle.

Employing his respectable military skills, Pontiac devised a scheme whereby members of his coalition would jointly move against British garrisons in May of 1763, with each tribe launching a surprise attack on the fort nearest its home turf. Pontiac's strategy generally worked as designed, as eight of the twelve posts his plan targeted quickly fell to Indian forces.

The entire action probably would have worked as conceived had not his tactic to capture the stronghold at Detroit been divulged in advance to the fort's commandant. Forewarned of a pending assault, the British troops at this key installation were able to foil Pontiac's trick to infiltrate the stockade. His hand revealed, the Indian leader was forced to undertake siege operations, a type of combat for which his braves were poorly suited.

Throughout the summer of 1763, Pontiac's

men surrounded but could not seize the all-important British military base at Detroit. With the arrival of autumn the frustrated league of Indian forces slowly dissolved, the land blockade was lifted, and the Europeans were left bloodied but still in control of the Great Lakes area and the Ohio River valley.

This brief period of conflict, variously known as Pontiac's Conspiracy or Pontiac's War, was as close as the Midwest's native peoples would come to halting the westward advance of another race into their homeland. The genius who almost carried out this remarkable feat was murdered by another Indian at 20 April 1769 at what is today East St. Louis. Someone later eulogizing Pontiac observed that his grand design was so bold that "history has retained his name, even if his actions did not achieve the result he anticipated."

As if to prove the merit of these words, when the present seat of Oakland County was established in 1818 it was called "Pontiac" in recognition of the great Indian chief's accomplishments. Settle-

ment of the surrounding area developed so quickly that with the passing of just ten years the Michigan legislature saw fit to authorize the building of a territorial road from this pioneer village southwest to Ann Arbor. In time, the route that was laid out between these two towns gradually became a major highway, and in 1934 much of the portion in Oakland County was designated trunk line M-218 (an identifier that remained at least in some fashion until 1963).

Seeking to give the road a more colorful and regionally appropriate name throughout its length, in February of 1938 the South Lyons Kiwanis Club proposed that the entire stretch of highway be called the "Pontiac Trail." This recommendation was approved by the Oakland County Road Commission on March 7 and by the Washtenaw County Road Commission on March 18 of that year, giving chief Pontiac one of only two memorial highways in our state paying homage to an authentic Native American person (the other being Tecumseh).

Coordinates: Southeastern Michigan Enlargement B-E/1-5

POW/MIA MEMORIAL FREEWAY

Since humans have fought throughout recorded history, it is probably safe to say there have been prisoners of battle since the beginning of recorded time. In some instances these captives have been killed, viewed as spoils of war, made into slaves, ransomed, or even exchanged. Early on, each victorious nation did pretty much as it pleased with POWs, as there were no uniform principles to govern behavior in this area.

The world's first treaty dealing with the treatment of POWs was made between the United States and Prussia in 1785. Thereafter, thoughts were given to establishing international rules for properly handling prisoners of war but nothing concrete materialized until the Geneva convention of 1929. This code required all signing nations to furnish information about POWs to the opposing side and permit representatives from neutral countries to visit prison camps and question the internees.

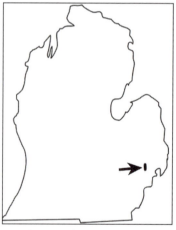

During World War II a number of governments (mainly on the Axis side) mistreated prisoners, showing that more rules or guidelines were needed to protect captives from harm. To provide additional standards for safeguarding POWs, the Geneva conventions of 1949 were drawn up.

These humanitarian norms for managing prisoners taken in war committed all signees to treat soldiers, news correspondents, civilian supply contractors, and members of labor service units with respect. All captives were to be removed from the combat zone; be required to give no more than name, rank, serial number, and date of birth; given adequate food and medical care in safe and sanitary camps; allowed to send and receive mail; have the right to engage in religious, intellectual and physical activities; and be free from acts of violence, intimidation, insults or public display.

A number of Michigan people have been prisoners of war or are still listed as being missing in action. However, poor record keeping prevents the statistics from being given at this time (it is said that 108 soldiers from the Wolverine State were made prisoners during the Korean War, but this figure seems much too low to be relied upon). As databases increase and improve, it will almost certainly be

possible to reveal these figures for all conflicts in which our citizens have fought and been captured.

The Legislature wanted to honor these "people who continue to be profoundly affected by the ordeal they underwent in the course of defending the nation, and those people who never returned." To achieve this goal, lawmakers passed Public Act 54 of 2003 creating the POW/MIA Memorial Freeway on route M-53 between 27 Mile Road and 34 Mile Road in Macomb County. At the time this book went to press, plans to dedicate the highway had not yet been completed.

Coordinates: L/13-14

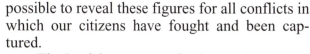

PRENTISS M. BROWN MEMORIAL HIGHWAY

Prentiss Marsh Brown was a member of the Mackinac Bridge Authority at its inception in 1951 and remained with that body until his death in St. Ignace on 19 December 1973.

According to one of his biographers, Brown's "most satisfying personal achievement came as chairman of the Mackinac Bridge Authority, when he secured financial backing to construct the five-mile-long Mackinac Bridge." At the time of its completion in 1957, this connection between Michigan's two great peninsulas was the longest total suspension span in the world.

But Brown was more than just a prime force behind the building of the Mackinac Bridge. His public service career on behalf of this state had many other dimensions.

Born in St. Ignace on 18 June 1889, Brown attended the local schools and then went on to Albion College where he graduated in 1911. After studying at the University of Illinois, Brown was admitted to the bar in 1914 and began practicing law with his father in St. Ignace.

He also immediately began working for local government, serving as prosecuting attorney of Mackinac County from 1914 to 1926 and city attorney of St. Ignace from 1916 to 1928.

In 1932, Brown became the first Democrat

from his district in the Straits region elected to the U.S. House of Representatives. Four years later the voters put Brown in office again, this time sending him to the U.S. Senate. His reelection bid in 1942 was unsuccessful.

After leaving Congress, Brown brought his skills to bear in the private sector. He was on the boards of at least a dozen companies, among them being the head of Detroit Edison, the National Bank of Detroit, and the Arnold Transit Company with its famous ferries to Mackinac Island.

It is understandable that the Michigan legislature would choose to honor someone of this caliber. And given Brown's major achievement in helping to build the Mackinac Bridge, it is not surprising that his tribute would be near that magnificent structure.

Recognition for a job well done came in the form of Senate Concurrent Resolution 560 of 1976. This document declared that the portion of I-75 between the Mackinac Bridge and Sault Ste. Marie would be known as the Prentiss M. Brown

Memorial Highway.

According to his family, there were none of the usual ceremonies to dedicate this action or unveil a commemorative marker. In essence, Brown's memorial monument is the "Mighty Mac," the link across the Straits that he felt was the greatest accomplishment of his life.

This stretch of Upper Peninsula concrete remained a tribute to Brown

for twenty-five years, until the Legislature decided to recodify the statutes governing Michigan's roads of remembrance. By the time this project was accomplished by virtue of Public Act 142 of 2001, the new language said that "the portion of highway I-75 in Cheboygan and Mackinaw counties shall be known as...the 'Prentiss M. Brown Memorial Highway'."

Coordinates: C-D/10-11

PRESTON SCHMIDT OVERPASS

Sometime in the early 1960s, constable Preston Schmidt "was responding to an emergency call when he was delayed while waiting for a train to clear the [Grand Trunk Western] railroad crossing at Bristol Road in Flint Township." After experiencing this interference, the frustrated police officer reportedly spent much of the remainder of his life working to get an overpass built at the site of the traffic holdup.

Preston Eugene Schmidt was born in Houston County, Tennessee, on 8 February 1929, eventually leaving the Volunteer State and coming to Flint, Michigan, in 1948. Schmidt found a job in the Buick plant, where for twenty years he labored as a tool-and-die man. During his tenure as a skilled tradesman, he also served fourteen years in the Michigan National Guard.

Following his departure from General Motors, Schmidt began a second career in public service. For fourteen years he was a member of the Flint Township Planning Commission and was Supervisor of that government entity during the period 1968-70. Advancing up the political ladder, Schmidt later wore the title of Genesee County Commissioner (1971-72), County Road Commissioner (1973-1992),

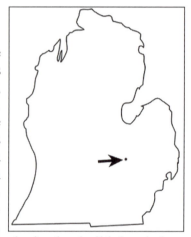

and member of the County Parks Board (1975-78, 1981-83, 1989-92). He still held some of these offices when he became a victim of cancer on 28 November 1992.

Some time after Schmidt's death, approval was finally obtained to build the viaduct that had been his dream for much of his adult life. Seeking "to recognize his many years of work advocating for its construction," the Genesee County Road Commission passed a resolution on 5 October 1999 proposing that the structure be named in Schmidt's honor. The Michigan Legislature obliged this request through Public Act 25 of 2000, a statute designating the Preston Schmidt Overpass on state highway M-121 near Flint's Bishop International Airport. When the multi-lane bridge was finished in the summer of 2000, it was dedicated in Schmidt's name in the usual fashion on June 30 of that year.

Coordinates: Flint Inset

PULASKI MEMORIAL HIGHWAY

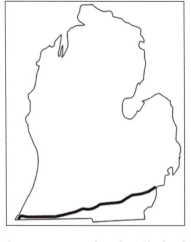

The American colonists did not single-handedly defeat the British during the Revolutionary War. A number of foreigners served with our armed forces, offering their military expertise (and in some instances their lives) to the cause of liberty.

Some of the more famous of these European soldiers were Marquis de Lafayette (France), Baron von Steuben (Prussia), and Count Casimir Pulaski (Poland). Of these three officers, only the latter has a Michigan state or federal highway named in his honor.

Pulaski was born into Polish nobility on 4 March 1748 at a time when Russia controlled Polish affairs. In 1768 he joined his father in a revolt against outside domination, and during this warfare he distinguished himself as a leader.

When Pulaski's uprising failed, he fled to France where he met Benjamin Franklin and offered his services to the cause of American independence. Armed with letters of recommendation from Franklin to George Washington, he sailed for Boston and joined the colonial army as a volunteer.

Pulaski's first battle action was at Brandywine, where he so acquitted himself that General Washington successfully persuaded Congress to appoint him brigadier general in charge of cavalry. To this day, Pulaski is known as the "Father of the American Cavalry."

As Pulaski's highly effective military exploits continued, Congress approved his plan to raise an independent corps of dragoons and light infantry. This fighting unit, comprised mainly of Pennsylvania Germans, became famous under the name of Pulaski's Legion.

The Polish Count saw his last martial engagement on 9 October 1779 at Savannah. There, while leading a charge of his Legion, he was severely wounded in the right thigh.

Pulaski was taken to the American warship Wasp for treatment, but he died of his wounds two days later on board the vessel. His body was buried at sea, but funeral services were held afterwards in the city of Charleston.

Because of his service and sacrifice for American independence, this country has bestowed more honors upon Pulaski than any other foreigner who fought in the Revolutionary War. Michigan joined in this tribute on 31 March 1953, when its legislature passed Public Act 11 designating present-day US-12 the Pulaski Memorial Highway (recognition reiterated nearly a half-century later by Act 142 of 2001).

This road of remembrance was dedicated in the presence of 100,000 people on 4 October 1953 at Detroit City Hall, with Mayor Cobo and Governor Williams presiding. Despite such a display of support at the eastern end of the route, the only place where maps still show US-12 as Pulaski Highway is along the western stretch of the trunk line in Berrien County.

Coordinates: M-N/7-13

PURPLE HEART HIGHWAY

The armed forces of the United States bestow many medals for individual heroism, bravery, and exemplary conduct in combat. In descending order of rank these awards are the Medal of Honor, Distinguished Service Cross/Medal, Silver Star, Legion of Merit, Bronze Star, commendation medals, and the Purple Heart.

Genealogically speaking, the Purple Heart can trace its lineage back to 1782 when it was created by General George

Washington as this country's first military decoration. Designed by Pierre Charles L'Enfant (who also planned the city of Washington, DC), the medal was originally presented only to those who had performed in action the most extraordinary deeds.

Following the Revolutionary War, the use of the Purple Heart's ancestor was discontinued. It was revived under its present name, however, on 22 February 1932, the 200th anniversary of Washington's birth. The reestablished decoration was to be given to "anyone wounded in action while serving with the U.S. armed forces and to the next of kin of those killed in action or dying of combat wounds."

The award--a purple heart-shaped badge with a profile relief bust of George Washington in a general's uniform--was first conferred retroactively to deserving World War I veterans. Thereafter it was presented to military personnel who, in the line of duty, required treatment by a medical officer as a result of an act by the enemy.

At about the same time this badge of merit was revived in 1932, a fraternal organization for those who had received the combat decoration was formed called the Military Order of the Purple Heart. The purpose of this national association was to pre-serve and strengthen comradeship among its members, work for the welfare of those who have received service-connected disabilities, represent former soldiers in the presentation of their claims before the Veterans' Administration, and perform assistance on behalf of needy servicemen and women.

It was in tribute to the recipients of the Purple Heart and their federally-chartered society that the Michigan Legislature considered House Bill 5162 of 2000. This proposed statute--encouraged by Lansing Chapter 37 of the Military Order of the Purple Heart--aimed to designate a short segment of I-69 in Clinton and Shiawassee counties as the "Purple Heart Highway." Though 51 lawmakers declared in support of the bill, the measure never made it out of committee and those who won the Purple Heart were left not with honor but with a purple rage.

The pain of having been rebuffed in the initial attempt to establish a Purple Heart Highway

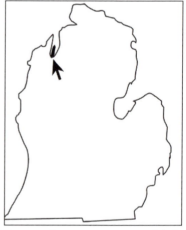

turned to joy two years later when the Governor signed Public Act 12 of 2002 officially bestowing this title upon "that potion of highway I-69 beginning at the intersection of I-69 east and US-27 north in Clinton County and extending east to exit 105 in Shiawassee County...."

Coordinates: L/11-12

QUEEN'S HIGHWAY

Above Traverse City, extending out into Grand Traverse Bay, exists the beautiful Old Mission Peninsula presently served by the northern extremity of M-37. Today, this stretch of trunk line is one of the most pleasant rides in Michigan, but it wasn't always so.

Back in 1933 the route had no number, but was simply known as Peninsula Center Road. It was characterized as "a dusty, twisting, narrow streak of gravel curving up hill and down dale over the rugged backbone of the Peninsula Country."

Not only was the road poorly constructed, it was in bad condition due to heavy use. Each year it served as the exit path for the rich agricultural harvest of the district, as trucks annually carried 6,000 tons of cherries and 500,000 bushels of ap-ples to market along its course.

In 1933 the farmers of the Peninsula approached the legislature in an effort to secure a hard surfaced highway over which their crops could be transported. Since "the road was not one which would form a link in a continuous highway system," the request was initially denied.

"However, by having the lighthouse property on Old Mission Point dedicated as a state park, it was then possible for the state to take over the Peninsula road." With this change in jurisdiction, government moneys to rebuild the highway were soon allocated.

As the improvement and paving of Peninsula Road neared completion in the fall of 1935, a number of names were suggested for the new trunk line. Of the many recommendations, "the state highway department oked Queen's Highway as its choice of names."

"It had been felt that the Cherry Queen, and the part she played in publicizing the industry and the region, might well be honored by having the new road named for her." Along with recognizing the annual Cherry Queen, a royally-titled motorway presented some additional promotional opportunities.

Locals reasoned that by "using the name Queen's Highway, many of the tourists and strangers who come here and hear the name will ask why it is called that. It will give the people an opportunity to explain that Old Mission peninsula is the home of the first of the commercial cherry orchards in the state, that it has 220 commercial orchards on the peninsula, representing almost half a million trees."

The Queen's Highway was officially christened and opened on 28 September 1935 at the junction of M-72 and M-37. The occasion was dedicated by the reigning Cherry Queen when she broke a bottle of cherry juice on the pavement. After the ceremony, cherry juice and doughnuts were served to those in attendance.

Coordinates: G/9

RAINBOW TRAIL

In November of 1917, the Saginaw Board of Trade proposed that a "trans-state pike" be created between its town and Muskegon. Such a road, the organization maintained, would help to develop Central Michigan as well as link two of the largest cities along the middle of the mitten.

The idea for a cross-state motorway was well-received by every affected community except one: Muskegon officials felt the time was not right to undertake such a project.

And so the cause for a trunk line connecting Saginaw and Muskegon remained dormant for a decade until, in November of 1927, the Fremont Chamber of Commerce began working toward the goal of resurrecting the concept.

In an effort to encourage tourist travel into and through the region, the businessmen of Fremont and surrounding towns began promoting part of trunk line M-46 as the "Saginaw, Stanton & Muskegon Short Line Highway." By using the initials of the three towns in the name, they came up with the motto of "Short & Safe for Motoring."

It did not take long for its backers to realize that they had christened their road with a title that

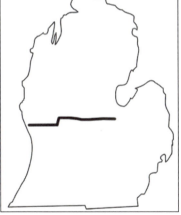

was more likely to put drivers to sleep than in a mood to travel its course. Consequently, on 19 June 1928 they met to make some much needed improvements.

First, the official route was established more along the lines of contemporary M-46. Next, new names for the road were sought, with the most popular being "Rainbow Trail" and the "Lake to Lake Trail." In a Solomon-like compromise, the backers of the highway decided to call it the "Rainbow Trail" with the motto "Lake to Lake."

With this task finished, the road's supporters proceeded to purchase 100 metal Rainbow Trail markers to guide travelers along the 140-mile way. These porcelain-surfaced signs, along with a dozen or so larger advertising billboards, were erected during the summer of 1928.

Under ordinary circumstances, the prospects

for the Rainbow Trail Association would have been bright. It had correctly recognized the need for a primary east/west connector linking the Lower Peninsula at its middle pinch-point. But the birth of the group was followed closely by the Crash of 1929, and the young body could not survive the effects of the Great Depression.

Today, the Rainbow Trail is gone

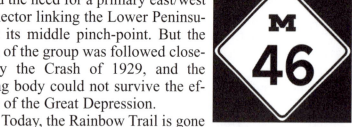

and forgotten by all save a few collectors who may have acquired one of the organization's distinctive, multicolored road signs. But the highway that it adopted has fared much better, currently thriving as a familiar and often used thoroughfare across the heartland of Michigan.

Coordinates: J-K/8-12

RANDOLPH STREET

The Ordinance of 1787--the one passed by Congress creating the Northwest Territory from which Michigan and four other states were carved--declared in Article 6 that slavery would not be allowed within the boundaries of this public domain. On 22 November 1802, the Governor of this Territory, William Henry Harrison, announced that an election would be held in three weeks for the purpose of electing delegates to a convention. This convention, to be held at Vincennes, would be for the purpose of considering whether or not Congress should be asked to repeal or suspend this prohibition on involuntary servitude.

Governor Harrison presided over this convention, and it was decided by the elected representatives to petition our national legislature to suspend Article 6 for a period of ten years. The chairman of the Congressional committee to whom the request was sent stated in response that "the labor of slaves is not necessary to promote the growth and settlement of the colonies in that region [known as the Northwest Territory. My] committee deem it highly dangerous and inexpedient to impair a provision wisely calculated to promote the happiness and prosperity of the northwestern country and to give strength and security to that extensive frontier." After hearing these words, Congress refused to suspend the article and the Northwest Territory was preserved for freedom.

It is ironic that the man who spoke so eloquently against human bondage was himself a plantation

owner with 400 slaves. He was John Randolph, a planter and politician who owned an 8,000-acre estate called Roanoke in Charlotte County, Virginia. Born in that state on 2 June 1773, Randolph received his collegiate education during periods of study at Princeton, Columbia, and William & Mary. He was a captivating speaker, great debater, and one of the most powerful orators of his time.

With the exception of two terms, Randolph served in the U.S. House of Representatives during the thirty-year period from 1799 to 1829. From 1825 to 1827 he was a member of the United States Senate. Noted in Washington DC for his colorful personality and championing of lost causes, he frequently appeared on the floor of the House in equestrian attire and flourishing a riding whip. Appointed minister to Russia in 1830, his health became broken and he died at Philadelphia on 24 May 1833.

In part because of his role in keeping the Northwest Territory free from slavery, the people of Detroit named one of their downtown streets after John Randolph in 1828. About a hundred years later (the authorizing letter from the late 1920s or early 1930s is undated), the Michigan State Highway Department incorporated part of this avenue into its trunk line system. Consequently, today this short inner-urban motorway still honors the memory of the Virginian slave owner who refused to allow this form of exploitation to reach the Old Northwest while it also serves as a small segment in the road known as route M-3 to drivers who are slaves to their cars.

Coordinates: Downtown Detroit Inset

RED ARROW HIGHWAY

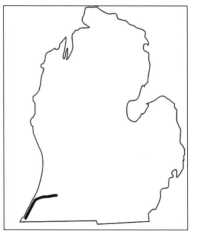

In southwestern Michigan, drivers see road markers for the "Red Arrow Highway." Since the route parallels I-94, it is not uncommon for exit signs along the interstate to display this intriguing name. Many thousands of people must have wondered how the thoroughfare got its name. Is it part of our Indian legacy, or did some travel promotionist coin the words because the mainly east-west road points like an arrow to the rising and setting suns?

The answer goes back 45 years, when a movement arose to honor the accomplishments of the 32nd U.S. Infantry Division. This military unit had been made up largely of soldiers from the Michigan and Wisconsin National Guards. The insignia of this Division was a red arrow, adopted to represent its piercing of the German Hindenburg line in World War I and its penetration of the many Japanese lines during the southwest Pacific campaigns of World War II.

In recognition of all the soldiers who fought with the 32nd Infantry Division--and especially in tribute to the 6,150 men who were killed while serving under its emblem--on 7 July 1930 a proposal was made to the State Administrative Board to name a trunk line "Road of [the] 32nd" from the Ohio border "north to the Straits and thence through the Upper Peninsula to the state of Wisconsin." This highway, to be marked with red arrows, was never designated.

A transportation salute to the 32nd Infantry Division finally did come on August 30, 1952, when State Highway Commissioner Charles M. Ziegler officially declared route US-12 the "Red Arrow

Memorial Highway." The actual dedication of this highway took place on 22 March 1953. Brief ceremonies were first held at the two extremities of the 200-mile route, New Buffalo and Detroit. Then the two parties converged by car at Jackson, where the formal activities took place.

Nearly eight years after these commemoration services, the path of obsolete US-12 was replaced by adjacent and modern I-94. The designation "US-12" was removed from the downgraded old road and applied to the route in southern Michigan that now bears that number. With this act, jurisdiction over what had been the Red Arrow Highway passed to the various county road commissions.

Through an understanding reached with the State Highway Department in 1959, those counties who wished to do so were allowed to continue calling the old road the Red Arrow Highway. In some cases this option was exercised, and thus we continue to see today on the transportation landscape the name of a memorial to one of Michigan's most renown combat forces. Consequently, today motorists can still go over the Red Arrow, which is something German and Japanese divisions couldn't do.

Coordinates: M-N/7-13

RED BUD TRAIL

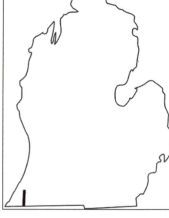

For years many citizens of Berrien County wanted a good road linking Buchanan with Berrien Springs. By 1926 this desire had reached the point that a petition campaign was launched in an effort to get county approval for construction of such a highway.

The promoters of this concept maintained that a thoroughfare between the two towns would help local farmers more easily get their goods to market, facilitate summer home development along the west bank of the Saint Joseph River, and attract motoring tourists to the region.

Though the rationale for a connecting route may have been right, the timing was wrong as other projects had higher priority for the Road Commission. Consequently, another petition campaign had to be launched in 1929, and this second appeal for an inter-city highway was approved by county officials.

Surveying of the entire route between Berrien Springs and Buchanan began early in 1931, and construction of the Oronoko Township portion of the project was actually finished late that year. However, the effects of the Great Depression caused setbacks in most road-building programs across Michigan, so the segment south of Buchanan was not completed until 1933.

The last stretch of road to be made ready was the division running north out of Buchanan, where activity commenced in December of 1933 using unemployed local men on government relief. The work force averaged 75 laborers per day, and their average individual compensation was just 44 cents per hour.

It was while this final phase of the Berrien Springs to Buchanan road was being prepared that a local resident suggested a name for the highway. This individual--noting the striking appearance of the flowering Red Bud--proposed that these trees be planted all along the route and that it subsequently be given the title of Red Bud Trail.

The originator of the idea pointed to the success of the Azalea Trail in Mobile, Alabama, which drew thousands of tourists annually to see its blossoms. He opined that if large numbers of Red Buds lined the course of Berrien County's new thoroughfare,

they would add to the road's drawing power and make it a regional attraction.

Most people in the area embraced this idea for brightening the landscape, but a few persons objected. The protesters pointed out the Red Bud is also known as the Judas Tree because Judas Iscariot, after betraying Jesus, supposedly hung himself on a Near-East variety of the plant. According to legend, the white flowers of the tree blushed red with shame over this act and have remained so ever since.

Opponents of the proposed trail name mentioned the myth that the heart-shaped leaves of the Red Bud have traditionally represented the hard heart of Judas. They also noted that the rose-colored flowers appear like drops of blood over the surface of most Red Bud branches, giving rise to the old belief that the tree hemorrhages each Spring in memory of Judas.

A tree with such a reputation, said a few, was not worthy of a place of honor along the flanks of, or bestowing its name upon, a Berrien County highway. These arguments were rejected by the vast majority of citizens, and the idea to create a Red Bud Trail was accepted.

The 14-mile long country lane was finished and opened to traffic in August of 1934 and the successful construction project, along with its colorful name, was dedicated in Buchanan on September 8 of that year. Close on the heels of this event ornamental Red Bud trees were set out along the right-of-way, beginning the process of beautifying the route.

For a short time thereafter a portion of the current Red Bud Trail was designated by the State Highway Department as M-174, but that status soon ended and the entire road was turned over to local control. Today, the Berrien County Road Commission welcomes travelers to drive the scenic path and see its showy profusion of flowers.

Coordinates: N/7

REMEMBRANCE ROAD

After World War I, many citizens of Michigan felt compelled to offer more than just words of thanks to the soldiers who had fought in that terrible conflict. Consequently, some communities erected memorial parks, buildings or monuments in honor of the local men and women who performed military duty for their country.

The residents of Kent County were also seeking a means of showing their appreciation to those who served in uniform. As early as 1918, some were suggesting that recognition be given soldiers by means of a memorial highway.

This idea, along with other proposals, was talked about until 30 January 1923 when the Grand Rapids Chapter of the Daughters of the American Revolution decided to take some action. On that date they went before the Kent County Road Commission to request public support for the development of a limited memorial highway.

The concept presented to the Commission was for 213 young elm trees--one for each Kent County soldier who died in World War I--to be planted along some well-traveled road as a tangible reminder of individual sacrifice. The Commission endorsed this proposal, thus giving life to "the first permanent war memorial in Kent County."

The plan that evolved from the meeting was for a double row of trees to extend along 1.5 miles of US-16 on the west side of Grand Rapids in what is now the

town of Walker. To ensure their vitality, each sapling was to be well along in growth with a height of from 20 to 25 feet and a trunk four inches thick.

The DAR agreed to spend over $1,500 to buy the trees, and in return the Kent County Road Commission said it would plant and care for them. The Road Commission also arranged to place a large boulder at the beginning of the memorial drive upon which the DAR could place a bronze tablet conveying a brief tribute.

Within the remarkably short span of three months all of this work was finished, and on 28 June 1923 the completed enterprise was dedicated. At that time the project was consecrated to those in whose memory it was built and the entire development formally turned over to the Kent County Road Commission for perpetual safekeeping.

Though the trees that were planted eventually succumbed to Dutch Elm disease and the trunk line designation US-16 was removed in 1963, the memorial route is still honored today in the name of the highway, Remembrance Road. And still surviving with this avenue of tribute is our freedom to drive it anytime we want.

Coordinates: Grand Rapids Inset

REO HIGHWAY

While Oldsmobile is a nameplate familiar to all, relatively few people know very much about the man who first produced the car.

Born in Geneva, Ohio, on 3 June 1864, Ransom Eli Olds moved to Lansing, Michigan, in 1880 when his father came to the

Capitol City and opened a machine shop.

Being of an inventive mind, Ransom began experimenting with steam-powered carriages at his father's business. Before long he had devised a horseless conveyance which functioned successfully at speeds of up to 10 miles per hour.

Later, after his initial creation was improved, it received world-wide exposure through an article in Scientific American. As a result of this publicity, in 1893 one of his vehicles was ordered by a concern in Bombay, India. This was the first U.S. car sold abroad.

By 1896, Ransom had abandoned steam power and constructed his first gasoline-operated vehicle. As this machine was refined, thoughts turned to mass producing the run-about for sale on a large-scale basis.

Toward this end, the Olds Motor Works was established in 1899. Its plant in Detroit was "the first American factory especially designed for automobile" manufacturing and the site "where the first assembly line system of production was installed."

Ransom sold his interest in the Olds Motor Works in 1904 and quickly formed the Reo Motor Car Company (from his initials) in Lansing. This firm soon became one of the leaders in the industry, making its founder a very wealthy man.

Seeking to use his substantial income in a positive way that would benefit his industry, Olds proposed to give the counties of Ingham, Livingston, and Oakland $300 for every mile of road they built in 1915 and 1916 on the main route between Detroit and Lansing.

There were just two conditions attached to this offer: the work had to meet established state highway construction standards and the road had to be named the Reo Highway.

The governing boards of all three counties agreed to these terms and subsequently collected thousands of dollars in bounties from Olds. But not one of them complied with the provision to put the name of his company on the road.

A man of grace and good will, Ransom Olds is not known to have taken offense at this failure to fulfill the terms of his offer. He, like everyone else, adopted the custom of referring to the road by the name still used today, Grand River Avenue.

Coordinates: L-M/11-13

ROAD OF MEMORY (BATTLE CREEK)

Early in 1922, the American Legion Headquarters suggested that a tree "be planted on Arbour Day this year for every American soldier who died overseas during the World War." These saplings, it was hoped, would grow into stately reminders of those in military uniform who gave their all that we residents of the United States "might enjoy the privileges of citizenship in the finest land of an unfettered world."

It was this spirit of tribute that prompted the members of American Legion Post 54 in Battle Creek to pass a resolution on 26 January 1922 asking that the two military highways leading to and from Camp Custer be dedicated to the memory of the city's ex-service men and women. The two streets recommended for this honor were Harmonia and Upton roads, avenues by which thousands of men entered the fort and over which they left for the fields of combat.

In addition to declaring the highways memorials, the Legionnaires endorsed setting a tree along the roadsides for every local person who served in World War I. Their idea was for each plant to be "marked by a suitable tablet for the living and being further designated by a distinguishing marker for the dead." The result would be a motorway "beautified in memory of the brave boys who went over there [to Europe] and did not return."

For two years this proposal remained just a dream, until January of 1924 when a chapter of the Michigan Nurses Association voted to plant memorial trees between Battle Creek and the fort's eastern boundary. Since the nurses did not want to spread their homage too thin, they elected to limit their venerating activities to the borders of what was then a longer Upton Avenue.

Joining the nurses in this noble effort was a local chapter of the Federation of Women's

Clubs. Together these groups planted maples and elms along the main access route to Camp Custer, dedicating the memorial project and the highway on 28 May 1924.

Today, much of Upton Road that once served as the gateway to Camp Custer has been supplanted by a street unimaginatively called "Avenue A". And the status of the former route as a memorial to brave soldiers and fallen warriors has disappeared from the city's consciousness and landscape, leaving evidence of this honorable gesture consigned to the pages of early nineteenth-century Battle Creek history.

Coordinates: Battle Creek Inset

ROAD OF MEMORY (SAGINAW)

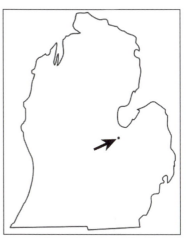

After World War I, many Michigan cities thought it proper to erect some permanent monument in tribute to the young spirits that had fallen in combat. They did so recognizing that such a gesture would not restore the lives they gave or relieve the grief of those they left behind. Rather, it was done to show respect and gratitude to those who went to their death for the cause of freedom and democracy.

One of the towns that elected to pay homage to those who made the supreme sacrifice was Saginaw. There, the Daughters of the American Revolution proposed a "Road of Memory" as a means of expressing a community's appreciation to its soldiers sent away on a trip from which there was no return.

The movement to create a fitting memorial of a grateful city to its wartime dead began in May of 1925. The motivating idea was to turn the portion of route M-46 that runs through Ezra Rust Park into a testimonial that Saginaw does not forget those who brought her honor.

This goal would be accomplished by erecting a bronze tablet on a concrete base for each of the 150 Saginaw County men who were killed while on military duty. The personal markers, individually placed beneath an accompanying tree, would flank both sides of the "Road of Memory."

To achieve this ambition, the community set out to raise the necessary $5,000 in a fund drive. Thanks to the efforts of numerous individuals-- along with businesses and various social, fraternal, patriotic and service or-

ganizations--the requisite sum was realized within a month.

With money in hand, Saginaw residents thought they could complete the tribute to their fallen Gold Star heroes by the Fall of 1925. However, when it was disclosed that the city had plans to widen route M-46 through Rust Park, it became apparent there would not be enough room left along the side of the road to accommodate tablets to each of the soldiers killed in service.

Since this news meant that Saginaw's deceased veterans could not be recognized individually, a change in plans was called for. Instead of having a marker for every person claimed by the War, it was decided to celebrate them as a group by erecting an inscribed granite shaft and a tall flag pole.

The county's modified tribute to its departed servicemen was finished by 1926, and on May 31 of that year the monument in Ezra Rust Park was dedicated. At that ceremony the people of Saginaw consecrated an enduring reminder of their men in uniform who brought glory to the community and themselves when they laid down their lives on behalf of country and humanity.

Coordinates: Saginaw Inset

ROAD OF REMEMBRANCE (IONIA)

In November of 1918, the month and year World War I ended, the American Forestry Association started a nationwide movement to plant memorial trees for our soldier dead. The organization contacted every governor in the country to promote the idea and ask for official support.

In Michigan, this cause was taken up by the Northern Nut Growers Association. They encouraged "the planting of trees in parks and along highways as a lasting testimonial of a grateful people to their defenders." While any type of memorial tree would be acceptable, the group obviously preferred those species that produced an annual fall harvest of edible delights in a protective shell.

The Michigan legislature tried to help the cause by passing some supportive enabling statutes. Public Act 36 of 1919, for instance, authorized the planting of "any ornamental, nut bearing, food producing or shade tree upon any public highway." And Public Act 325 of the same year, seeking to aid municipalities in their efforts to pay homage, authorized any city to acquire land "for the erection of memorials to soldiers and sailors."

In Ionia County, it was the Daughters of the American Revolution who took initial advantage of this law to create "Ionia's first memorial to the soldiers, sailors and marines who fought in the World War." On Arbor Day--6 May 1921--they planted fifteen trees along the river bank near the east end of the fair grounds and associated park.

Given the success of this gesture and the public support it generated, the

DAR engaged in a similar exercise two years later. In September of 1923, the members planted a row of seven walnut trees near the old Session school house not far from the present intersection of Riverside Drive and M-66. It was the goal of the group to continue the activity "until there shall be a long stretch of trees along this highway."

Though this was obviously not the first memorial planting in Ionia County, it was the first road of remembrance within its jurisdiction. The Ionia newspaper, in commenting upon this accomplishment, noted that in planting these trees the DAR "will have erected the finest of all monument[s]--not alone to the hero of a war--not alone as shelter for generations to come--but [as] a living sentinel" that we give to nature that she might give back again in abundance to others who come after.

In this way the community's heroes were honored with a form of life that required some upkeep and attention, a periodic reminder to those caretakers who might otherwise forget the sacrifices the trees honored. And these stately roadside fruitbearing monuments also gave of themselves, just like the deceased soldiers they honored.

Coordinates: K/10

ROAD OF REMEMBRANCE (SAULT STE. MARIE)

In 1921, the Chicago Tribune began advancing the idea of planting trees along highways to perpetuate the memory of those who fought in World War I. These arbor-lined motorways were to be called "roads of remembrance."

The concept was "to plant trees in memory of every person, either men or women who served honorably in the World War, under military oath. In cases where the person honored with a tree lost his or her life in the service of the country, the fact [was] to be designated on [a] bronze marker."

Promoters traveled all across the Midwest encouraging individuals, groups and communities to participate in the project. Their slogan was, "If you had a soldier in your family, don't let his name be missing from the sentinel trees that will stand guard against the nation's forgetfulness."

While news of the Tribune's plan reached Sault Ste. Marie during the year of its debut, it was not until the Spring of 1926 that the town finally adopted the proposal. At that time the community decided to declare 29 miles of M-129 a "Road of Remembrance" to its veterans.

The route of tribute was to run from the city's southern boundary to Rockview Road, about five miles south of Pickford. Along this stretch was envisioned an "avenue of elms," one for every soldier who served on active duty from Chippewa County.

It was decided to do the undertaking in phases, with the first mile south of town to be planted in 1926. To achieve this goal, school children donated pennies and adults contributed dollars to buy 250 trees in memory of

specific veterans.

The county road commission marked out the places where each tree should go and on the appointed day 200 people turned out to dig the necessary holes and put the saplings in the ground. This process was repeated in the Spring of the following year when the second mile of highway was planted with another 250 memorial trees.

The tradition of annually setting out living reminders for those who defended democracy did not survive into 1928. By then, community interest had turned to other matters and nearly everyone who wanted to participate in the project had already done so.

Thus, the envisioned beautiful trunk line flanked with shady ornaments never extended more than a few miles from Sault Ste. Marie. But during the brief time the community developed its Road of Remembrance, it managed to create a landscaped highway thoughtfully dedicated "to the lasting memory of those who fought and lived, and those who fought and died; to those who gave much and those who gave all."

Coordinates: C/11

ROBERTS-LINTON HIGHWAY

In 1910 it was found necessary to deepen the channel of the Saginaw River. The prospects of the enterprise being completed, however, were not good because the project estimates were way over budget. The expense of carrying the removed river bed dredgings out to Saginaw Bay were so high the undertaking might have to be canceled.

Two Saginaw men stepped forward to rescue the project. William Seelye Linton and Rolla W. Roberts suggested that the excavated earth be deposited all along the vacant east bank of the River between Saginaw and Bay City. This scheme would avoid the costly need to transport spoils to Lake Huron, while the deposited materials could be later used as a base for a new highway between Saginaw and Bay City.

This idea was approved, and the dredging activities were conducted during the years 1912-1913. But the road-building portion of the pro-

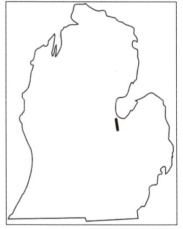

posal was not commenced because the necessary moneys were not available.

In 1923, leaders in Bay City and Saginaw attempted to resurrect the dormant second phase of the Roberts-Linton concept. They chartered a special train and 600 of the top citizens got on board for a trip to Lansing, where they petitioned and lobbied to have state financial assistance for the River Road. Unable to resist such an organized appeal, the Governor agreed to their plan.

After a period of budgeting, planning and surveys, the filling and grading of the road was finished in 1927. The first concrete was poured on 6 July 1928, and the entire highway was completed and dedicated on 27 October 1929.

The opening ceremonies took place on the Saginaw-Bay county line, with about 20,000 local residents in attendance. The citizens turned out to see and celebrate the completion of a million dollar pavedway--free of crossroads, railroad tracks, advertising or filling stations--that cut three miles off the distance between their two towns.

Of the two men who had made this day possible, Linton--born on 4 February 1856 in St. Clair, Michigan--had come to Saginaw with his parents in 1859. Later, as an adult, he found success there in the lumber business. In addition, he was a member of the city council (1884-1885), mayor (1892-1894), member of the state house of representatives (1887-1888), representative to Congress (1893-1897), postmaster of Saginaw (1898-1914), and on the board of state tax commissioners (1919-1925). He died in Lansing on 22 November 1927.

His associate, Roberts, was born in Wheatville, New York, on 14 No-

vember 1858, coming to Saginaw in 1881. He worked first for the Flint & Pere Marquette Railroad (1881-1886), then as city engineer (1886-1912), and finally as an engineer for the state highway department beginning in 1912. He died as the result of a car accident on 15 June 1931.

The death of Roberts made the legislature realize that he and Linton had never been given their due for conceiving of and making possible the river parkway. In posthumous recognition of their contributions, Senate Resolution 35 of 1931 declared "that the section of US-23 between Saginaw and Bay City commonly called the River Road be officially designated as the Roberts-Linton Highway."

The description of this tribute was slightly modified in 2001 with the passage of Public Act 142. This piece of legislation declared that "the portion of highway I-75 and US-23 beginning in the city of Saginaw and extending north to the city of Bay City shall be known as the 'Roberts-Linton Highway'...."

Coordinates: J/12

ROGERS MEMORIAL HIGHWAY

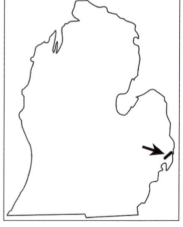

From 1950 through 1960, the official state highway maps listed the memorial trunk line roads in Michigan. This compilation identifies M-28 from Wakefield east to Sault Ste. Marie as the Frank Foster Rogers Highway and US-25 from Port Huron to Detroit as the Rogers Highway. Both claims, while having some basis in fact, are probably in error.

The person being celebrated by these roads is Frank Rogers, a man born in Raisin Township of Lenawee County on 20 August 1858. Educated in the rural schools, Rogers went on to graduate from what today is Michigan State University with a Bachelor of Science degree in 1883.

Professionally, Rogers found employment as a surveyor in Sanilac County until 1890, when he moved to Port Huron. He served as city engineer there from 1891 to 1899 before leaving to work for a local road-building firm. In 1905 he was appointed Michigan's first deputy state highway commissioner, a position he held until 1913

when he moved up to become head of the State Highway Department.

Rogers remained as state highway commissioner until 1 January 1929, when he retired from office to become a consultant. During his tenure he was so successful at building roads that he became known as the "father of the state highway system." After a long and distinguished career, he died in Lansing on 30 April 1942 at the age of 83.

The first and perhaps only road named for Frank Rogers is old US-25 in Saint Clair County. Because of his previous connection with Port Huron, the County Road Commission named what is now Gratiot Avenue in Rogers' honor on

7 December 1920. There was talk of extending this memorial highway north into the Thumb as far as Pointe Aux Barques, but there is no evidence that this was actually done.

The next attempt to christen a road for Frank Rogers began in June of 1921. This effort envisioned the creation of a highway that would start at Port Huron and proceed from there west through seven contiguous counties to the shores of Lake Michigan. The ambitious project, which was never undertaken, was to connect the eight county seats of Port Huron, Mt. Clemens, Pontiac, Howell, Mason, Charlotte, Hastings, and Allegan.

The third movement to designate a road for Rogers commenced in December of 1922 when a group of Upper Peninsula road builders suggested all of route M-28 bear his name. Though initial reaction was positive, the idea was eventually rejected for fear that anytime Rogers authorized expenditures on the road he would be open to the charge of favoritism.

Two other considerations played minor roles in the loss of a road of remembrance for Rogers in the Upper Peninsula. Some said the route was in such bad shape that naming it for the highway commissioner would cause him embarrassment. Others, noting that the trunk line had already been designated part of the Theodore Roosevelt Memorial Highway, were afraid that declaring it for a second person would cause the national group to choose another path through Michigan.

A compromise solution was found to the problem in February of 1923. Instead of a Frank Foster Rogers Highway, it was suggested that a monument of tribute be erected in his honor. The Northern Michigan Road Builders Association acquired the necessary land about eight miles northwest of Saint Ignace, and boulders were brought to the location from all of the counties in the UP. A suitable marker was built from this raw material, and the resulting stone base with tablet was dedicated on 4 June 1930.

The last known effort to name a highway for Frank Rogers began in October of 1928. Interests in the south-central Lower Peninsula began lobbying for a road that would run from Metamora near the Ohio boundary north to Lansing through Ogden Center, Palmyra, Holloway, Tecumseh, Clinton, Manchester, Chelsea, Stockbridge, and Mason. It was deemed appropriate to assign Rogers' name to the road because it passed within half a mile of his boyhood home.

There was probably little chance under normal circumstances that the desired road would ever be built, but the Great Depression, which began the following year, ensured that funds for such a route would not be forthcoming. Thus, Rogers had his name proposed for more highways than any other person in Michigan history and yet the state never designated a single trunk line in his honor.

Coordinates: K-L/14

RUST STREET/DRIVE

It has been said that "no name has been more prominent in the history of Saginaw than that of Ezra Rust." If this man indeed holds such an important position in the annals of the community, then it is necessary to perform at least a cursory examination of his life.

The subject of this review was born in Wells, Vermont, on 23 September 1832, but five years later moved with his family to Marine City on the St. Clair River. Rust spent his boyhood doing chores on his father's farm, but at the age of fourteen he left agriculture and began working for his brothers in their nearby saw mill. His exposure to the instruments of commercial lumbering taught him so much about mechanics that in 1849 he left the mill and began a six-year career as engineer on various Great Lakes steamboats.

In 1855 he left the maritime life and returned to work in his brothers' saw mill. By 1859, however, the timber resources of the St. Clair River district were exhausted, forcing Rust to ply his craft elsewhere. With his siblings as partners he acquired a new saw mill at what is today Saginaw, and in 1862 he added a salt works at the same site. The scope of his business quickly grew, requiring the addition of a saw mill at Zilwaukee in 1865 and another at Bay City in 1871. These efficiently-run operations--fed by the great pine forests of the Saginaw Valley--produced vast quantities of sawn lumber for a wood-hungry nation, eventually making Rust one of the wealthiest men in Michigan.

Rust did not keep all of his riches to himself. He was very generous in sharing the monetary fruits of his labors with the city of Saginaw. One example of this largess occurred in 1905, when he purchased for his fellow-residents a large island in the Saginaw River and donated $50,000 to have it turned into a nicely landscaped public gathering place. In gratitude for this magnanimous gesture, the city council named a nearby street "Rust Avenue" and christened the newly-created pleasuring grounds "Rust Park."

Though Ezra Rust died in 1918, he was still on the minds of Saginaw's inhabitants as late as 1934. In that year the city built a broad boulevard through Rust Park using

$100,000 in federal funds to create the beautiful roadway. Since the construction was a source of community pride--and since the pavement traversed common property acquired and developed by Mr. Rust--the city council decided to name the street "Ezra Rust Drive in honor of the memory of the man who gave the city the land through which the newly improved highway passes."

This great improvement to Saginaw's transportation system was dedicated on 23 August 1934, an event attended by 25,000 people, the "largest single outpouring of citizenry that Saginaw ever has witnessed." Because the celebrated artery was a part of route M-46, a number of state government officials were present to participate in the day's parade, concert, speeches and entertainment.

In 1961 the path of M-46 in downtown Saginaw was changed. Ironically, the course of the trunk line was diverted from Ezra Rust Drive and Rust Park south to another of the town's main arteries, Rust Avenue. Thus, it looks like M-46 through Saginaw may wear out but it will apparently never Rust out.

Coordinates: Saginaw Inset

SAGINAW TRAIL

Everyone in Michigan is familiar with the name Saginaw. What is uncertain is just what the word means. According to some sources, the term translates into "Land of the Sauks," in reference to the Indians who are said to have occupied the area in former times.

The moccasined feet of these and other native Americans beat a path from Detroit to Saginaw Bay that the European settlers called the Saginaw Trail. As the American frontier spread west and pioneers came to live in the southern Lower Peninsula, they too began to use this ancient foot path.

It quickly became the principal route into the interior of Michigan and the chief axis of settlement out of Detroit. As covered wagons, ox carts, and supply vehicles trundled along the trail, it became obvious to government officials that the narrow track had to be improved.

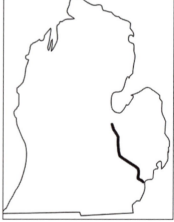

The first step in this process was to conduct a survey of the route, a task authorized by the Territorial Legislature on 7 December 1818. When this job was finished, Governor Lewis Cass established by proclamation on 15 December 1819 the route of the trail from Detroit to Pontiac. Laying out the Pontiac to Saginaw portion of the road was not approved by the Legislature until 12 June 1822.

It was one thing to designate a highway and survey its course, and quite another thing to actually build it. Given the meager financial resources of Michigan Territory, such an undertaking could only be accomplished by the federal government.

With this realization in mind, in 1826 Michigan interests went to Washington D.C. seeking appropriations for the purpose of improving the Saginaw Trail. After giving the matter due consideration, Congress gave its blessing to the idea on 2 March 1827.

Soon thereafter work began on the construction project, and by 1833 the road was finished as far as Flint. The entire 92-mile project was completed in 1841, when what had started out as barely a bridle path was finally transformed into a serviceable highway.

Though resources had been found to improve the Saginaw Trail, there were inadequate public funds to maintain it. Consequently, in 1848 and 1850 Michigan turned the Detroit to Saginaw route over to private plank road companies who, in return for up-

keep of the artery, were allowed to levy fees upon all those who used it.

The charters of these toll companies expired at the end of 60 years, at which time the Saginaw Trail reverted back to being a freely accessible public highway. The benefits of this changed status can be seen in I-75, the modern successor to the Trail, which stands today as the most heavily traveled route in the state.

Presently, the only traces of the Saginaw Trail are on road signs in Genesee County along route M-54. But just like in pioneer times, the general course of the old Saginaw Trail is still the principal path into the interior of Michigan. And while the traffic load of today is much greater than in the frontier period, during rush hour it sometimes seems to move at the pace of centuries past.

Coordinates: J-M/12-13

SAGINAW VALLEY TRAIL

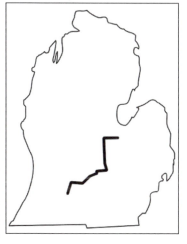

The north-flowing Saginaw River, with a total distance of only around 22 miles, is probably the shortest river in Michigan (water courses of such modest extent are usually called creeks or streams). But with a depth of from 15 to 20 feet and an average width of 670 feet, it is probably the biggest river for its length in the country.

The Saginaw River is formed by the confluence of its four main branches, the Cass, Flint, Shiawassee and Tittabawassee rivers. Its slow-flowing channel, which empties into Saginaw Bay, is navigable along its entire length for Great Lakes shipping.

With a watershed of 6,222 square miles, the Saginaw River has the largest drainage basin in the state (the Grand River valley surface area is next in size). Its fan-shaped tributary realm is approximately the same maximum extent north and south as it is east and west, about 122 miles each way.

Within the collection zone of the Saginaw River there exists such highly industrialized urban sites as Flint, Saginaw, Bay City, and Midland. Also embraced by its hydrologic sphere is some of the best farmland in Michigan, with one-

third of the surface area devoted to agriculture.

Given the size and importance of the Saginaw River basin, it is not surprising that it would eventually be memorialized by a highway. This event occurred on 19 September 1917 in Lansing, at which time and place the Saginaw Valley Pike Association was formed. The purpose of this organization was to promote a route between Saginaw and Battle Creek, and the name they chose for this road was the Saginaw Valley Trail.

One should not assume that a good thoroughfare already existed between these two towns. To the contrary, the intervening transportation network was abysmal by contemporary standards. It was hoped, however, that by naming a specific artery and thus encouraging motorists to follow it, the increased traffic would force authorities to improve the chosen highway.

The course selected by the founders of the Saginaw Valley Trail was reportedly shown to and approved by the state highway commissioner. It generally followed contemporary M-66 from Battle Creek north to M-78, M-78 east to I-69, I-69 northeast to Perry, M-52 north from Perry to M-46, and M-46 east into Saginaw.

Since road signs did not then exist as we know them today, the route of the Trail was identified by a special symbol painted on flanking telephone poles. The mark for the route was a ten-inch band of black topped by a ten-inch band of white. Upon this back-

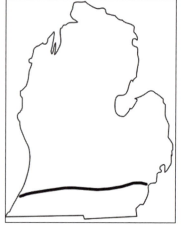

SAGINAW VALLEY ROUTE

ground was painted the monogram SVT to assure travelers they were on the right path.

With all of this preparation, one would think that the prospects for the Saginaw Valley Trail were quite promising. Unfortunately, the sponsors were good with planning but poor in timing. The First World War came soon after their organization, and by the time hostilities were over so was interest in promoting the trunk line. Consequently, while the name "Saginaw Valley" still graces many businesses, institutions, and even a state university, it can no longer can be found on the road maps of Michigan.

Coordinates: J-M/10-12

SAINT JOSEPH ROAD

When the Europeans came to what is now Michigan, they found a well-developed network of Indian footpaths. One of these beaten tracks, connecting Detroit with the mouth of the St. Joseph River along the approximate course of present-day I-94, was not surprisingly called the Saint Joseph (or Joseph's) Trail.

As pioneers began to settle in the western Great Lakes region, the federal government authorized the construction of a few military roads to help in the defense of the region. One of the oldest and most important of these routes was the Detroit to Chicago Road, known today as US-12, running southwest from the alignment of the Saint Joseph Trail.

Though ostensibly built for conveying men and supplies to forts and places of conflict, this military highway was heavily used by immigrants coming to live in the frontier area. Following this strategically located route, the bulk of early settlers taking up residence in Michigan Territory concentrated along the Detroit to Chicago Road in the most southern tier of counties.

This pattern of development concerned those who wished to promote the interests of the second layer of counties across Michigan, being the area within Wayne, Washtenaw, Jackson, Calhoun, Kalamazoo, Van Buren and Berrien counties. What was needed, they felt, was a competing route north of the Detroit to Chicago Road to

draw people into the east/west corridor between Detroit and contemporary Benton Harbor.

To deflect the tide of newcomers away from the south border region, it was proposed to make the St. Joseph Indian trail into a road. A petition was circulated encouraging the Territorial Legislature to take this step, supposedly signed "by every man on the contemplated route."

Responding to this popular sentiment, Michigan lawmakers passed an act on 4 November 1829 authorizing a survey of the envisioned route. The course as laid out went across the heart of the southern Lower Peninsula generally following the old Indian trail, passing through the seats of all seven counties touched by the road.

The survey was finished in December of 1830, and on 3 March 1831 the Territorial Legislature passed a second act formally declaring the route established and designating the road a public highway. People responded immediately to this new means of access to Michigan's interior, traveling its path in great numbers and quickly taxing the carrying capacity of the road.

To keep the heavily traveled highway in adequate repair, in 1834 the U.S. government stepped in and authorized the then-substantial sum of $20,000 to help improve the route for bearing the weight of passing settlers' wagons. These federal enhancements, plus the attractions of the country through which it ran, helped to make the Saint Joseph Road the main territorial artery in Michigan.

Because it was such "an avenue of great consequence," people began referring to it as the "Territorial Road" since it was the most important of all the territorial roads in existence. Before long this descriptive title became the highway's name, and the phrase "Saint Joseph Road" slowly slipped into obscurity.

Eventually, "Territorial Road" was viewed as too general to be meaningful and it was dropped in favor of more specific identifiers. Beginning around World War I the route was unimaginatively characterized on auto maps as the Michigan-Detroit-Chicago Road, but by the late 1920s this lengthy moniker was beginning to evolve into the shorter and more familiar title of Michigan Avenue. Today, the name of our territory

and state is still present on the transportation landscape of this travel corridor, but the current preference is for trunk lines to be known by numbers rather than words.

Saint Joseph, too, is still a famous term in the southern Lower Peninsula, as it is remembered in the form of a city, a county, two rivers, a lake, and a township. It's just unfortunate that such an important part of the Lower Peninsula's heritage cannot also be preserved as a name for at least a part of what was once the premier territorial road in early Michigan.

The journal American Motorist predicted this would happen in its issue of December, 1923. The periodical "deplored that there is a tendency on the part of some States in adopting this most excellent plan of [numerical] road marking to ignore the well established name of some historic trail or National highway created as a memorial.... The [editor] earnestly requests the State Highway Departments, where they can legally do so, to preserve the name designation of established routes as well as the number." In this particular instance, Michigan unfortunately could not oblige.

Coordinates: M-N/7-13

SAINT JOSEPH VALLEY PARKWAY

The Saint Joseph River is born near Hillsdale and, after flowing west 210 miles, discharges into Lake Michigan between the cities of St. Joseph and Benton Harbor. Draining an area of about 4,300 square miles (60% of which is in Michigan), it is one of the largest rivers in our state.

Over the years, the banks of the Saint Joseph became increasingly settled and the adjacent territory downstream heavily developed. Two major communities situated along this lower course are South Bend and Niles, between which there has grown a substantial flow of road traffic.

The most congested of these linking highways was US-31, the main route connecting the two communities. With the bulk of the traffic concentrated on this thoroughfare, movement was relatively slow and driving hazardous.

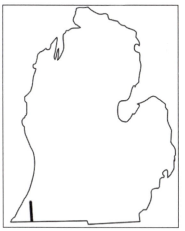

Bumper stickers advertising this fact became popular with many of the area's citizens, as the rears of their cars declared "I Drive US-31. Pray for Me."

To alleviate this problem, the Transportation Departments of Indiana and Michigan began building a bypass that would allow non-local traffic to get around the congested zone. By 1992 this construction project had progressed to the point that a name had to be found for the new highway. Should it simply be called the "US-31 Bypass" or would some other title be more appropriate?

To answer this question, during the Fall of 1992 business organizations in the Michiana region held a contest. They jointly solicited the populace to suggest a name for the freeway loop. The winning submission would be selected by representatives from the chambers of commerce in Elkhart, Mishawaka, South Bend, Niles, Berrien Springs, and St. Joseph/Benton Harbor.

The idea was to have a name that "rolls off the tongue and [is] representative of all the areas" traversed by the highway. Unacceptable were names of people or anything that would favor some part of the larger community, like "Four Flags" or "Blossomland."

Over 125 entries were submitted, including such ideas as Potawatomi Parkway, Bi-State Thruway, Valleyview Parkway, Sunset Parkway, and Great Northern Parkway. From this mix was chosen St. Joseph Valley Parkway because it was easily pronounceable, highly descriptive, and "something the whole area is comfortable with."

Once this decision had been made, the next step was to give it official status. Toward this end the local state representative introduced House Concurrent Resolution 26 of 1993, a measure quickly approved by the Michigan legislature. The Indiana lawmakers were a little slower in responding, waiting until 1995 to pass HCR 52 which bestowed the same designation on their stretch of the highway.

Though the Hoosiers started late, they did beat Michigan across the finish line. Indiana dedicated its portion of the St. Joseph Valley Parkway on 25 July 1995. North of the border, road signs were not erected on the upgraded route until four months later and the dedication ceremonies were delayed until 1 December 1995 at Berrien Springs. Finally, the prayers of motorists had been answered.

As time passed, the road that had originally been a high speed bypass around the congested flow of Niles/South Bend traffic was built further north and made of part of Michigan's interstate highway network. To reflect this change in status and purpose, the Legislature in 2001 passed Public Act 142 which bestowed the name "St. Joseph Valley Parkway" upon the portion of trunk line US-31 beginning at the northern Indiana border and "extending north to the intersection with I-94 in Berrien County."

Coordinates: N/7

SAVIDGE STREET

At any moment in time, nearly every community has its foremost citizen. For each town along the continuum of its history there seems to be one person who is temporarily paramount in its social, political and business activities. In the village of Spring Lake during the early twentieth century, that eminent person was William Savidge.

Born in Spring Lake on 30 September 1863, Savidge was educated in Grand Rapids before going on to higher learning at the University of Michigan. After graduating from the Ann Arbor college in 1884, he proceeded to spend two years at the Harvard law school before permanently returning to Spring Lake and taking an active roll in managing his father's lumber firm of Cutler & Savidge.

In addition to taking care of his family's business concerns, Savidge was also involved in outside commercial interests. For example, at various stages of his career he was director of the Grand Haven State Bank, the Grand Rapids Fire Insurance Company, the Michigan Trust Company, and the Spring Lake Bank as well as President of the U. of M. Alumni Association (1892), and State Senator in Lansing (1897-98).

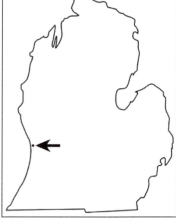

When Savidge died prematurely on 9 May 1916, his passing was a shock to the residents of West Michigan and a blow to the interests of the Spring Lake area. On the day of his funeral all local business was suspended for the afternoon, schools closed, flags were lowered to half mast, and a special railroad car was run over from Grand Rapids to accommodate the many mourners from that city.

The Savidge family looked for some appropriate way to pay tribute to its lost member. Not long after William's death, his sister Esther gave Spring Lake its first pavement in her brother's memory. This gesture was particularly appropriate, since during his life Savidge had been an active supporter of good roads and was a director of the Wolverine Pavedway Association, the West Michigan Pike Association, and the

Grand Highway Association.

In appreciation for the mile-long ribbon of hardtop, Spring Lake informally rechristened its main avenue from State Street to Savidge Street in 1916. However, this title alteration was not made official by local authorities until 6 February 1935 and the switch in designation was finally dedicated on 22 June of that year. As testimony to this event today, on the north side of highway M-104 in Spring Lake stands two markers telling all witnesses that the adjacent busy road is named for a local man of letters, finance, and a favorite son, William Savidge.

Coordinates: K/8

SCHAEFER ROAD

In the middle of what is now Dearborn, six miles west of the Detroit City Hall on a route formerly called the Old Chicago Road, a German immigrant operated an inn appropriately called the Six Mile House. This was the first stop for travelers heading inland from the Detroit River along what we know today as Michigan Avenue.

The owner of this combination tavern, restaurant and hotel was Joseph Schaefer, a man born in Germany on 24 October 1833 and a subsequent immigrant to America around 1860. Upon arrival in the United States he located in the Upper Peninsula's Copper Country where he briefly worked as a miner. Not long after the Civil War started, Schaefer left the ore fields and enlisted at Houghton as a private in Company I of the 23rd Michigan Infantry.

Upon receiving his discharge from the military in July of 1865, Schaefer settled at the site of contemporary Dearborn where he operated his roadhouse at what is now the northeast corner of Schaefer Road and Michigan Avenue. The former highway was named by local citizens in Mr. Schaefer's honor to acknowledge his service in the War Between the States and, quite likely, because it also passed by his place of business and residence.

Joseph Schaefer continued catering to weary

Detroit Area

travelers and slaking the thirsts of regular customers until 1891, when the establishment was taken over by his son, John, who assumed these duties. The father remained in retirement until his death at home on 18 January 1897.

John, who inherited the Six Mile House, was born in Springwells Township on 16 December 1866 and educated in the district schools where he was a classmate of Henry Ford. This friendship endured over the ensuing years, eventually leading John to abandon the family hostelry business in 1918 to establish the Schaefer Lunch Company for the purpose of making box meals for employees at Ford's Rouge plant. Over 100,000 of these meals were supplied daily, with each worker getting soup, three sandwiches and a pie for just 15 cents.

As John's packaged meal venture grew, it became necessary to enlarge his facilities. He constructed the Schaefer Building on the site of the old Six Mile House, creating in the process what was said to be the largest office complex between Detroit and Chicago on route US-12. As John's success grew and he became one of the foremost members of the community, many people assumed that Schaefer Road was named after him, and this mistaken belief can be found stated in a variety of printed sources.

As important as the Schaefer name was in the Dearborn area, it was not immune from threats. In August of 1926 some members of the city council suggested changing the title of Schaefer Road to Coolidge Highway in favor of the man who was then President. When members of the Schaefer family objected, the matter was temporarily shelved. An identical proposal resurfaced in February of 1931, and again the heirs of Joseph protested the obliteration of "a historic land mark." One member of the Dearborn City Council decried that approving the measure would deprive "one of the pioneer and most honored families in the vicinity of a birthright obtained through the patriotic [military] service of their ancestor." By such

words the issue was permanently settled and the Schaefer name left on the signboards.

As the Detroit metropolitan area expanded inland, Schaefer Road grew into a major north/south thoroughfare. In July of 1937, a seven-mile stretch of the highway was made a trunk line route and given the identity M-39. The street retained this status until 1962, when the designation was transferred west to the Southfield Freeway.

When John Schaefer died on 6 June 1941, he had become so famous that the Dearborn City Hall closed for the day and the town's flags were flown at half-staff. His funeral, attended by over 300 people, was one of the largest in the history of the community. Despite these tributes to the son, it is the name of the man's relatively unknown father that appears on the road maps of Wayne County and with which thousands of drivers in southeastern Michigan are familiar.

Coordinates: Southeastern Michigan Enlargement D-F/7

SEAWAY FREEWAY

The St. Lawrence Seaway is a navigable waterway connecting the Great Lakes with the Atlantic Ocean. It extends 182 miles from Montreal, Canada, to the eastern-most point of Lake Ontario.

This maritime passage is not a natural route to the heart of North America. It had to be artificially developed to overcome a series of rapids along the St. Lawrence River that barred most shipping from the Great Lakes.

For centuries mankind had dreamed about having ocean-going vessels sail inland 2,300 miles to the head of Lake Superior. Opening up the interior of the continent to seafaring navigation would greatly reduce transportation costs and increase international trade.

Construction on this great engineering project began in August of 1954. The effort was a cooperative one between the United States and Canadian governments.

Our friends north of the border carried most of the financial burden, paying about 70% of the

$500,000,000 cost. They also made the greatest physical sacrifices for the cause, losing 60 square miles of farmland and seven towns as con-

Detroit Area

struction reshaped the landscape to allow ships to sail the upper reaches of the St. Lawrence River.

This aid to navigation was finished and opened to waterborne traffic on June 26, 1959. Attending the dedication ceremonies and representing the two participating countries were Queen Elizabeth II and President Eisenhower.

With the completion of this giant undertaking at hand, the subject was on many people's minds. Thus, when in May of 1959 the Highway Department was planning part of I-75 in southeastern Michigan, commissioner John C. Mackie decided to name a section of it the Seaway Freeway in honor of the great engineering feat that allowed high-seas shipping access to the Great Lakes State.

The highway was to run in Wayne County from Sibley Road north to the Detroit city limits at Outer Drive, connecting the Detroit-Toledo Freeway with the Fisher Freeway. This 9.5-mile stretch of pavement extended through the communities of

Southgate, Allen Park, Lincoln Park, and Melvindale.

Construction on this section of Interstate began in July of 1962 and was finished on 28 December 1966. When it was dedicated on that day, it was the longest section of urban freeway ever opened at one time in Michigan.

Coordinates: Southeastern Michigan Enlargement F-G/7

SHERIDAN ROAD

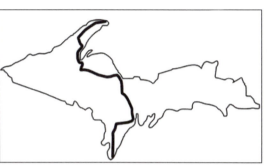

He was the best cavalry commander on the Union side in the Civil War, having never been defeated in combat. His start as a successful battlefield officer in 1862 was as leader of the Second Regiment of Michigan Cavalry. It is not surprising, then, that this state would have a highway named in his honor.

The man of attention is Philip Henry Sheridan, born 6 March 1831 in Albany, New York, and graduate of the United States Military Academy at West Point in 1853. His life as a career soldier was uneventful until the outbreak of the War Between the States, and by the end of this conflict he had so distinguished himself that he held the rank of major general.

After the Civil War Sheridan was sent to the Gulf of Mexico region to restore order. His rule as military governor in Texas and Louisiana was so harsh that President Andrew Jackson relieved him in 1867. He was subsequently sent to Chicago, where he commanded the Military Division of the Mississippi which was engaged in various Indian campaigns.

While in the Windy City between 1867 and 1883, Sheridan developed strong social contacts with many of the local residents. After he died on 5 August 1888, this friendship led the community to name a new fort to the north of town after the popular Civil War general.

Appropriately, the highway con-

necting Chicago with the just-finished Fort Sheridan was called Sheridan Road. In time, this route was extended to Milwaukee, becoming the first paved link between the two lake ports. Not satisfied with this accomplishment, as early as 1916 promoters began seeking extension of the road north of Milwaukee. This notion was delayed, however, by the outbreak of World War I.

By 1922, events had normalized to the point that the Greater Sheridan Road Association started promoting an extended thousand-mile Sheridan Road from St. Louis, Missouri, through Chicago to the tip of the Keweenaw Peninsula. In Michigan, the highway followed contemporary US-41 from Menominee to Fort Wilkins.

To help publicize this great north/south artery, all of the bordering Upper Peninsula cities and villages were encouraged to change the names of their streets on this route to "Sheridan Road." Labor Day of 1923 was set as the date for the switch, and the event was celebrated by participants as the beginning of big things for the region.

To promote the cause, the Greater Sheridan Road Association widely advertised the highway to attract tourists and other travelers. It also erected numerous road signs along the trail, its logo being a silhouette of Sheridan mounted upon his famous jet-black charger "Rienzi."

This memorial highway was actively touted until the early 1930s, when the severe national economic depression left few funds for promotional activities. With no continuing public visibility, the route soon faded into obscurity. Today, about the only remnant of the thoroughfare in Michigan is some small print on signboards in the town of Menominee which indicate that First Street was formerly named Sheridan Road.

Coordinates: A-F/4-5

SIDNEY OUWINGA MEMORIAL BYPASS

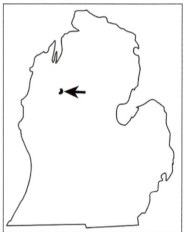

In recent years it has become customary to name new stretches of major federal highways as quickly as they are built or even before they are finished. One example of this practice can be seen in the US-131 diversion around Cadillac, a road designated as a memorial one year prior to its completion.

The person celebrated by this interstate-type pavement--Sidney Ouwinga--was born in Marion on 24 August 1927 and spent his life as a resident of that town. He began working at the age of 12 in his father's local general store, and then later went into agriculture where he specialized in growing potatoes. He was known for his practice of annually giving friends and colleagues complimentary bags of his best potatoes.

Ouwinga's career in public service began as township supervisor. From there he went on to the Osceola County Board of Commissioners (1972-1982) and then the Michigan State House of Representatives (1982-1991). He died while in legislative office on 17 July 1991 after a long bout with cancer.

Over 500 people attended his funeral, including the Governor and Lieutenant Governor. His colleagues in the lower chamber honored him through House Resolution 396 of 1991, adopted unanimously by standing vote. But many felt something more was called for in paying respects, and so another suitable form of recognition was explored.

For years Ouwinga had been a member of the US-131 Association, a group devoted to getting the highway upgraded to freeway status. Furthermore, as a lawmaker he had "worked tirelessly" to get the trunk line diverted around Cadillac and advanced north of the town. Therefore, it seemed only natural to name the Wexford County portion of route between M-115 and Boon Road in his honor.

This commemoration was accomplished through the authority of Public Act 174 of 2000, a measure that paid tribute to "one of the finest, most influential northern Michigan legislators ever." Declaring the road to be the Sidney Ouwinga Memorial Bypass, the route was officially dedicated to the former lawmaker with "the usual ribbon-cutting, dignitaries and speeches" on 27 October 2001.

Coordinates: H/9

SOJOURNER TRUTH
MEMORIAL HIGHWAY

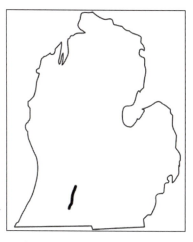

Her real name was Isabella Baumfree, but everyone knows her as Sojourner Truth. Born as a slave around 1797 in Ulster County, New York, she became free in 1828 when a new law in the Empire State banned involuntary servitude.

Sometime in the 1840s, the path of this emancipated black woman led her to Battle Creek, Michigan. From this town she traveled widely through New England and the Midwest speaking out against slavery and for women's rights.

Though Sojourner Truth never learned to read or write, she was an effective orator combining homely remarks with a quick wit. Her lectures were very popular in reformist circles, and until her death at Battle Creek in 1883 she was a national leader in the abolitionist and early feminist movements.

A person of this stature could not be buried on Michigan soil without someone wanting to name a highway in her honor. This very idea arose in 1976 when the state's American Revolution Bicentennial Commission urged the legislature to take such action as a proper tribute to a deserving woman.

In response, the solons in Lansing passed Act 93 of 1976 declaring that "the portion of state highway M-66 located in Calhoun County shall henceforth be known as the Sojourner Truth Memorial Highway." On May 21 of the same year, the specified route was dedicated to the former slave who had adopted Michigan as her home.

Perhaps surprisingly, the legislature later passed another law relating to the Sojourner Truth trunk line. This time the action was undertaken at the request of the Cereal City Development Corporation.

The CCDC wanted some statutory revisions because a section of the Sojourner Truth Memorial Highway had "become better known to local residents as the 'Penetrator'." To change this habit and restore attention to one of Battle Creek's famous historical figures, the CCDC asked the legislature to rename the Penetrator--a portion of "M-66 between Interstate I-94 and Hamblin--as the Sojourner Truth Downtown Parkway."

Granting this request, said the CCDC, "would serve to emphasize in a highly visible way the link between Sojourner Truth and the City of Battle Creek, which was once the center of abolitionist sentiment in the state." Convinced by this argument, the legislature obliged by passing Public Act 208 of 1993.

As a result of this modifying language, Michigan residents and visitors can now travel on a Sojourner Truth Highway or a Sojourner Truth Parkway. They can also use this great woman as a role model and strive to become sojourners along the road of truth.

Coordinates: Battle Creek Inset

SOLDIERS' MEMORIAL HIGHWAY

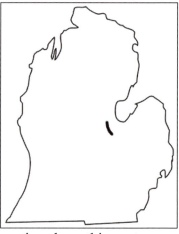

It is said that the first war memorial was probably a cairn or heap of boulders erected over the common grave of men killed in battle. Later in history these cairns were replaced by monuments of stone or masonry, with commemorative shafts and columns set up in special places of honor.

Eventually this custom gave way to statues of kings and generals--the "bronze man on a bronze horse"--that were often established in public squares or at the intersections of principal city avenues. Communities that could not afford cast figures of their heroes settled for displays of guns, pyramids of cannon balls, garlands of chains, or similar martial structures.

By the twentieth century, a movement had developed to make war memorials not only beautiful but also useful. It was increasingly felt that if money was going to be spent on some gesture of remembrance, the product should pay tribute to fallen soldiers and at the same time contribute something to the community.

The result of this philosophy was called the "living" memorial, in contrast to the traditional "dead" objects of metal and stone. Living memorials, which we recognize and accept today, are things like parks, recreational areas, wildlife sanctuaries, game preserves, flower gardens, landscaped waysides, and forests dedicated to the human cost of war.

Subscribing to this concept of living memorials, in January of 1922 chapters of the American Legion and Daughters of the American Revolution jointly endorsed a "road of memory" for those soldiers and sailors "who rendered their final account" in World War I. As originally conceived, the dedicated highway was to extend from Saginaw to Houghton Lake via Midland, Edenville and Gladwin, but there is no evidence to indicate that the two most northern counties along this route ever participated in the project.

Acting in unison, Saginaw and Midland counties chose a twenty-mile stretch of road paralleling the Tittabawassee River as their common living memorial. The two governments decided to enhance this scenic drive by planting trees along most of its length to help keep green in the minds of citizens the collective accomplishments of local soldiers and the price they paid fulfilling their mission.

Wishing to promote the living memorial concept, the Forestry Department at what is now Michigan State University furnished the trees for this project at cost. Eager to do its part to promote alternative forms of tribute, the State Highway Department paid 60% of the expense of planting the trees and also supervised putting them in the ground. The fruits of this cooperation appeared on 5 May 1922 when the first of 500 black walnut and 1,000 white pine trees were set out along the Tittabawassee River drive, officially placing M-47 among Michigan's roads of remembrance.

Coordinates: J/11-12

SOUTHFIELD FREEWAY

Detroit Area

Southfield Township, Oakland County, was organized in 1830. Just two years later the officials of this governmental unit began opening highways along the section lines, a practice common in areas that have been laid out according to the Congressional survey system. One of these routes of communication, running south from around the community of Birmingham, was called Southfield Road in honor of the Township.

Over time, these parallel ruts in the dirt were continued by a similar bridle and wagon path extending down to Dearborn and beyond in Wayne County. By the end of the first quarter of the twentieth century, the former country trail had become a popular north/south rural thoroughfare. Because of its increasing use and good location, in 1926 the Wayne County Road Commission decided to turn much of Southfield Road into a wide superhighway.

Envisioned as a bypass around congested Detroit from the downriver area north to Oakland County, the Wayne County Road Commission gradually made Southfield into a belt line artery. By 1942 this agency had finished turning most of Southfield Road under its jurisdiction into a broad dual-lane, divided, high-speed motorway.

Then, in 1952, the Wayne County Road Commission began studying the feasibility of converting the Southfield Highway with its ample right-of-way into an expressway from contemporary I-94 north to Base Line Road. The idea was to build three lanes in each direction with continuous adjacent service drives for local traffic. The proposed freeway was to have a "rolling grade" design running at or slightly below surface level. The pavement would be depressed at all overpasses, which meant a dip in the profile every one-half mile.

Since Southfield Highway was under county and city control at that time, attempting such a major construction effort would require deep-pocket reinforcements. The additional help appeared in November of 1958 when Michigan authorities determined that Southfield from I-94 to Northwestern Highway would become a limited access route as part of the state trunk line system. Accordingly, on 31 March 1959 Southfield Highway became M-39 and six months later construction began on the $40,000,000 upgrade project.

Road building activities generally proceeded from south to north, with the federal government picking up 50% of the tab, the state covering 37.5%, Wayne County contributing 6.5%, and the cities of Detroit and Dearborn financing the remainder. The first section of the 14-mile-long route was opened in December of 1961 and the final link was finished on 29 October 1964. Though the Southfield Freeway was dedicated on that autumn date, the ceremonies were overshadowed by the completion and celebration of the Lodge Freeway on that same day. With the large volume of traffic using the Southfield Freeway thereafter, in 1966 it became necessary to extend M-39 south of I-94 to Fort Street, creating the situation pretty much as it stands today.

Coordinates: Southeastern Michigan Enlargement D-F/7

STEPHENSON HIGHWAY

Detroit Area

Memorial highways in Michigan are generally named after people or groups of individuals who performed great deeds. However, in at least one case a road of remembrance in our state honors the man who donated the land upon which it was built.

The story goes back to 13 October 1881 when Burnette Fechet Stephenson was born at Port Huron. He moved to Detroit in 1906, and within two years was established in the real estate business where he specialized in developing land in and around the Motor City.

In 1916 he spent over $1,500,000 to buy around 1,800 acres of contiguous farm land east of Woodward Avenue between Highland Park and Royal Oak. Within this tract he plated at least a dozen subdivisions and opened up 5,000 home sites in Berkley, Ferndale, Highland Park, Madison Heights, Pleasant Ridge, and Hazel Park (a town he founded and named after his wife).

Since these dwellings were constructed some distance from the major places of employment, Mr. Stephenson donated a 75-foot right-of-way to the Detroit United Railway so a street car track could be built to connect his property with the city's transportation network. This railroad, known as the Stephenson Line, was the last interurban route built in Michigan.

Trolley cars were the primary means of getting to and from work in pre-World War I urban Michigan, but by the 1920s the private automobile was increasingly serving as the main form of conveyance. With a growing number of vehicles traveling inadequate roads, movement in and about Stephenson's extensive subdivisions was becoming a major headache.

To solve this problem, Stephenson donated a 204-foot right-of-way through the middle of his real estate holdings for the building of a "super highway." Construction of this multilane thoroughfare was started in 1924, and the first section was dedicated in Hazel Park on September 27 of that year in the presence of the governor and thousands of spectators.

Because of his generosity and concern for the public's welfare, this new avenue extending north from Base Line Road was named the Stephenson Highway. As use of this principal street grew, late in 1931 it became incorporated into the state trunk line system as route M-150.

Stephenson Highway remained a prominent feature on the road maps of greater Detroit until 1969, when I-75 was superimposed upon its southern-most three miles and the state trunk line designation was removed. Today, only the northern portion of the Stephenson Highway still exists, running from about 12 Mile Road in Madison Heights up to Rochester Road in Troy.

As for Mr. Stephenson, he also fared well after the creation of his highway in 1924. He finished developing his properties in southeastern Oakland County, making a fortune in the process. Following his accomplishments in real estate, he briefly entered politics with an unsuccessful race for Congress in 1932, a stint on the State Liquor Control Commission during 1933-1935, and an aborted run for governor in 1938.

In 1941, Stephenson bought what was said to be the largest cherry orchard in the state situated on 240 acres northwest of Lexington in Sanilac County. To market the harvest from his 18,000 trees, Stephenson reportedly installed the first plant in the country to quick-freeze cherries in 30-pound containers for use in the bakery trade.

Like many others growing old, Mr. Stephenson eventually turned his gaze toward the congenial climate of Florida. He moved to St. Petersburg, where he again became involved in real estate matters and created several large subdivisions.

Remaining active almost up to the end, Mr. Stephenson died in St. Petersburg on 14 May 1954 at the age of 72. His body was returned to Michigan, where it now lies in Roseland Park Cemetery, just three miles from the road that bears his name.

Coordinates: Southeastern Michigan Enlargement C/8

STRAIGHT TO THE STRAITS ROUTE

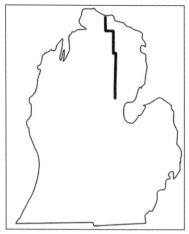

Contemporary M-33 started out much like any other road in the northern half of the Lower Peninsula. It began as little more than a cow path that scarcely knew where it was going, evolved into a sandy track for horse-drawn vehicles, and eventually became a gravel trail for automobiles.

By 1929, residents along M-33 were promoting the route as the quick way for drivers from southeastern Michigan to reach the Straits of Mackinac. According to their calculations, the highway was 48 miles shorter than the other popular options like US-23 (along the Huron shore) or US-27 (up the middle of the state).

To draw attention to M-33, boosters tried to give it a title that would make it popular with the motoring public. Many names were suggested, like Big Dipper Drive, Meridian Route, Planetoid Passage, Michigan's Roof Garden Avenue, The Ne Plus Road, Drive of the Great Bear, Al Fresco Turnpike, Solar Avenue, Empyrean Boulevard, and Paul Bunyan Highway.

Finally, on 12 May 1939, a name was chosen and the Straight-to-the-Straits Association was formed. The group adopted the slogan "It's M-33 for me", and to guide travelers along the way it used the emblem MSS (Michigan Straight to the Straits).

To help spread its message, the Association issued a ten-cent monthly magazine called <u>The Northern Light</u> which promoted the highway, advertised local businesses, and offered stories about the area's attractions. It also served as a forum for airing the group's desires for improvements to M-33 like paving and widening.

The Association lauded M-33 as the fastest and most convenient way to the Straits by sponsoring caravans of cars along the road to get attention, erecting signs to entice traffic, and holding special sales in towns along

the route where everything was priced at 33 cents. Operating funds were raised by holding picnics, dances, and similar community events.

The Straight to the Straits group was active until 1940, when the national defense buildup and ensuing World War diverted attention to more pressing matters. In 1947, as the country returned to normal, the Association was reorganized and its promotional activities resumed.

By 1960--after the building of the Mackinaw Bridge and the related improvement of US-27--it was clear to the Association that M-33 would never be a major highway carrying traffic to the Straits. The members realized that to survive they would have to change the objectives of their organization.

Adjusting to new realities, the Strait-to-the-Straits people began to tout M-33 as a good two-lane scenic route for the leisurely traveler. Instead of focusing on direct paths and shorter distances, the emphasis turned to such assets as wilderness, open spaces, serenity and sightseeing.

But the relatively few people who wanted these qualities in an itinerary could find them with or without enticements, and so the need for a Straight-to-the-Straits Association gradually waned. Though the organization ceased to exist around 1966, a now fully paved and popular M-33 stands as a testament to their faith in the merits of the route.

Coordinates: E-H/11-12

SWEETWATER TRAIL

We are all familiar with the oceans, those briny bodies of water that occupy about 70% of this planet. But there are also lakes on the various continents so large that they can, without doing injustice to the term, be called inland seas. Unlike their larger and salty counterparts, however, these interior basins contain fresh water or, in more poetic language, sweet water. This fact has provided identification for one of our state's motor routes.

This vehicular byway was created by the Michigan Historic Preservation Network, a non-profit organization founded in 1979 for the purpose of protecting and highlighting the old-time physical and cultural assets of our two peninsulas. Feeling the best way to safeguard these natural and manmade treasures is by making people aware of them, the Network decided to focus its attention on saving and promoting Michigan's maritime heritage.

This hydrological orientation was adopted because, historically speaking, our state's population has tended to locate along the shoreline. Centuries ago our water features were the main highways for travel, so settlement was initially almost solely confined to the coasts of lakes and the mouths of large rivers. With more than 3,200 miles of beach surrounding the margins of Michigan, there are obviously many historical sites to see where the Great Lakes meet the land.

To help people become familiar with how our peninsulas' inhabitants have lived and worked in the zone of interaction between water and earth, the Preservation Network established in 1991 the Sweetwater Trail. This route, laid out so as to follow as closely as possible Michigan's peripheral shoreline, was designed to guide people to--plus help them to understand and appreciate--the best remaining features of our state's long-time relationship with its coastal geography.

Specially designed logos along the way guide travelers as they seek to journey back into history by following the Sweetwater Trail. The marked path leads drivers to such aquatic sites as lighthouses, lifesaving stations, harbors of refuge, marinas, fishing villages, nautical museums, waterfront industries, underwater preserves, and pleasing coastal landscapes. This system of roadside signage not only enhances the experience of general travelers but also helps to promote the increasingly popular pastime of heritage tourism.

Eventually, the plan is to have the Sweetwater Trail completely surround the shoreline margins of Michigan. For now, however, the Trail is established in just the northeastern of the state. There, it traces the track of US-23 between Standish and Mackinaw City. In the extreme eastern Upper Peninsula the course takes in all or parts of trunk lines M-129, M-134, M-221, and US-2.

Visually stimulating and educationally rewarding historic resources can be found in communities all along the Great Lakes' littoral with Michigan and even in between the centers of population. To find these treats for the eye and brain, one should forsake the yellow brick road and follow instead the path of the Sweetwater Trail.

Coordinates: C-I/10-13

TAHQUAMENON FALLS MEMORIAL HIGHWAY

It is not common to find cartographic depictions of individually named or memorial highways. The state or federal government has not been known to produce such maps for Michigan, leaving the field in sole possession of private interests.

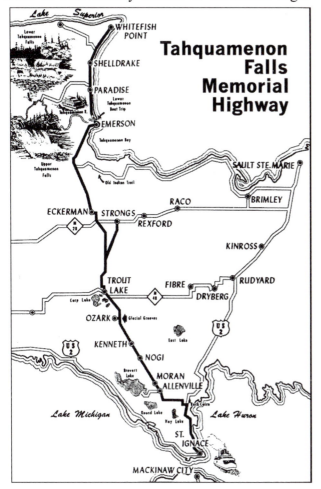

Since most of the early named highways were founded by organizations seeking to entice motorists to visit their realms for commercial gain, these business-supported groups would sometimes use their own money to publish and distribute literature showing the paths of their adopted routes of travel.

Some of the best early examples of this practice came off the presses on behalf of the West Michigan Pike and the Dixie Highway. These two pioneering channels of traffic issued promotional brochures and single folded maps showing motorists how to follow their respective north/south drives. Other sponsoring bodies, less well endowed financially, saved money by incorporating a crude map of their pet project into the named road's emblem or logo.

As time passed and independent publicity expenses grew, backers of particular highways increasingly resorted to placing advertisements in tourist periodicals to reach their intended audience. The adjacent map from the 1950 Upper Peninsula Lure Book is an example of how such efforts could be effective in bringing a specific highway to the attention of those behind the wheel.

TAHQUAMENON FALLS MEMORIAL HIGHWAY

Formally established in January of 1947, Tahquamenon Falls State Park is the most popular park in the Upper Peninsula with over 500,000 visitors annually. Embracing nearly 40,000

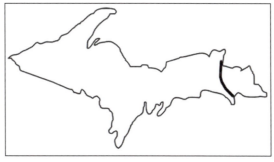

acres, it is second only to Porcupine Mountains State Park in size.

The main feature of the park is the 200-foot-wide Tahquamenon River with its 50-foot upper falls and 23-foot lower falls.

With a flow of 50,000 gallons of water per second, the upper falls is the second largest east of the Mississippi River in water volume and third in size, as only Niagara Falls and Cumberland Falls (Kentucky) have greater drops.

As is often the case with Native American names, the true meaning of "Tahquamenon" is uncertain. The literature issued by the Michigan State Parks claims the word is Indian for "marsh of the blueberries." Whatever its meaning, the name became immortalized when Henry Wadsworth Longfellow wrote of Hiawatha building his canoe alongside "the rushing Tahquamenaw."

Years before a state park was established around the lower Tahquamenon River, people were drawn to the beauty of this stream. To accommodate this growing body of tourists, secondary roads were built to the site. Access to the region was further expedited when, in 1938, Mackinac and Chippewa counties finished building a cut-off road that ran from St. Ignace to about Eckerman.

When the Tahquamenon Falls area became part of Michigan's state park system, many residents in the

eastern UP wanted the most direct road from St. Ignace to Whitefish Point taken over by the Highway Department and paved. Local chambers of commerce and other business interests felt this could best be done by getting more people to use the route through coordinated promotional activities.

A special meeting to develop publicity plans was called at Trout Lake on 5 February 1947, and there an association was formed for the purpose of encouraging north-bound tourists to travel the cutoff road. In an effort to call attention to the route while at the same time paying homage to the region's veterans, a decision was made to dub the shortcut the Tahquamenon Falls Memorial Highway.

This strategy proved to be effective, for the increase in traffic year by year and the pending construction of the Mackinaw Bridge eventually led the state to take over the road in May of 1954 and declare it M-123. Ironically, once the state acquired jurisdiction over the trunk line, it creased to be called the Tahquamenon Falls Memorial Highway and this honorary designation is unknown today.

Coordinates: B-D/10

TAWAS-MANISTEE TRAIL

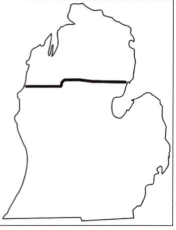

In 1871 commissioners authorized and began laying out the Tawas to Manistee State Road, a 150-mile-long connector between two towns on opposite sides of the southern Michigan mitten. Surveying and construction of the route continued through the decade and into the 1880s before a crude, bumpy, winding dirt wagon path was created athwart the middle of the Lower Peninsula.

This barely improved link between Lakes Huron and Michigan served the region's needs until the advent of the motor vehicle, when better transportation facilities were called for. As the state began to develop a system of highways to aid travel and commerce, its attention eventually turned to the old track through the extensive forests separating Manistee and Tawas City.

Between 1914 and 1920 government officials gradually incorporated parts of the trail into the state trunk line network, incrementally extending M-55 east to west across the state. By 1925 a serviceable highway was completed between Tawas and West Branch and two years later nearly everything east of Cadillac was finished.

The problem segment of the route was between Manistee and Cadillac, where factions were arguing over which course the motorway should take. One camp wanted a northern passage that went through Brethren, Harrietta and

Boon. This option required the construction of only eight miles of new road, needed relatively few bridges, and served a more populous area.

A second group backed a more southerly path that essentially followed the present alignment of M-55 through "25 miles of jack pine, scrub oak and pine barrens" but with a terminus closer to the town of Manistee. Not until 1927 did these contesting forces reach a compromise which made the northern option a county road and the southern choice a state trunk line.

But this meeting of the minds did not result in the immediate completion of the western extremity of M-55. For years thereafter parties argued over the exact alignment of the southern route, local courts had to settle numerous right-of-way disputes, and the hardships wrought by the Great Depression claimed most of the moneys that were formerly allocated for road construction.

Work on the last leg of M-55 west of Cadillac did not begin until late in 1930. The section within Manistee County was finally completed in September of 1932 and the Wexford County portion was opened in July of 1933. Thus, two-thirds of a century after it was first established, the road between Tawas and Manistee became a modern trans-state thoroughfare.

In the process, the highway exchanged the familiar title "Tawas-Manistee Trail" for the rather impersonal identifier "M-55." While being christened with a number was certainly less romantic, it was a more contemporary type of name that reflected the route's final elevation to one of Michigan's better class of country roads.

Coordinates: H/8-12

TECUMSEH TRAIL

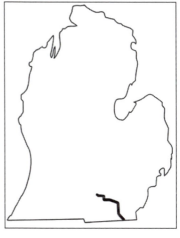

Tecumseh, a Shawnee chief whose name meant shooting star, was born in March of 1768 near what is today Springfield, Ohio. Though the details of his youth are generally unknown, it is certain that in adulthood he became one of the greatest of American Indians.

This man was recognized by all parties as a superb warrior, orator, strategist, and charismatic leader. He used these skills in an effort to get his fellow Indians to return to the ways of their forefathers and preserve their lands from encroachments by the white man.

At first Tecumseh thought incursions of settlers could be prevented, and the Indian way of life maintained, by peaceful means. But he eventually concluded that force would be necessary to achieve these goals, and he set out to establish a single alliance of nearly all tribes east of the Mississippi to halt the American advance.

By the time of the War of 1812, Tecumseh had created a confederacy of the Midwestern bands and was in command of over one thousand braves. Allying his forces with those of the British, he was given the rank of brigadier general in the royal army.

Tecumseh ably led his men against the United States during this period of hostilities, ultimately losing his life on 5 October 1813 at the battle of the Thames River in Ontario. With his death the intertribal alliance fell apart, mainly bringing an end to Indian resistance.

Since Tecumseh was an "enemy" of our nation, some may wonder why he was held in such high regard by his adversaries that a town in Michigan would be named in his honor. The answer lies in the fact that, though an opponent of this country in combat, he was considered a noble and honorable man on both sides of the battle line.

His arch-enemy, Governor William Henry Harrison of Indiana, said that Tecumseh was "one of those uncommon geniuses which spring up occasionally to produce revolutions and overturn the established order of things. If it were not for the [close] vicinity of the United States, he would, perhaps, be the founder of an empire that would rival in glory Mexico or Peru."

Given the high universal esteem for Tecumseh, it is not surprising to find a road named in his honor. This tribute occurred on 28 September 1917 when the Tecumseh Commerce Club called a meeting to designate and mark a named highway between Jackson, Michigan and Toledo, Ohio.

Following what are now just back roads, the chosen path ran southeast from Jackson through the towns of Napolean, Manchester, Clinton, Tecumseh, and Blissfield, then across the state line through Sylvania to the Lucas County seat. Since the idea for the road originated in Tecumseh, and since that town was about midway along the route, the title of the highway was almost a foregone conclusion.

A black and white sign bearing the profile of an Indian head was chosen as the identifying symbol for marking the road. Such are the vagaries of fate, however, that today the twentieth-century sign and its associated highway have lost their fight with time and it is Tecumseh, the old defeated chieftain, who has won the battle with history.

Coordinates: M-N/11-13

TELEGRAPH ROAD

Since many people enjoy playing Trivial Pursuits, here are some questions about Michigan transportation. What is the only even-numbered federal route in our state that goes north and south (the rest all go east and west)? What was the first federal aid road built in Wayne County? What trunk line was at one time the longest highway in Michigan, running from Toledo to Mackinaw City? The answer in every instance is US-24 and its Telegraph Road segment.

Obviously, Telegraph Road gets its name from the communication system invented by Samuel F.B. Morse in 1837. His method of transmitting and receiving information was not commercially established in our state until 1847, when the first telegraph line was installed between Detroit and Ypsilanti along the line of the Michigan Central Railroad. In 1848 a competing company completed a telegraph line between Buffalo and Detroit, and soon thereafter another firm ran a line from Detroit to Chicago via Monroe. All of these businesses merged in 1856 to form the Western Union Telegraph Company.

When considering the subject of telegraphy, most people think of railroad right-of-ways which are lined with poles and wires. In earlier times, however, it was not uncommon to run the lines straight across the countryside, away from railroads but near some avenue of land transportation whenever possible to simplify the job of accessing and supplying the chosen communication route. It appears as though the telegraph line stretching from about Trenton to Pontiac was strung up around 1868. Not surprisingly, some of the rural roads adjacent to this line eventually came to be named after the conspicuous electric superstructure adorning their flanks.

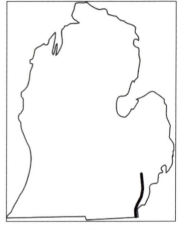

Originally, just the portion of US-24 south of Dearborn was called Telegraph Road. It remained a second-class provincial route until 1919, when state, federal and Wayne County officials decided to make it into a major north/south trunk line. At that time, nearly all traffic heading north of Detroit had to go directly through the city, a traffic design that resulted in terrible vehicle congestion downtown. To help solve this problem, authorities decided to build a bypass around the Motor City by upgrading the status of Telegraph Road.

The first portion of the new highway to be completed was in 1922 when the segment between Dearborn and Flat Rock was opened. Next in succession came the portion from Flat Rock south to Stony Creek in Monroe County (1923), between Michigan Avenue and Grand River Avenue in Wayne County (1924), Stony Creek to the Ohio State Line in Monroe County (1925), and from Grand River Avenue to the Dixie Highway northwest of Pontiac in Oakland County (1930).

This more direct route to points north that avoided the clogged streets of Detroit quickly became a popular thoroughfare for motorists to follow, eventually turning Telegraph Road itself into a rather congested artery. Today, the multi-laned trunk line is a busy urban motorway over most of its length, and drivers bypass its traffic problems by traveling where possible on nearby interstate systems. But with all of its modern characteristics, the memory of an historic transmission line from the past remains embodied in the name of Telegraph Road.

Coordinates: Southeastern Michigan Enlargement A-H/6

THEODORE ROOSEVELT INTERNATIONAL HIGHWAY

Theodore Roosevelt, the 26th president of the United States, was born in New York City on 27 October 1858. As a gifted child in a wealthy family, Theodore studied under tutors until he entered Harvard University at the age of 18.

After graduating from college in 1880, Roosevelt entered politics. He first served in the New York State Assembly, then later with New York City government, and finally as the assistant secretary of the Navy.

In May of 1898, he resigned his secretaryship to become lieutenant colonel of the First U.S. Volunteer Cavalry, popularly known as the Rough Riders. Due to his leadership and bravery in the ensuing Spanish-American War, Roosevelt became a national hero.

Capitalizing upon this fame, Roosevelt won election as governor of New York State in 1898 and in 1900 was chosen to be William McKinley's vice-presidential running mate. This political team won the national election, but when McKinley was assassinated in the Fall of 1901, Roosevelt became the youngest person ever to hold the presidency of the United States.

During his nearly eight years in the White House, Roosevelt had many accomplishments. Domestically, he was known for busting trusts, resource conservation, and giving people a "square deal." Internationally, he won the Nobel prize for ending the Russo-Japanese War, began building the Panama Canal, and developed "Speak softly and carry a big stick" diplomacy.

America's affection for the man is manifested by the teddy bear, which is named in his honor. Roosevelt's likeness is also one of the four faces carved into Mount Rushmore in South Dakota.

When "Teddy" Roosevelt died on 6 January 1919, many people sought ways to perpetuate his memory. One group, meeting in Duluth about six weeks later, decided to do this by promoting an international, transcontinental highway from Portland, Maine, to Portland, Oregon.

As finally laid out, the route crossed Ontario between Buffalo and Detroit, this Canadian stretch also known as the Lake Erie North Shore Trail. Once in Michigan, it followed the approximate path of I-75 north from the Motor City to US-23, and then stayed on that trunk line all the way to the Straits of Mackinac.

Crossing the Straits, the Roosevelt Highway continued west on US-2. The northern tier of counties in the Upper Peninsula objected to this choice, since it left them out of the picture. As a compromise, the organizers agreed to make M-28 part of the Roosevelt Highway system too, giving Michigan northern and southern routes which merged into one at Wakefield.

Michigan completed construction on its portion of the Roosevelt Highway in late summer of

1926. The final link in the 4,060-mile route was not finished in Montana until August, 1930, with dedication ceremonies occurring at that site fourteen months later.

Today, no one hears the name "Roosevelt Highway" associated with a route number in our state. The reason may be found in a column that appeared in <u>Michigan Roads & Pavements</u> some years ago. The editors noted that "a great deal of local pride had to be overcome...before the present uniform [road numbering] plan could be adopted. Objection was met, and strenuous objection at that, from cities and highway associations when

the subject [was raised] of dropping the official name-route designation in favor of the plain numeral one."

"Local money and local energy had gone into more than one road project, it was pointed out by the local associations, and they did not feel that their labor and money should be buried under a cross-country numeral. But 'for the good of the order' argument was advanced by the state and federal highway officials and in time it prevailed." Thus, alas for backers of the Roosevelt Highway, their number was up.

Coordinates: B-M/1-13

TOM BOLT HIGHWAY

On 19 September 1922, the portion of M-46 from Muskegon east to Casnovia was opened to the public. At the time it was said to be the first completed route in the county and "the longest single unbroken stretch of improved highway in any county in Michigan."

Initially, this 23-mile-long ribbon of concrete was known as Cedar Springs Road. But some people yearned for a less prosaic title.

Action toward developing a more impressive identity was soon initiated by the Greater Muskegon Chamber of Commerce, which proposed that the newly paved way be named after the "Father of Good Roads in Muskegon County." On 28 June 1923 the Muskegon County Board of Supervisors agreed, unanimously resolving that the thoroughfare be known as the "Tom Bolt Highway."

Who was Tomas J.G. Bolt, and why did he deserve to have a highway named after him? The answer is a highly respected public servant who was a pioneering booster for good roads in Western Michigan.

Bolt's list of accomplishments includes serving for approximately 50 years as Moorland Township's repre-

sentative to the Muskegon County Board of Supervisors. In addition, he was a township treasurer and supervisor, county school inspector, member of the county road commission, and a state senator during the years 1909-1910.

After a long and distinguished career, Tom Bolt died on 27 May 1933 at the age of 85. As the ensuing years passed, the name of this famous local politician slowly faded from memory and "his" road became known as Apple Avenue.

Today, no evidence remains of the Bolt Memorial Highway except for two stone markers with metal plaques at either end of the route. Though the man celebrated by M-46 has long departed, the busy highway remains as a tribute to the person who first presented the resolution urging that the cross-county road be built.

Coordinates: K/8

TOP OF MICHIGAN TRAIL

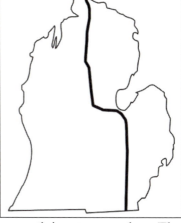

The central Lower Peninsula north of about Clare has long been known as one of the great playgrounds of Michigan. As weekend traffic along I-75 demonstrates, many people find year-round recreational pleasure in the area's hills, forests, lakes and streams.

Before the advent of the automobile, most tourists to this region had to rely upon the services of the Michigan Central Railroad to reach their destinations. But as the privately-owned, motorized vehicle became increasingly capable of traveling long distances, agitation arose for good quality roads to accommodate easy access into areas previously reserved to the iron horse.

The call for an interior road from about Bay City to the Straits began in May of 1917 when petitions were filed with the state highway commissioner. These written appeals for such an improved route were signed by all of the affected county road commissions, all appropriate county officers, the members of the state military board, and most city and village leaders in the region.

In less than half a year the recommended path had been mapped out and the highway named. Since the destination of the proposed route was the top of the Lower Peninsula, the road was dubbed the Top of Michigan Trail. In approximate terms, its course followed contemporary US-23 from Toledo to Bay City, US-10 from Bay City to North Bradley, M-18 from North Bradley to Roscommon, and I-75 from Roscommon to Mackinaw City.

The promoters of this highway, in an effort to give the road identity, wanted to create an insignia by which the Trail would be known and marked. They chose the monogram TMT flanked on either side by a pine

tree, the conifer deemed to be emblematic of northern Michigan.

In keeping with this arboreal theme, plans were made to plant pine trees along much of the road's 333-mile length to make the route more enticing to travelers The idea was to create an attractive Trail similar to the famous tree-lined highways of Europe

While the purpose of the road was certainly to provide local public convenience, stimulate commerce, and assist in the region's development, perhaps the primary consideration was to attract vacationers to the realm. Consequently, in February of 1918 an effort was made to change the rather peculiar name of the highway to the more alluring title, Northern Michigan Tourist Pike.

This modification did not catch on, but in the final analysis it didn't matter. Mainly during the period 1919-1921, as the road was incorporated into the state transportation system, trunk line numbers were assigned to segments of the route and the quirky phrase "Top of Michigan Trail" quickly faded from general use.

Today, modern ribbons of concrete have replaced the original primitive track into the heartland south of the Straits. So, while there is still a top to the Lower Peninsula, you can no longer take just an old trail from the south to get there.

Coordinates: E-N/10-13

TOWNSEND NATIONAL HIGHWAY

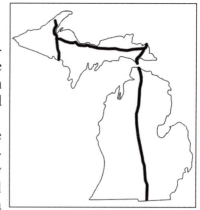

Charles Elroy Townsend resided in Michigan all of his life. He was partially responsible for the establishment of the national highway system across America. He once had a number of major roads in both the Upper and Lower Peninsulas named for him. Despite all of this, he is probably a stranger to nearly everyone reading these words.

Born in a rural setting near Concord, Michigan on 15 August 1856, Townsend had to help run the family farm as a youth, an activity that prevented him from finishing high school until the age of 21. Following graduation, he taught school in Jackson County from 1878 through 1886.

In 1887, Townsend permanently left education to become the Jackson County Register of Deeds. Surrendering this public office at the end of 1896, he joined a Jackson law firm and became a practicing attorney. He remained in the legal profession until 1903, when he entered the political arena.

Townsend was first elected as a Representative to Congress in 1903, a position he held for four terms. In 1911 he left the House to become one of Michigan's two United States Senators. He served in this capacity until 1923, when he was defeated in a bid for reelection.

Following his departure from Washington, Townsend was made a member of the International Joint Commission on Canadian/US boundary problems. He remained an active member of this body until his death in Jackson, Michigan on 3 August 1924.

During his tenure on Capitol Hill, Townsend was especially interested in matters relating to transportation. In particular, he energetically promoted better highways and took the lead in advancing legislation that would provide federal funds for road building.

While in the Senate, in 1919 he introduced the so-called federal highway aid bill (S.5626). The concepts embodied in this measure ultimately provided financial assistance from Washington to benefit road construction throughout the country. The result of this law was the eventual development of a great network of US trunk lines across the land creating our first system of interstate routes.

In recognition for his work to further the establishment of better highways by means of public tax dollars, in the summer of 1920 the Michigan Good Roads Association approved the creation of the Townsend National Highway. This road was to go from Mobile, Alabama, to extreme northern Michigan, connecting the realms of the palm and the pine.

At the time, linking the waters of the Gulf and the Great Lakes was a popular notion. With Mobile supposedly being the nearest subtropical port to Michigan, it was selected as the southern terminus of the Townsend National Highway.

Generally speaking, this road of tribute followed contemporary I-65 north to Indianapolis and then I-69 to Fort Wayne. Within Michigan, its course included US-127 from the border to Higgins Lake; I-75 from Higgins Lake to Sault Ste. Marie; M-28 from the Soo to Marquette; US-41 from Marquette to Calumet; and all of US-141.

This layout was approved in 1921 by the Director General of the United States Good Roads Association, but his blessing apparently did little to advance public acceptance of the plan. Unfortunately, the Townsend National Highway just never caught on as a named thoroughfare, leaving the road even less well known than the now relatively obscure man it was meant to honor.

Coordinates: A-N/4-11

U.A.W. FREEWAY

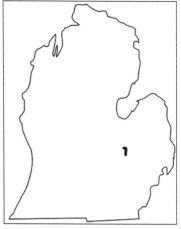

The UAW is one of the largest labor unions in the United States, with over 1,000 locals and 775,000 members around the country. An abbreviation for United Automobile Workers, the UAW is now far more encompassing, representing workers in the auto, aerospace, agricultural implement, parts, and supply industries as well as technical, office and professional workers in the private and public sectors.

The labor union was founded in Detroit on 26 August 1935, but initially had trouble getting recognized as a bargaining agent by the auto manufacturers. This situation changed in January of 1937 when the UAW engaged in a sit-down strike at the Chevrolet plants in Flint.

A concept imported from France, the sit-down strike occurred when employees sat down at their jobs and refused to work or leave the plant. By utilizing this technique, the UAW won recognition as a bargaining agent from General Motors in February of 1937, with Chrysler agreeing to terms shortly thereafter and Ford following suit in 1941.

As the union representing most workers in the automobile industry, the UAW did much to improve the economic well-being of its members. It also played a major role in helping labor in general through the backing of such issues as better health and safety, increased minimum wage, civil rights, and fair employment practices.

Since the UAW was born in Michigan and reached maturity in Flint, it is not surprising that certain elements in Genesee County were interested in giving some recognition to the union. These parties thought that a highway should be named for the UAW, but all suitable roads had already been designated for someone else.

Flint's major east-west thoroughfare, M-78, had previously been acknowledged as the Chevrolet Freeway, and the town's principal north/south route, I-475, had been declared the Buick Freeway. It would be impossible to name either of these highways for the UAW without dishonoring two men who were important to the local community.

A local legislator solved this dilemma when he introduced House Concurrent Resolution 583 of 1980. The measure proposed making Flint's east/west artery the Chevrolet-Buick Freeway and I-475 the UAW Freeway. This compromise was quickly approved by the Michigan House and Senate and their sentiments were dedicated, appropriately, on Labor Day of 1981.

Coordinates: Flint Inset

UNDERGROUND RAILROAD MEMORIAL HIGHWAY

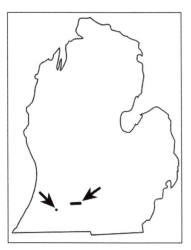

Prior to the American Civil War, a system was devised for surreptitiously moving slaves from the South to freedom in the abolitionist North. This clandestine method of human transportation, operating from about 1830 to 1860, was called the Underground Railroad.

Neither subterranean nor a railroad, the collective escape routes got this name because they were operated in secrecy and used railway terms to covertly describe their activities. For example, stopping places along the way were called "stations," people who aided fugitives were known as "conductors," and the runaway slaves were referred to as "packages" or "freight."

In 1990, Congress authorized the National Park Service to study the operations and identify the routes of the Underground Railroad. Since Michigan was an active participant in aiding this movement, representatives from this government agency examined our state for sites worthy of federal recognition. Two such places were identified, one in Detroit and the other in Schoolcraft.

Dr. Nathan Thomas and his wife, Pamela, were participants in the Underground Railroad. They fed and sheltered up to 1,500 slaves in their Schoolcraft home between 1838 and 1860 before sending the escapees on to the next "station" down the line in Battle Creek. So important was the role of this residence in the Underground Railroad system that it has been preserved and opened to tourists.

The Legislature felt this facet of Michigan history needed promotion, so in 2004 it passed Public Act 139 to help bring attention to the local role in freeing people from bondage. Lawmakers passed a statute declaring that "the portion of highway US-131 in the township of Schoolcraft, beginning at the intersection of US-131 and West U Avenue in Kalamazoo County and continuing south to the intersection of West XY Avenue and US-131, shall be known as the 'Underground Railroad Memorial Highway'."

Because the National Park Service had to investigate the Underground Railroad on almost a countrywide scale, its progress in identifying important elements of the network was understandably slow. In part to expedite this process in our state, in 1998 the Legislature created the Michigan Freedom Trail Commission. The purpose of this body was to preserve the history of the Underground Railroad in our two peninsulas, promote its legacy, and encourage markers identifying and explaining the nature of this sub rosa organization.

In looking for significant places in Underground Railroad history, it is natural that the attention of the Freedom Trail Commission would be drawn to Battle Creek. There one can find a monument to local resident Erastus Hussey, who helped over 1,000 slaves escape involuntary servitude prior to the Civil War. Also in the same town is a monument to former slave Sojourner Truth, a widely known female abolitionist who, upon gaining her freedom, made Battle Creek her home until her death in 1883.

In an effort to highlight the part played by Battle Creek in rescuing blacks from forced labor in the South, the Michigan Legislature passed Public Act 140 of 2004. This law declared that "the portion of highway I-94 beginning at exit 98 in Calhoun County and continuing east to exit 110 in Calhoun County shall be known as the 'Underground Railroad Memorial Highway,.'"

These roads of remembrance were created just as this book was going to press, so their dates and places of dedication cannot be included.

Coordinates: M/9-10

UNITED SPANISH WAR VETERANS MEMORIAL HIGHWAY

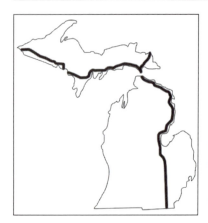

After World War II, many governments around the country expressed an interest in giving tangible public recognition to those who had served in that conflict. The most popular manner of tribute by far was the municipal auditorium or civic center, followed in order of preference by memorial parks, athletic fields and stadiums, monuments, and hospitals. Only 2% of these gestures of gratitude came in the form of highways.

Ironically, one of these roads of remembrance was dedicated to a group of men who never fought in World War II. Instead, some Michigan routes were named in honor of soldiers who had previously been overlooked by a state that had been remiss in giving thanks to its United Spanish War Veterans.

Immediately after the Spanish-American War, many of those who took part in the conflict felt the need for a fraternal organization. Several groups came into existence around the country, but none of them were big enough to be effective or enduring. In 1904 the leaders of these various entities met and decided to merge into a single body called the United Spanish War Veterans.

The purpose of the USWV--aside from that of providing comradeship--was to gain government benefits for its members, help needy veterans and their families, and promote the general welfare of those who fought in the War against Spain. In Michigan, a maximum of 4,650 men belonged to local chapters of the association, which was 72% of those who were eligible. The last United Spanish War veteran in this state died in 1984.

As postwar governments got active in paying respects to their uniformed men and women, some also made amends to those soldiers of past conflicts who had yet to receive such honors. This is what motivated the Michigan legislature to pass Public Act 207 of 1945, which made US-23 from Toledo to Mackinaw City the United Spanish War Veterans Memorial Highway.

This gesture pleased the Spanish War veterans of the Lower Peninsula,

but those in the U.P. felt they had been left out of the picture. To placate these individuals, the legislature passed Public Act 104 of 1949 creating a United Spanish War Veterans Memorial Highway for the Upper Peninsula. (These two laws were combined and essentially reiterated by Public Act 142 of 2001).

Since the goal of the lawmakers was to have the route run through as many U.P. counties as possible, the path of the road approximately followed contemporary I-75 from the Soo to St. Ignace, US-2 from St. Ignace to Iron Mountain, M-95 from Iron Mountain to Sagola, M-69 from Sagola to Crystal Falls, and US-2 from Crystal Falls to Ironwood.

While the enabling legislation required that suitable markers be placed along these memorial highways, for years this stipulation was overlooked. Finally, in response to complaints from Spanish American War veterans and their families, Governor George Romney had two signs erected in July of 1968, one at Mackinaw City and the other at Saginaw.

Over the years, perhaps due to road widening or the effects of time, these signs disappeared. To correct this problem, in January of 1993 the Department of Transportation was asked to put up markers at Mackinaw City, Standish, Flint, and the Michigan/Ohio boundary line. The agency complied with this request, allowing even those unfortunate people who do not read this article to know there is a United Spanish War Veterans Memorial Highway in Michigan.

Coordinates: C-N/1-13

UNITED STATES ROAD

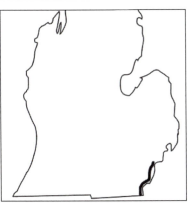

Since prehistoric times there has been a land route connecting the contemporary towns of Detroit and Toledo. For the Indians the link was just a foot trail, and after the Europeans arrived it was slightly enlarged by first the French and then the British into a bridle path.

When the Americans finally occupied what is now Michigan in 1796, they yearned for better communications with the more settled portions of the Union to the south. In an effort to achieve this goal, the territorial legislature passed an act in 1808 establishing a lottery for the purpose of raising money to build a road between Detroit and Toledo.

Before anything came of this scheme the War of 1812 broke out and, so that military supplies could be brought to Detroit, the U.S. Army hurriedly built a road a short distance back from Lake Erie in present-day Monroe and Wayne counties. But this near-shore track was constructed in a temporary fashion to meet the needs of an emergency, and within a few years it was impassable to traffic.

Not long after the end of hostilities the people of Michigan sought help in repairing the military road, and assistance came from the Secretary of War who in 1816 directed Major General Alexander Macomb (of Macomb County fame) to use his troops at Detroit to make the needed improvements. For two years from 150 to 200 soldiers were assigned to this task, and by 1819 they had put the entire length of highway back in a useable state.

The rehabilitation work of the Detroit garrison was of a cursory nature that, at best, turned an overgrown swath through the wilderness into a rough trail. Since much of the road was built across low, wet land, its maintenance was very difficult. By 1822 the route was said to be "almost impossible for wagons (even in good weather) on account of logs, stumps and deep holes, and in the fall and spring it is almost impossible to travel it on horseback."

The following year local residents again petitioned our nation's capitol for relief with the poor transportation system, and the desired response came from Congress on 26 May 1824 when it passed an act declaring the first federal highway in Michigan to be the tie between Detroit and Toledo. For the next five years soldiers and private contractors worked to put the route in shape, and by 1829 they had finished building a primitive road one to three miles inland from the waterfront.

This artery--variously called the Detroit-Frenchtown Road or the Toledo & Detroit Turnpike-- slowly evolved from a track of mud and mire to an important avenue of settlement and commerce. In time it developed into a major thoroughfare for travelers southbound from Detroit, finally leading to the complete paving of the trunk line on 15 October 1918.

When traffic along the former Detroit to Toledo military road eventually exceeded its carrying capacity it was replaced by the I-75 expressway, the last segment of which was opened on 17 September 1970. But remnants of the old route still exist in the transportation network of southeastern Michigan in such isolated Monroe and Wayne County street names as River Road and US Turnpike.

Coordinates: M-N/13

VAN DYKE ROAD

M-53 is the longest highway in Michigan actually named after an individual, extending from Detroit north to the tip of the Thumb at Port Austin. In all but one of the five counties through which it extends, it is known as Van Dyke Road.

The namesake of this thoroughfare, James Adams Van Dyke, was born in Mercersburg, Pennsylvania, on 10 December 1813. Somewhat of a child prodigy, at the age of fifteen he entered Madison College at Uniontown, from which he graduated four years later with high honors.

After earning his bachelor's degree in 1832, Van Dyke commenced the study of law. Two years later he came to live in Detroit, where in 1835 he was admitted to the Michigan bar and entered into general practice.

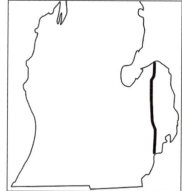

Van Dyke quickly made his mark in his newly adopted home, being appointed city attorney of Detroit in 1835 and 1839. From this job he advanced to Wayne County prosecuting attorney, a position he held from 1840 to 1842. Continuing his move up the public-service chain of command, Van Dyke was next chosen city council alderman in 1843-44 and then elected mayor in 1847.

Following his term as Detroit's chief executive, Van Dyke founded and served as head of the city's fire department from 1847 to 1851, even helping to build its permanent quarters. Possessed of seemingly inexhaustible energy, he was also chosen as a member of the first board of commissioners of the Detroit water works, a post he filled from 1853 to 1855.

This continuous public service was interfering with his private law practice, so in 1852 Van Dyke took down his shingle and became general counsel for the Michigan Central Railroad Company. However, a distinguished past and a bright future was no protection from the vagaries of life, and he was killed by an unknown, quick-acting disease on 7 May 1855 at the young age of 43.

Van Dyke left to his family an estate comprising hundreds of acres northeast of what was then downtown Detroit. When, exactly a decade later, this property was first subdivided for

development, one of the major streets running inland from the River was Van Dyke Avenue.

As Detroit grew in size and population, Van Dyke Avenue expanded with it. Eventually, the street became a major access road to and from the city, a fact which lead to its establishment as state trunk line M-53 around 1920. Bit by bit the highway was improved northward, the project being completed to the Lake Huron shore in 1927.

Today, at least in its southern reaches, a congested Van Dyke Road is slowly giving way to adjacent limited access arteries that enable drivers to speed along at a modern clip. And as the bypassed old route gradually fades from the roster of principal thoroughfares, so too, unfortunately, does the memory of the remarkable man whose name identifies the highway.

Coordinates: I-M/13-14

VERNIER ROAD

When the French colonized what is now Michigan, they gave property to Gallic pioneers as an inducement for them to come and live in the Great Lakes frontier. Even some of those individuals who arrived after the British took control in 1760 were allowed to continue this practice and take a small piece of real estate for their own.

The pattern of settlement in this era was one of long, narrow lots often referred to as ribbon or strip farms. These linear agricultural units were typically about 150 to 600 feet wide and up to three miles deep, a width to depth ratio averaging 1:10. The unusually-shaped fields formed extended rectangles with their long axes perpendicular to the water, creating a distinctive pattern on the landscape that can still be seen from just south of Monroe to nearly as far north as Port Huron.

This seemingly strange arrangement offered a number of advantages to the occupants of rural Michigan living under the banner of the fleur-de-lis. It provided as many people as possible with water frontage, an important consideration when lakes or rivers were the main means of trans-

portation in all but winter, at which time the inhabitants resorted to a primitive road that usually ran parallel to the water. The system also allowed set-

Detroit Area

tlers--who almost always cultivated the near-shore areas--to have residences in tight proximity to one another, unlike the later American system of land division which often had the closest neighbor a quarter-mile distant. And finally, the long lots usually cut across the grain of the land, giving each farmer a variety of soil and vegetation types.

One of the persons who acquired a long lot in eighteenth-century Michigan was John Baptiste Vernier, a man born in Montreal in 1763 and married in Detroit in 1790. His tract of land, comprising 419 acres, eventually came to be identified by the Americans as Private Claim 156 and it comprised part of what we know today as Grosse Pointe Shores. As the family of Vernier grew, the additional members acquired lands adjacent to or not far from the original farmstead, eventually forming a congregation of relatives living along the eastern Macomb/Wayne County boundary.

Representatives of this bloodline were still residing in the vicinity when, years later, the Michigan Legislature passed Public Act 250 of 1849 authorizing "commissioners to lay out and establish a state road on the most eligible route from some point on the Lake St. Clair, in the Township of Grosse Point[e...], northwesterly to the Gratiot Road, so called." One of the three commissioners appointed to this task was a member of the extended Vernier kin group. This is significant because the route ultimately chosen for the new road went direct-

ly through lands owned by descendants of John Baptiste Vernier. Since the patriarch had died in 1834, it is likely the highway was named after the clan and not for a particular individual.

Vernier Road remained pretty much a country byway until 1916 when it was taken over and improved by the Wayne County Road Commission. Jurisdiction over this route was changed in the summer of 1939 when the State Highway Department was given supervisory authority and quickly designated the thoroughfare M-29. Vernier Road remained a trunk line until 1971, at which time it reverted back to its present status as just a modern American street with an old French name.

Coordinates: Southeastern Michigan Enlargement D/10

VETERAN'S MEMORIAL HIGHWAY (ITHACA)

Michigan as a state has honored its men and women who served on active duty with some commemorative monuments. The oldest of these tributes is the Soldiers' and Sailors' Monument in Detroit (dedicated in 1872), which pays homage to the Wolverine veterans of the Civil War.

The next major conflict after the War Between the States was the Spanish-American War (1898) and the subsequent Philippine Insurrection. The Michigan military personnel involved in this strife were later celebrated with the "Hiker Memorial" (dedicated 1946), which stands in front of the Capitol building in Lansing.

The ensuing twentieth century saw a number of major military encounters, the worst for America being the clashes known as World War I, World War II, Korean War and the Vietnam War. Saluting the Michigan citizens who participated in this combat is the Michigan Veterans Memorial (dedicated 1982), which also stands on the foregrounds of the State Capitol.

Although the previously referenced Michigan Veterans Memorial included within its embrace those who fought in Vietnam, the veterans

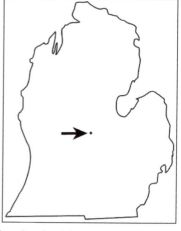

of that Southeast Asian struggle wanted their own structure of appreciation. This wish was realized in 2001 with the completion of the Michigan Vietnam Monument about four blocks west of the Capitol in Lansing.

Building these kinds of stone tributes to Michigan's men and women in uniform can be an expensive and time-consuming affair. A much cheaper and simpler approach is to name a particular stretch of road in their honor. This idea was adopted by the Ithaca post of the Veterans of Foreign Wars, which sought to recognize all veterans of our armed forces by declaring Business Route US-27 through the town to be the Veteran's Memorial Highway.

Resident members of the VFW lined up support for this project by obtaining resolutions of approval from the City of Ithaca, Emerson Township, and the Gratiot County Board of Commissioners. Armed with these endorsements, local politicians submitted a bill to the Michigan Legislature seeking state acceptance of the concept, official consent for which came in the form of Public Act 142 of 2001.

One of the sponsors of the enabling law summed up the purpose of the effort by saying that "proclaiming

this route as 'Veterans Memorial Highway' serves to keep fresh in our minds the great sacrifices that have been made to allow us to live the lives of freedom with which we in the United States are blessed." The named road that these sentiments spawned was dedicated at a brief sign unveiling on May 24, 2002.

Coordinates: K/11

VETERANS MEMORIAL DRIVE

A publication issued by the Michigan Legislature stated that "veterans of the armed services have made sacrifices for the American people and for democratic ideals so that Americans may live, work, and play in the way few citizens of the world are able. The sacrifices made by veterans should remain prominent in the collective memory of the nation, and veterans who have acted in the nation's behalf should be held in high esteem."

Having made this observation, the printed release went on to say that "in order to pay tribute to those who have fought and sometimes died to uphold American values, and also to help young Americans remain mindful of the tragic consequences of war and the need to pursue peace, many communities have designated a portion of their street-scape to honor veterans. To memorialize veterans by designating a portion of the highway system in their honor is a viable way for citizens within a community to testify to each other, and also to those who visit, that service and commitment to others, and to ideals, are clearly valued."

Taking these words to heart, the citizens of Ogemaw and Oscoda counties decided to establish within their collective jurisdictions a "Veterans Memorial Drive." The chosen route was a twenty-mile-long stretch of M-33 running from Houghton Creek Road (near Rose City) to Miller Road or M-72 (north of Mio). Supporting this concept was the Rose City Council, Rose Township Board, Oscoda County Board of Commissioners, the Mio Veterans of Foreign Wars, the Michigan Department of the American Legion, and over one hundred residents who lived

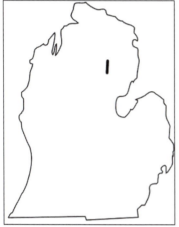

along or near the proposed trunk line of tribute.

A number of reasons were put forth in support of a local road of remembrance. Some believed "it will serve as a reminder to motorists using the highway of the sacrifices veterans made on behalf of our country." Others said "the highway memorial designation is only a small [but important] token of the appreciation and recognition we owe to our veterans who have given so much." And still others felt "we need this [expression] of thanks in place for [veterans] so they know their efforts are remembered and honored."

As the movie "Saving Private Ryan" (1998) seemed to raise patriotic feelings in this country while providing the public with a realistic understanding of what soldiers experience in combat, the people of the Ogemaw and Oscoda region felt the time was right to push for an official acceptance of their goal to create a paved salute to those who served in our armed forces. These thoughtful citizens took their case for a bi-county avenue

of gratitude to their elected representatives, who responded by officially establishing the desired highway under authority of Public Act 174 of 2000. This designation was soon after dedicated on 14 October 2000, with appropriate ceremonies occurring at both ends of the Veterans Drive.

As an aside, it should be noted

that the transportation literature will show another "Veterans Drive" in Michigan. This appellation appeared at Coldwater in 1935 with the blessing of the State Highway Commissioner. The reader will search in vain for such a road, however, because the title is a misnomer. For reasons that are now lost to time, the people of the Depression era in Branch County chose "Memorial Drive" as the name for the bridge on US-12 crossing the Coldwater River.

Coordinates: G-H/11

VETERANS MEMORIAL FREEWAY (M-59)

In July of 1919, not long after the end of World War I, a procession of trucks from the War Department set out from Washington D.C. for a cross-country trip to San Francisco. The purpose of this transcontinental jaunt was "to arouse national interest in a series of 'Roads of Remembrance,' roads stretching away across the country dedicated to the remembrance of the boys who drove the trucks in the war and their comrades."

This mobile effort by the federal government to honor our nation's veterans bypassed Michigan, so three years later local efforts were commenced to accomplish this same goal. The project started in Adrian, where an attempt was initiated to interest "the American Legion posts of the entire state in naming its [county and township] roads after Michigan men who gave their lives in the World War and after events and organizations associated with the state's participation in the conflict...".

This well-intentioned concept generated little support across the state, and so Michigan's veterans remained without a road dedicated to their memory. As time passed, the number of Wolverine soldiers deserving of such recognition continued to grow as America deployed its uniformed sons and daughters into hostile situations around the world in defense of liberty. By the end of the Vietnamese War, Michigan had sent the following numbers of its citizens to fight in our country's major military engagements (figures in parentheses represent the number of persons from our state who died on active duty from all causes):

War of 1812:	1,532	(17)
Black Hawk War:	1,826	
Toledo War:	1,177	
Patriot War:	436	
Mexican War:	2,085	(355)
Civil War:	90,119	(14,855)
Spanish War:	6,948	(701)
World War I:	135,485	(5,000)
World War II:	658,108	(15,415)
Korean War:	210,000	(2,500)
Vietnam War:	400,000	(2,654)

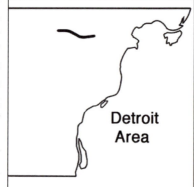

Aware of these statistics, the Michigan legislature finally decided that the state's veterans had waited long enough for their avenue of tribute. At last giving our fighting men and women their due, the lawmakers in Lansing passed House Concurrent Resolution 691 of 1978 designating "that portion of the M-59 Freeway located between the City of Pontiac and the City of Utica as the Veterans Memorial Highway."

Due to an error in drafting the resolution, this road of remembrance actually ended up with two names. In the preliminaries of the enabling text it is said the designated portion of M-59 will be called the "Veterans Memorial Freeway" and in the conclusion of the document the trunk line is referred to as the "Veterans Memorial Highway." To correct his dual-identity problem, the Legislature passed Public Act 142 of 2001 which cured the split personality of the road by designating it the "Veterans Memorial Freeway.".

Coordinates: Southeastern Michigan Enlargement A-B/6-9

VETERANS MEMORIAL HIGHWAY
(ALPENA)

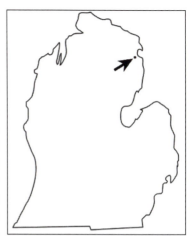

Every year the Office of Veterans Affairs in Washington, DC, compiles various statistics on former military personnel in this country. As of 1 July 2000, this agency's figures show that in Michigan there are now living 95,700 Persian Gulf War veterans, 281,500 Vietnam War veterans, 128,100 Korean War veterans, 191,900 World War II veterans, and 100 World War I veterans. Another 210,00 of our state's current residents served in uniform during peace time.

Believing that these individuals deserved some kind of recognition for their support and defense of this country, the commander of the Alpena Post of the Military Order of the Purple Heart began a campaign to have a neighborhood road designated in their collective honor. For years he worked on this project, slowly gaining the support of the community and other veterans' organizations in the vicinity.

Finally, by the turn of the century, the commander had marshaled the necessary local backing for his enterprise and he took his idea to the Legislature for action. This body, impressed with the man's diligence and arguments in defense of his cause, responded by passing Public Act 174 of 2000 which designated "the part of highway M-32 located between Ripley boulevard and Bagley street in the city of Alpena as the 'Veterans Memorial Highway'."

This triumph in memory of those who answered our government's call to arms was, appropriately, dedicated in Alpena on 11 November 2000, also popularly known as "Veterans Day." The road was welcomed "as an important reminder of the tremendous sacrifice made by our servicemen and women for the good of their nation."

As one of the featured speakers that day aptly put it, "the dedication of this stretch of thoroughfare...will forever stand as the testimony of the people of Alpena of the highest regard we hold for our men and women who serve in American uniforms. It is [our] hope that the generations that come after us will understand that we've set this special place apart to honor the very best in our nation and will, perhaps, be inspired to emulate their courage and sense of duty."

As the ceremonies drew to a close in front of the cemetery chapel along route M-32, an observer properly summed up the purpose of the new trunk line of tribute. He said, "Our veterans backed up their declarations to cherish this land by risking the very real possibility of serious harm to themselves. Some...made the supreme sacrifice itself and gave their very lives for their families, their homes, and their belief in America. Let this ground and this highway stand as a sacred way of remembering them."

Coordinates: F/13

VETERANS MEMORIAL HIGHWAY
(I-69)

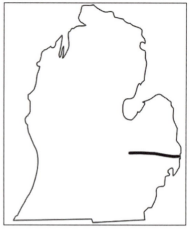

There are hundreds of veterans organizations in the United States comprised of former military personnel and/or their families and heirs. The oldest of these associations at the national level is the Society of Cincinnati, formed in 1783 as a fraternal body for those men who served in the Revolutionary War.

Next in succession came the Military Society [of the] War of 1812 (established in 1826), followed by the Aztec Club of 1847 and the National Association of Veterans of the Mexican War (respectively founded in 1847 and 1873 for men who fought in the Mexican-American War).

The American Civil War gave rise to the Grand Army of the Republic (1866) to represent those who wore the blue uniforms of the North and the United Confederate Veterans for those from the South who dressed in gray. The Spanish-American War was the next great conflict after the war between the states, and the U.S. soldiers participating in this contest later banded together to form the United Spanish War Veterans (1899).

The Twentieth Century saw four major military actions, the first of which was World War I which produced the veterans' group known as the American Legion (1919). A generation later World War II enveloped the planet, and in its wake came an organization for its U.S. participants called AMVETS (created in 1944 as American Veterans of World War II).

Scarcely had the world caught its breath when the Korean War broke out, a hostile action which gave rise to the Korean War Veterans Association (1985). The most recent major military undertaking in United States history was the Vietnam War, and this prolonged struggle eventually gave birth to the Vietnam Veterans of America (1978).

While the organizations just mentioned are generally open to all ex-soldiers who served in a particular war, there are other groups that restrict their membership to those with certain specific characteristics. For example, there are veterans' associations based on religion (Jewish War Veterans, 1896), physical condition (Disabled American Veterans, 1920), race (Tuskegee Airmen, 1972), awards (Military Order of the Purple Heart, 1932), and unit (101st Airborne Division Association, 1945).

Perhaps seeking to subsume all of these defenders of democracy under one umbrella, the Michigan Legislature decided to create a tribute to them as a class of appreciated soldiers regardless of their rank, unit, or period of service. To this end the lawmakers passed Public Act 142 of 2001 which recognized that "the portion of highway I-69 between the western city limit of the

city of Flint and the eastern city limit of the city of Port Huron shall be known as the 'Veterans Memorial Highway'." Because this designation simply replaced the Veterans of Foreign Wars Memorial Highway, there is no evidence that a dedication ceremony ever took place.

Coordinates: K/12-14

VETERANS MEMORIAL HIGHWAY
(LUDINGTON)

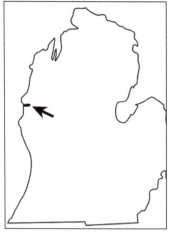

Soldiers who have served in combat have commonly desired to interact with their comrades in arms after the conclusion of hostilities. These relationships are usually established on an individual basis, but for each conflict there also exists a formal organization to accommodate socializing and to represent the interests of veterans from a particular war.

Large numbers of former Michigan servicemen have joined these associations of ex-military personnel over the years. A listing of these groups and their membership numbers (for the year 2000) in our state provides a measure of the degree to which fighting Wolverines have defended the American flag when our nation's opponents have wanted to trample on that honored banner.

In December of 2002, an analysis by the gain, often extracting a high cost in terms of physical and emotional well-being, is to designate public works in their memory. To that end,...veterans groups in the western counties of Michigan's Lower Peninsula have indicated to a state senator that they would like to designate a memorial highway to honor all veterans in their region. At their request, legislation [was] introduced to name a portion of a highway in Mason County in tribute to the veterans of the armed services."

The Legislature realized that "historical

Organization	Michigan Posts	Michigan Members
AMVETS	90	12,000
American Legion	455	87,000
Disabled American Veterans	75	40,000
Grand Army of the Republic	463	88,000
Korean War Veterans Association	4	900
United Spanish War Veterans	69	4,650
Veterans of Foreign Wars	380	75,000
Vietnam Veterans of America	56	3,300

Michigan House of Representatives observed that "it is appropriate that the state recognize the extraordinary contributions of those who have served as soldiers in the armed services of the United States, whether or not they were injured or mortally wounded in service to our country. The state's recognition is appropriate for two reasons: First, it allows citizens to honor those among them who were willing to disregard personal gain and fight for the freedoms and liberty that are promised by the constitutional form of government here in the United States. Further, the state's recognition makes an ongoing public dialogue possible as it keeps citizens mindful about the horror of war and the importance of an unrelenting effort to seek peaceful solutions to social and political problems."

The release continued by saying "Among the ways that the state can recognize those who put their duty to their country before personal events and prominent citizens deserve recognition in our communities. One way to commemorate events and people and to ensure ongoing public awareness is to place a sign along a public roadway." In consideration of this tradition, our state's lawmakers passed Public Act 651 of 2002 making the portion of route US-10 between Scottville and Ludington the Veterans Memorial Highway. This law, said thankful supporters, allows "the citizens of Michigan, and in particular the citizens of Mason County, to express their appreciation for the courage of freedom fighters. Naming a well-traveled portion of the state's busy road system in their honor gives the veterans of all wars the public recognition they deserve." This gesture of appreciation by a grateful populace was dedicated on 13 June 2003 with the man who spearheaded the project--former serviceman Bob Gancarz--as master of ceremonies.

Cordinates I/7-8

VETERANS MEMORIAL HIGHWAY (UPPER PENINSULA)

The most highways named for a single person is four, this being the number of state and federal roads in Michigan honoring Martin Luther King. The greatest number of trunk lines bearing the same name is six, with a half-dozen motorways in our state being designated "Veterans Memorial Highway."

Many of these appellations have been assigned in recent times, meaning that the duplication is actually by design rather than ignorance. When this redundancy is brought to the attention of legislators, those lawmakers that speak to the issue claim no suitable alternative language or phrasing can be found to adequately recognize the men and women who have served our country in uniform.

The sixth road to be called "Veterans Memorial Highway" came about because it was observed that no Michigan trunk line in the Northern Peninsula carried this title. To rectify this perceived deficiency and to honor all past and present members of our armed forces who have seen combat, groups of former soldiers in the western UP asked that a Veterans Memorial Highway be established in their region.

The rationale for this request claimed that "naming a well-traveled portion of the state's busy road system in their honor gives the veterans of all wars the recognition they deserve. While this recognition allows citizens to honor those among them who demonstrated courage in defense of freedom, it also makes possible an ongoing dialogue about the horrors of war and the importance of an unrelenting effort to seek peaceful solutions to social and political problems."

To oblige the wishes of these Upper Peninsula patriots, the legislature passed Public Act 10 of 2003 which made route M-28 from Ishpeming west to its terminus at US-2 the Veterans Memorial Highway. Placard boards testifying to this deed were erected everywhere M-28 met or intersected a trunk line highway, requiring the installation of eleven roadside signs. This tribute was appropriately dedicated in Wakefield on Memorial Day, 31 May 2004.

Coordinates: B-C/1-5

VETERANS MEMORIAL PARKWAY

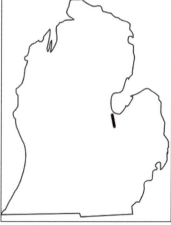

Though Saginaw and Bay City are situated relatively close to one another, movement between them was difficult early in this century because of the poorly developed transportation network that connected the two cities.

As early as 1913, a solution to this problem was proposed in the form of a shoreline highway linking the towns along the east bank of the Saginaw River. As time passed and the need for improved roads increased, more local groups began endorsing the idea of an intercity artery.

Two of these supporters were the Saginaw and Bay City American Legion posts. As early as 1922 they expressed a desire for the new waterside thoroughfare, suggesting that it be designed to honor "the soldiers, sailors and marines of the two counties who died in their country's service."

The initial vision for this "road of memory" was a beautiful parkway embracing trees planted "in honor of those who went over[seas] and will never come back." As a special added touch, impressive memorial arches were proposed for both ends of the motorway.

Once these and other ideas had put most Saginaw Valley residents in favor of the road, it remained for these citizens to gain state funding for the project. This goal was achieved on 23 October 1923, when 700 people from the region descended upon the state Capitol to successfully lobby for the riverside drive.

Highway construction began on 1 June 1925, when dredges seeking earth for road fill began excavating material from the bottom of the Saginaw River. This channel-deepening and shore-building activity continued through 1926, and then most work ceased for a year so the fill could fully drain and settle.

Grading activities commenced in 1928, and by October of 1929 all paving was done and the new route was open to traffic. Later, 80,000 trees and shrubs would be added to

the Parkway, and wildlife preserves for waterfowl created along its flanks.

Though the shorter and faster route between Saginaw and Bay City had now become reality as US-23 (a segment known today as M-13), the concept of an official bicounty memorial highway remained just a dream. However, veterans and military organizations continued to push for this recognition, and their wish was finally granted by the Michigan legislature in February of 1935 through the passage of Senate Concurrent Resolution 9.

The road of remembrance, as decreed by state government officials, was dedicated on 10 November 1935 in ceremonies taking place along the Parkway exactly midway between between Saginaw and Bay City. By this act, the people of the lower Saginaw Valley gave their soldiers a tribute more serviceable than any monument of metal or stone.

Coordinates: J/12

VETERANS MEMORIAL HIGHWAY/ROAD (MONROE)

I n September of 1989, members of various veterans groups in southeastern Michigan requested that the Monroe County Road Commission consider naming some major thoroughfare "Veterans Memorial Road." The Commission supported this idea, and suggested route M-125 as being one of the likely prospects to receive this tribute.

Since route M-125 was a state trunk line, any action dealing with the road would first have to obtain approval from government officials in Lansing. In an effort to receive this blessing, the Monroe County Road Commission enlisted the support of the area's representative and senator at the state capitol.

These two lawmakers introduced to the legislature House Resolution 365 and House Concurrent Resolution 414, both in the 1989 session. These measures directed the Michigan Department of Transportation to "designate a road in Monroe County as Veterans Memorial Road in honor of the many Michigan citizens who served

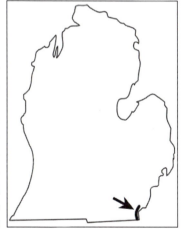

with valor in the United States Armed Forces."

The Department of Transportation, in collaboration with the Monroe County Road Commission, chose to bestow the title "Veterans Memorial Highway" upon all of route M-125. Though the actual name of the road would not be changed and no addresses affected, a few signs would be erected telling motorists of the designation.

There was some opposition to this decision. The major local newspaper, for instance, correctly pointed out that M-125 was already known at various points along its length as Monroe Street and South Dixie Highway. Adding another name to the route would just create more confusion, it said.

It is understandable that people would resist giving another appellation to a road that already had too many names. However, their cause was doomed on 14 May 1990 when the Monroe City Council passed a resolution supporting the actions of the County Road Commission.

With the last obstacle to the memorial highway removed, its once-controversial signs were placed at selected spots along the 13-mile stretch of M-125. Special ceremonies in recognition of the occasion were

held at both ends of the trunk line on 30 August 1990, officially establishing what at the time was said to be Michigan's "ninth state roadway dedicated to a veterans group."

The matter remained uneasily settled for about a decade, when the Legislature intervened again, probably for the last time. By authority of Public Act 142 of 2001, the lawmakers in Lansing declared that "Highway M-125 in Monore county shall be known as 'Veterans Memorial Road'."

Coordinates: N/13

VETERANS OF FOREIGN WARS MEMORIAL HIGHWAY

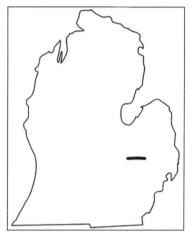

Nearly everyone has seen the men with service caps selling little red poppies each May. These paper flowers, made by disabled veterans to resemble the blossoms that once covered the battlefields of France, are sold by the Veterans of Foreign Wars to raise money for their various community projects.

The VFW is a fraternal, patriotic and educational organization open to all members of the American Armed Forces who fought in any foreign military campaign undertaken by the United States government. Its main purposes are to assist needy veterans and their dependents, organize memorial services for deceased soldiers, promote patriotism, and perpetuate the memory and history of those who defended liberty in uniform.

The first full foreign military engagement for the Stars and Stripes was the Spanish-American War of 1898. Following this conflict in 1899, three different national societies were established for the benefit of those Americans who had participated in the hostilities. In 1914 these separate organizations merged to form the Veterans of Foreign Wars, and the unified body was then officially chartered by Congress on 28 May 1936.

Today, the VFW consists of 10,900 local posts comprised of over 2,000,000 members. Because the association traces its genealogy back to 1899, this year marks the 105th birth-

day of America's second largest veterans' organization.

Michigan has a special relationship with the VFW, for Eaton Rapids is the location of its national home for children of deceased or totally disabled overseas veterans. Youngsters qualified for admission receive their education, food, clothing and medical care free of cost. Those graduates who desire college or special vocational training also get financial assistance.

Because the VFW has done so much for the nation and this state, the Michigan legislature sought to express the public's gratitude by naming a road in honor of the group. This was accomplished by House Concurrent Resolution 545 of 1980, which designated M-21 between Port Huron and the eastern city limits of Flint as the VFW Memorial Highway.

Unfortunately, to many people VFW was not an abbreviation but just three meaningless letters. Consequently, the message that the lawmakers hoped to convey was lost to some of the citizenry. In an effort to correct this problem, the legislature subsequently passed Senate Concurrent

Resolution 914 of 1984 making route M-21 between Lapeer and Flint the Veterans of Foreign Wars Memorial Highway.

All of this work ultimately came to naught, for both of these VFW resolutions were repealed in 2001. In their place, under the force of Public Act 142, was substituted the overused name of "Veterans Memorial Highway." According to the authorizing legislation, this generic title was to apply to "the portion of highway I-69 between the western city limit of the city of Flint and the eastern city limit of the city of Port Huron...." With this statute, the Veterans of Foreign Wars became veterans foreign to Michigan's roads of remembrance.

Coordinates: K/12-13

VETERANS OF WORLD WAR I MEMORIAL HIGHWAY

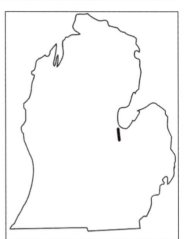

Other than World War II, the First World War (originally called the Great War) involved more countries and caused greater destruction than any other conflict in history. This titanic struggle was ignited in Sarajevo on 28 June 1914 when the visiting Austrian Archduke and heir to the throne was assassinated there by a Serb.

Believing that the Serbian government was behind the attack, Austria-Hungary soon declared war on the neighboring country. Because of the entangling alliances then in place on the Continent, this military action quickly drew many other nations into the fighting. Before long the Central Powers (Germany and Austria-Hungary) were in full armed conflict with the Allies (Britain, Russia and France).

At the start of the war the United States was neutral and most Americans were opposed to involvement in European affairs. But when, with passing time, Germany began to sink our unarmed ships and encourage Mexico to attack us, those who lived under the Stars and Stripes had no choice but to take up the cudgels.

Congress declared war on Germany 6 April 1917, and by June 24 of that year the first of about two million U.S. soldiers began landing in France. The members of this American Expeditionary Force made the difference in what had nearly become a stalemated contest, and by 11 November 1918 an armistice brought on by the presence of Yankee doughboys concluded the hostilities. The war that was supposed to end all wars had lasted four years, lead to the death of nearly ten million troops, and resulted in the wounding of 21 million other soldiers.

Michigan's support for the cause of freedom consisted of vast amounts of raw materials and an impressive quantity of military industrial products. In addition, the Selfridge air field (Mount Clemens) was opened on 8 July 1917 and Camp Custer (Battle Creek) was built in the summer of the same year at a cost of $10,000,000. But by far the state's greatest contribution was in manpower, with 175,000 soldiers coming from within our borders. Many of these individuals paid dearly in their efforts to make the world safe for democracy, with 5,000 dying in service and another 15,000 suffering wounds.

The state legislature was not unmindful of these sacrifices and felt they deserved some expression of gratitude. To help the citizens of our two peninsulas say thanks to those who so nobly represented Michigan on active duty, the lawmakers in Lansing passed Public Act 142 of 2001. This statute disclosed that "the portion of highway I-75 and US-23 beginning in the city of Saginaw and extending north to the city of Bay City shall be known...as the 'Veterans of World War I Memorial Highway'."

Coordinates: J/12

VICTORY HIGHWAY

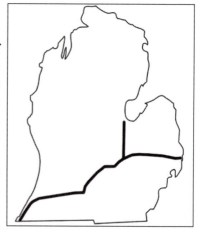

A few months before the end of World War I, the Michigan Good Roads Association began giving some thought to how our state should honor its participants in that conflict. Since the organization promoted the improvement of land transportation, it was no surprise when the group suggested a memorial highway as a token of our collective appreciation.

With this purpose in mind, representatives from around the state met in Lansing on 29 January 1919 and formed the Victory Highway Association. The purpose of this body was to encourage development of a memorial highway as a lasting testament to the sacrifices of those who served and the triumph of democracy over tyranny.

The route chosen for this commemoration roughly paralleled present-day I-94 from New Buffalo to Marshall, then I-69 on to Port Huron. A branch of this lake-to-lake motorway extended off of the main line, approximately following M-13 as far north as Bay City. All told, the route extended 343 miles across the state and was portrayed on the 1919 edition of the Rand McNally road map.

The plans for this memorial highway were staggering. Each city and township through which the road passed was encouraged to erect markers and tablets identifying by name their residents who fought for the cause of liberty. In addition to these monuments, governments were encouraged to construct adjacent parks, camping places, shrines, and other enhancements. War trophies, like captured German cannon and tanks, were to be acquired from the War Department and placed at intervals along the thoroughfare of freedom.

A great deal of emphasis was to be placed on beautification of the route. Supporters envisioned an avenue bordered with 100,000 trees, plus shrubbery, flowers, and similar scenic effects. People living along the highway were encouraged to improve their properties, and farmers were asked to keep the roadside free of weeds to enhance appearance.

Donations were solicited from the public to help fund some of these improvements and ensure that the effort was crowned with success. An attempt was even made to interest the Canadians in the project, hoping they would extend the route from Port Huron on to Toronto, Montreal, Quebec and Halifax, thus making the highway an international tribute.

Despite the investment of all this energy, only one instance of the road being improved by a group has been found. On 4 May 1923, The Daughters of the American Revolution planted 114 walnut trees along the trunk line between Kalamazoo and Oshtemo. This was done in memory of the 114 men from Kalamazoo County who died in World War I.

The saplings were all raised from seeds obtained from walnut trees growing at Mount Vernon, Virginia, and with an expected life span of 300 years they were considered enduring monuments to the local heroes. Over 300 people came out to see the arboreal planting ceremonies about three miles west of Kalamazoo and extending for 1.5 miles on either side of the road.

Support for the Victory Highway continued until about 1930 before gradually disappearing as a cause. The goals of those who conceived the idea were too overwhelming to accomplish, and the stringencies of the Great Depression ended further prospects for activity.

However, the memorial avenue enterprise was not entirely a bust, for the promoters of the road did get Michigan government to include all of the designated mileage in the state's system of paved trunk line highways. Those in whose honor this deed was done would be pleased to know that millions of motorists have subsequently experienced driving pleasure on the routes dedicated to their accomplishments.

Coordinates: J-N/7-14

VICTORY MEMORIAL HIGHWAY

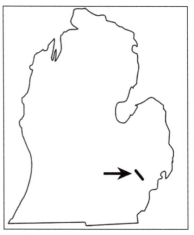

On 28 October 1922, the Pontiac Press carried an article encouraging the planting of trees. This act was advocated not just for the noble cause of reforestation, but also for such worthy purposes as ornamentation, shade, food, and symbolic recognition.

In addressing this latter virtue, the newspaper observed that one of the strongest boosts to the greening of our nation was the recent "effort to have thousands of trees planted along the waysides as memorials to the soldiers of America in the late war. Under the stimulus of this movement, many thousands of trees have been planted, of sorts and in positions that will bring grateful thought from a future generation."

The cause of using vegetation to pay homage could, if done wisely, yield multiple benefits to those involved, said the newspaper. "Nut trees, shade trees, and fruit trees along many roads will be flourishing in years to come when the last of the survivors of the war will have passed on," not only remaining as living memorials but also providing comfort and sustenance to our heirs.

The members of the Pontiac Kiwanis Club, reading these words, took the idea to heart and unanimously agreed "to start planting trees in memory of local boys who lost their lives in the world war." They decided to place these trees along route US-24 from Pontiac north to the Oakland County line and, following this beautification, to christen the road the Victory Memorial Highway.

The next day the Pontiac city manager voiced his support for the project, and thereafter similar endorsements came from state officials and the county road commission. To help raise money for the undertaking, the Pontiac Kiwanis brought in the glee club, band, and orchestra from what is now Michigan State University and sold tickets to a concert and dance music performed by the college singers and musicians.

When sufficient funds had been acquired in 1923, work started on creating an arboreous avenue in honor of local World War I veterans. Ten-foot high American elms were planted at fifty-foot intervals on both sides of the designated road. Each tree was supplied with a bronze plate bearing the name and legend of a deceased Oakland County soldier.

The results of these labors were quite impressive, leading some to consider replicating the enterprise elsewhere around the state. One of these believers was Governor Alexander Groesbeck who, in January of 1924, suggested that Woodward Avenue from Detroit to Pontiac have victory arches erected at either end and then be named as a street dedicated "to the memory of Michigan's heroes who fought in the World War."

This idea was apparently never acted upon, for stone monuments are much more expensive to create than those of living trees. But marble lasts longer than woody plants and, had the Governor's proposal been adopted, there would probably be, unlike today, some evidence left of a community proclaiming its debt to those fellow-citizens who risked and sometimes gave their lives for the cause of freedom.

The American elms that once graced the old Dixie Highway heading northwest out of Pontiac have long since been lost to disease and subsequent road-widening efforts. Now, if Oakland County residents seek some public expression of gratitude to those who served in World War I, they can still drive along the upper reaches of US-24 but they will not find any tangible evidence that it is or was a Victory Memorial route.

Coordinates: L/13

VIETNAM VETERANS
MEMORIAL HIGHWAY

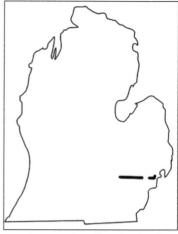

It was the longest war in which the United States has taken part, lasting from 1957 to 1975. Four times as many bombs were released by our planes during the conflict than the Allies dropped on Germany during all of World War II. The struggle cost our country about $200 billion, 8,500 aircraft, 58,000 lives, and 365,000 wounded. It was the Vietnam War.

All of Vietnam was originally governed by the French until 1939, when the country was occupied by the Japanese army. After Japan's defeat in 1945, the French tried to reestablish control over their former colony. This action led to a revolt in the north, and the first phase of the Vietnam War began.

The fight between the French and Vietnamese nationalists lasted until July of 1954 when the two parties signed a peace treaty agreeing to divide the territory into two parts, a communist north and a republican south. Some elements in South Vietnam soon became dissatisfied with the people in power there, so in 1957 a guerrilla-type civil war broke out in parts of the countryside.

The United States--a friend of the South Vietnamese government--sent military advisors to help soldiers of the Saigon regime suppress this insurgency movement, marking the beginning of American armed forces in that country and phase two of the Vietnam War. Members of our uniformed services remained on active duty there until 29 March 1973, when our last ground troops left Vietnam.

With the departure of U.S. combatants, the South Vietnamese army lost the will or ability to win the war. In just two years the protracted conflict was over, and our former battlefield allies surrendered to North Vietnam on 30 April 1975. Since that date nearly one million Vietnamese have fled their country, most coming to live in the land of Uncle Sam.

During the period of hostilities the Pentagon sent 2,700,000 troops to Vietnam, of which over 300,000 were Michigan citizens. Of this Wolverine contingent, 2,646 died while on active duty ranking us seventh among the fifty states in the number of veterans killed during that conflict. Given our involvement in and sacrifices for the war, it was felt that Michigan should pay some kind of homage to those who fought in that Southeast Asian campaign.

Impetus for a specific tribute finally came from Chapter 154 of the Vietnam Veterans of America, a Roseville organization said to be the largest of its kind in the country. This body proposed that all of route M-59 in Macomb County be designated the Vietnam Veterans Memorial Highway, an idea that was subsequently endorsed by the city councils of Warren and Sterling Heights, the township boards of Clinton, Harrison, Macomb and Shelby, along with the Macomb County and Livingston County Boards of Commissioners.

With such widespread support for the idea, it was not long before the Michigan legislature took notice of popular sentiment. Consequently, in 1989 the Senate passed Concurrent Resolution 332 declaring M-59 in Macomb County to be a highway of commemoration for those who served in Vietnam.

But the House refused to approve the measure because in 1978 a former legislature had declared M-59 between Utica and Pontiac to be the Veterans Memorial Freeway, meaning a portion of this road would now have two different names. Not wanting to bestow duplicate titles on a state highway, in 1992 the Michigan legislature found a compromise solution to the problem by passing Public Act 240 which made all of M-59--except the previously designated segment between Pontiac and Utica--the Vietnam Veterans Memorial Highway.

Unfortunately, according to one of the promoters of this road of remembrance, there were no cere-

monies dedicating this important honor. Instead, then, we as individuals should dedicate ourselves to defending the noble principles that motivated Americans to fight and die in a foreign land seeking to preserve for another country the kind of independence that we so often take for granted here.

Coordinates: L/12-14

WALTER P. CHRYSLER FREEWAY

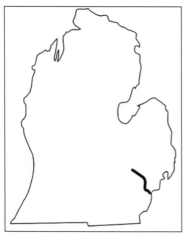

When I-75 was being planned for Detroit, the road was referred to as the "proposed Hastings-Oakland Expressway" after two major streets along its path. For many people, this title was descriptive and adequate. Not so for the Detroit Board of Commerce.

This trade-promotion group petitioned the Detroit Common Council to officially name the new trunk line the "Walter P. Chrysler Expressway." After briefly considering the matter the aldermen agreed, and on 6 November 1957 they unanimously voted to honor the famous auto magnate with a freeway in his name.

While the word Chrysler is well known as one of the "Big Three" car manufacturers, it is not well known as a person. The man behind the name, Walter Percy Chrysler, was born 2 April 1875 in Kansas, a state in which he spent his youth.

After graduating from high school, Chrysler went to work in the mechanical departments of a variety of Midwestern railroads. In 1912 he left railroads to become plant manager for the Buick Motor Company. By 1916 he was named president of Buick and a vice-president of General Motors.

Chrysler did not get along well with the head of General Motors, so in 1920 he resigned from the company. Soon thereafter Chrysler was hired to reorganize the failing Maxwell Motor Corporation. He put this business back on a sound financial footing and then, with the support of the company, he reestablished the firm in 1925 as the Chrysler Corporation.

In 1928, Chrysler acquired the Dodge Brothers Company, an act that put him in a position to challenge the leadership of Ford and General Motors. He remained president of the Chrysler Corporation until 1935, when he retired to become chairman of the board. He held this post until his death

at Great Neck, Long Island, on 18 August 1940.

On 30 January 1959, groundbreaking occurred for the construction of the Chrysler Expressway. The first section of the freeway was opened to traffic on 26 June 1964. The entire superhighway was finished on 6 December 1971 when the I-75 and I-696 interchange was opened.

While the Detroit Common Council named the Chrysler Expressway, its authority ceased at the municipal boundaries. As the length of the road increased, it eventually extended beyond the Motor City and into different jurisdictions. Theoretically, any of the other governmental units through which the Chrysler freeway passed could bestow a new name upon the route.

To prevent this scenario from occurring, in 1990 the Michigan legislature passed Senate Resolution 435 permanently establishing the name of the trunk line. According to the language of the document, "I-75 from downtown Detroit north to the northern boundary of the County of Oakland [will be known] as the Walter P. Chrysler Freeway in recognition of the role that he and the company he founded have played in the development of this region and all of Michigan."

This designation was slightly expanded under Public Act 142 of 2001, which declared that "the portion of highway I-75 that is within [all of] Wayne and Oakland counties shall be known as the 'Walter P. Chrysler Freeway'."

Coordinates: Southeastern Michigan Enlargement D-E/8-9

WALTER P. REUTHER HIGHWAY

Most people have heard of Walter Reuther, but few know very much about him. Since Michigan has a highway named in his honor, a brief get-acquainted session may be in order.

The son of two German immigrants, Walter Philip Reuther was born on 1 September 1907 in Wheeling, West Virginia. At the age of sixteen, he left high school to become an apprentice die maker with a local concern.

He soon mastered his chosen craft, and in 1927 he moved to Detroit where his talents were in greater demand. In the Motor City he found work at the Ford automobile plant, where he quickly acquired the high rating of supervisory die maker.

Reuther worked in this capacity until 1933, when he was laid off from Ford as a result of declining sales in the Great Depression. He remained active in labor affairs, however, and in 1936 he was elected to the general executive board of the United Automobile Workers.

He rapidly moved up the ranks of the UAW, acquiring more power and influence along the way. By skillfully using these assets he became president of the Union in 1946, a position he held for the rest of his life.

During his career Reuther bargained for and won from the automakers such benefits as employer-funded pensions (1950), medical insurance (1950), supplementary unemployment benefits (1955), and cost-of-living allowances.

On the political scene, Reuther was equally effective. He was instrumental in helping John F. Kennedy get elected to the presidency in 1960 and in shaping much of the civil rights and welfare legislation proposed by Lyndon Johnson's administration.

Reuther's impact as a labor leader and promoter of liberal causes ended on 9 May 1970 when he and his wife were killed in a plane crash near Pellston, Michigan.

Within a week of his death, the authorities planning the Pontiac Silverdome agreed to name the structure the "Walter P. Reuther Memorial Stadium." Concurrently, some cities along the route of proposed I-696 were passing resolutions to have the highway named the "Walter P. Reuther Memorial Freeway."

In the race to pay tribute to the deceased union leader the road warriors won, for under Senate Concurrent Resolution 57 of 1971 the Michigan legislature declared that I-696 when built would be called the "Walter P. Reuther Highway." More than eighteen years later--14 December 1989--the final stretch of this memorial trunk line was finished and opened to traffic.

Coordinates: Southeastern Michigan Enlargement C/5-10

WASHINGTON BOULEVARD/ROAD

Just about everyone knows that George Washington was a general during the Revolutionary War and our nation's first President. It is also pretty much common knowledge that his birthday is celebrated every February as a public holiday, that his image appears on the quarter coin and our $1.00 bill, that he is the only President to have a state named after him, and there is a tall monument in his honor in the District of Columbia. After this, most people start to struggle a bit, so perhaps a review of the man's life is appropriate here.

Entering this world on 22

February 1732 at Wakefield, Virginia, Washington received a basic education near his birthplace before entering the profession of surveyor. By 1752 he had abandoned this line of work to become an officer in the Virginia militia. He remained in uniform until 1758, when he left the army and took up farming.

Recipient of a substantial inheritance and the husband of a wealthy widow, Washington owned thousands of acres. On the portion of this land that was cultivated, he pioneered in scientific farming. Progressive in the ways of agriculture, he was early to practice crop rotation, advanced livestock management, and field fertilizing techniques. His success in these endeavors helped to make him one of the richest country gentlemen in America.

Ownership of large tracts of land in that era carried with it political responsibility. Therefore, Washington served as a member of the Virginia house of representatives at Williamsburg from 1758 to 1775. He was also selected as one of Virginia's delegates to the Continental Congresses in Philadelphia. It was at this assembly in 1775 that he was chosen commander of the Continental armed forces, a post he agreed to accept without pay.

Once Washington commenced combat in the Revolutionary War, he saw his home at Mount Vernon just once in the next six years. After leading the Continental Army that won independence from England, he resigned his military command in December of 1783 and returned to his estate near the Potomac River. He remained a Virginia planter until 1787, when he was called upon to preside over the Constitutional Convention in Philadelphia.

When the document that gave birth to the United States was finally written, Washington was the unanimous choice to be President of the new country. Consequently, in April of 1789 he returned to public life and served two terms as our first chief executive. Refusing to serve a third time, he retired to his plantation in 1797 and died there on 14 December 1799. The 67-years-old veteran was given a military funeral and laid to rest in the family tomb at Mount Vernon.

During his impressive career, Washington's highest military rank was Lieutenant General. Over the years, as our armed forces grew, other U.S. Army officers came to outrank him. To correct this somewhat disrespectful situation, in 1976 Congress granted Washington our nation's highest military title: General of the Armies of the United States, making him the senior officer on all Army rolls. With this gesture, Washington could be first in command as well as "first in war, first in peace, and first in the hearts of his countrymen."

When Augustus Woodward was called upon the lay out the city of Detroit in 1807, he wanted to honor the "father of our country." He did so by naming one of the streets in the town center after George Washington. This avenue--eventually called Washington Boulevard--carried the trunk line number US-16 during the decades of the 1930s, 1940s and 1950s, temporarily making the short stretch of pavement one of Michigan's oldest federal memorial highways.

Another short segment of federal motorway in our state once bore Washington's name. In April of 1942, the governing authorities of Gratiot County decided to designate most of their east/west roads after presidents of the United States. Under this new system, about two miles of Washington Road coincided with route US-27, a happy pairing that remained until 1961 when the main highway was rebuilt to its present configuration and its twenty-year union with George discontinued.

Coordinates: Downtown Detroit Inset; K/11

WAYNE HIGHWAY

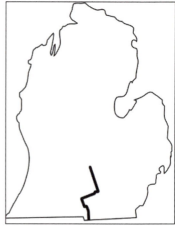

With Michigan's most populous county named in his memory--plus a township, a village and a state university--it is probably not surprising that there would also be a road in tribute to Anthony Wayne. To understand the reason for this distinction one must first go back to Chester County, Pennsylvania, where the subject of honor was born on 1 January 1745.

In was in this part of the Keystone State that Wayne reached manhood and became a practicing surveyor. When the revolutionary War commenced in 1775, he left his seat in the Pennsylvania colonial assembly and raised a regiment of men to fight in the conflict.

Wayne's performance as a military officer was strikingly daring, cool and courageous, giving rise to his popular nickname of "Mad Anthony." On account of his exploits on the battlefield, by 1777 he was made a brigadier general and assigned to General Washington's staff.

It is said that Wayne was particularly talented at motivating soldiers, and a good example of how that was done can be seen in his behavior during the famous bivouac at Valley Forge. There, throughout the terrible winter of 1777-1778, Wayne stayed in the field with his men even though his comfortable home was just five miles away.

Wayne continued to lead troops throughout the War, finally leaving the military in 1783. He remained in civilian life, serving variously as state representative and member of Congress until April of 1792, when President Washington recalled him to active duty as major general and commander in chief to deal with a crisis in what is now the Midwest.

Native Americans had been attacking settlers in the region for years, and expeditions by U.S. forces had been unable to end the depredations. To accomplish this task, Wayne was given the Army of the Northwest, which he trained in Indian warfare techniques for two years. Once his soldiers had been adequately drilled, he met the Indians in August of 1794 and defeated them at the Battle of Fallen Timbers near present-day Toledo.

Following this engagement, Wayne convinced the Indians to return to the ways of peace at the Treaty of Greenville, Ohio, one year later. He was then given the assignment of taking possession of Detroit in 1796 when the British yielded their forts on the southern side of the Great Lakes. It was while returning from this mission that Wayne died on December 15 at what is now Erie, Pennsylvania.

In recognition of "Mad" Anthony's accomplishments, in 1915 the approximate route of contemporary US-127 from Cincinnati to about Defiance, Ohio, was designated the Wayne Highway. In September, two years later, this road of tribute was extended northward to Michigan's capital via present-day M-99 from the state line north to Homer, M-60 east to Jackson, and then US-127 north to Lansing. An attempt was made to advance the highway from Lansing to Petoskey, but apparently that effort came to naught (although some early Rand McNally maps show the route briefly extending as far north as Cadillac).

While the Wayne Highway was formally established and marked, as a named route it never really caught on with the traveling public. Consequently, in 1938 when Congress was holding hearings on the establishment of a permanent federal memorial to Wayne, it was suggested that he be honored by the construction of a broad motor parkway along the General's line of march between Cincinnati and Detroit.

For more than a decade Ohio and Indiana tried to get Michigan interested in this joint project, but officials in Lansing never supported the grand boulevard scheme because Wayne traveled

from Toledo to Detroit by water, thus diminishing the significance of a highway monument to the man in our state. Consequently, while more than two centuries ago Wayne paved the way for westward expansion into Michigan, today any real or proposed Michigan pavements named for the General have waned.

Coordinates: L-N/10-11

WEST MICHIGAN PIKE

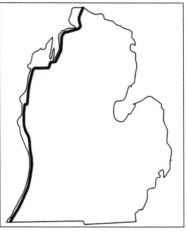

Since the advent of the automobile, there have been dozens of organizations created in this state to promote the establishment of various highways. The oldest of these entities is the West Michigan Pike Association.

This pioneer Association traces its roots back to 10 January 1912, when the West Michigan Lake Shore Highway Association was founded for the purpose of improving the road between Chicago and Mackinaw City. It was believed that a better motorway would encourage more tourists to visit the eastern coast of Lake Michigan, turning that region into the playground of the Middle West.

While the goals of the newly formed group were sound, its choice of a name proved to be too long and cumbersome. Consequently, on 30 May 1913 it reorganized as the West Michigan Pike Association and adopted the slogan, "Lake Shore All the Way."

Immediately the Association began issuing an annual guidebook to the resort and fruit-growing region of western Michigan. This publication, now a collector's item, provided a detailed map of the 400-mile route along with information about hotels, service stations, and general points of interest.

To make it easier for visitors to travel the Lake Shore route, the promoters decided in 1916 to erect concrete markers along every mile of its length. These posts, numbered consecutively from the southern border of Michigan, weighed 350 pounds, were eight feet tall (five of which was above ground), and had the words "West Michigan Pike" cast upon their face (a sample of this monument has been preserved at the corner of Fulton and Seventh streets in Grand Haven).

The guidebooks and the mile

posts greatly expedited travel along the West Michigan Pike, soon making it one of the most popular drives in the state. In part on account of this high vehicle use, in 1926 most of the road was incorporated into the federal highway system as route US-31.

When the coastal trunk line became a number rather than a name, the West Michigan Pike Association began to slowly disappear. The group had been formed to develop a road to the Lake shore region, and with that mission accomplished its purpose seemed fulfilled.

But by the late 1920s, traffic on US-31 had at times grown so heavy that motorists could travel no more than 20 miles per hour. The congestion had become so bad that tourists were vacationing elsewhere or avoiding the coastal highway enroute to their lakeside destinations.

To help solve this problem, the West Michigan Pike Association was reborn and reorganized in early 1929. This time the purpose of the group was not to push for the building of a shoreline road, but for its broadening, straightening, and relocation along a more scenic course.

The West Michigan Pike Association, always dependent upon donated funds and services, did not survive the Great Depression. But the cause for which it labored continues, as our Department of Transportation slowly develops US-31 as a freeway between Indiana and Mackinaw City.

Coordinates: E-N/7-10

WESTNEDGE AVENUE

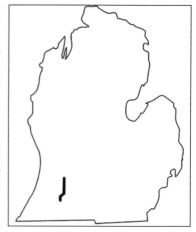

For years Kalamazoo had a major north/south thoroughfare called West Road that went to the center of town. Now, if at the time there was a cookbook for confusion, this would certainly be one of the included recipes. This baffling situation was finally corrected on January 12, 1920, when the Kalamazoo City Council rechristened the main artery Westnedge Avenue.

Linguistically, moving from West to Westnedge was not much of a change. But the mental concept produced by the new name went from being directional to one that was inspirational. This is because the new street title was the surname of a Kalamazoo native "whom the whole great state of Michigan considers its most illustrious World War hero."

Joseph Burchnall Westnedge was born in Kalamazoo on 16 August 1872 and spent the rest of his civilian life in and around the city. As a young man he attended nearby Kalamazoo College and then, as a fully-employed adult, found managerial work with the local paper manufacturing industry.

But Westnedge is honored not for his performance in the private sector but for his accomplishments in public military service. He joined the Michigan National Guard in 1894 as a private, and within a few years had risen to the rank of Lieutenant. By the outbreak of the Spanish-American War in 1898, he had attained the rank of Captain and commanded Company H of this state's 32nd Regiment.

Continuing his advance up the promotional ladder, Westnedge was made Lt. Colonel in 1911 and carried this rank when he accompanied Michigan forces to Texas during the 1916 Mexican Border Campaign against Pancho Villa. The following year he advanced to the rank of Colonel and was given command of the 126th Regiment in the United States 32nd Infantry Division. This unit was sent overseas early in 1918 to fight on the battlefields of France.

It was in Europe that Westnedge's abilities as a commander were most in evidence, a performance that won him the distinguished service medal and the hearts of his men. An officer who was frequently on the front lines and under fire, he managed to make it through World War I unscathed by shot or shell but was killed by disease in Nantes, France, on 29 November 1918. He was the only regimental leader in the 32nd Division to retain his command from the beginning of the War until the 1918 Armistice.

When news of Westnedge's death reached Kalamazoo, his fellow-citizens resolved that there would be some "proper public acknowledgment of the community's debt to the memory of this great soldier and leader." The town's American Legion post suggested this gesture be a road of remembrance, and so the city fathers chose to alter the name of West Road.

The route variously known as West and Westnedge was made a state trunk line in 1913, status it retained until 1964 when the US-131 bypass was opened west of Kalamazoo. Though no longer a numbered highway, the road through town is undiminished in status for it still carries the name of a man who brought glory to himself

and the cause that he represented. And to this day the stretch of US-131 in Kalamazoo County that is not up to Interstate highway standards is still known as South Westnedge Avenue, a continuing tribute to one of the area's World War I heroes.

Coordinates: Kalamazoo Inset

WILLIAM HOWARD TAFT
MEMORIAL HIGHWAY

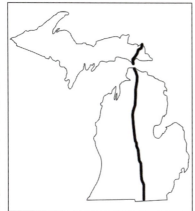

Standing six feet tall and weighing 300 pounds, he was the largest man ever to serve as President of the United States. While in the White House, he started the custom of throwing out the first ball at the opening of each major league baseball season. Furthermore, he is the only man in our nation's history to serve first as President and then as Chief Justice of the Supreme Court. And he was the first President ever buried in Arlington Cemetery (the only other one is John F. Kennedy).

This man of great stature and accomplishment is William Howard Taft, who entered this world at Cincinnati, Ohio, on 15 September 1857. Educated in the local public schools, he went on to graduate from Yale University in 1878 and the Cincinnati Law School in 1880.

With a doctorate of jurisprudence in hand, Taft set out on an ascending career of public service. He successively held such posts as county prosecuting attorney, collector of internal revenue, practicing lawyer, superior court judge, solicitor general, court of appeals judge, first civilian governor of the Philippines, secretary of war and, in 1908, president elect of the United States.

After serving one term as chief executive, Taft was defeated in a reelection bid by Woodrow Wilson. Upon leaving Washington, he became professor of constitutional law at Yale University and president of the American Bar Association.

In 1921, Taft was appointed Chief Justice of the Supreme Court, a position he held until poor health forced him to retire from the bench on 3 February 1930. He died in our nation's capital about one month later, 8 March 1930, a victim of heart disease.

On the day Taft died, some friends in his home town suggested that a national highway be named in his honor. In less than three weeks the William Howard Taft Memorial Highway Association was formally organized, a group which ultimately proposed that a road from Sault Ste. Marie to Fort Myers, Florida, perpetuate the former President's memory.

As laid out, the Michigan portion of this 1,710-mile-long route closely paralleled contemporary I-75 from the Soo to about Higgins Lake. There it diverted to US-127, which it followed south to the Ohio border.

In all of the states through which this memorial highway passed, the respective legislatures endorsed naming the road for the ex-president and even the seventy-third Congress was asked to support the idea through House Joint Resolution 194. Michigan's blessing came via House Concurrent Resolution 9 of 1933, a gesture which unanimously approved designating a north/south route from the St. Marys River to the Gulf of Mexico in tribute to William Howard Taft.

Though the Taft Memorial Highway still exists as law and concrete, few if any drivers are aware of the fact because no one sees any road signs. Which is rather ironic, given that the huge man himself would have been very had to miss.

Coordinates: C-N/10-11

WILLIAM P. ROSSO HIGHWAY

He was the first road commissioner for Macomb County and considered by many to be the father of the area's fine road system. Furthermore, he was one of the organizers of, and first president of, the Michigan Association of Road Commissioners and Engineers. It is not surprising that a person with these accomplishments would have a Macomb County road named in his honor.

Such is the case of William Philip Rosso, a man born near Mount Clemens on 23 June 1865. Initially satisfied to be just a farmer, he eventually became involved in public life by first serving as a trustee of his township school district and then as one of the township highway commissioners.

So well did Rosso discharge these duties that when the Macomb County Road Commission was created in 1912, the County Board of Supervisors appointed him to organize the office. His subsequent tenure with the Road Commission covered nineteen years, embracing the periods 1912-1925 and 1931-1936.

On Rosso's last day in office, the Road Commission passed a resolution thanking him for his many contributions to the county and its transportation network. A year later, in response to the worsening health of their former colleague, the Road Commission passed another tribute to Rosso by renaming Hall Road between Gratiot Avenue and Lake Saint Clair in his honor.

Seven months later--on 27 July 1939--Rosso died after a long illness

at the age of 74. It is appropriate that his departure from this world occurred on the family farm at the western end of the William P. Rosso Highway.

In 1989, a bill was presented to the Michigan legislature designating Hall Road the Vietnam Veterans Memorial Highway. There was some concern by residents of the Mount Clemens area that this would eliminate the existence of the William P. Rosso Highway. Resolutions were passed by the four townships abutting the street asking that the Rosso name not be removed from its signboards. Their appeals were effective, as the ensuing legislation for the Vietnam Veterans Memorial Highway had it terminate at the point where the Rosso road begins.

When, in 1937, the Macomb County Road Commission christened a road in Rosso's honor, the route was entirely within its jurisdiction. In 1949, however, the predecessor of today's Department of Transportation made it part of an extended trunk line M-59. Rosso Highway remained in this elevated status-- thus making it a state road of remembrance--until 1961, when it reverted back to its original character as a local avenue of commemoration.

Coordinates: Southeastern Michigan Enlargement B/11

WILLOW RUN EXPRESSWAY

Before the United States entered World War II, it was clear that global conditions required this country to prepare for the possibility of involvement in a major armed conflict. With the goal in mind of readying this nation for any hostilities to come, it was announced in February of

1941 that the largest plant ever built under one roof would be constructed just east of Ypsilanti near a stream called Willow Run.

The land had been owned by the Ford Motor Company for years, and was used by the firm in the recent past for the experimental cultivation of soy beans.

Now, the government revealed, the site was going to be developed by Ford into a gigantic factory to build four-motored, B-24 Liberator bombers using assembly line methods.

Though the great industrial complex was envisioned to require 100,000 hired hands, there was no major labor supply in the immediate vicinity. The biggest pool of workers for running the plant was at least twenty miles away in the Detroit metropolitan area.

In theory these employees could be brought in by mass transit, but the existing buses were already full to capacity and the roads on which they traveled were either antiquated or congested with normal traffic. It was calculated that a thousand buses would be required to transport the personnel necessary for this airplane manufactory, and not only were this many vehicles unavailable, those that did exist could more usefully be operated within cities rather than on long rural trips.

Since the main line of the Michigan Central Railroad went close by the bomber plant, some thought workers could be brought to the site on flanged wheels. It was discovered that to do this would require twenty trains of eighteen cars each. Not only did consists of this nature not exist, even if they magically appeared there were no passenger facilities in existence and the line of the Michigan Central was already being worked to near overload.

As plans for the bomber-building facility advanced, it became clear that 65% of the inbound freight and 69% of the outbound movements would be dependent on trucks. It was estimated from this math that 500 freight haulers would arrive at the plant each day. So many vehicles bringing in raw materials and taking out finished products would necessitate a major upgrade of the local transportation network. If superhighways were going to be constructed to help feed supplies to the factory, then authorities decided the same roads could be used to bring humans to the job in their private cars.

The road commissions for Wayne and Washtenaw counties, the State Highway Department, and representatives from the Ford Motor Company conferred on how best to accommodate the traffic to be generated by the bomber plant. On 21 August 1941 they agreed on a plan, the federal government approved the concept on August 26, and trunk line construction started soon thereafter.

The work that ensued represented "the nation's most extensive highway project undertaken to provide access to an industrial plant." Half of a normal year's road-building activities for the State Highway Department were channeled into this single enterprise. Nearly three-quarters of the agency's engineers were assigned to the job, and it occupied the attention of 125 Michigan government employees from all divisions.

The goal of these public servants and their associates was to build a multi-lane divided thoroughfare across a 120-foot right-of-way adjacent to the bomber plant. Because of the high water table in the area, the road elevation had to be three feet above ground to avoid weight restrictions during the period of spring breakup. To bring in this much fill, up to 7,000 truckloads of dirt were moved daily at the height of grading operations.

With work proceeding around the clock, seven days a week, paving activities were able to begin on 22 October 1941. Since it was so late in the construction season, the aggregates and water in the concrete had to be preheated and calcium chloride added to the mix to expedite setting. To insulate the pours from cold weather, fresh concrete was covered with two feet of hay or straw at a rate of 100 tons to the mile.

Each lane of traffic was eleven feet wide and nine inches deep. Because of shortages and rationing, no steel was used to reinforce the concrete saving thirty-six tons of metal per mile. During favorable weather the crews were able to lay down about 2,600 feet of concrete per day, a rate which enabled them to finish the last pour on 17 December 1941.

Much additional work needed to be done on the $7,500,000 project, and thus it was not dedicated and placed into service until 12 September 1942. Today the fruits of these labors are still called the Willow Run Expressway on some maps, but most people just know the road as the stretch of pavement between exits 185 and 194 of route I-94 in Michigan.

Coordinates: Southeastern Michigan Enlargement: G/3-5

WILSON AVENUE

It was not until the twentieth century that an identification system for Michigan's highways was developed. Prior to that time, most channels of traffic were either known by the two nearest towns they connected (like the Niles-Buchanan Pike) or by some local title that continually changed as an individual progressed along the trail from one district to another. This chaotic approach to road designation was supposedly addressed by Public Act 282 of 1915, which required that all roads built with some state funds be named and signed.

Though as late as 1942 Kent County was still working to comply with this statute in certain rural areas, it appears that in the county there was some initial effort to follow the spirit of the law. This conclusion is drawn from the fact that within one year of the Legislature's requirement that certain roads be named, the highway known today as Wilson Avenue was christened.

The tag applied to this thoroughfare was apparently supposed to celebrate the accomplishments of Samuel H. Wilson, a well-known local realtor and property developer. A life-long resident of Kent County, Wilson began building tract housing west of Grand Rapids in 1903 and continued in this line of work until his death in September of 1931. His biggest undertaking was Wyoming Park, a subdivision which included

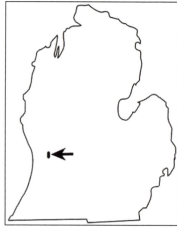

2,500 fully-developed lots. In addition to land issues, Wilson was also active in community banking, politics and civic affairs.

When the Belt Line loop was partially established around Grand Rapids in 1928, the western segment was run along part of Wilson Avenue and given the trunk line number of M-114. In 1942 the route code was changed to US-16, and this in turn was altered to the current M-11 in 1962. With all of these digits serving as identifiers over the years, the name of Wilson Avenue was all but forgotten along the state highway portion of its length. Only south of the Grand River, where the motorway falls under county jurisdiction, does Mr. Wilson still receive his due through what in essence are road-sign memorials.

As an aside, the route number M-11 has had a long history in our state, once covering much more mileage than at present. For decades it has been a favorite with motorists who have affectionately referred to the trunk line as a female named Emma Leven.

Coordinates: Grand Rapids Inset Map

WOLVERINE PAVEDWAY

The unofficial nickname of Michigan is "Wolverine State." The appellation apparently stems from our struggle with Ohio over control of Toledo and adjacent territory to the west.

It seems some citizens of the Buckeye State wanted to insult us in the battle of words known today as the Toledo War. Searching for the worst thing they could call us short of a four-letter word, the Ohioans said we were as lowdown as wolverines

Now, in some quarters a wolverine is a despised animal because it periodically kills more

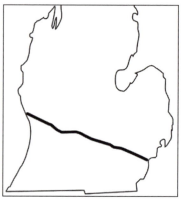

than it eats, will even consume human flesh if a corpse is found, and it has a highly offensive odor. Clearly, calling someone a wolverine could be viewed as something other than a compliment.

But the Michiganers of the 1830s saw things differently. They knew the wolverine was also noted for its strength, cunning and fearlessness.

In fact, this "skunk bear," as the creature is sometimes called, is so tough that no animal except man hunts it. Sure, our ancestors said proudly, we are wolverines.

It was in tribute to this pugnacious beast and our common nickname that a group of men formed the Wolverine Pavedway Association in Lansing on 4 September 1915. The purpose of this organization was to build a concrete path 185 miles long between Detroit and Grand Haven.

The route--which essentially followed the Grand River Avenue of today--would be the first road to cross the state, essentially linking Lakes Erie with Lake Michigan. Its cost was estimated at $2,000,000, and its name would be the Wolverine Pavedway.

Financing for this mammoth undertaking was to come from a variety of sources. The State Highway Department would pick up about 25% of the tab, with other moneys coming from local governments, private donations, and maybe a $50 contribution by automobile manufacturers for every car sold along the route.

The promoters of this enterprise came very close to accomplishing their goal, but the dream was not to be realized. The reasons for the failure were too many directors (50), insistence upon all pavement rather than allowing some crushed stone or gravel, and the emergence of competing highway projects that siphoned off interest and funds.

The most serious obstacle, however, was the inability to agree upon a route between Lansing and Grand Rapids. Half wanted a northerly course through Ionia and the rest wanted a southerly path through Lake Odessa. It was this disagreement more than anything else that led to the demise of the Wolverine Pavedway.

Before all hope was abandoned for the concept, it was decided to build a model stretch to serve as an example and inspiration for others. "Inasmuch as Lansing has the permanent offices of the association," supporters said, and "as the 'Capital City' is gaining direct benefits, local good roads enthusiasts feel that Ingham County should be foremost to launch actual construction work."

The president of the Wolverine Paved Way Association selected the 3-mile road between Lansing and East Lansing to serve as a demonstration project. After about a year of construction, the only segment of concrete attributable to the Wolverine Pavedway opened for traffic on 21 December 1916. And this may have been the only time a Wolverine was cordially welcomed near the home of Michigan State University.

Coordinates: K-M/8-13

WOODWARD AVENUE

As a glance at any Michigan road map will show, the "Number One" street in Detroit is Woodward Avenue. It has even been given the honor of being designated M-1 by the state highway department.

Woodward Avenue, one of the busiest arterial thoroughfares in Detroit, has a long history of being "Number One." In 1909, for instance, it boasted the first mile of concrete laid anywhere in America, covering the distance between Six and Seven Mile Roads.

Five years later, at the corner of Grand Boulevard, Woodward Avenue acquired the first traffic signal in Michigan. On 9 October 1917, at the intersection of Woodward and Michigan avenues, Detroit installed the country's first "Crowsnest" traffic tower, an elevated perch from which a police officer could direct approaching vehicles. And in October of 1920, at the same intersection, Detroit authorities erected the world's first four-way traffic signal light.

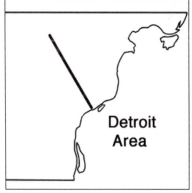

Detroit Area

Woodward Avenue's pioneering litany extends right up to the present, as on 13 June 2002 it became the first National Scenic Byway in Michigan, a tribute dedicated (according to the Michigan Department of Transportation) on 20 August 2003.

This stellar record begins in 1806, about a

year after Detroit was almost completely destroyed by fire. Wishing to build the town anew in a more spacious fashion, the governor of Michigan Territory charged Augustus Brevoort Woodward with the task of designing an improved street plan.

Woodward, a friend of Thomas Jefferson, had been appointed by the President to be a United States Judge in Detroit. He held this position from 1805 to 1824, when he was reassigned in a similar capacity to Tallahassee, Florida, where he died on 12 June 1827.

Born in New York City in 1774, Woodward graduated from Columbia College in 1793 and then went on to practice law near the nation's capital. There he met Charles L'Enfant, the architect who designed Washington, D.C. Impressed with the Frenchman's plan of the city, Woodward decided to use a variation of the same

layout for his map of Detroit.

When the plat of new Detroit was presented to the citizens, Woodward was criticized for naming one of the main streets after himself. "Not so," he replied, tongue firmly planted in cheek. "The avenue is named Woodward because it runs wood-ward, toward the woods."

Several attempts were subsequently made to remove his name from Woodward Avenue. Court House Street and Market Street were proposed as substitutes, but rejected. The portion of the route emanating from the downtown area was variously called Congress Street, Witherell Street and Saginaw Road or Turnpike. Despite these efforts, "Woodward" prevailed in the end, adding its name to the memorial highways of Michigan.

Coordinates: Southeastern Michigan Enlargement B-E/6-9

WORLD WAR II VETERAN'S MEMORIAL HIGHWAY

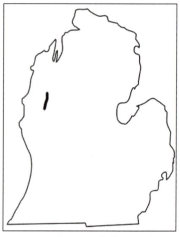

When war broke out in Europe in September of 1939, the United States almost immediately initiated a program of defense in case hostilities expanded to include this country. As part of this preparedness effort, in August of 1941 the government ordered the automobile companies in Michigan to reduce the number of cars assembled so they could instead turn out more weapons.

After Japan bombed Pearl Harbor on 7 December 1941, our nation's industries devoted their full attention to winning what by then had become a global struggle called World War II. The last cars for private use were completed on 10 February 1942 and civilian truck assembly ceased on May 31 of that year. From then on, Michigan's manufacturing might was almost solely directed at contributing arms to America's "Arsenal of Democracy."

During the course of the war, Michigan supplied more munitions than any other state. Our factories turned out nearly 8,700 B-24 bombers at Willow Run, tens of thousands of tanks from arsenals around Detroit, millions of engines, and a large quantity of other products to equip our military forces. When combat finally ended on 14 August 1945, thousands of people flocked to the downtown sections of their cities to celebrate the peace and Michigan's great industrial effort that had helped bring it about.

But the happiness of these late summer festivities was somewhat muted by the fact that of the roughly 650,000 Michiganians who served in the armed forces during World War II, nearly 15,500 had died in service and in excess of 29,000 were wounded in action. So while our working men and women on the home front had performed well and rightfully rejoiced in the fruits of their labors, the real heroes of the moment were those mainly absent individuals from our state who had worn a military uniform.

As early as October, 1940, members of the Michigan National Guard had been activated into federal service as part of the famous 32nd Infantry "Red Arrow" Division. As subsequent events called for additional soldiers and sailors, about 150,000 of our citizens volunteered for battle duty while another 500,000 or so were chosen to fill the ranks by local draft boards. Thus, of the approximately 13,000,000 men and women who served this country in World War II, about five percent came from Michigan.

Wishing to pay tribute to these honorable souls, VFW Post 5315 in Baldwin proposed that part of a state highway in Lake County be designated in their memory, sentiments that were endorsed on 4 May 1995 by the Commissioners of that county. To give official status to this public gesture of appreciation, Senate Resolution 203 was later introduced in the state legislature for the purpose of recalling "the valor of those [World War II veterans] who made enormous personal sacrifices for freedom."

After due deliberation, on 9 November 1995 the lawmakers in Lansing officially declared that "M-37 from its intersection with US-10 north

to the Lake/Wexford county line [be named] in honor of the veterans of World War II." This recognition, coming on the fiftieth anniversary of that terrible conflict's end, was dedicated on location in May of 1996.

In the interest of thoroughness, it should be noted that there was another "World War II Commemorative Highway" in Michigan, though it never received official sanction from state authorities. The story begins on 12 May 1994, when the Howell VFW post convinced the Livingston County Road Commission to make the one-mile length of "Grand River Avenue between Burkhart Road and State Highway M-59" a street of remembrance for only the years 1994-1995 in honor of the end of the Second World War a half-century earlier. At that time the Road Commission also offered to make and install the necessary notification signs, a project the agency finished about two weeks later. Though the period of recognition has long past, to this day (2004) one of the markers still stands just west of route M-59 on Grand River Avenue declaring that stretch of pavement to be the "World War II Memorial Highway."

Coordinates: I/8

DO
NOT
STOP

POSTSCRIPT
Highways Envisioned But Not Born

This book has identified those state and federal routes which bear a name as well as a number, or had legislation introduced to give them this status. There are, however, some memorial highways that never got beyond the idea stage which have not been mentioned in the text. In the interest of giving every potential candidate for a Michigan road of remembrance their due, this section will briefly review those trunk lines of tribute that were intellectually conceived but never given birth.

1916: Perhaps the oldest of these "wanna bees" is Metzger Drive, an appellation touted in 1916 for the route between Detroit and Toledo. This link was once referred to in a travel guide as the "worst road in America." So bad was this dirt trail that some motorists "even shipped their cars to Toledo...by boat to avoid driving over this stretch of roadway." Determined to remove this stain from Michigan's reputation, William Metzger--Detroit's first retail car dealer, organizer of the Cadillac Motor Car Company, and founder of the Detroit Automobile Club--raised enough funds from private sources to provide a concrete thoroughfare from Wayne County's southern border to Monroe. For this accomplishment some wanted to name the pavement in his honor, but Mr. Metzger was "inclined to drop everything and run when anyone...mentioned such a thing as that."

1917: Second in the chronological listing of named lanes of traffic that might-have-been is the Lincoln Highway. This motorway--formed in 1913 and headquartered in Detroit--was the first continuous improved road across the American Continent, extending from New York City to San Francisco. Its path did not enter Michigan but instead passed just to our south in Ohio and Indiana. However, efforts were apparently made in 1917 to develop branch lines in the Lower Peninsula leading to the main artery, with segments designated between Port Huron and Harbor Beach and from Oshtemo west to the Kalamazoo County line. There is no evidence that these actions were ever approved by the sponsoring body of the Lincoln Highway or that these stretches of pavement ever formally bore the name of our sixteenth president.

1921: Third in the continuum is the Superior Trail, the title suggested in September of 1921 for what is now highway US-41 between the Windy City and the tip of the Keweenaw Peninsula. According to its proponents, this moniker would appeal to sweltering urbanites suffering from the summer heat in such steamy metropolitan areas as Chicago and Milwaukee. These townfolk, looking for relief from uncomfortably high temperatures, would want to take a road to northern Michigan whose name suggests "the greatest body of fresh water in the world, cooling breezes and an invigorating climate." Unfortunately, tourist promotion is not that simple, and the concept came to naught after a year of so of attempted salesmanship by the Upper Peninsula Development Bureau.

1921: Tied for third place is a highway named for the first railroad in Michigan, the "Erie & Kalamazoo Trail." The E & K Railroad was completed in 1836 as a link between Toledo and Adrian. When the original route of this line was changed slightly, the chairman of the Lenawee County Automobile Club suggested that a commemorative highway be built on the old right-of-way. The idea was for a thoroughfare between Toledo and Kalamazoo marked with signs showing the profile of an antique wood-burning locomotive. The Trail was to approximately follow US-223 from Toledo to its termination near Somerset then west on US-12 to Moscow. At that point its course took what today are secondary roads through Litchfield, Tekonsha, Burlington, Athens and Vicksburg to Kalamazoo. Unfortunately, this great scheme had to be abandoned as better alternative trunk lines made its development unnecessary.

1923: Placing fourth in the temporal listings is a memorial highway whose identity is unknown. Its apparent existence began in May of 1923, when school children attending township schools in Gogebic County planted 150 white elm trees along what today is route US-2. Plans were for each tree to be "named after a soldier of the Civil War, the Spanish American and the [First] World War," with the Ironwood American Legion post and County Road Commission providing assistance. Reference is made in the historical record to the enactment of these deeds, but the actual title bestowed upon this road of recognition is never mentioned.

1924: Next in the order of succession is the Knickerbocker Highway, proposed early in 1924 as the name for a road connecting Holland with the northern Indiana border. Had this moniker actually been accepted, the designated route would have gone along M-40 from Holland to Allegan, M-89 from Allegan to Battle Creek, secondary roads from Battle Creek through Union City to Coldwater, and I-69 from Coldwater to the Hoosier state.

1924: Another route was proposed late in 1924 that affected our state. It was called the "Lake-to-Ocean Highway," and its Michigan segment was from Detroit (its most northerly terminus) south to Toledo. After leaving the Lower Peninsula, the road approximately followed I-75 to Lexington KY, secondary motorways from Lexington to Kingsport TN, US-23 from Kingsport to Asheville NC, I-26 from Asheville to Charleston SC, US-17 from Charleston to Savannah GA, and I-95 from Savannah to Jacksonville FL.

1926: A few years later Chicago interests proposed "an all-rural boulevard 200 feet wide" from Milwaukee south around the Windy City and then east to southwestern Michigan near New Buffalo. This belt line was to carry motorists unimpeded (much like contemporary Interstates) "around Chicago and suburban towns, thus avoiding street congestion...and obstructions to speed." Because the anticipated route touched Wisconsin, Illinois, Indiana and Michigan, a suggested name for the thoroughfare was "Four State Boulevard." The envisioned Midwest metropolitan bypass was not constructed until relatively modern times when major federal arteries by custom bear white numbers on red and blue shields, and so the original name became lost in transportation's obscure past.

1927: Next on the seniority list of rejected memorial highways is Green Avenue. This was the suggested name for the section of M-66 that runs from I-96 north to Ionia. The idea, made in 1927, was to honor then-Governor Fred W. Green, at the time "Ionia's first citizen." Green may have deserved to have a strip of pavement christened on his behalf, but the traffic artery that was to bear his name is known today by the unimaginative title of State Road.

1928: Close on the heels of the proposed trunkline recognizing Governor Green came a similar call on behalf of former Governor Chase S. Osborn. In 1928 the Sault Ste. Marie newspaper began publishing articles on the merits of naming the route between St. Ignace and the Soo after their hometown hero. This campaign continued without success into 1932, which is why today I-75 in the Upper Peninsula is not known as the Osborn Highway.

1928: Also in 1928 words were written in favor of making former US-27 in Michigan part of the "Bee Line Highway." This named route began at the Gulf of Mexico and closely followed contemporary I-65 north to Indianapolis. The idea was to extend the "Bee Line" road approximately along the present course of I-69 to Lansing, then over current US-127 to I-75, from which point the highway would proceed to a high-latitude terminus at either St. Ignace or Sault Ste. Marie. The negative outcome of this proposition proved the old adage that talk is indeed cheaper than action.

1930: The 32nd Infantry Division of World War I was mainly comprised of National Guard units from Michigan and Wisconsin. As a memorial to the wounded and dead of this military outfit, in July of 1930 the State Administrative Board was asked to "designate a through route from the southern state line north to the Straits, then westward through the Upper Peninsula to connect with a similarly designated Wisconsin highway, to be known as the 'Road of the 32nd' and marked with red arrows, the insignia of the division." The Board never acted on this request, but in 1952 a "Red Arrow Highway" was established in the southern Lower Peninsula, identified remnants of which remain to this day.

1931: In 1931, the women's auxiliary of the Samuel W. Wheeler Post of the United Spanish War Veterans obtained permission from the State Highway Department to make a "memorial roadside planting" along the western approach to the city of Marquette. The trees and shrubs proposed to border the first quarter mile of US-41 coming into town were intended to honor soldiers of the Spanish-American War, and the vegetation in tribute to these veterans was incrementally put in the ground during the growing seasons of 1932-1936. Perhaps because these undertakings took place over an extended period of time, the effort never received local official blessing nor was the stretch of memorial highway ever given a name.

1931: James Abram Garfield (1831-1881) was the twentieth President of the United States. Just four months after taking office--while walking through a railroad station in Washington DC--he was shot and killed by an assassin. When, in 1886, Bay County set off a new township, it named the administrative unit "Garfield" in honor of the slain chief executive. By 1897, a hamlet had developed near the middle of this township, and understandably it also chose to remember Garfield in its name. One will not be surprised to learn that the north/south road passing through the middle of the settlement and the township was called Garfield Road. In 1931, the supervisors of Bay County tried to encourage the state to extend M-33 south from Alger to Saginaw, creating a bypass of congested Bay City and giving road work to local unemployed residents. This new route was to be called the "Garfield Highway," but hard times brought on by the Depression and competing higher priorities prevented it from ever being built.

1932: In this year it was proposed that a scenic parkway be built around Lake Superior. The circle route was to begin at the Straits of Mackinac and then head north to Whitefish Bay. From there it would proceed west, in turn passing by or through the Tahquamenon Falls, Grand Marais, Munising, Marquette, the Huron Mountains, L'Anse, Houghton, Fort Wilkins, Ontonagon, and the Porcupine Mountains before continuing on to Ashland, Wisconsin. Because the projected path of this road was to meander through three states and one Canadian province, it was called the Lake Superior International Highway. Due in part to thrift required by the Great Depression, funds were never available to construct this ambitious scheme.

1933: John J. and George Edwin Reycraft were brothers who both graduated from the Detroit College of Medicine, both came to Petoskey in the 1890s, both served at different times as mayor of the community, and both founded and operated the town's hospital. It was said that they did "more for Petoskey than any other two residents of the city." In May of 1933, after both men had died, it was proposed that a small stretch of US-31 between Petoskey and Bay View be named the Reycraft Memorial Highway. No evidence can be found to show that this noble sentiment was actually accomplished.

1935: In the summer of 1935, President Roosevelt signed the document making Isle Royale the country's twenty-fifth National Park. Soon after this act took place, a proposal was made to designate US-41 the Isle Royale-Smokies-Everglades National Parks Trail. Often referred to as just the "National Parks Trail," US-41 then began at Naples Florida (near Everglades National Park) and ended at Copper Harbor (the closest one could approach by land to Lake Superior's Isle Royale National Park). In addition to linking America's two great peninsula states, US-41 passed by or through Kenesaw Mountain, Chicamauga and Chattanooga Civil War battlefields, Great Smoky Mountains National Park, and Mammoth Cave. But the meanders of the highway near the parks, monuments and historic sites of the Southeast and Midwest was viewed by motorists as more of a travel itinerary than a federally numbered route, and with an unwieldy title to carry as well the name of the Trail never caught on with the traveling public.

1939: In 1939 the Automobile Club of Michigan, in its magazine Motor News, hinted that it might be appropriate to name the access road to the Lake of the Clouds in Ontonagon County. This highway into the Porcupine Mountains is currently known as M-107, but back then the people at "Triple A" thought Sky Line Drive would be a nice title. Over sixty years later, they may still be right.

1940: Thomas Conlin, for 38 years editor and publisher of the Crystal Falls Diamond Drill weekly newspaper, died on 24 August 1935. Slightly more than a half-decade later, after about ten miles of route US-2 from Crystal Falls south to the Wisconsin border had been rebuilt, the citizens of the area decided it would be fitting to dedicate this segment of highway in honor of Mr. Conlin. They sought the support of government officials in Lansing for this idea, but in 1940 the state's leaders were more interested in exiting the Depression than they were in naming roads for people long deceased. For this reason, Thomas Conlin appears in local history books and US-2 can be found on contemporary travel maps.

1943: In 1943, during the height of the Second World War, Michigan began making plans for road construction projects it would undertake at the end of hostilities. One of the enterprises being considered was called the "Erie-Huron Scenic Highway," a stretch of multi-lane pavement running from Toledo (Lake Erie) to Port Huron (Lake Huron). Though never built, the path of the 120-mile sightseeing route was generally south from Port Huron along present-day M-29 to I-94, I-94 to I-75, I-75 to M-85 and back to I-75 until Toledo.

1945: In 1938, civic-minded people in Monroe proposed the creation of an Historic Trail as an "effective means of acquainting out-of-town visitors--and local residents, too--with the sites and buildings which have figured prominently in the rich and colorful history of Monroe." This Trail was to feature thirty-five significant places in Monroe's past that were strung along the paths of routes M-50, M-125 and US-24. By 1945, manifesting the impact that World War II had on thinking, the name of the contemplated motorway had been changed to Monroe County Historic Trail and Memorial Parkway. Unfortunately, due to a variety of distractions, the envisioned program was not completed until the late 1950s. By then the urge to honor past military exploits had dimmed, so the words "Memorial Parkway" were dropped from Monroe County's Historic Trail.

1946: Born in Lansing on 23 February 1880, Roy Dikeman Chapin went to work for the famous Ransom Olds twenty-one years later. In 1901 he drove an Oldsmobile from Detroit to New York City in just seven days, the first car to make that journey. Chapin subsequently became sales manager for the Olds firm, and then in 1909 he was made president of the Hudson Motor Car Company in Detroit. By 1923, Chapin had moved up to chairman of the board at Hudson Motors, before becoming Secretary of Commerce in 1932 for the Hoover administration. He died prematurely in Detroit on 16 February 1936 after a highly distinguished career. Because of his contributions to Detroit and the automobile industry, certain interests wanted what is today metropolitan I-94 named the "Roy D. Chapin Highway." This movement did not meet with success, and the road is shown on contemporary maps as the Edsel Ford Expressway.

1951: In 1951, the Huron-Clinton Metropolitan Authority announced it was going to build a nine-mile, four-lane divided motorway east from

Kent Lake in Oakland County's Kensington Park region. This road, designed to be another access route to the popular recreation area, was to be called the "Sidney Waldon Parkway." Mr. Waldon, who had died in 1945, was an original member of the Metropolitan Authority and at different times was chief engineer for both the Cadillac and Packard car companies. Unfortunately for the legacy of Mr. Waldon, the superhighway that was to bear his name was never built.

1953: In this year the state legislature passed Public Act 176 which created the Michigan Turnpike Authority. The purpose of this entity was to "construct, maintain, repair and operate [two] turnpike projects" in the southern Lower Peninsula. The first of these undertakings was to run from Toledo to Bay City, generally along the present path of I-75. This toll road was informally called the "Michigan Turnpike." The second proposed pay-to-drive route was to stretch from Detroit west to the Indiana line near New Buffalo, pretty much covering the course of contemporary I-94. The working name for this highway was the "Trans-Michigan Turnpike." It is possible that the labors of this Authority would ultimately have produced a toll road or two, but the Federal Aid Highway Bill of 1956 provided for the Interstate Highway System, greatly diminishing the need for privately-funded expressways. Consequently, the limited access trunk lines were built with public money as freeways and the Turnpike Authority was disbanded by Public Act 13 of 1962.

1958: Readers of an article in the January, 1959, issue of Inside Michigan Magazine might understandably conclude that the beautiful shoreline road along M-119 between Harbor Springs and Cross Village is also known as the Swift Memorial Drive. This designation was bestowed by the Emmet County Road Commission in 1958 to honor Albert Thorne Swift, a prominent resident of Harbor Springs who, before his untimely death, worked to develop the summer tourist trade of the region. In fact, Swift Memorial Drive is just another name for Lower Shore Road, the secondary highway that continues along the Lake Michigan coast in the section where route M-119 runs inland.

1967: During his 48-year career as a public servant he was Deputy State Highway Commissioner, head of the Wayne County Parks program,

Director of the Wayne County sewage disposal and water supply system, manager of the Wayne County airport, and engineer/manager of the Wayne County Road Commission. Once considered the most powerful man in all of Michigan county government, his name was Leroy C. Smith. Because he had done so much for Wayne County transportation, Senate Concurrent Resolution 36 was introduced to name the Southfield Freeway (M-39) in tribute to him. This measure could not muster the necessary votes to pass, and so the intended beneficiary of this gesture died having built many highways but having none named in his honor.

1975: Trunkline M-115 is said to be Michigan's "only true diagonal road for its nearly 100-mile length." Running from approximately Clare to Frankfort, the cross-peninsula artery was authorized in 1934 in part to give motorists from the southeastern portion of the state easier access to the northwestern resort district. In summer, these vacationers headed straight for the setting sun on this route which, like a beacon, drew them to the region's woods and waters. This phenomenon prompted the Automobile Club of Michigan in July of 1975 to dub the two-lane pavement the "Going-to-the-Sun Highway." This title never caught the public imagination, however, and so the thoroughfare remains today a three-digit number rather than an euphonious name on the map.

1980: Paul Goebel, Sr., was born and raised in Grand Rapids and then spent the rest of his life serving the people of that town. During his career in the community as a businessman, he also performed as Director of the Peoples National Bank (1936-1950), Mayor of the City of Grand Rapids (1950-1954, 1956-1958), Kent County Supervisor (1950-1954, 1957-1958), delegate to the Michigan Constitutional Convention (1960-1961), and Regent of the University of Michigan (1961-1970). Because of his many accomplishments, a bill was submitted in the Legislature to "make part of US-131 in Kent County the Paul Goebel Sr. Highway." With insufficient support to pass the measure, when Goebel died in 1988 he was remembered at his funeral by many friends and beneficiaries but not by a memorial highway.

1981: David Shepherd served on the Oak Park City Council for fourten years and as the town's mayor for ten years. When this relatively young man died in office, members of the community wanted to pay tribute to him in some fashion. There evolved from this desire a consensus that nearby I-696 "from Lahser Road east to I-75 in Oakland County [should] be renamed in honor of" the deceased. House Concurrent Resolution 361 was introduced to accomplish this goal, but it never passed the legislature because the route in question had already been dedicated to the memory of Walter Reuther.

1984: Austin Blair served as Governor of our state during the time of the Civil War, guiding our two peninsulas through a period of national crisis. Under his leadership, Michigan exceeded its quota of money and men as set by officials in Washington and provided vast quantities of raw materials to further the war effort. Blair also liberally spent his own funds in support of the Union cause, a generosity that nearly reduced him to financial ruin by the time he left office. To commend this man for his public service, a bill was introduced in 1984 to designate "the Jackson County portion of I-94 as the Austin Blair Memorial Highway." But because Blair had already been honored by a statue on the Capitol grounds, there was little inclination to name a road for him, too.

1985: Representatives from Alger, Chippewa and Luce counties tried to create a 175-mile long Superior Scenic Drive in this year. The route was to begin in Munising and travel east along H-58 to Deer Park; from Deer Park south on H-37 to M-123; M-123 east to Lake Shore Drive; Lake Shore Drive east to Six Mile Road; Six Mile Road east to I-75; and I-75 north to Sault Sainte Marie. The tourist highway was never built because of its price tag (about $13,000,000) and the need to construct twelve miles of new pavement in the protected Pictured Rocks National Lakeshore.

1994: In the summer of 1994, Michigan hosted the World Cup finals soccer matches at the Silverdome. In April of that year, during a speech in Monroe, Governor Engler opined that this upcoming "prestigious event [was] worthy of remembering through a special roadway designation." It was his suggestion that portions of I-94 be labeled the "World Cup Highway." However, the Governor could not find anyone in the Legislature willing to sponsor such legislation, and so the proposed name was never applied to our state's main east/west thoroughfare.

1999: Douglas Carl was a complete Michigan man. He was born in Almont in 1951, educated at Romeo schools and MSU (class of 1973), and died in Macomb County in 1997. During his short 46 years on this earth Carl spent most of his adult life in the public arena. To wit, he served his fellow citizens as Macomb County Commissioner (1980-82), State Representative (1985-1987), and State Senator (1987-1997). After his untimely death, certain parties sought to honor Carl with a highway of tribute in his district. A bill was introduced to make route M-53 between 27 Mile Road and 34 Mile Road the "Doug Carl Memorial Freeway," but sufficient support could not be found in the Legislature to get the measure passed into law.

1999: As readers of this book can appreciate, most of Michigan's memorial highways are unknown to the general public. This fact was demonstrated in 1999 when a lawmaker from southeastern Michigan expressed a desire to name route I-275 the "Reagan Freeway" after this country's fortieth President. The notion never went anywhere for, not only was it poorly received by residents of the region, it was subsequently learned that the targeted road had already been designated by the Legislature in memory of Philip A. Hart.

2000: In 1861 Congress authorized the Medal of Honor, the foremost distinction conferred upon someone serving in the U.S. armed forces. The award is made in the name of Congress to any person who has distinguished themselves in conflict with the enemy by fearless daring, at the risk of life above and beyond the call of duty. This most prestigious of all decorations, the Medal of Honor is at the pinnacle of America's pyramid of military tributes. The standards for receiving this highest of commendations are so rigorous that 55% of the medals presented since World War I have been posthumous. Of the approximately 3,400 men and one woman who have earned the Medal of Honor, 109 (3%) were from Michigan (two soldiers from our state won the Medal twice). It was in tribute to these courageous individuals that the Legislature passed House Bill 5028 of 2000 making route I-75 in Monroe County a memorial to the most valorous of those who have fought for this country. This noble gesture was vetoed by the Governor on 27 December 2000, not because of any reluctance to bestow recognition upon our national heroes, but because

I-75 in Monroe County had already been named the "American Legion Memorial Highway" by an earlier session of the Legislature.

2001: According to some sources, the most decorated soldier in American history was Matt Louis Urban. An Army Captain who served in North Africa and Europe during World War II, Urban was wounded seven times and received 29 medals, including the coveted Medal of Honor. Most of his exploits occurred between June 14 and September 3, 1944, when he "distinguished himself by a series of bold, heroic actions" in France. Once a resident of Monroe, Michigan, Urban spent his last years living along the east coast of Lake Michigan in Holland, dying there in 1995. In tribute to this gallant figure, a bill was introduced to name route M-50 in Monroe County the "Matt Urban Memorial Highway." Unfortunately, there was not enough support in the Legislature to get this measure passed.

2002: Phoebe Anne Oakley (Annie Oakley) was one of the greatest markswomen the world has ever seen. At 30 paces she could hit the thin edge of a playing card, shoot a dime from a brave soul's fingers, or nick the end of a cigarette held between someone's lips. She assumed international fame during the seventeen years she toured with Buffalo Bill's Wild West Show as a trick-shot artist. The popular musical comedy "Annie Get Your Gun" (1946) was loosely based on her life. In part because she performed on occasion in Michigan, a bill was introduced in 2002 to name most of highway US-127 the "Annie Oakley Memorial Pike." But the dead-eyed woman's connection to this state was apparently too tenuous to merit a road of remembrance, for the Legislature failed to endorse the tribute.

2003: Born in Gratiot County on 10 July 1939, Larry L. DeVuyst was educated at Ithaca High School and Michigan State University. As an adult, DeVuyst became a farmer and equipment business owner before entering public service. He was a member of the Natural Resource Commission from 1991-1996, at which point he successfully ran for state Representative from Montcalm and Gratiot counties. Late in 2003 a bill was introduced in the Michigan Senate proposing that the portion of US-127 a quarter-mile either side of Junction M-57 be designated the "Larry and Joanne DeVuyst Highway and Interchange."

APPENDIX 1

NAMED HIGHWAYS IN EACH COUNTY

Alcona (8)
  Blue Water Trail
  Dixie Highway
  East Michigan Pike
  Huron Shore Highway
  Michigan Pike
  Sweetwater Trail
  Theodore Roosevelt International
    Highway
  United Spanish War Veterans
    Memorial Highway
Alger County (6)
  Cloverland Trail
  Great Lakes Automobile Route
  Jacobetti Highway
  Sheridan Road
  Theodore Roosevelt International
    Highway
  Townsend National Highway
Allegan County (10)
  Blue Star Memorial Highway
  Dixie Highway
  Gerald R. Ford Freeway
  Great Lakes Automobile Route
  James Whitcomb Riley Memorial
    Highway
  Mackinaw Trail
  Michigan Pike
  Michigan Trail
  Michigan-Erie Highway
  West Michigan Pike
Alpena County (10)
  Blue Water Trail
  Dixie Highway
  East Michigan Pike
  Huron Shore Highway
  Michigan Pike
  Michigan Polar-Equator Trail
  Sweetwater Trail
  Theodore Roosevelt International
    Highway
  United Spanish War Veterans
    Memorial Highway
  Veterans Memorial Highway
Antrim County (10)
  Blue Star Memorial Highway

  Cairn Highway
  Dixie Highway
  Green Arrow Route
  James Whitcomb Riley Memorial
    Highway
  Mackinaw Trail
  Michigan Pike
  Michigan Polar-Equator Trail
  Michigan Trail
  West Michigan Pike
Arenac County (11)
  American Legion Memorial
    Highway
  Bicentennial Freedom Way
  Blue Water Trail
  Dixie Highway
  East Michigan Pike
  Huron Shore Highway
  Michigan Pike
  Straight to the Straits Route
  Sweetwater Trail
  Theodore Roosevelt International
    Highway
  United Spanish War Veterans
    Memorial Highway
Baraga County (7)
  Cloverland Trail
  Great Lakes Automobile Route
  Isle Royale Trail
  Memory Lane
  Theodore Roosevelt International
    Highway
  Townsend National Highway
  Veterans Memorial Highway
Barry County (4)
  Colgrove Highway
  Custer Trail
  Green Arrow Route
  Paradise Trail
Bay County (19)
  Algonquin Trail
  American Legion Memorial
    Highway
  Bay City Historic Heritage Route
  Bicentennial Freedom Way
  Blue Water Trail
  Dixie Highway
  East Michigan Pike

Historic Heritage Route II
Huron Shore Highway
Huron Shore Pike
Liberty Highway
Michigan Pike
Roberts-Linton Highway
Theodore Roosevelt International
  Highway
Top of Michigan Trail
United Spanish War Veterans
  Memorial Highway
Veterans Memorial Parkway
Veterans of World War I
  Memorial Highway
Victory Highway
Benzie County (9)
  Blue Star Memorial Highway
  Chippewa Trail
  Dixie Highway
  Great Lakes Automobile Route
  Manitou Trail
  Michigamme Trail
  Michigan Pike
  Michigan Trail
  West Michigan Pike
Berrien County (24)
  Blossom Highway
  Blue & Gray Trail
  Blue Star Memorial Highway
  Chicago Road
  Detroit-Lincoln-Denver Highway
  Dixie Highway
  Dunes Highway
  Gerald R. Ford Freeway
  Great Lakes Automobile Route
  Iron Brigade Memorial Highway
  LaSalle Trail
  Liberty Highway
  Martin Luther King Drive
  Michigamme Trail
  Michigan Avenue
  Michigan Pike
  Michigan Trail
  Pulaski Memorial Highway
  Red Arrow Highway
  Red Bud Trail
  Saint Joseph Road
  Saint Joseph Valley Parkway
  Victory Highway
  West Michigan Pike

Branch County (4)
  Chicago Road
  Custer Trail
  Iron Brigade Memorial Highway
  Pulaski Memorial Highway
Calhoun County (28)
  Blossom Highway
  Capital to Capital Highway
  Carleton Road
  Colgrove Highway
  Custer Trail
  Detroit-Lincoln-Denver Highway
  Dickman Road
  Erie & Kalamazoo Trail
  Fort Custer Memorial Highway
  Green Arrow Route
  Kalamazoo-Deering Trail
  Liberty Highway
  Marshall's Territorial Road
  Martin Luther King Jr. Memorial
    Highway
  Michigan Avenue
  Michigan Trail
  Michigan-Erie Highway
  94th Combat Infantry Division
    Memorial Highway
  Paradise Trail
  Pioneer Trail
  Red Arrow Highway
  Road of Memory
  Saginaw Valley Trail
  Saint Joseph Road
  Sojourner Truth Memorial
    Highway
  Underground Railroad Memorial
    Highway
  Victory Highway
  Wayne Highway
Cass County (7)
  Cass County Veterans Memorial
    Highway
  Chicago Road
  Colgrove Highway
  Detroit-Lincoln-Denver Highway
  Dixie Highway
  Iron Brigade Memorial Highway
  Pulaski Memorial Highway
Charlevoix County (9)
  Blue Star Memorial Highway
  Dixie Highway

Green Arrow Route
James Whitcomb Riley Memorial
  Highway
Mackinaw Trail
Michigamme Trail
Michigan Pike
Michigan Trail
West Michigan Pike
Cheboygan County (17)
  American Legion Memorial
    Highway
  Arctic-Tropic Overland Trail
  Bicentennial Freedom Way
  Blue Water Trail
  Center Line Highway
  Dixie Highway
  East Michigan Pike
  G. Mennen Williams Highway
  Huron Shore Highway
  Michigan Pike
  Straight to the Straits Route
  Sweetwater Trail
  Theodore Roosevelt International
    Highway
  Top of Michigan Trail
  Townsend National Highway
  United Spanish War Veterans
    Memorial Highway
  William Howard Taft Memorial Highway
Chippewa County (18)
  American Legion Memorial
    Highway
  Arctic-Tropic Overland Trail
  Bicentennial Freedom Way
  Blue Star Memorial Highway
  Blue Water Trail
  Cloverland Trail
  "Curley" Lewis Memorial
    Highway
  Dixie Highway
  Jacobetti Highway
  Meridian Road
  Prentiss M. Brown Memorial
    Highway
  Road of Remembrance
  Sweetwater Trail
  Tahquamenon Falls Memorial
    Highway
  Theodore Roosevelt International
    Highway

Townsend National Highway
United Spanish War Veterans
  Memorial Highway
William Howard Taft Memorial
  Highway.
Clare County (5)
  Arctic-Tropic Overland Trail
  Center Line Highway
  Kevin Sherwood Memorial
    Highway
  Townsend National Highway
  William Howard Taft Memorial
    Highway
Clinton County (13)
  Amvets Memorial Highway
  Arthur Vandenberg Memorial
    Highway
  Center Line Highway
  Central Michigan Pike
  Dexter Trail
  Gary Priess Memorial Highway
  Glacial Trail
  Grand River Avenue
  Great Lakes International
    Highway
  Michigan Trail
  Purple Heart Highway
  Townsend National Highway
  William Howard Taft Memorial
    Highway
  Wolverine Pavedway
Crawford County (7)
  American Legion Memorial
    Highway
  Arctic-Tropic Overland Trail
  Bicentennial Freedom Way
  Center Line Highway
  Top of Michigan Trail
  Townsend National Highway
  William Howard Taft Memorial
    Highway
Delta County (11)
  Amvets Memorial Drive
  Blue Water Trail
  Bohn Highway
  Cloverland Trail
  Great Lakes Automobile Route
  King's International Highway
  Memory Lane
  Oscar G. Johnson Memorial

Highway
Sheridan Road
Theodore Roosevelt International
  Highway
United Spanish War Veterans
  Memorial Highway
Dickinson County (8)
  Bohn Highway
  Cloverland Trail
  Great Lakes Automobile Route
  King's International Highway
  Leif Erickson Highway
  Memorial Drive
  Oscar G Johnson Memorial
    Highway
  United Spanish War Veterans
    Memorial Highway
Eaton County (7)
  Capital to Capital Highway
  Clinton Trail
  Fitzgerald Memorial Highway
  Hartel Road
  Liberty Highway
  Saginaw Valley Trail
  Victory Highway
Emmet County (7)
  Blue Star Memorial Highway
  Chippewa Memorial Pike
  Dixie Highway
  Mackinaw Trail
  Michigamme Trail
  Michigan Pike
  West Michigan Pike
Genesee County (28)
  American Legion Memorial
    Highway
  Arctic-Tropic Overland Trail
  Bernie Borden Memorial
    Overpass
  Bicentennial Freedom Way
  Bristol Road
  Buick Freeway
  Central Michigan International
    Highway
  Central Michigan Pike
  Chevrolet Expressway
  David Dunbar Buick Freeway
  Disabled American Veterans
    Highway
  Dixie Highway

Dort Highway
East Michigan Pike
Flint Trail
Great Lakes International
  Highway
Liberty Highway
Michigan Trail
Miller Road
Pearl Harbor Memorial Highway
Saginaw Trail
Theodore Roosevelt International
  Highway
Top of Michigan Trail
U.A.W. Freeway
United Spanish War Veterans
  Memorial Highway
Veterans Memorial Highway
Veterans of Foreign Wars
  Memorial Highway
Victory Highway
Gladwin County (2)
  Meridian Road
  Top of Michigan Trail
Gogebic County (9)
  Bohn Highway
  Cloverland Trail
  Coolidge Trail
  Great Lakes Automobile Route
  King's International Highway
  Memory Lane
  Theodore Roosevelt International
    Highway
  United Spanish War Veterans
    Memorial Highway
  Veterans Memorial Highway
Grand Traverse County (13)
  Blue Star Memorial Highway
  Chippewa Trail
  Dixie Highway
  Grand Traverse Memorial
    Highway
  Hamilton Way
  James Whitcomb Riley Memorial
    Highway
  Mackinaw Trail
  Michigamme Trail
  Michigan Pike
  Michigan Trail
  Paradise Trail
  Queen's Highway

West Michigan Pike
Gratiot County (14)
    Bagley Road
    Center Line Highway
    Central Michigan International
      Highway
    Cleveland Avenue
    Colgrove Highway
    Glacial Trail
    Luce Road
    Memorial Row
    Michigan Trail
    Monroe Road
    Rainbow Trail
    Townsend National Highway
    Veteran's Memorial Highway
    William Howard Taft Memorial
      Highway
Hillsdale County (11)
    Carleton Road
    Center Line Highway
    Chicago Road
    Erie & Kalamazoo Trail
    Iron Brigade Memorial Highway
    Kalamazoo-Deering Trail
    Memory Mile
    Meridian Road
    Michigan-Erie Highway
    Pulaski Memorial Highway
    Wayne Highway
Houghton County (7)
    Cloverland Trail
    Great Lakes Automobile Route
    Memorial Road
    Sheridan Road
    Theodore Roosevelt International
      Highway
    Townsend National Highway
    Veterans Memorial Highway
Huron County (9)
    Algonquin Trail
    Blue Water Highway
    Blue Water Trail
    Dixie Highway
    Earle Memorial Highway
    Huron County Memorial
      Highway
    Huron Shore Pike
    Michigan Pike
    Van Dyke Road

Ingham County (23)
    Amvets Memorial Highway
    Arthur Vandenberg Memorial
      Highway
    Capital to Capital Highway
    Center Line Highway
    Dexter Trail
    Fitzgerald Memorial Highway
    Fred L. Kircher Freeway
    Gary Priess Memorial Highway
    Grand River Avenue
    James M. Pelton Firefighters
      Memorial Highway
    Liberty Highway
    Logan Street
    Mackinaw Scenic Shortway
      Route
    Martin Luther King Jr. Boulevard
    Michigan Trail
    Olds Freeway
    Reo Highway
    Saginaw Valley Trail
    Townsend National Highway
    Victory Highway
    Wayne Highway
    William Howard Taft Memorial
      Highway
    Wolverine Pavedway
Ionia County (13)
    Amvets Memorial Highway
    Arthur Vandenberg Memorial
      Highway
    Blue Water Highway
    Central Michigan Pike
    Colgrove Highway
    Dexter Trail
    Glacial Trail
    Grand River Avenue
    Great Lakes International
      Highway
    Green Arrow Route
    Michigan Trail
    Road of Remembrance
    Wolverine Pavedway
Iosco County (9)
    Blue Water Trail
    Dixie Highway
    East Michigan Pike
    Huron Shore Highway
    Michigan Pike

Sweetwater Trail
Tawas-Manistee Trail
Theodore Roosevelt International
  Highway
United Spanish War Veterans
  Memorial Highway
Iron County (10)
  Bohn Highway
  Cloverland Trail
  Coolidge Trail
  Great Lakes Automobile Route
  Isle Royale Trail
  King's International Highway
  Memory Lane
  Theodore Roosevelt International
    Highway
  Townsend National Highway
  United Spanish War Veterans
    Memorial Highway
Isabella County (5)
  Arctic-Tropic Overland Trail
  Center Line Highway
  Michigan Trail
  Townsend National Highway
  William Howard Taft Memorial Highway
Jackson County (18)
  Austin Blair Memorial Highway
  Blossom Highway
  Center Line Highway
  Clinton Trail
  Colgrove Highway
  Detroit-Lincoln-Denver Highway
  Haskell L. Nichols Memorial
    Highway
  Jackson County Roadside
    Memorial
  Mackinaw Scenic Shortway
    Route
  Meridian Road
  Michigan Avenue
  Michigan Trail
  Red Arrow Highway
  Saint Joseph Road
  Tecumseh Trail
  Townsend National Highway
  Wayne Highway
  William Howard Taft Memorial
    Highway
Kalamazoo County (21)
  Amvets Memorial Parkway

Blossom Highway
Colgrove Highway
Detroit-Lincoln-Denver Highway
Dixie Highway
Eire-Kalamazoo Trail
James Whitcomb Riley Memorial
  Highway
Kalamazoo County Memorial
  Highway
Kalamazoo-Deering Trail
King Highway
Liberty Highway
Mackinaw Trail
Michigan Avenue
Michigan Trail
Michigan-Erie Highway
Ohio-Indiana-Michigan Way
Red Arrow Highway
Saint Joseph Road
Underground Railroad Memorial
  Highway
Victory Highway
Westnedge Avenue
Kalkaska County (4)
  Green Arrow Route
  James Whitcomb Riley Memorial
    Highway
  Mackinaw Trail
  Michigan Trail
Kent County (23)
  Amvets Memorial Highway
  Arthur Vandenberg Memorial
    Highway
  Central Michigan International
    Highway
  Central Michigan Pike
  Cesar E. Chavez Way
  Custer Trail
  Dixie Highway
  Gerald R. Ford Freeway
  Glacial Trail
  Grand Highway
  Grand River Avenue
  Great Lakes International
    Highway
  James Whitcomb Riley Memorial
    Highway
  Lake Michigan Drive
  Mackinaw Trail
  Michigan Trail

126th Infantry Memorial
    Boulevard
Paradise Trail
Paul B. Henry Freeway
Rainbow Trail
Remembrance Road
Wilson Avenue
Wolverine Pavedway
Keweenaw County (4)
    Brockway Mountain Drive
    Cloverland Trail
    Great Lakes Automobile Route
    Sheridan Road
Lake County (2)
    Paradise Trail
    World War II Veteran's Memorial
        Highway
Lapeer County (11)
    Central Michigan International
        Highway
    Central Michigan Pike
    DeWayne T. Williams Memorial
        Highway
    Earle Memorial Highway
    Great Lakes International
        Highway
    Liberty Highway
    Michigan Trail
    Van Dyke Road
    Veterans Memorial Highway
    Veterans of Foreign Wars
        Memorial Highway
    Victory Highway
Leelanau County (4)
    Chippewa Trail
    D.H. Day Highway
    Manitou Trail
    Michigamme Trail
Lenawee County (15)
    Carleton Road
    Center Line Highway
    Chicago Road
    Erie & Kalamazoo Trail
    Hoosier Highway
    Iron Brigade Memorial Highway
    Kalamazoo-Deering Trail
    LaPlaisance Bay Turnpike
    Mackinaw Scenic Shortway
        Route
    Meridian Road

Michigan-Erie Highway
Pulaski Memorial Highway
Tecumseh Trail
Townsend National Highway
William Howard Taft Memorial
    Highway
Livingston County (13)
    Amvets Memorial Highway
    Arctic-Tropic Overland Trail
    Arthur Vandenberg Memorial
        Highway
    Dexter Trail
    Flint Trail
    Grand River Avenue
    Korean War Memorial Highway
    Michigan Trail
    Reo Highway
    Top of Michigan Trail
    United Spanish War Veterans
        Memorial Highway
    Vietnam Veterans Memorial
        Highway
    Wolverine Pavedway
Luce County (5)
    Cloverland Trail
    Jacobetti Highway
    117th Quartermaster Battalion
        Highway
    Theodore Roosevelt International
        Highway
    Townsend National Highway
Mackinac County (18)
    American Legion Memorial
        Highway
    Arctic-Tropic Overland Trail
    Bicentennial Freedom Way
    Blue Star Memorial Highway
    Blue Water Trail
    Bohn Highway
    Cloverland Trail
    Dixie Highway
    King's International Highway
    Meridian Road
    117th Quartermaster Battalion
        Highway
    Prentiss M. Brown Memorial
        Highway
    Sweetwater Trail
    Tahquamenon Falls Memorial
        Highway

Theodore Roosevelt International
  Highway
Townsend National Highway
United Spanish War Veterans
  Memorial Highway
William Howard Taft Memorial
  Highway
Macomb County (22)
  Algonquin Trail
  Base Line Road
  Blue Water Trail
  Bluewater Circle Drive
  Christopher Columbus Freeway
  Columbus Memorial Highway
  Dixie Highway
  Earle Memorial Highway
  Gratiot Avenue
  Groesbeck Highway
  Hall Road
  Henry B. Joy Road
  James G. O'Hara Freeway
  Jefferson Avenue
  Lakes & River Drive
  Michigan Pike
  Michigan Trail
  POW/MIA Memorial Freeway
  Veterans Memorial Highway
  Vietnam Veterans Memorial
    Highway
  Walter P. Reuther Highway
  William P. Rosso Highway
Manistee County (10)
  Blue Star Memorial Highway
  Chippewa Trail
  Dixie Highway
  Great Lakes Automobile Route
  Manitou Trail
  Michigamme Trail
  Michigan Pike
  Michigan Trail
  Tawas-Manistee Trail
  West Michigan Pike
Marquette County (9)
  Cloverland Trail
  Great Lakes Automobile Route
  Jacobetti Highway
  Leif Erickson Highway
  Memorial Highway
  Sheridan Road
  Theodore Roosevelt International

Highway
  Townsend National Highway
  Veterans Memorial Highway
Mason County (9)
  Blue Star Memorial Highway
  Dixie Highway
  Great Lakes Automobile Route
  Michigamme Trail
  Michigan Pike
  Michigan Trail
  Pere Marquette Memorial
    Highway
  Veterans Memorial Highway
  West Michigan Pike
Mecosta County (4)
  Green Arrow Route
  James Whitcomb Riley Memorial
    Highway
  Mackinaw Trail
  Michigan Trail
Menominee County (9)
  Blue Water Trail
  Bohn Highway
  Cloverland Trail
  Great Lakes Automobile Route
  King's International Highway
  Oscar G. Johnson Memorial
    Highway
  Sheridan Road
  Theodore Roosevelt International
    Highway
  United Spanish War Veterans
    Memorial Highway
Midland County (5)
  Arctic-Tropic Overland Trail
  Mackinaw Scenic Shortway
    Route
  Meridian Road
  Soldiers' Memorial Highway
  Top of Michigan Trail
Missaukee County (2)
  Green Arrow Route
  Tawas-Manistee Trail
Monroe County (23)
  Algonquin Trail
  American Legion Memorial
    Highway
  Arctic-Tropic Overland Trail
  Bicentennial Freedom Way
  Carleton Road

Clara Barton Memorial Highway
Custer Road
Dixie Highway
East Michigan Pike
Erie & Kalamazoo Trail
Flint Trail
Historic Heritage Route I
LaPlaisance Bay Turnpike
Michigan Pike
Michigan Trail
Michigan-Erie Highway
Monroe Historic Heritage Route
Philip A. Hart Memorial Highway
Telegraph Road
Top of Michigan Trail
United Spanish War Veterans
   Memorial Highway
United States Road
Veterans Memorial Highway
Montcalm County (8)
   Central Michigan International
      Highway
   Colgrove Highway
   Green Arrow Route
   Korean War Veterans Memorial
      Highway
   James Whitcomb Riley Memorial
      Highway
   Mackinaw Trail
   Michigan Trail
   Rainbow Trail
Montmorency County (2)
   Michigan Polar-Equator Trail
   Straight to the Straits Route
Muskegon County (16)
   Amvets Memorial Highway
   Arthur Vandenberg Memorial
      Highway
   Blue Star Memorial Highway
   Central Michigan International
      Highway
   Dixie Highway
   Great Lakes Automobile Route
   Memorial Drive
   Michigamme Trail
   Michigan Pike
   Michigan Trail
   Moses J. Jones Parkway
   Muskegon County Memorial
      Causeway

Rainbow Trail
Tom Bolt Highway
Veteran's Memorial Causeway
West Michigan Pike
Newaygo County (3)
   Korean War Veterans Memorial
      Highway
   Mason Drive
   Paradise Trail
Oakland County (27)
   Adler Memorial Highway
   American Legion Memorial
      Highway
   Arthur Vandenberg Memorial
      Highway
   Base Line Road
   Bicentennial Freedom Way
   Boy Scout Trail
   Cesar E. Chavez Avenue
   Columbus Memorial Highway
   Coolidge Highway
   Disabled American Veterans
      Memorial Highway
   Deacon Memorial Highway
   Dixie Highway
   East Michigan Pike
   Grand River Avenue
   Michigan Trail
   Pontiac Trail
   Reo Highway
   Saginaw Trail
   Stephenson Highway
   Telegraph Road
   Theodore Roosevelt International Highway
   Veterans Memorial Highway
   Victory Memorial Highway
   Vietnam Veterans Memorial
      Highway
   Walter P. Reuther Highway
   Wolverine Pavedway
   Woodward Avenue
Oceana County (9)
   Blue Star Memorial Highway
   Dixie Highway
   Great Lakes Automobile Route
   Hayes Road
   Michigamme Trail
   Michigan Pike
   Michigan Trail
   Pere Marquette Memorial

Highway
West Michigan Pike
Ogemaw County (5)
  American Legion Memorial
  Highway
  Bicentennial Freedom Way
  Straight to the Straits Route
  Tawas-Manistee Trail
  Veterans Memorial Drive
Ontonagon County (5)
  Cloverland Trail
  Joseph H. Meagher Memorial
  Highway
  107th Engineers Memorial Road
  Theodore Roosevelt International
  Highway
  Veterans Memorial Highway
Osceola County (4)
  Green Arrow Route
  James Whitcomb Riley Memorial
  Highway
  Mackinaw Trail
  Michigan Trail
Oscoda County (2)
  Straight to the Straits Route
  Veterans Memorial Drive
Otsego County (9)
  American Legion Memorial Highway
  Arctic-Tropic Overland Trail
  Bicentennial Freedom Way
  Center Line Highway
  G. Mennen Williams Highway
  Michigan Polar-Equator Trail
  Top of Michigan Trail
  Townsend National Highway
  William Howard Taft Memorial Highway
Ottawa County (17)
  Amvets Memorial Highway
  Arthur Vandenberg Memorial Highway
  Blue Star Memorial Highway
  Central Michigan Pike
  Cleveland Street
  Dixie Highway
  Gerald R. Ford Freeway
  Grand Highway
  Great Lakes Automobile Route
  Great Lakes International Highway
  Lake Michigan Drive
  Michigamme Trail
  Michigan Pike

Michigan Trail
Savidge Street
West Michigan Pike
Wolverine Pavedway
Presque Isle County (9)
  Blue Water Trail
  Dixie Highway
  East Michigan Pike
  Huron Shore Highway
  Michigan Pike
  Straight to the Straits Route
  Sweetwater Trail
  Theodore Roosevelt International
  Highway
  United Spanish War Veterans
  Memorial Highway
Roscommon County (8)
  American Legion Memorial
  Highway
  Arctic-Tropic Overland Trail
  Bicentennial Freedom Way
  Center Line Highway
  Tawas-Manistee Trail
  Top of Michigan Trail
  Townsend National Highway
  William Howard Taft Memorial
  Highway
Saginaw County (25)
  American Legion Memorial
  Highway
  Arctic-Tropic Overland Trail
  Bicentennial Freedom Way
  Central Michigan International
  Highway
  Colgrove Highway
  Dixie Highway
  East Michigan Pike
  Glacial Trail
  Hoffman Road
  Liberty Highway
  Mackinaw Scenic Shortway Route
  Michigan Trail
  Rainbow Trail
  Road of Memory
  Roberts-Linton Highway
  Rust Street/Drive
  Saginaw Trail
  Saginaw Valley Trail
  Soldiers' Memorial Highway
  Theodore Roosevelt International

Highway
Top of Michigan Trail
United Spanish War Veterans
  Memorial Highway
Veterans Memorial Parkway
Veterans of World War I
  Memorial Highway
Victory Highway
Saint Clair County (21)
  Algonquin Trail
  Blue Water Highway
  Blue Water Trail
  Bluewater Circle Drive
  Central Michigan International
    Highway
  Central Michigan Pike
  DeWayne T. Williams Memorial
    Highway
  Dixie Highway
  Gratiot Avenue
  Great Lakes International
    Highway
  Green Drive
  Huron Shore Pike
  James G. O'Hara Freeway
  Lacroix Road
  Lakes & River Drive
  Liberty Highway
  Michigan Pike
  Michigan Trail
  Rogers Memorial Highway
  Veterans Memorial Highway
  Victory Highway
Saint Joseph County (10)
  Capital to Capital Highway
  Chicago Road
  Colgrove Highway
  Gold Star Memorial Highway
  Green Arrow Route
  Iron Brigade Memorial Highway
  James Whitcomb Riley Memorial
    Highway
  Mackinaw Trail
  Ohio-Indiana-Michigan Way
  Pulaski Memorial Highway
Sanilac County (9)
  Algonquin Trail
  Blue Water Highway
  Blue Water Trail
  Colgrove Highway

Dixie Highway
Earle Memorial Highway
Huron Shore Pike
Michigan Pike
Van Dyke Road
Schoolcraft County (10)
  Blue Water Trail
  Bohn Highway
  Cloverland Trail
  Great Lakes Automobile Route
  Hiawatha Road
  Jacobetti Highway
  King's International Highway
  Theodore Roosevelt International
    Highway
  Townsend National Highway
  United Spanish War Veterans
    Memorial Highway
Shiawassee County (8)
  Central Michigan Pike
  Great Lakes International
    Highway
  Liberty Highway
  Mackinaw Scenic Shortway
    Route
  Pearl Harbor Memorial Highway
  Purple Heart Highway
  Saginaw Valley Trail
  Victory Highway
Tuscola County (6)
  Algonquin Trail
  Blue Water Trail
  Colgrove Highway
  Dixie Highway
  Huron Shore Pike
  Michigan Pike
Van Buren County (16)
  Blossom Highway
  Blue Star Memorial Highway
  Detroit-Lincoln-Denver Highway
  Dixie Highway
  Dunes Highway
  Gerald R. Ford Freeway
  Great Lakes Automobile Route
  Liberty Highway
  Michigamme Trail
  Michigan Avenue
  Michigan Pike
  Michigan Trail
  Red Arrow Highway

Saint Joseph Road
Victory Highway
West Michigan Pike
Washtenaw County (19)
   American Legion Memorial
     Highway
   Arctic-Tropic Overland Trail
   Blossom Highway
   Chicago Road
   Detroit-Lincoln-Denver Highway
   Flint Trail
   Ford Road
   Hoosier Highway
   Iron Brigade Memorial Highway
   Michigan Avenue
   Michigan Trail
   Pontiac Trail
   Pulaski Memorial Highway
   Red Arrow Highway
   Saint Joseph Road
   Tecumseh Trail
   Top of Michigan Trail
   United Spanish War Veterans
     Memorial Highway
   Willow Run Expressway
Wayne County (60)
   Algonquin Trail
   American Legion Memorial
     Highway
   Amvets Memorial Highway
   Arthur Vandenberg Memorial
     Highway
   Base Line Road
   Bicentennial Freedom Way
   Blossom Highway
   Blue Water Trail
   Bluewater Circle Drive
   Charles J. Rogers Interchange
   Chicago Road
   Chrysler Freeway
   Clara Barton Memorial Highway
   Columbus Memorial Highway
   Coolidge Highway
   Disabled American Veterans
     Memorial Highway
   Davison Limited Highway
   Detroit Industrial Expressway
   Detroit-Lincoln-Denver Highway
   Dix Avenue
   Dixie Highway

Earle Memorial Highway
East Michigan Pike
Edsel Ford Expressway
Fisher Freeway
Ford Road
Fort Street/Road
Grand River Avenue
Gratiot Avenue
Hoosier Highway
Hoover Drive
Iron Brigade Memorial Highway
James Couzens Highway
Jefferson Avenue
Lakes & River Drive
Leroy C. Smith Freeway
Lodge Expressway
Matt McNeely Boulevard
Michigan Avenue
Michigan Pike
Michigan Trail
Pan American Highway
Philip A. Hart Memorial Highway
Pulaski Memorial Highway
Randolph Street
Red Arrow Highway
Saginaw Trail
Saint Joseph Trail
Schaefer Road
Seaway Freeway
Southfield Freeway
Telegraph Road
Theodore Roosevelt International
   Highway
United States Road
Van Dyke Road
Vernier Road
Washington Boulevard
Willow Run Expressway
Wolverine Pavedway
Woodward Avenue
Wexford County (6)
   James Whitcomb Riley Memorial
     Highway
   Mackinaw Trail
   Michigan Trail
   Paradise Trail
   Sidney Ouwinga Memorial
     Bypass
   Tawas-Manistee Trail

APPENDIX 2

Wolverine Pavedway
M-17
  American Legion Memorial
    Highway
M-18
  Top of Michigan Trail
M-19
  Gratiot Avenue
  Lakes & River Road
M-20
  Hayes Road
  Michigan Trail
M-21
  Blue Water Highway
  Central Michigan Pike
  DeWayne T. Williams Memorial
    Highway
  Glacial Trail
  Great Lakes International
    Highway
  Veterans of Foreign Wars
    Memorial Highway
M-22
  Chippewa Trail
  Great Lakes Automobile Route
  Manitou Trail
  Michigamme Trail
M-24
  Boy Scout Trail
M-25
  Algonquin Trail
  Bay City Historic Heritage Route
  Blue Water Highway
  Blue Water Trail
  Dixie Highway
  Huron County Memorial
    Highway
  Huron Shore Pike
M-26
  Memorial Road
M-28
  Jacobetti Highway
  Great Lakes Automobile Route
  Theodore Roosevelt International
    Highway
  Townsend National Highway
  Veterans Memorial Highway
M-29
  Algonquin Trail
  Blue Water Trail

Bluewater Circle Drive
Jefferson Avenue
Lakes & River Drive
Vernier Road
M-30
  Meridian Road
M-32
  Michigan Polar-Equator Trail
  Veterans Memorial Highway
M-33
  Straight to the Straits Route
  Veterans Memorial Drive
M-34
  Carleton Road
M-35
  Amvets Memorial Drive
  Blue Water Trail
  Great Lakes Automobile Route
M-37
  Custer Trail
  Mason Drive
  Paradise Trail
  Queen's Highway
  World War II Veteran's Memorial
    Highway
M-38
  Joseph H. Meager Memorial
    Highway
M-39
  Southfield Freeway
M-40
  Michigan-Erie Highway
M-43
  Colgrove Highway
  Fitzgerald Memorial Highway
M-45
  Lake Michigan Drive
M-46
  Central Michigan International
    Highway
  Colgrove Highway
  Liberty Highway
  Michigan Trail
  Monroe Road
  Rainbow Trail
  Road of Memory
  Rust Street/Drive
  Saginaw Valley Trail
  Tom Bolt Highway

M-47
  Soldiers' Memorial Highway
M-50
  Clinton Trail
  Custer Road
  LaPlaisance Bay Turnpike
M-51
  Detroit-Lincoln-Denver Highway
M-52
  Hoffman Road
  Liberty Highway
  Mackinaw Scenic Shortway
    Route
  Saginaw Valley Trail
M-53
  Christopher Columbus Freeway
  Earle Memorial Highway
  POW/MIA Memorial Freeway
  Van Dyke Road
M-54
  Dort Highway
  Saginaw Trail
M-55
  Tawas-Manistee Trail
M-57
  Bernie Borden Memorial
    Overpass
  Cleveland Avenue
  Central Michigan International
    Highway
M-59
  Hall Road
  Veterans Memorial Highway
  Vietnam Veterans Memorial
    Highway
  William P. Rosso Highway
M-60
  Colgrove Highway
  Wayne Highway
M-62
  Cass County Veterans Memorial
    Highway
M-66
  Colgrove Highway
  Green Arrow Route
  Martin Luther King Memorial
    Highway
  Road of Remembrance
  Saginaw Valley Trail
  Sojourner Truth Memorial

Highway
M-69
  Great Lakes Automobile Route
  Oscar G. Johnson Memorial Highway
  United Spanish War Veterans
    Memorial Highway
M-78
  Capital to Capital Highway
  Liberty Highway
  Saginaw Valley Trail
M-82
  Korean War Veterans Memorial
    Highway
M-85
  Algonquin Trail
  Fort Street/Road
  Matt McNeely Boulevard
M-89
  Michigan-Erie Highway
M-94
  Great Lakes Automobile Route
  Hiawatha Road
M-95
  Great Lakes Automobile Route
  Leif Erickson Highway
  United Spanish Veterans Memorial Highway
M-96
  Dickman Road
  Fort Custer Memorial Highway
  King Highway
M-97
  Groesbeck Highway
  Hoover Drive
M-99
  Carleton Road
  Logan Street
  Martin Luther King Jr. Boulevard
  Memory Mile
  Wayne Highway
M-100
  Hartel Road
M-102
  Base Line Road
  Columbus Memorial Highway
M-104
  Cleveland Street
  Grand Highway
  Great Lakes International
    Highway
  Savidge Street

M-107
    107th Engineers Memorial Road
M-109
    D.H. Day Highway
M-117
    117th Quartermaster Battalion
    Highway
M-119
    Chippewa Memorial Pike
M-120
    Muskegon County Memorial
    Causeway
    Veteran's Memorial Causeway
M-121
    Bristol Road
    Disabled American Veterans
    Highway
M-123
    Tahquamenon Falls Memorial Highway
M-125
    Clara Barton Memorial Highway
    Monroe Historic Heritage Route
    Veterans Memorial Highway
M-129
    Brockway Mountain Drive
    Dixie Highway
    Meridian Road
    Road of Remembrance
    Sweetwater Trail
M-134
    Dixie Highway
    Sweetwater Trail
M-139
    Martin Luther King Drive
M-150
    Stephenson Highway
M-153
    Ford Road
M-154
    Green Drive
M-160
    Henry B. Joy Road
M-174
    Red Bud Trail
M-218
    Pontiac Trail
M-221
    Sweetwater Trail

US-2
    Amvets Memorial Drive
    Blue Star Memorial Highway
    Blue Water Trail
    Bohn Highway
    Cloverland Trail
    Coolidge Trail
    Great Lakes Automobile Route
    King's International Highway
    Memorial Drive
    Memory Lane
    Theodore Roosevelt International
    Highway
    United Spanish War Veterans
    Memorial Highway
US-10
    Arctic-Tropic Overland Trail
    Dort Highway
    Top of Michigan Trail
    Veterans Memorial Highway
US-12
    Chicago Road
    Hoosier Highway
    Iron Brigade Memorial Highway
    Michigan Avenue
    Pulaski Memorial Highway
    Red Arrow Highway
US-16
    Arthur Vandenberg Memorial
    Highway
    Grand River Avenue
    Washington Boulevard
US-23
    Arctic-Tropic Overland Trail
    Blue Water Trail
    Dixie Highway
    East Michigan Pike
    Huron Shore Highway
    Michigan Pike
    Roberts-Linton Highway
    Saginaw Trail
    Sweetwater Trail
    Theodore Roosevelt International
    Highway
    Top of Michigan Trail
    United Spanish War Veterans
    Memorial Highway
    Veterans Memorial Parkway
    Veterans of World War I
    Memorial Highway

US-24
    Clara Barton Memorial Highway
    Dixie Highway
    Telegraph Road
    Victory Memorial Highway
US-24BR
    Cesar E. Chavez Avenue
US-25
    Blue Water Highway
    Clara Barton Memorial Highway
    Dix Avenue
    Fort Street/Road
    Rogers Memorial Highway
US-27
    Arctic-Tropic Overland Trail
    Center Line Highway
    Luce Road
    Townsend National Highway
    Veteran's Memorial Highway
    William Howard Taft Memorial
        Highway
US-31
    Blue & Gray Trail
    Blue Star Memorial Highway
    Cairn Highway
    Dixie Highway
    Dunes Highway
    Grand Traverse Memorial
        Highway
    Great Lakes Automobile Route
    Hamilton Way
    LaSalle Trail
    Michigamme Trail
    Michigan Pike
    Michigan Trail
    Pere Marquette Memorial
        Highway
    Saint Joseph Valley Parkway
    West Michigan Pike
US-33
    Blue & Gray Trail

US-41
    Amvets Memorial Drive
    Great Lakes Automobile Route
    Memory Lane
    Sheridan Road
    Townsend National Highway
US-127
    Bagley Road
    Center Line Highway
    Fred L. Kircher Freeway
    Gary Priess Memorial Highway
    Haskell L. Nichols Memorial Highway
    James M. Pelton Firefighters Memorial
        Highway
    Kevin Sherwood Memorial Highway
    Meridian Road
    Townsend National Highway
    Wayne Highway
    William Howard Taft Memorial Highway
US-131
    Central Michigan International Highway
    Colgrove Highway
    Gold Star Memorial Highway
    James Whitcomb Riley Memorial Highway
    Mackinaw Trail
    Michigan Trail
    Sidney Ouwinga Memorial Bypass
    Underground Railroad Memorial Highway
US-141
    Coolidge Trail
    Isle Royale Trail
    Memory Lane
    Townsend National Highway
US-223
    Carleton Road
    Eire & Kalamazoo Trail
    Kalamazoo-Deering Trail
    Michigan-Eire Highway

APPENDIX 3

NAMED HIGHWAYS BY YEAR OF
FOUNDING

1913
  Huron Shore Highway
  Meridian Road
  West Michigan Pike
1914
  Grand Highway
1915
  Cloverland Trail
  Dixie Highway
  East Michigan Pike
  Mackinaw Trail
  Michigan Pike
  Reo Highway
  Wolverine Pavedway
1916
  Arctic-Tropic Overland Trail
  Custer Road
  Huron Shore Pike
1917
  Central Michigan Pike
  Custer Trail
  Dickman Road (Battle Creek)
  Great Lakes Automobile Route
  Henry B. Joy Road (Mount
    Clemens)
  Hoosier Highway
  Lakes & River Drive
  Saginaw Valley Trail
  Tecumseh Trail
  Top of Michigan Trail
  Wayne Highway
1918
  Center Line Highway
  Liberty Highway
  Ohio-Indiana-Michigan Way
1919
  Glacial Trail
  Theodore Roosevelt International
    Highway
  Victory Highway
1920
  Detroit-Lincoln-Denver Highway
  King's International Highway
    (Canadian)
  Memorial Highway

  (Ishpeming/Negaunee)
  Rogers Memorial Highway (Saint
    Clair County)
  Townsend National Highway
  Westnedge Avenue (Kalamazoo)
1921
  Colgrove Highway
  Erie & Kalamazoo Trail
  Hamilton Way (Grand Traverse
    County)
  Kalamazoo-Deering Trail
  Memorial Drive (North
    Muskegon)
  Memorial Road (Houghton)
1922
  Michigan Avenue
  Pioneer Trail (Calhoun County)
  Sheridan Road
  Soldiers' Memorial Highway
  Victory Memorial Highway
    (Oakland County)
1923
  Grand Traverse Memorial
    Highway (Traverse City)
  Memorial Row (Alma/Saint
    Louis)
  Remembrance Road (Grand
    Rapids)
  Road of Remembrance (Ionia)
  Tom Bolt Highway (Muskegon
    County)
1924
  Bohn Highway
  Boy Scout Trail (Oakland
    County)
  Gold Star Memorial Highway
    (Saint Joseph County)
  Hoffman Road (Saginaw County)
  Road of Memory (Battle Creek)
  Stephenson Highway
1925
  Carleton Road
  Coolidge Highway (Wayne
    County)
  Groesbeck Highway (Macomb
    County)
  James Whitcomb Riley Memorial
    Highway

Muskegon County Memorial
   Causeway
Pan American Highway
Road of Memory (Saginaw)
1926
   Base Line Road (Wayne County)
   Capital to Capital Highway
   Dort Highway (Flint)
   Green Drive
   Road of Remembrance
      (Sault Ste. Marie)
1927
   Dunes Highway
   Paradise Trail
   Hiawatha Road
1928
   Coolidge Trail
   Great Lakes International
      Highway
   Lake Michigan Drive
   Rainbow Trail
1929
   Algonquin Trail
   Blossom Highway
   Haggerty Road
   Hoover Drive (Detroit)
   Memory Lane (Escanaba)
1930
   American Legion Memorial
      Highway (Ann Arbor)
   Chippewa Trail
1931
   Memorial Drive (Iron Mountain)
   Memory Lane (Crystal Falls)
   Roberts-Linton Highway (Bay
      City/Saginaw)
1932
   Isle Royale Trail
   LaSalle Trail (Berrien County)
1933
   Brockway Mountain Drive
      (Keweenaw County)
   William Howard Taft Memorial
      Highway
1934
   Central Michigan International
      Highway
   Michigan-Erie Highway
   Red Bud Trail
   Rust Street/Drive (Saginaw)

1935
   King Highway (Kalamazoo)
   Queen's Highway (Grand
      Traverse County)
   Veterans Memorial Parkway (Bay
      City/Saginaw)
1937
   James Couzens Highway (Detroit)
   William P. Rosso Highway
      (Macomb County)
1938
   Blue-Gray Trail
   Blue Water Highway
   Mackinaw Scenic Shortway
      Route
   Pontiac Trail
1939
   Earle Memorial Highway
   Fitzgerald Memorial Highway
   Straight to the Straits Route
1940
   Blue Water Trail
   Hartel Road (Eaton County)
1941
   Davison Limited Highway
      (Detroit)
   Willow Run Expressway
1942
   Bagley Road
   Cleveland Avenue (Gratiot
      County)
   Detroit Industrial Expressway
   Luce Road
   Monroe Road

1944
   Lodge Expressway (Detroit)
1945
   Cass County Veterans Memorial
      Highway
   Jackson County Roadside
      Memorial
   Kalamazoo County Memorial
      Highway
   Mason Drive
   Memory Mile (Litchfield)
   United Spanish War Veterans
      Memorial Highway (Lower
      Peninsula)

1946
  Cleveland Street (Ottawa County)
  Edsel Ford Expressway (Detroit)
  Memory Lane (Baraga)
1947
  Bluewater Circle Drive
  Tahquamenon Falls Memorial
    Highway
1948
  Blue Star Memorial Highway
  Blue Water Highway (Ionia
    County)
  Hayes Road
1949
  Memory Lane (Bessemer)
  United Spanish War Veterans
    Memorial Highway (Upper
    Peninsula)
1951
  Leif Erickson Highway
1952
  Arthur Vandenberg Memorial
    Highway
  Red Arrow Highway
1953
  Manitou Trail
  Pulaski Memorial Highway
1954
  Clara Barton Memorial Highway
  107th Engineers Memorial Road
    (Ontonagon County)
  Pere Marquette Memorial
    Highway
1955
  Columbus Memorial Highway
    (Wayne County)
1957
  Chrysler Freeway (Detroit)
1958
  Fisher Freeway (Detroit)
1959
  Amvets Memorial Drive
    (Escanaba)
  Green Arrow Route
  Jeffries Expressway
  Seaway Freeway (Wayne County)
1963
  Amvet Memorial Parkway
    (Kalamazoo)
  Michigamme Trail

1966
  Adler Memorial Highway
    (Southfield
1967
  Fred L. Kircher Freeway
    (Lansing)
1969
  American Legion Memorial
    Highway
  Buick Freeway (Flint)
  Chevrolet Expressway (Flint)
1971
  Charles J. Rogers Interchange
    (Detroit)
  Michigan Polar-Equator Trail
  Walter P. Reuther Highway
1972
  Olds Freeway (Lansing)
1973
  Martin Luther King Drive (Benton
    Harbor)
1974
  Gerald R. Ford Freeway
1975
  Bicentennial Freedom Way
1976
  Amvets Memorial Highway
  DeWayne T. Williams Memorial
    Highway
  G. Mennen Williams Highway
  Prentiss M. Brown Memorial
    Highway
  Sojourner Truth Memorial
    Highway (Battle Creek)
1977
  Philip A. Hart Memorial Highway
1978
  Christopher Columbus Freeway
    (Macomb County)
  Veterans Memorial Highway
1980
  UAW Freeway (Flint)
  VFW Memorial Highway
1981
  Curley Lewis Memorial Highway
    (Chippewa County)
1984
  Veterans of Foreign Wars
    Memorial Highway
1985

Dr. Martin Luther King, Jr.,
  Memorial Highway (Albion)
1986
  Jacobetti Highway
1988
  Fort Custer Memorial Highway
    (Calhoun County)
1989
  Martin Luther King, Jr., Boulevard
    (Lansing)
  Moses J. Jones Parkway
    (Muskegon)
  Veterans Memorial Highway
    (Monroe County)
1990
  Amvets Memorial Highway
  Disabled American Veterans
    Highway (Burton)
1991
  Martin Luther King Memorial
    Highway (Battle Creek)
  126th Infantry Memorial
    Boulevard (Wyoming)
  Sweetwater Trail
1992
  Haskell L. Nichols Memorial
    Highway
  Joseph H. Meagher Memorial
    Highway
  Vietnam Veterans Memorial
    Highway
1993
  117th Quartermaster Battalion
    Highway
  Saint Joseph Valley Parkway
    (Berrien County)
1994
  Iron Brigade Memorial Highway
1995
  Cesar E. Chavez Avenue (Pontiac)
  World War II Veterans Memorial
    Highway (Lake County)
1996
  Disabled American Veterans
    Memorial Highway (Livonia)
  Monroe Historic Heritage Route
1997
  Bay City Historic Heritage Route
  James G. O'Hara Freeway
  Matt McNeely Boulevard

(Detroit)
1998
  Paul B. Henry Freeway
    (Grand Rapids)
1999
  Deacon Memorial Highway
    (Farmington Hills)
2000
  Marshall's Territorial Road
  Sidney Ouwinga Memorial
    Bypass (Wexford County)
  Veterans Memorial Drive
  Veterans Memorial Highway
    (Alpena)
2001
  Bernie Borden Memorial
    Overpass
  D.H. Day Highway (Leelanau
    County)
  David Dunbar Buick Freeway
  Pearl Harbor Memorial Highway
  Veteran's Memorial Causeway
  Veteran's Memorial Highway
    (Ithaca)
  Veterans Memorial Road
  Veterans of World War I Memorial
    Highway
2002
  Cesar E. Chavez Way
  Gary Priess Memorial Highway
  Korean War Veterans Memorial
    Highway
  94th Combat Infantry Division
    Memorial Highway
  Oscar G. Johnson Memorial
    Highway
  Purple Heart Highway
  Veterans Memorial Highway
    (Mason County)
2003
  James M. Pelton Firefighters
    Memorial Highway
  POW/MIA Memorial Freeway
  Veterans Memorial Highway
    (Upper Peninsula)
2004
  Kevin Sherwood Memorial
    Highway
  Underground Railroad Memorial
    Highway

BIBLIOGRAPHY

Much of the information for this book came from scores of articles that were extracted from dozens of newspapers published all across the state. Whether small-town weekly or big-city daily, this was probably the best source of data on the memorial highways of Michigan.

The next most useful storehouses of relevant facts were a pair of periodicals devoted in large part to highway construction in our state. Probably the superior of the two started out as Michigan Roads & Forests (1907-1922), becoming Michigan Roads & Pavements (1922-1929), then Michigan Roads & Airports (1930-1935), and ending up as Michigan Roads & Construction (1936-present). Coming in a close second in the fruitful journal category was the Michigan Contractor & Builder (1907-present).

Government records were another rich source of details on Michigan's roads of remembrance. City council proceedings, county road commission minutes and annual reports, biennial reports of the State Highway Department, and state legislative journals all proved to be invaluable in tracking down official actions in the creation of these special highways. Of all the measures passed in Michigan pertaining to trunklines of tribute, probably the most important and far-reaching is state statute 142 of 2001, also known as the Memorial Highway Act. This law consolidated and codified most of the previous decrees creating named roads under a single title and into one convenient place.

A good foundation for this project was established by two reference tools created by the Michigan Department of Transportation and its predecessors. First and foremost was a book published in 1967 by the State Highway Department titled "Michigan's Memorial Highways and Bridges." The other useful support was a web site giving particulars about our state's memorial highways at:

http://www.mdot.state.mi.us/misc/memhiways.htm

Lists of the early named highways in Michigan, depictions of the routes they took, and examples of their respective symbols can be found on the Rand McNally Auto Trails Maps starting in 1918 and running through nearly all of the 1920s. The most comprehensive collection of these cartographic productions is housed in the Rand McNally Company Map Collection at the Newberry Library in Chicago. An abbreviated inventory of the named roads for the entire country can be found on the national listing of North American Auto Trails: http://www.owu.edu/~deschul/trails/trails.html

Another database that proved to be quite rewarding in this undertaking was the website: www.michiganhighways.org. This site offers a detailed history of every state and federal highway within the boundaries of our two peninsulas. A somewhat less elaborate treatment for named national roads throughout the entire country can be found at: www.us-highways.com/; www.byways.org/travel/designated_byways.html; and www.marion.ohio-state.edu/fac/schul/trails/trails.html. Illustrations and text pertaining to road signs can be reached at: www.ugcs.caltech.edu/~jlin/signs/

An organization exists for those who are interested in the named roads of the past. This association is called the Society for Commercial Archeology, and its semi-annual Journal not infrequently runs articles on some of these highways that are identified by more than just a route number. Additional information on this group can be found at its website: SCA@sca-roadside.org

Very few articles have been written about our state's memorial highways. Some authors have studied individual roads and published their findings as pieces devoted to a single specific route (like Gratiot Avenue, the Sauk Trail, Woodward Avenue, etc.), but there are barely a handful of stories done on portions of the genre or the theme as a whole. One or two of the major roads--like the West Michigan Pike or the Dixie Highway--published guidebooks to their routes in the early years which are now collectors' items.

Perhaps the best coverage of the topic can be found in an account of Michigan's Military Highways that appeared in a newsletter called "Voice of the Volunteers" (volume 3, numbers 2 & 3), a 1997 Bulletin published by the Michigan Emergency Volunteers. Another broad-based treatment of this subject was offered by Michigan History Magazine, July-August 2002 (volume 8, number 4), pages 20-21.

For the country as a whole, the best place to look for articles on named routes is the Mount Clemens-based periodical called American Road. This journal is almost solely devoted to writing about the historic highways of our nation and features found along their paths. Its stories not only identify and describe the popular two-lane thoroughfares of the past, they also tell readers how to best drive them today to relive the motoring experiences of the "good old days." Since this is a recent quarterly (about two years in age), it is quite possible that few libraries have the magazine. For more information visit www.mockturtlepress.com.

It is worth mentioning here a periodical that should not be consulted for relevant facts, its title not withstanding. From 1989 to 2004, an annual release came out of Shelby (in Oceana County) called "A Motoring Guide to Historic Pathways of Michigan" While its name would lead people to believe that facts on old highways could be found therein, such a conclusion would be in error as it is a statewide tourist promotional publication and not something devoted to old roads.

The materials gathered in the course of researching this book filled twenty-three manuscript boxes. These records are on permanent deposit at the State Archives of Michigan where, once they have been processed, anyone may gain access to them during normal business hours.

```
┌─────────────────┐
│   ┌─────────┐   │
│   │   NO    │   │
│   │ READING │   │
│   │ BETWEEN │   │
│   │  LINES  │   │
│   └─────────┘   │
└─────────────────┘
```

INDEX

ADDENDA

Chicago Road (Page 50): This route in Michigan--represented by highway US-12--was recently declared a Historic Heritage Trail in recognition of its importance since recorded time. This honor was formalized on 9 June 2004 at Cambridge Junction, when dedication ceremonies were held at Walker Tavern.

Huron Shore Highway (Page 110): Recently, the 200-mile stretch of US-23 from Standish north to Mackinaw City was designated the "Sunrise Side Coastal Highway" in a cooperative promotional effort between MDOT and local commercial interests. This event was dedicated on 21 May 2004 in successive ceremonies that day at Standish, East Tawas, and Harrisville.

Kevin Sherwood Memorial Highway (Page 126): This road is scheduled to be dedicated on 8 October 2004 at the Clare rest area along US-127.

Michigamme Trail (Page 153): According to a map of the northwestern Lower Peninsula published in 1957 by the Michigan Indian Foundation in Detroit, the stretch of US-31 between Charlevoix and Petoskey was apparently once known as the Chief Blackbird Trail. No other evidence can be found of this name.

Michigan Avenue (Page 154): As the number of motor vehicles increased after the Korean War, Michigan Avenue--the principal latitudinal street through Jackson--gradually became overwhelmed with congestion. To alleviate this situation, in 1965 the city began creating a perimeter loop around the central commercial district. The upper leg of this little downtown bypass became a one-way street carrying traffic from east to west. Also known as part of Business Route I-94 and M-50, the northern portion of this new main road was designated Glick Memorial Drive by the city council on 5 March 1968. The thoroughfare honors Louis Glick, a local business pioneer and philanthropist, who died the previous year.

Purple Heart Highway (Page 179): As this book goes to press, the Michigan Legislature appears poised to approve Senate Bill 1243 of 2004 making I-69 in Branch County the Purple Heart Trail.

Washington Boulevard (Page 234): At least three other roads fall under this heading. Route M-32 follows Washington Avenue in the town of Alpena, Business Route US-41 traces the path of a similarly named street in Marquette city, and trunk line M-13 does the same in the municipality of Saginaw.